AF608073

Playing Games

in Nineteenth-Century Britain and America

SUNY series, Studies in the Long Nineteenth Century

Pamela K. Gilbert, editor

Playing Games

in Nineteenth-Century Britain and America

edited by

ANN R. HAWKINS,
ERIN N. BISTLINE, CATHERINE S. BLACKWELL,
and MAURA IVES

Published by State University of New York Press, Albany

Printed in the United States of America

For information, contact State University of New York Press, Albany, NY
www.sunypress.edu

Library of Congress Cataloging-in-Publication Data

Names: Hawkins, Ann R., editor | Bistline, Erin N., editor | Blackwell, Catherine S., editor | Maura Ives, editor.
Title: Playing games in nineteenth-century Britain and America / edited by Ann R. Hawkins, Erin N. Bistline, Catherine S. Blackwell, and Maura Ives.
Description: Albany : SUNY Press, 2021. | Series: SUNY series, studies in the long nineteenth century | Includes bibliographical references and index.
Identifiers: LCCN 2021028910 (print) | LCCN 2021028911 (ebook) | ISBN 9781438485553 (hardcover : alk. paper) | ISBN 9781438485560 (ebook)
Subjects: LCSH: Games—Great Britain—History—19th century. | Games—United States—History—19th century. | Amusements—Great Britain—History—19th century. | Amusements—United States—History—19th century. | Great Britain—Social life and customs—19th century. | United States—Social life and customs—19th century.
Classification: LCC GV75 .P63 2021 (print) | LCC GV75 (ebook) | DDC 790.0941—dc23
LC record available at https://lccn.loc.gov/2021028910
LC ebook record available at https://lccn.loc.gov/2021028911

10 9 8 7 6 5 4 3 2 1

To the ever inventive and lovely Ann Donohue.
This book began with her idea and encouragement.

Contents

List of Illustrations xi

Acknowledgments xv

Introduction
From Snapdragon to Three-card Loo: Rediscovering Nineteenth-Century Games 1
Ann R. Hawkins, Miles A. Kimball, Erin N. Bistline, Allison Whitney, and Catherine S. Blackwell

Section I: Games in Motion

Chapter One
Bodies in Play: Boxing, Dance, and the Science of Recreation 41
Kristin Flieger Samuelian and Mark Schoenfield

Chapter Two
Baseball in the Frame of Gilded-Age America 69
Matthew Von Vogt

Chapter Three
"We are only horses and don't know": Sport and Danger in Fox Hunting 87
Erin N. Bistline

Section II: Communal Games

CHAPTER FOUR
"The Memory Game": Play, Trauma, and *Great Expectations* 111
Sean Grass

CHAPTER FIVE
Seeing Victorian Culture through Croquet's "Treacherous Wire Portal" 129
Catherine S. Blackwell

CHAPTER SIX
Acting Charades in 1873: Girls and the Stakes of the Game 153
Heather Fitzsimmons Frey

Section III: Playing the World

CHAPTER SEVEN
Dangerous Games: The Advent of Wargaming in the Nineteenth Century 175
Andrew Byers

CHAPTER EIGHT
The United States as Wonderland: British Literature, U.S. Nationalism, and Nineteenth-Century Children's and Family Board and Card Games 193
Michelle Beissel Heath

CHAPTER NINE
Gaming the Great Exhibition of 1851: Children's Board Games, Display, and Imperial Power 215
Megan A. Norcia

CHAPTER TEN
Teetotum Lives: Mediating Globalization in the Nineteenth-Century Board Game 243
Siobhan Carroll

Section IV: Books, Boards, and Other Objects

Chapter Eleven
What Did They Play, and What Does This Say?: A Quantitative and Cultural Analysis of British Collected Games in the Nineteenth Century through the *Games Research Database* 265
Maurice Suckling

Chapter Twelve
Professor Hoffmann's Victorian Puzzles and Stage Magic 293
Andrew Rhoda

Chapter Thirteen
"An Endless Round of Delights": Materializing the Toy Theatre 307
Jennie MacDonald

Chapter Fourteen
The Game of Authors, 1861–1900: A Case History 331
Maura Ives

Contributors 351

General Index 357

Games Index 377

Illustrations

Figures

2.1 Captain Adrian C. Anson of the Chicago White Stockings appears in a suit rather than a uniform. 71

2.2 In Goodwin's 1888 chromolithograph, Captain Anson, in a brilliant blue shirt, is identified by his position (1st base) and his team, Chicago White Stockings. 77

2.3 The reverse of Goodwin's 1888 card shows Anson among other "Champions" from baseball and other sports. 77

2.4 In Goodwin's 1888 chromolithograph, King Kelly, wearing a red tie, is identified by his position (center field) and his team, the Boston Beaneaters. 78

2.5 The reverse of Goodwin's 1888 card shows Kelly among other "Champions" from baseball and other sports. 78

2.6 Captain Adrian C. Anson holds a bat aloft in Allen & Ginter's 1887 card. 79

2.7 The reverse of Allen & Ginter's 1887 card shows Anson among other "World's Champions" from baseball and other sports. 79

2.8 King Kelly is presented here against the pastoral baseball diamond common in the 1887 Gold Coin card set. 80

2.9 The reverse of Buchner's Gold Coin 1887 image of Kelly reminds purchasers: "Continue to save the wrappers. They are valuable." 80

5.1 "Croquet" from an 1863 issue of *Punch's Almanack* depicts several women playing croquet with their skirts lifted to show their ankles. 131

5.2 "Oh, How Kind!!" from an 1865 *Punch, or the London Charivari* pokes fun at unattractive "goloshes." 133

5.3 "The Game of Croquet" from an 1865 *Peterson's Magazine* featured striped, bordered, *and* embroidered petticoats. 135

5.4 In this untitled image from the 1869 *Girl of the Period Miscellany*, a flirtatious "Mai[d] of the Mallet" taps her male partner's ball with her toe. 139

9.1 Henry Smith Evans identifies himself as a Fellow of the Royal Geographic Society on his *Crystal Palace Game*. 218

9.2 Henry Smith Evans's *Crystal Palace Game* depicts the deaths of Englishmen at the hands of South Pacific islanders. 223

9.3 Henry Smith Evans's *Crystal Palace Game* includes a scene of the taking of slaves. 227

9.4 William Spooner's *A Comic Game of the Great Exhibition of 1851* satirizes the Exhibition, its goals, and its visitors. 230

9.5 In William Spooner's *A Comic Game of the Great Exhibition of 1851*, players "take" or "pay," adding value to the life of humanity or detracting from it. 233

9.6 William Spooner's *A Comic Game of the Great Exhibition of 1851* highlights how technological innovation can destroy humanity. 234

10.1 The advertisement on the slipcover for *Walker's New Geographical Game Exhibiting a Tour Through Europe* directed interested players to the publisher's wares. 246

10.2 *Walker's New Geographical Game Exhibiting a Tour through Europe* required players to compete to be the first to successfully land on the final square. 248

10.3 The McLoughlin Brothers's 1890 *Game of Round the World* capitalizes on the press generated by Nellie Bly's successful whirlwind tour of the globe. 257

11.1 Data from Tables 11.1 and 11.2 represented in percentages. 274

11.2 Data from Tables 11.3 and 11.4 represented in percentages. 275

11.3 Data from Table 11.5 represented in percentages. 278

13.1 On the left, Captain Clarence presents a miniature theatre to Master Jacky, and on the right, the boys work on their performance. 311

13.2 On the right of John Leech's illustration for *Young troublesome*, the boys set their toy theatrical on fire. 313

13.3 Title sheets, such as this one from *The Castle of Otranto; or, Harlequin & the Giant Helmet*, highlight the practices of nineteenth-century pantomimes. 321

13.4 The scenery sheets from J. K. Green's 1841 *The Castle of Otranto; or, Harlequin & the Giant Helmet*, were adapted from the original theater backdrops. 323

13.5 Sheets from J. K. Green's 1841 *Harlequin & the Giant Helmet* suggest how some of the pantomime "tricks" looked in performance. 323

Tables

11.1 Game types shown in the 873 nineteenth-century listings on GARD 273

11.2 A categorization of listings with unclear game types on GARD 273

11.3 Categories for the listings that are described as "probably" 274

11.4 Breakdown of unclear listings in GARD 275

11.5 Board games breakdowns from previous tables organized in order of frequency 275

Acknowledgments

Our thanks to Richard E. Porter for his careful reading of the full manuscript and his thoughtful copyediting and to Allison Whitney, who began the project with Ann Hawkins before other obligations drew her away. Ann Hawkins would like to also thank Miles Kimball who never fails to offer support and who reads everything well.

Introduction

From Snapdragon to Three-Card Loo: Rediscovering Nineteenth-Century Games

ANN R. HAWKINS, MILES A. KIMBALL, ERIN N. BISTLINE, ALLISON WHITNEY, AND CATHERINE S. BLACKWELL

> They met for the sake of eating, drinking, and laughing together, playing at cards, or consequences, or any other game that was sufficiently noisy.
>
> —Jane Austen, *Sense and Sensibility*[1]

Readers of nineteenth-century literature and letters—or twenty-first-century Regency romance[2]—encounter a world filled with games. Consider Anthony Trollope's *The Warden*, where the progress of a game of whist is described with a rhetoric reminiscent of the *Iliad*:

> With solemn energy do they watch the shuffled pack, and, all-expectant, eye the coming trump. With what anxious nicety do they arrange their cards, jealous of each other's eyes! [. . .] Now thrice this has been done, thrice has constant fortune favored the brace of prebendaries, ere the arch deacon rouses himself to the battle; but at the fourth assault he pins to the earth a prostrate king, laying low his crown and sceptre, bushy beard, and lowering brow, with a poor deuce. (51)

Or consider Jane Austen's *Pride and Prejudice*, where card games reveal character and deepen situation.[3] Lady Catherine De Bourgh prefers the complicated strategies of *quadrille*, while her daughter Anne plays the less rigorous *cassino* (Austen, *Pride* 172; Hoyle).[4] Mrs. Bennet has a "rapacity for whis[t]," while Lydia Bennet loves the luck involved in "a noisy game of lottery tickets" (Austen, *Pride* 350, 76). Jane Bennet and Mr. Bingley "both like Vingt-Un better than Commerce," while neither Elizabeth Bennet nor Mr. Darcy has a fondness for cards (Austen, *Pride* 25).[5] Austen's letters to her sister Cassandra mention a dozen or more games in passing, including cribbage, brag, speculation, whist, billiards, charades, "bilbocatch, [. . .] spillikins, paper ships, riddles, conundrums, and cards" (150). Such "amusements," as Austen calls this range of games, were as familiar to her contemporaries as *Monopoly* or *Go Fish* are to us. But, as we look at Austen's world, we find a wonderland of unfamiliar games. *Snapdragon*—where players thrust their fingers into a low bowl of flaming brandy to capture raisins. *Hot cockles*—where a blindfolded player knelt, face in another player's lap, hands behind the back, and guessed who struck them. *Bullet pudding*—where a bullet or marble sat on top of a pile of flour and players sliced the flour, then, with only their lips, retrieved the marble from wherever it fell ("Charades").

This collection takes as its territory that unfamiliar wonderland. We focus on games in nineteenth-century transatlantic culture, examining the games themselves as they appeared in popular magazines, engravings, and art of the period and demonstrating the ways in which games reflect, permeate, and influence culture. While some essays might include criticism of specific literary texts, that is not our primary purpose. Instead, we hope to open up the field of nineteenth-century games for further study. For the nineteenth-century scholar relatively new to the study of games, we survey the importance of games both historically and for our present moment. And for the scholar of games, we overview the ways the historical record shows that nineteenth-century people used the terms *games*, *sport*, and *play*. Finally, as is traditional for publications of the sort, we summarize in this chapter the contributions of our essayists whose work follows.

Playing Games

Playing games is as old as human history itself and as new as the game of the week in the Apple app store. Archaeological excavations routinely find games or depictions of games included in burial sites. Ancient Egyptian tombs have included a variety of such pastimes from guessing games, to board and ball games, to representations of sports such as boxing and wrestling; and many of these games are still played in some form across the world (Brewster 27).[6] Game courts (such as those of the Maya and Aztecs) and game boards carved into stone (from Thebes to Moscenice, Croatia, to an ancient carving of "Hounds and Jackals" in Gobustan, Azerbaijian) all testify to the human interest in playing together (Gurevich). Mencius, Herodotus, Plato, Ovid, and Tacitus all record this passion, describing games and game play in their works. Even Shakespeare records the importance of games: in *Henry V*, the French Dauphin sends Hal a "tun" of tennis balls; and in *King Lear*, Kent calls an angry servant a 'base football player," accusing the servant of playing an illegal game (1.2.255; 1.4.85).

More recent history (and scholarship) has focused on video games, dating at least to their popular advent in the 1970s and 1980s—from *Pong* to *Donkey Kong*, from *Oregon Trail* to *Zork*, from Ms. *Pac-Man* to *Super Mario Brothers*. Simply mentioning these titles today fosters nostalgia from those of a certain age, as evidenced by the tone of the 2015 IEEE Historic Gaming Timeline, which "invit[ed]" users "to get gaming nostalgic by exploring and engaging with our homage to console gaming history!"[7] It is by now a truism that the gaming industry has eclipsed the film, television, and music industries in terms of its sheer presence and economic impact in most American household. According to the Entertainment Software Association's 2020 demographic survey, "three quarters of all U.S. households have at least one person who plays video games, and 64 percent of U.S. adults and 70 percent of those under 18 regularly play video games," including 41 percent of all women ("2020" 3, 5). Moreover, Americans spent a total of $35.4 billion on gaming in 2019, underscoring this pastime's priority in many household budgets ("U.S. Video" 4).

Such investment has spurred both technological advances (enabling players to adopt play roles in increasingly lifelike and diverse scenarios) and broad expansion of the sorts of topics suitable for game play, leading to controversy about the role of games in society and private life. While the growing graphic realism of "first-person" games—such as "shooter," "fight," and "combat" genres—have caused concern, that same technology has also allowed players with disabilities—who number some "42 million"—to experience virtual professional athleticism ("2020" 4). Such "first-person" games blur the lines between "games" and "sports"—a trend that echoes the nineteenth century's own broad definitions—and many have developed into competitive and lucrative spectator sports involving leagues, televised tournaments, and betting lines. While gamers can be personally isolated from one another, their play can be strongly communal, with team-based multimedia communication: 65 percent report playing 6.6 hours playing online with others and 4.3 hours playing in person ("2020" 6). Teachers have gamified the classroom at every level, and more than half of parents play video games with their children at least weekly, making gaming a social experience that most parents feel is a "good opportunity to socialize with their children" ("2020" 13). Finally, the growth in video games has also led to cross-media pollination, as moviemakers have created motion pictures based on games. Examples include *Lara Croft: Tomb Raider* and *Prince of Persia*, both of which led to movie spin-offs while also echoing such earlier cinematic productions as *She* (1935), *Beau Geste* (1939), and *Gunga Din* (1939). These games thus connect video gaming in the twenty-first century with the colonialism of the nineteenth and twentieth centuries.

Despite video games' market dominance, board, card, and dice games have remained a staple in many modern households. And the board game market, which topped 9.6 billion dollars in sales in 2016, was expected to reach "more than 12 billion by 2023" ("$12").[8] While *Clue* (or *Cluedo*) and *Yahtzee* are more familiar to us than such nineteenth-century titles as *The Mansion of Happiness* or *Game of the District Messenger Boy*, many family game nights and informal get-togethers still feature low-tech amusements. And groups still gather to play communal games, whether outside of downtown store fronts, at the local diner or bar, or in board game parlors. People gather to play games such as checkers or dominoes, or older games like *Monopoly*; games developed in parallel with the video-game age, such as Gary Gygax's popular *Dungeons & Dragons* series; and newer games, such as *Settlers of Catan*. Card-trading games such as *Pokémon* have helped children practice not only basic arithmetic, but important social skills (its app version in *Pokémon Go* fosters physical activity). Building on this burgeoning interest, International Table-top Day, founded in 2012, provides a day worldwide for groups to build community and play board games.

Seeing a way to use games to generate foot traffic, museums have frequently included board games in their programming. We saw this development, for example, from 2013 at the Monterey County Youth Museum in California, 2016 at the Cleveland Museum of Art, and

2017 (and following) at the Rubin Museum in New York City ("Fun"; "Then"; "Board"). From family game nights, museums moved to other population segments. The 2020 Grand Rapids Public Museum's LaughFest Game Night allowed players-of-age to sample local wines and beers, and the North Carolina Museum of Natural Sciences virtual Adult Nights added a Game Night lecture series with interactive gaming ("LaughFest"; "Adult"). Whether for children or adults, these popular programs have become regular features of museum programming, such as the Amon Carter Museum of Art's Game Night in Fort Worth, Texas ("Game"). As part of this trend, some museums have even opened up their collections for play: the Stuhr Museum of the Prairie Pioneer in Grand Island, Nebraska, for example, from 2017 to 2019, allowed patrons to play dozens of historic games ("Special").[9]

As museums use game play to draw in patrons, those with substantial collections of historic games have built exhibitions around them. One of the oldest of these collections—and exhibitions—was associated with the University of Waterloo, which still hosts the Elliot Avedon Virtual Museum of Games, whose robust collection of online exhibitions includes a section of scholarly papers on games from various countries.[10] The San Francisco Museum hosted the 2012–13 exhibition *Let's Play: 100 Years of Board Games* which examined mass-produced games from the 1860s, 14 of which are still featured on their website. The Victoria and Albert Museum of Childhood's 2016–17 touring exhibition *Game Plan: Board Games Rediscovered*, highlighted 100 game objects from around the world, with an emphasis on those which were beautifully designed and produced.[11] Most recently, the British Museum's 2019 exhibition "Playing with Money: Currency and Games," curated by Robert Bracey, examined how modern board games shape players' understanding of money and economics (Pierre). Even the Louvre provides a virtual selection of its games ("Selected").[12]

Perhaps the best known board-game collection is the New York Historical Society Museum and Library's Liman Collection—an archive of more than 500 items donated by Arthur and Ellen Liman. The Liman Collection provides important access to nineteenth- and twentieth-century board games. As a regular rotating exhibition, *The Games We Played: American Board and Table Games* focuses on a different set of games every four months. Objects from the Liman Collection have appeared in a number of catalogues, including Marisa Kayyem and Paul Sternberger's 1991 *American Board and Table Games of the Nineteenth Century from the Liman Collection*, Margaret Hofer and Kenneth Jackson's 2003 *The Games We Played: The Golden Age of Board and Table Games*, and Ellen Liman's 2017 *Georgian and Victorian Board Games: The Liman Collection*. The Liman catalogues join earlier descriptive collections based in the nineteenth century, specifically including Olivia Bristol's 1995 *Victorian Board Games* and 1996 *Six Edwardian and Victorian Board Games* and Jill Shefrin's 1997 *Ingenious Contrivances: Table Games and Puzzles for Children*, an exhibition from the Toronto Public Library's Osborne Collection of Early Children's Books.

And so here we are: we make electronic games central to our social lives, assisted by a massive video game industry, and we look back into the (mostly recent) past with an unavoidable air of nostalgia, prompting (or reinforcing) our renewed interest in games of the past, such as board games. This combination is so potent that several universities now offer the full range of academic programs (from baccalaureate to doctoral) in the field. Little wonder, then, that scholars have grown interested in the broader history of games in human culture. These factors tend to drive the cycle of scholarship: as interest builds, and resources become more publicly available, research becomes increasingly possible, thus increasing awareness and making resources available, and so on). UPenn's CFP list routinely includes calls for papers and presentations on games (though most focus on video games and online culture). Academia.edu, which allows scholars to self-archive their work, shows researchers tagging their work with at least 23 headings having to do with games, including history of games, games in pedagogy, and video games. Of the self-archived published articles, conference presentations and other works in progress, we find more than 140 articles on board games. This kind of sociological evidence shows that our contemporary interests in games is growing.

Yet, despite this expanding interest in games, gaming history, and gaming culture, *nineteenth-century* games haven't received substantial scholarly attention.[13] This is despite the consistent popularity of games based in the nineteenth century, such as classic games like *Oregon Trail*, *The Yukon Trail*, and *Gold Rush!* which pit players against the landscape and dangers of nineteenth-century U.S. westward migration, or those that reflect an ongoing interest in nineteenth-century transatlantic history and literature, including the history-infused *Victoria: an Empire Under the Sun* or *Victoria II* but also the literature-oriented *Adventures of Tom Sawyer*, *Dr. Jekyll and Mr. Hyde*, or the many Sherlock Holmes–inspired games.

It's not that interest in the nineteenth century has waned; but it's possible that the corresponding scholarship on games has not kept up with the scholarship of other aspects of Romantic and Victorian culture, or that nobody has been keeping track as well as we do with other fields of scholarship. It is remarkably difficult even to locate research on nineteenth-century games. A perusal of the *Modern Language Association's International Bibliography (MLA-IB)* yields some interesting data. Of the 24 published works in English tagged by *nineteenth-century* and *games* in the *MLA-IB*, two focus on literary texts as games, while 13 (almost 60 percent of the remainder) focus on sports and sporting life (baseball, cricket, lacrosse, highland games, archery, shooting, fox hunting, horse racing, even bull- and cockfighting). The remaining nine divide across toys (four, including dolls, blocks, etc.); specific games in literature and culture (four, including chess); and sewing (one). *Board games* more broadly generates only 94 articles (two from Ann R. Hawkins and Erin N. Bistline's 2017 special issue of the CEA *Critic* on games and gaming). *Games and nineteenth-century literature* generates only five results; *games and nineteenth-century culture*, four; and *board games and nineteenth-century literature*, only one. In Worldcat, *board games* combined with both *nineteenth-century* and *Great Britain* yields only 12 records for historical games: two for reproductions of games, two catalogues of exhibitions, three versions of Hoyle's instructional books, and one critical work, Megan Norcia's 2019 *Gaming Empire in Children's British Board Games, 1836–1860*, an extension of her article in this collection. Using the Library of Congress subject heading *Games—Social Aspects—United States—History—19th Century* yields only three works on baseball, one on the bicycle, and Doug Guerra's 2018 *Slantwise Moves: Games, Literature and Social Invention in Nineteenth-Century America*, which discusses commercially produced games to understand the cultural intertextuality of Nathaniel Hawthorne's, Herman Melville's, and Walt Whitman's literary texts.

The field for studies of sport is generally more robust than the scholarship of parlor games. But even so, the combined Library of Congress search heading *Sports—Great Britain—History—Nineteenth-century* garners fewer than 25 titles, including two bibliographies. Most allied to our interest are those studies which base their examinations in contemporary literature and periodicals. The first group of studies offer more historical than literary arguments. Mike Huggins's 2004 *The Victorians and Sport* examines the complex history of sport in Victorian society, tracing the changing relationship people had with sport during the time and connects those changes to the massive social upheavals occurring simultaneously. Adrian Harvey's 2004 *The Beginnings of a Commercial Sporting Culture in Britain, 1793–1850* examines the shifting approach to sports in Britain, using detailed periodical and quantitative research to make arguments about professional sports and changing our ideas about commercialized sports. Nancy Fix Anderson's 2010 *The Sporting Life: Victorian Sports and Games* intertwines discussions of sport with larger social issues, providing along the way fascinating historical details and insights into the increasing importance of sport in the Victorian era. The second set situate their studies more in literary texts. Kathleen Blake's 1975 *Play, Games, and Sport: The Literary Works of Lewis Carroll* offers a close reading of Lewis's Alice books and his lesser-known work. Michael Oriard's 1991 *Sporting with the Gods: The Rhetoric of Play and Game in American Culture* ambitiously approaches a study of play and game, through literature, history and theory. Malcolm Cormack's 2007 *Country Pursuits: British, American, and French Sporting Art from the Mellon Collections in the Virginia Museum of Fine Arts* focuses on the art of sport, and its sections—"Animals, Horse racing, Foxhunting and Coursing, Shooting and Fishing, Coaching and Carriages, and Other Country Pastimes"—offer a fascinating overview of sporting as the nineteenth-century viewer would have seen it (97). Finally, Sharon Harrow's 2015 edited collection *British Sporting Literature and Culture in the Long Eighteenth Century* shares many of our own aims, though focusing on sports in the eighteenth century. Her collection covers a breadth of topics—sport overall, clothes, tennis, archery, horse culture, swimming, and boxing—from a variety of theoretical standpoints.

Even with the recent growth of study on nineteenth-century sport, research on nineteenth-century games remains still in its infancy. Other literary and historical periods generated considerable amounts of scholarship, *MLA-IB* recording 291 articles and books on medieval games; 124 for renaissance; 85 for eighteenth-century; and 112 for twentieth-century. Studies of medieval and renaissance games can find homes in two publishers's series: University of Amsterdam's Cultures of Play, 1300–1700 and the Medieval Institute Publications's Ludic Cultures 1100–1700. And of course there is a robust field of book series and journals examining digital game studies. But, clearly, the contemporary interest in games has not yet fostered adequate basic research on the nature and significance of nineteenth-century games and gaming.

Our collection steps into this gap in nineteenth-century and games scholarship, exploring the role of games and play in nineteenth-century society in the United Kingdom and the United States. But before we lay out the terrain we undertake to traverse, we should point out the terrain we leave to others to explore. We value works that theorize the nature of games, of play, of the ludic nature of human experience, of literary texts as games—but that is not our focus. Instead, we examine specific moments in the historic record, drawing on descriptions of games and gaming in contemporary periodicals, engravings, and other ephemera as well as in the physical evidence of the games themselves. Our approach draws on the methods of bibliography, book history, and textual criticism in considering specific games and their historical, cultural, literary, and social contexts.

Our focus on the nineteenth-century transatlantic culture thus recognizes the roots of current games and gaming practices in the narratives of print culture, particularly the production of printed ephemera, and we suggest that it participates as fully in the formation of transatlantic culture as scholars have long suggested is the case with cultures of print. After all, most board games were printed; Milton Bradley, the well-known producer of board games, began as a maker and seller of lithographic prints. The nineteenth century's visual and print technologies allowed people to visualize play in new ways—both to render them as part of scientific discourse and to discover new levels of aesthetic features in the playing body. Meanwhile, developments in print culture allowed for ever greater distribution and ownership of play materials—for those who could afford them.

Games and the Nineteenth-Century Consumer

Therefore, it is not only the game and the players that we must attend to, but the entire culture of new middle-class consumers flexing their purchasing power in order to amuse themselves in socially appropriate ways, as well as the emerging industry that produced games for a rapidly growing gaming culture. To build an authentic sense of the role of games in everyday life, we must track their economic cost and contemporary value to the people who bought and played them. Therefore, we focus on ephemera to reveal the importance of games in everyday British and

American lives. Games and play were integral to nineteenth-century culture in Britain and the United States, building on their historical antecedents, yet leaving a dynamic inheritance to games in later centuries, even today. Briefly, technological advances during the nineteenth century allowed for easier and cheaper manufacturing and distribution of board games and books about games, while the changing economic conditions created a larger market for games as well as more time in which to play them. These changing conditions not only made games more profitable, but they also increased the influence of games on many facets of culture.

Defining Games

So, what resources would a nineteenth-century game player need to have in order to play games? To answer this question, we must first address another: What do we mean—and more importantly, what did their original audiences mean—by "games" and associated terms such as games, sport, and play, which were related in ways that might seem alien to twenty-first-century scholars? To get a sense of the nineteenth century's definitions of and distinctions between these terms, we examined Gale's *Nineteenth-Century Collections Online* (NCCO) as well as the nineteenth-century holdings of the *British Newspaper Archive* (BNA), paying close attention to the use of the word *game* in its various forms.[14] We reviewed thousands of page images, collecting evidence for how the nineteenth-century authors published in those periodicals or the nineteenth-century advertiser hawking books, games, and other wares might have used the terms. Though it's not easy to trace references to particular games at any given moment or across the century, we did find references to a variety of games. Many, such as cricket, chess, billiards, darts, and cribbage, are familiar to us, at least by name. Others are less so, like "three-card loo."

But we also discovered that *games* as a term was both more broad and more narrow than we find it today. In the 1849 *Social Sports; or Holiday Amusements*, the narrative categorizes as "sports," a range of activities from hoops, jumping rope, cup and ball to enigmas, charades, and see-saw. Likewise, though periodicals commonly used the word *game* in ways that seem familiar to us, they also used that word with enough slippage that it seems useful to notice its nineteenth-century breadth. In the July 1821 *La Belle Assemblée*, for example, an English antiquarian traces the range of "English sports and amusements" from 1698 to 1759 ("Recollections" 7–9). In that essay the author lumps together sport, games, play, and the arts somewhat willy-nilly, discussing (in this order) chess, dice, ball, trundling the hoop, riding, horse races, hunting, hawking, singing, archery, racing, leaping, throwing stones, baiting bulls and bears, cockfighting, spear throwing at a shield in the Thames to win a prize (and avoid dunking), Quintain (hitting a bag of sand attached to a spindle with a spear while on horseback), tournaments, keeping fools, leaping on and off of horses as at Astley's, masquerading in the streets, wrestling, back-sword and football, boxing, singing ballads, going to the theater, and masked balls. It's a dizzying level of granulation, making it easy to see why more scholarship hasn't yet been attempted. But it also shows that the nineteenth century's view of *games* wasn't distinct from other forms of what most today might call *play* or *physical sport.*

Below, we order our discussion of the word *game* and its meanings, roughly according to our perception (given our search results) of how frequently forms of that word appear in *BNA* periodicals. Though this is a problematic measure, it is the only one we have. We also focus our discussion below on the early years of the nineteenth century, leaving it to our contributors to draw the conversation through the rest of the century.

To Hunt Game: Sports in Field and Pasture

Most frequently in the periodicals, *game* refers to animal stock, whether cultivated through animal husbandry or living wild on the property, and the sports—hunting, fishing, fox-chase—associated with it. Owning game, hunting game, consuming game, all are a function of property ownership, making this *game* the realm of the wealthy and aristocratic male. The person who owns the land is understood to also own the wildlife on it, making roaming animals like deer and rabbits often contested property. This use of *game* appears frequently: in articles on game laws, various field sports, and animal husbandry; in notices indicating which estates are open or closed to hunting or fishing; and as the century progresses, in articles and notices protesting the inhumane treatment of such animals. This *game* is the territory of wealthy men, as Longman, Hurst, Rees, and Orme's advertisement addressed "To Sportsmen" shows[15] (1e). Taking up two-thirds of a newspaper column, the advertisement appeared multiple times in multiple newspapers across England and Scotland. Both the size of the advertisement and its widespread use suggest that its publishers expected the books to perform well in terms of sales. The first section of the advertisement describes five books on sport and animal husbandry, devoting between five and eight lines to each; the second section describes several volumes on game laws. The five sporting books are well produced, lavishly illustrated, and expensive:

- William Barker Daniel's new three-volume edition of *Rural Sports*, boasting seventy-three fine engravings by John Scott, Edwin Landseer, John Tompkins and others, is priced at £7 17s 6d in quarto, and £5 5s in octavo.

- William Taplin's two-volume *The Sportsman's Cabinet; or, a correct Delineation of the various Dogs used in the Sports of the Field, including the Canine Race in general* published under the pseudonym "A Veteran Sportsman" includes engravings of each dog breed, taken from original paintings by Philip Reinagle and engraved by John Scott, and accompanied by "beautiful vignettes engraved on wood." In quarto, Taplin's *Cabinet* costs £7 7s.

- Richard Badham Thornhill's one-volume *The Shooting Directory* is available with "elegant engravings by Medland" for £1 11s 6d and with "the plates coloured after life," for £3 3s.

- Delabere Blaine's two-volume large-octavo *The Outlines of the Veterinary Art, or the Principles of Medicine, as applied to a knowledge of the structure, functions, and economy of the Horse, the Ox, the Sheep, and the Dog; and to a more scientific and successful manner of treating their various diseases* capitalizes on Blaine's status as a "professor of animal medicine," includes anatomical plates and costs £1 5s.

- An Amateur Sportsman's one-volume *Sporting Anecdotes, original and select; including Characteristic Sketches of eminent Persons who have appeared on the Turf*, published under the pseudonym is illustrated with "several engravings." An octavo, the book costs 10s 6d. ("To Sportsmen" 1e)

The Cost of Games

So much for the definitions, how much did these things cost?

Thirty-six billion dollars—or 36,000 million—seems an unimaginably large number for most twenty-first-century people to contemplate, except to recognize that a $36 billion annual outlay means that many Americans spend lavishly on video games and equipment—about $108 for each adult per year. Of course, the top-down statistical data provided today by nations, trade agencies, importers, and exporters was not for the most part available either during the nineteenth century or after; we simply don't have accurate categorical data about trade until the early twentieth century. However, we can make some educated guesses to determine what monetary resources were needed to enjoy games in the nineteenth century. We can use data from advertisements to find the raw costs of games, but we need to know whether a game costing six shillings or a game-related book costing seven pounds was cheap or expensive and who could have afforded either or both. William St. Clair in his landmark study *The Reading Nation in the Romantic Period* offers a useful method for determining what was affordable and wasn't, based on pay rates. Using the British government's 1816 pension and half-pay rates, St. Clair predicts that a "reasonable but not extravagant income for members of the upper- or upper-middle classes" would be 100 shillings (or £5) per week (194). For "younger sons, clergymen, officers, doctors, merchants, widowed ladies on annuities, journalists, university students," and others in the lower-middle classes, St. Clair estimates weekly incomes between 100 shillings (or £5) and 50 shillings (or £2 10s) (195). After 1810, printers—among the highest-paid skilled workers—earned around 36 shillings a week (or, £1 16s); carpenters earned 25 shillings (or, £1 5s); and law clerks around 10 1/2 shillings (St. Clair 195–96). For the rest of the "employed population"—"journeymen, tradesmen, farm workers, factory worker, domestic servants, and others"—"only a few earned as much as ten shillings a week" (St. Clair 196).

What could nineteenth-century people have purchased with these earnings? St. Clair converts the cost of any item into shillings, then estimates that cost as a percentage of a worker's weekly pay. The weekly four shillings a bookseller's apprentice earned could buy him a shared boarding-house bedroom, meals, and the "right to sit by the fire" (St. Clair 195). But the six-shilling "pint of wine served in a provincial hotel" would have cost the maid who served it the "equivalent of three weeks' wages," and a "copy of [George Gordon, Lord Byron's] *Childe Harold's Pilgrimage a Romaunt* would have cost six week's income" (St. Clair 196). Admission to the English Opera House in 1823 cost "five shillings for a box, three for the pit, two for the gallery, and one shilling for the upper gallery" (St. Clair 368). An individual printed Shakespeare play cost half a shilling. By St. Clair's calculations, the majority of the working population would have found most popular entertainments, including board games, out of reach. But we'll examine the costs of games more below.

Prefaced to each of the advertisements—perhaps for ease of changing the list between newspapers—is a long list of those booksellers publishing these books. Given the hefty cost of the volumes and the variety of publishers named on the title pages, these are most likely members of a consortium sharing the cost of producing and distributing the books, not simply booksellers keeping the books in stock. Taken collectively, the advertisements placed across a range of regional papers from an 1806 *York Herald and Caledonian Mercury* to an 1807 issue of the *Bury and Norwich Post*, the consortium included publishers in at least eight cities, one each in London, Bury, Hadleigh, Ipswick, Woodbridge, and Witham; eight in Edinburgh alone; and an additional six sales partners in York and Doncaster. Clearly, the books—however expensive—appeared to be a good investment, offering a strong return.

But who could afford these volumes? And who would want them? To answer that, we use St. Clair's 100-shillings-a-week gentleman. Daniel's two-volume *Rural Sports* and Taplin's one-volume *Sportsman's Cabinet*, cost 157.5 and 147 shillings, respectively: either one would cost a bit more than and a bit less than a week-and-a-half's income. Thornhill's one-volume *The Shooting Directory*'s 31½ shillings costs only two day's income, but if one chooses the colored illustrations, the price jumps to 63 shillings, almost a week's wages. Blaine's *Outlines of the Veterinary Art*, with anatomical plates, costs 25 shillings, somewhat reasonable if our gentleman is also to care for estate animals. The cheapest of the lot (but likely the smallest book), *Sporting Anecdotes* costs only a little more than a tenth of our gentleman's weekly income: at that cost, a book is a manageable, if not a frequent, purchase. Clearly, St. Clair's gentleman is not the intended purchaser of these books. Those who could afford the books on sport are most certainly landowners who would care about preserving their game. This likely audience explains why second section of the advertisement lists a series of books on game laws. But no one outside the upper or upper-middle classes could hope to afford even that one. The law clerk dreaming of a future country estate would have to devote almost a full month's pay to buy *Sporting Anecdotes*, and the other four books would be far out of reach. Clearly, game, as in game and field sports, was a lucrative subject, garnering strong interest from those most able to purchase the books.

Given the interests of this market, publishers developed other products for the "sportsman" who owned an estate and the game on it. By 1804, a number of publishers kept in stock a "sporting or game book," fashioned "on the plan of a book kept at Chevely Hall by the Duke of Rutland" ("This" 4b). Such a book by the help of "printed tables" "enables the lover of Field Sports to keep a daily Register of Sporting Occurrences; an accurate account of Game; the different kinds; when and where killed, where sent, (as presents), and various other particulars" (York). The 1808 version of this "sporting annal" allowed the purchaser to keep five years of records and was priced according to the book's size and other amenities, at seven shillings; ten shillings and six pence; fourteen shillings; twenty-one shillings; or forty-two shillings ("This"). Given the buying power of this market segment, it's no wonder that their interests appear robustly in every newspaper, if not on every page.

To Play Sports: Rustic and Ancient Games

Game is also used to designate athletic events or sports, though that context was narrower in the nineteenth century than it is for us. These sort of games fall broadly into several (sometimes overlapping) categories:

- ancient games such as the "Olympic, Pythian, Nemean, and Isthmian" games;[16]
- games played in rustic settings; and
- what we would call sporting events.[17]

Discussions of ancient games in periodicals is often tied to considerations of classical authors, such as Pindar. Rustic games are typically mentioned in articles extracted from or indebted to Joseph Strutt's *Sports and Pastimes of the People of England*. Boasting 21 editions between 1801 and 1903, Strutt's book considers the full range of "rural and domestic recreations," including "[m]ay-games, mummeries, pageants, processions, and pompous spectacles, from the earliest period to the present time," and his books were often copiously illustrated with engravings from ancient paintings depicting these events (title-page). The third category—references to sporting events—should be more robust, as Harvey argues that such events in England took place every day of the week. But our examination focuses on how the periodicals use the word *sports* or *sport* in general contexts, while Harvey counted references to specific sports (boxing, fox hunting, bear-baiting). A subset of the books on sporting events includes discussions of games played in various educational contexts as with the 1810 anonymously authored *A book of games, or A history of juvenile sports, practised at a considerable academy near London.* These juvenile games became, by mid-century, less play and more a form of physical and moral training, encouraged by the muscular Christianity movement. By 1867, *The Young Englishman's Journal* provided descriptions and illustrations of a variety of games intended to "develop the muscular system, and otherwise promote health, whilst they afford amusement to our young friends" ("British" 421). The games themselves emphasize physical ability: in *Saddle my Nag,* one team plays the role of the nag and the other team piles on top to see how many bodies the 'nag' can hold; in *Beating the Bear* (or "bast[ing]" as in the *Boy's Own Book*), a boy (the bear) is led about by a partner (his master) and attempts to tag another boy in order to make him the bear ("British" 421; Williams 32). The other boys may elude the bear by beating him with knotted handkerchiefs (the article cautions that the handkerchiefs should not contain "stones or hard substances" lest the bear be "seriously hurt" ("British" 421).

To Game and Gamble in the Hell and the Drawing Room

Both our prior senses of game tend to fall the province of men. Even Strutt's rural amusements, such as Morris dancing, focus on the activities of men, though in communal contexts. But with card and other gambling games (whether played for money or not), *gaming* cuts across gender and social class. At the same time, card games most often associated with locations in which women could play them—like whist—tend to be presented as more innocent in the periodicals of the time. Consider, for example, this tartly amusing dialogue from "A Game of Skill," published in the 1893 *Bristol Magpie*:

"I do wish you wouldn't gamble, Harry, dear."

"I don't, I only play Whist, my darling, and that is a game of skill."

"I am sure it isn't. Not as you play it, anyhow"

The distinction here between games of skill and games of chance is an important one, for games of chance played for money were often illegal. On 11 November 1748, for example, *The Derby Mercury* records the Lord Mayor of Ireland's actions in enforcing the anti-gaming laws: he "burnt a Rowley-powley table, and two shuffle-boards on Cork-hill" and "intended to suppress the billiard-tables, and other gaming diversions" ("Ireland" 2c). While one could play games of chance, one was forbidden to bet or wager on them, and across the nineteenth century, the periodicals frequently recount the often dire consequences of playing forbidden games of chance for money.

But to play games of skill well requires a thorough knowledge of the rules. And publishers' advertisements of the period show a robust trade associated with gaming manuals. The most famous are those of Edmond Hoyle (1672–1769), whose 1740 *Short Treatise on the Game of Back-gammon* was followed by his 1744 *Short Treatise on the Game of Quadrille*, and his more substantial 1745 *The Polite Gamester, containing short treatises on the game of whist, quadrille, backgammon, piquet, and chess. Together with* [. . .] *the game of whist*. By the beginning of the nineteenth century, Hoyle appears in as many permutations as publishers can hope to sell, and by 1800 (as we mentioned before) that involves a dramatic expansion of games. Here are some examples from a single advertisement, published in multiple newspapers, in order of price point:

- For three shillings, *Hoyle's Games Improved and selected as a Companion to the Card Table*, consisting of practical treatises on twenty-two Fashionable Games, wherein are comprised calculations for betting upon equal or advantageous terms, in 18mo, "sewed in a case like an Almanack, with gilt edges."
- For two shillings, *Hoyle's Game of Chess, now first including his Chess Lectures, and some selections from other Amateurs*, "in extra boards," which, according to John Carter, appears to signal a cloth binding.

- For six pence, sewed, *Hoyle's Treatise on Backgammon, as improved and corrected by Charles Jones, Esq.*
- For one shilling, *Introduction to Payne's Games of Draughts*, with additions, extracted from Hoyle's *Games*, improved by Charles Jones, Esq. ([Advertisement] 2e).

Clearly this coalition of nineteen London and five Manchester publishers wished to produce a Hoyle for every audience. That audience, at least in this advertisement, seems to be decidedly aristocratic: for the advertisers place at the head a description of the newest (fourth) edition of *Longmate's Pocket Peerage, of Great Britain and Ireland, continued to March 1808: containing an account of the Descent, Connections, Marriages, and Issue of every noble Family, with the Blazonry of their Arms*. Priced at 18s, Longmate's appeared in "two volumes, 12mo, printed on wove paper with fine ink, illustrated by above 1200 Arms, Crests, &c. recently engraved on Copper-plates" ([Advertisement] 2e). The juxtaposition of this book with the various Hoyles suggesting that the rule books were expected to find an audience among those who wished to have a pocket peerage as well.[18]

But Hoyle was not the only rule book. Across the nineteenth century, newspapers frequently announced publication of rule books for every game imaginable. In chess, for example, we find J. H. Sarratt's eighteen-shilling two-volume octavo *Treatise on the Game of Chess, containing a regular system of Attack and Defence*; or in billiards, E. White, Esq's 10s illustrated *A Practical Treatise on the Game of Billiards, with Calculations for Betting, Tables of Odds*. Some of the more interesting rule books also promise to help players avoid the unfair practices of professional players, as does Antony Pasquin's two-shilling and six pence *Treatise on the Game of Cribbage; shewing the Laws and Rules of the Game, as now played* [. . .] *with the best method of laying our your Cards, and exposing all the unfair Arts practised by Professional Players, or such men as are generally known by the appellation of BLACK LEGS*.

Games on Linen and Board

While games in the sense of sport, gaming (as in hunting), and gaming (as in gambling) were most often the province of men, board games were frequently part of the territory of the nursery and the drawing room. An advertisement in 1805 *Derby Mercury* for Parke's Shew Room makes game's delegation to the terrain of women quite clear. Parke advertises a wide and varied stock in household items, tucking a "[g]reat variety of Fine and Common Toys, Maps, *Games*, Alphabets, and various diverting and instructive Toys, for the Improvement of Youth" neatly beneath the notices for pearl, amber, coral, and cornelian jewelry, tea urns, japanned trays, knife cases, writing desks, Tunbridge Ware, umbrellas and parasols, fans and combs, but above hair powder, pomatum, soap and perfumes (emphasis added; d4). Likewise, J. Harris, the London successor to Newbery, advertises children's books and Christmas games "for the instruction and amusement of young persons" ("Christmas!" 1c). His advertisement includes two types of board games: three whose purpose is largely entertainment, and three whose purpose is explicitly educational. The "entertaining" or "interesting" board games are the following:

- *The Panorama of London, or a Day's Journey round the Metropolis; being an entertaining and instructive Game, exhibiting fifty views of the exterior or the interior of the principal buildings in London, with suitable directions, and the apparatus for playing* (price nine shillings including a case);
- *Geographical Recreations, or A voyage round the Habitable World; an instructive game, consisting of one hundred and twenty representations of the manners and customs of the inhabitants of the different parts of the globe, accompanied with directions, a short system of geography, and an apparatus for playing*; and
- *The Jubilee!! An interesting game, intended to exhibit the remarkable events, from the accession of his majesty King George the third, to the 25th of October, 1809, when he entered into the fiftieth year of his reign, and which was celebrated by every class of his subjects as a day of Jubilee; the whole elegantly engraved from 150 drawings, made for the purpose accompanied with a book descriptive of them, rules and directions, and apparatus for playing* (also nine shillings in a case). ("Christmas!" 1c)

While these "entertaining" games might teach players about the habits and customs of peoples around the world or the reign of King George, they are clearly less educational than the three games produced under the aegis of Mrs. Lovechild, a well-known children's author. Two of Lovechild's games—*A secret worth knowing* and *Friendly whispers for youth of both sexes*—involve play with a pack of "curious" cards (whatever *curious* means). Priced at one shilling each, these games are easily within the reach of well-to-do women, purchasing Christmas gifts with pin money. The third game, priced more expensively at six shillings, is a *Box of Grammatical amusement* includes a series of "sportive exercises" "intended to enable Ladies [. . .] to instil in the minds of youth the first rudiments of English grammar" ([Parke's] d4). The advertisement also includes two books by Lovechild—for two shillings, *The family miscellany; in prose and verse; a new and improved edition*, and for one shilling and six pence, the new and improved edition of *A Birth Day Present, or Nine Days Conversation between a Mother and her Daughter, on interesting subjects*. These books by Lovechild make the distinction between her games and the others in the advertisement clear.

The rest of Harris's advertised stock are children's books priced from one to five shillings. While most of the 21 books and games are anonymously authored, eight are explicitly identified with women (five with Mrs. Lovechild, and one each with Mrs. Dorset, Emma Hamilton, and Miss Lefanu), two more associated with a woman (Miss Sandham, whose name appears on the books' title pages), and only two with men (Mr. Roscoe and John Sabine). This suggests (as Stephanie Eckroth has discussed in her studies of the early-nineteenth-century novel's market) that, when signed, woman-authored books were more valued. But though Harris's advertisement is as long as Longmans's "To Sportsmen" and "Game Laws," it packs in far more titles, each one garnering three typographic lines or fewer.

By mid-century, the explicit distinction between board and other games began to fade. In 1857, an advertisement in the *Worcester Herald* for Birley's "presents for the new year" lumps all types of games together: "race and steeple chase games, bagatelle, backgammon, & chess boards, chess and draught men," "playing cards, conversation," "Cribbage and Pope Joan boards" ("Merry" 3e).

Addressing the Knowledge Gap

Playing Games in Nineteenth-Century Britain and the United States considers the material and visual culture of both American and British games, examining how cultures of play intersect with evolving cultural and social movements. With a particular interest in material and visual culture, the essays in this collection explore how games and play reveal cultural values or anxieties, whether through the performance of gender in social games (Blackwell, Bistline), in charades (Fitzsimmons Frey) and in home theatricals (MacDonald); in the rhetoric of patriotism and fantasies of virtual travel (Beissel Heath, Norcia, and Carroll); in the alignment of sport and recreation with scientific discourses on the body (Samuelian and Schoenfield, Von Vogt); and in the gamification of military strategy (Byers)—the chutes and ladders that emblematize the vicissitudes of the world. Our essayists examine the forces that undergird the development of many varieties of games, be they the fascination with the unknown (Rhoda), with the private practices of family life (Grass, Ives), or with the surviving artifacts of the game market (Suckling and others). The essays derive their accounts of games from publishing histories of game texts and materials; literary and visual representations of games; and the letters and diaries of players. The visual and material aspects of the games play an important role in their use, and the essays frequently engage with how these objects were designed, seen, and used.

In the following fourteen chapters, our contributors examine a wide variety of games and their cultural impact from a convergence of scholarly methods and approaches, including history of the book, media archaeology, literary studies, and the emerging foci on games, ephemera, visual and material culture, and the study of sport and leisure. We divide the collection into four sections: "Games in Motion," "Communal Games," "Playing the World," and "Books, Boards, and Other Objects."

Section I: Games in Motion

The essays in this section focus on the more physical games and sports played in the nineteenth century. We begin with Kristin Flieger Samuelian and Mark Schoenfield's examination of how nineteenth-century discourse, particularly that found in literary texts and in the increasing number of periodicals devoted to sporting culture, framed the idea of movement in games or sports. In "Bodies in Play: Boxing, Dance, and the Science of Recreation," Samuelian and Schoenfield examine the alliances between dancing and boxing, arts that both relied on "performance or spectacle." Both also depended on the relationship between the professional actors and their public personas and the "enthusiastic," "avid," and "knowledgeable" amateurs, or connoisseurs, who consumed the sports. In tracing the movement of these two sports, Samuelian and Schoenfield draw connections to poets and poetry—Lord Byron boxed, training with John "Gentleman" Jackson—and to the idea of both sports being a sort of (to use Byron's phrase) "poetry in motion." This "aesthetic" of motion "depended on marshaling a rhetoric of science"—one where boxing drew on dancing's "cachet" to "insist on the grace and legitimacy of the sport." Samuelian and Schoenfield, then, offer a starting point for our examination of the other sorts of movements games inspire or require in the nineteenth century.

While Samuelian and Schoenfield examine movement and how its representation in engraved images at the beginning of the century revealed (and fostered) increasingly professionalization of boxing and dancing, Matthew Van Vogt's "Baseball in the Frame of Gilded-Age America" carries that consideration into the photographic age. Focusing on the introduction of full-size pictorial baseball cards, Von Vogt considers the interplay with Eadweard Muybridge's stop-motion technologies and the increasing professionalism that the cards brought to baseball. Von Vogt poses two questions: What cultural images did the baseball cards offer? and "How do those images of baseball change when we view the baseball cards not only as visual but also as material (cardboard) objects?" To answer these, Von Vogt focuses on the representations of the players themselves, in their stances that appear to capture the moment of movement, to argue that "the photographic cards modernized the sport though imbuing it with the visual vocabulary of the pictorial archive" and that "the mass cultural anchoring of the cards in cigarette packages demonstrated the inseparability of baseball from the consumer economy."

Issues of movement and burgeoning professionalism undergird Erin N. Bistline's "'We are only horses and don't know': Sport and Danger in Fox Hunting" as well. Like Blackwell's consideration of croquet, Bistline traces another group game—fox hunting—through the conversations in periodicals and literature to highlight the place of the game among the gentry and aristocracy. Our ideas of the hunt rely heavily on nineteenth-century illustrations, which feature idyllic scenes full of hounds and men on horses, gazing into the distance. Even when the participants are depicted as in motion, the scenes are frequently serene. But for nineteenth-century readers, the game was far more nuanced, with constant reminders of the costs (in human life, livestock, and crops). Beginning with William Spooner's 1839 board game *The Funnyshire Fox*

Chase, Bistline discusses "both the cultural significance of fox hunting as well as [. . .] the complicated discourse surrounding it." As Bistline shows, from the earliest years of the century, the voices of those opposed to the hunt (citing issues of ethics, animal rights, and economics) appear alongside more sunny views.

Section II: Communal Games

Here we move from the playing fields to the parlor and nursery, examining the social games played with family or friends as part of a private circle. In "'The Memory Game': Play, Trauma, and *Great Expectations*," Sean Grass examines a game that Charles Dickens loved to play and its place in Dickens's fiction. The Memory Game involved each person reciting from memory a long series of words created by the group, then adding one of his own to the end. In careful examinations of key moments in *Great Expectations*, *Hard Times*, *David Copperfield*, and even *Edwin Drood*, Grass argues that play and games in Dickens serve purposes beyond simply entertainment. Instead, as Grass tells us, Dickens puts the game to use in his fiction, not to reveal the social or class implications of game play, but rather to "expres[s] and cordo[n] off ungovernable traumas and desires." In Dickens's works, "play—especially if taken to mean not just games and recreations but also imaginative fancy, linguistic invention, clowning, and play-acting—appears so often in his fiction, most memorably when, as in the famous opening of *Hard Times*, it provides a ludic antidote to the 'Facts' of a rigid and objectivizing industrial culture." As Grass reveals, Dickens required the "orderly space of play" in order to articulate and manage trauma.

While few of us would see the trauma inherent of a game of croquet, Catherine S. Blackwell in "Seeing Victorian Culture through Croquet's 'Treacherous Wire Portal,'" reveals that for nineteenth-century players (and readers) the game offered multiple pitfalls and opportunities for injury (both physical and psychological). Using literary texts and periodicals, particularly those from the 1860s when the passion for croquet appears to have been at its height, Blackwell traces the ways that discussions of croquet across the nineteenth century reveal important shifts in gender roles and expectations. Like boxing and dancing, croquet was both a casual pastime and an increasingly regulated "science," and games were often depicted as battles between individual players or teams. The movement of the game and its sounds—from the pop of a fair stroke to the quiet of the deceitful push—become important measures of fairness. Since the game allowed men and women to play together, novelists such as Charlotte Yonge, Anthony Trollope, Louisa May Alcott, and Lewis Carroll found the game a "perfect vehicle" for revealing character. Allowing public flirtations, the croquet grounds were frequently depicted in the periodical press as "honey traps": locations where one might easily throw over a betrothal and escape across the green with a new beau. While debates about the value of the sport were common, Blackwell reveals the ubiquity of the game as periodicals included advertisements for a range of croquet necessities, including petticoats, boots, and other items.

While the memory game required an agile mind and croquet agile feet, charades—or "acting charades" as they were performed in the mid-century—required costumes, props, curtains, and a groups large enough to compete. As Heather Fitzsimmons Frey shows in her "Acting Charades in 1873: Girls and the Stakes of the Game," an acting charade falls "somewhere between a riddle, a participatory game, and a private theatrical performance." In the game, "teams chose a word in secret, divided it into syllables, then played it out in scenes for the party as a whole." Using the private newspaper of the children of George MacDonald, Fitzsimmons Frey examines the perspective of Grace MacDonald, an unmarried nineteen-year-old. MacDonald's viewpoint allows a lens into the differences in gender expectations surrounding the popular party game: "Even when the subject was not provocative, while men and boys might be willing to dress in foolish ways, girls might worry about how they looked when they put themselves on display, thinking about issues such as 'correctness,' as well as showing off their own specific charms to advantage." Indeed, Fitzsimmons Frey argues that while the game could offer opportunities to explore behaviors that were normally considered unacceptable, the game "could just as easily reinforce status quo ideas about gender roles, the imperial project, and social institutions such as marriage."

Section III: Playing the World

Our third section discusses games transatlantically, addressing questions of empire and its effect on games. By considering cultures of play across the Atlantic, our essayists reveal radical shifts in games and their cultural meaning across the nineteenth century. In Britain, the expansion of mass education and literacy transformed the schedule of the day and the structures around leisure, particularly for children, whose lives were increasingly ordered around demarcations of work, study, and play (Jordan 196). On the American side, the period saw rapid transformations of game culture, with the development, refinement, institutionalization, and standardization of many sports and games, including the formation of league structures and infrastructure for the creation of sporting audiences (Pope 3). At the same time, the growth in print media, with an explosion in publishing targeting both middle-class and working-class readers, cultivated both game and sport culture, and makes certain types of game-related ephemera, from baseball cards to party games, available to larger groups of people (Pope 7).

While most of the games in our collection don't have the fate of nations at stake, Andrew Byers turns our attention to games with a more deadly purpose. In "Dangerous Games: The Advent of Wargaming in the Nineteenth Century," Byers traces the nineteenth-century development of the war game. While Byers notes that war games have a long history, dating to at least the development of the Chinese game of *Go* and were "intended to teach nobles, rulers, and military leaders the fundamentals of strategic problem solving," he identifies Prussia as the nineteenth-century innovator. Byers defines war games as those which "simulate or model the kinds of problems that military officers face in real-life situations for explicitly pedagogical, analytical, and professional development purposes," and he argues that "the creation of the influential Prussian wargame, Kriegsspiel [and] the transnational transmission and reception of Kriegsspiel (and related wargames) among the major powers and the United States" led to innovations in war games across the world and to invaluable military strategy for the forthcoming world wars.

While Byers traces the transnational movement of war games, Michelle Beissel Heath focuses on the transnational transmission of children's games. In "The United States as Wonderland: British Literature, US Nationalism, and Nineteenth-Century Children's and Family Board and Card Games," Beissel Heath examines an early example of cross-media transmission: Anne Abbot's 1844 book *Doctor Busby and His Neighbors*, which began life as a card game. In Abbot's and others' works, both literary and games, the United States is presented as "a place of fantastic potential for youth," with "inhabitants [that are] moral, good, patriotic-minded citizens unafraid of adventures and exploration or the public eye," and with "literary creations" that are "like their creators, in every way equal to or better than their British peers and predecessors." As

Beissel Heath argues, "games were recouped to render them 'appropriate' for youth and families," reimagining "the United States [. . .] as especially fitting for those same audiences." Through this shift and reinvention as family friendly, "literary themes, nationalism, and competition ran rampant, rendering games, play, and literature battlegrounds in a (cultural) revolutionary war."

Megan A. Norcia expands this focus to examine imperial power writ large. In "Gaming the Great Exhibition of 1851: Children's Board Games, Display, and Imperial Power," Norcia considers two important figures in nineteenth-century game culture—Henry Smith Evans and William Spooner—and their games responding to the Crystal Palace. Billed as an opportunity to promote international harmony through exposure to a range of cultures and cultural artifacts, the Crystal Palace exhibition offered a tour of the world (and the British empire), allowing the British to experience the products of various cultures. Valuing "opportunities for colonial development," Evans's game offers a "straightforward celebration of imperial power" and positions its child-players as "future imperial stewards," while Spooner's take in the Comic Game of the Great Exhibition is decidedly jingoistic. But both men make the imperial narrative "visible" for those playing, offering opportunities for "showcase and critique."

Siobhan Carroll then continues the discussion of games worldwide in "Teetotum Lives: Mediating Globalization in the Nineteenth-Century Board Game." Carroll focuses on the teetotum and its cultural significance even beyond the game board. The teetotum—a spinner commonly used in nineteenth-century board games (as today)—guided the players around the board. She argues that "the material artifact of the nineteenth-century board game encoded Britons' attitudes towards the accelerations, circulations, and space-time compressions of incipient globalization." The teetotum, Carroll continues, "was ideally suited to expressing the bewilderment and powerlessness felt by nineteenth-century Britons in an increasingly internationalized world." The games as physical objects offer representations of the empirical structure of the British world.

Section IV: Books, Boards, and Other Objects

In our final section, we consider a range of game-objects found in the nineteenth century from books about games, to playing or collecting cards, to toys. Maurice Suckling gives us a view into the nineteenth-century games market through a quantitative examination of the contents of the Games Research Database (GARD), some more than 3000 entries which help "tackle [the] question: what did they play and what does this say?" While empirical studies are uncommon in discussions of games, Suckling undertakes the necessary work of categorizing and schematizing the range of games available for play in the nineteenth century alongside periodic cultural analysis in relation to game types, themes, and mechanics. While GARD's holdings (drawn from personal collections) may be "skewed by personal interests or chance," the database still offers "a fair sample of British manufactured indoor games." Suckling's schema offers an essential groundwork for further scholarly examinations, allowing scholars and critics to understand the actual terrain of the nineteenth-century game. Without such analytical approaches to what the market actually included, games studies will remain, as William St. Clair puts it in his discussion of studies of readership, in the position of "economics before [the development of] statistics" (9).

Similarly, Andrew Rhoda, in "Professor Hoffmann's Victorian Puzzles and Stage Magic," examines the legacy of a single, significant author, Angelo John Lewis, whose works are best known for their schematization of the disparate fields of puzzle games and magic. To protect his professional identity as a barrister, Lewis published his many texts under the pseudonym of Professor Hoffmann. His 1878 *Modern Magic* "was one of the few publications on the practice of stage conjuring when it was published," and "Modern Magic did for stage magic what *Puzzles Old and New* did for mechanical and pencil and paper puzzles about seventeen years later." These texts, Rhoda argues, endure as classics to both puzzle collectors and magicians because of Hoffmann's ability to codify their materials into accessible categories.

In keeping with Fitzsimmons Frey's examination of children's acting charades, Jennie MacDonald in "'An Endless Round of Delights': Materializing the Toy Theatre" examines both the history and cultural significance of the toy theater, from "its beginnings as a live theatre souvenir, as an early form of fan culture, and as an emblematic example of nineteenth-century popular culture." So popular at mid-century were these toys that publishers went to great lengths to make their scenery, costumes, and even scripts parallel those of their "live" counterparts. The toy theaters "succeeded best as a vehicle for visually spectacular plays featuring courageous heroes and heroines; outrageous villains; supernatural figures and remarkable locations; battles, chases, and other exciting events;

and magic and special effects." In some instances, materials published for the toy theater market are the only remaining evidence we have for live performances. But as with Beissel Heath and Norcia, whose essays examine the lessons children learned from their board games, MacDonald argues that toy theaters taught children the "value of money," "patience, fortitude, and something of aesthetics and artistic materials."

Our final essay, Maura Ives's "The Game of Authors, 1861–1900: A Case History" provides a case study and model for how researchers can approach "the history, production and reception of the games prior to 1900." The Game of Authors (which also receives notice in Beissel Heath's essay) was "one of the most popular and commercially successful card games in nineteenth-century America." With at least 76 versions published by 1900, the Game of Authors required players to "matc[h] cards to form a set," and publishers claimed that the activity of "memorizing the names of the authors and the titles of their works" offered an educational value. Tracing the game through its origins in Salem, Massachusetts, with G. M. Whipple and A. A. Smith to its continued popularity in an increasingly crowded market, Ives indicates that the manufacturing and marketing of the game provided publishers with an opportunity to benefit from shifting customer expectations. Ives highlights—as we do in this collection overall—the gap in scholarship on games of this period, and her depth of archival research spotlights the wealth of riches yet to be discovered.

~

We hope that the essays in this volume will justify our argument that the role of games is so significant that any claim to analyze and understand a people, a culture, or an age without considering games is bound to create distortion. Games reveal the intricate relationships among large cultural, political, and social phenomena and the immediate lived experience of individuals and communities. Games offer a combination of physical and intellectual exercises that allow players to entertain hypotheses, theorize real-world phenomena, and in turn make concrete those theoretical concepts, to practice, enact, and revisit social relations, to imagine history, and to develop or refine disciplines of mind and body. Games are central to human experience—and to the lived experience of our nineteenth-century forebears—and any scholar interested in any other aspect of a culture would be remiss to set games aside as frivolous or irrelevant. As Mr. Sleary puts it in Dickens's *Hard Times*: "People mutht be amuthed" (Dickens 345).

Notes

1. See p. 79.

2. Twentieth- and twenty-first-century romance and historical novels set in the early nineteenth century regularly incorporate games to further plots. Rachael Miles makes use of a range of nineteenth-century games in her historical romances, incorporating toy soldiers and the board game *The Magic Ring* in *Jilting*; bocce, enigmas, and fetch in *Chasing*; quoits and word games in *Tempting*; and treasure hunts in *Charming*. And the blogs of published or aspiring authors often provide useful information about nineteenth-century cultural and social practices as do sites focused on Jane Austen, whether managed by loving readers or academics. See, for example, "Games," Kane, Glover, Abella, or Sanborn. These sites often provide useful historical information about games that by being readily accessible to general readers are influential in shaping understanding of historical games and their practices.

3. A number of Austen critics have pointed out this relationship, among them Benson, Brumit, and Vignaux.

4. A complicated game of strategy, *quadrille* uses a forty-card deck from which the tens, nines, and eights have been removed; cards have an established order and rank, depending on whether they are being used as trumps (see Hoyle 236–74). *Cassino*, conversely, is far more straightforward: players collect tricks by matching face value or by combining the face value of the card in the hand to those on the table (see Hoyle 70–88). A player who holds a ten, then, may collect all those cards that together add to ten.

5. As its title page announced, Hoyle's *Games* expanded in 1800 to include eighteen games, with *vignt-un* (or *twenty-one*) joining old standards *whist*, *quadrille*, and *cassino*. In *vignt-un*, players compete against each other and the dealer, taking cards until they reach or exceed 21 (see Hoyle 229–31). As Hoyle said of *Quinze* (a game "that very much resembles" *vingt-un*), the game "depending entirely upon chance, [. . .] not requiring that attention which most other games of the cards do, and therefore calculated for those who love to sport upon an equal chance" (229).

6. Brewster's prolific research on the folklore of games worldwide—along with that of other earlier twentieth-century researchers—is indexed at the Elliott Avedon Virtual Museum of Games.

7. Sadly, the IEEE 2015 timeline is no longer available.

8. Final figures will almost certainly be lower than this 2018 prediction, given the dramatic increase in purchasing (and playing) of board games during

the global COVID-19 pandemic. As Sarah Butler reported for the *Guardian* in April 2020, "sales of boardgames and jigsaw puzzles soared 240% during the first official week of coronavirus lockdown in the UK."

9. This resurgence of interest in board games extends to making them: in January 2019, for example, the Seattle Museum of History and Industry hosted a maker day, collaborating with a design studio to help attendees "design, prototyp[e], and tes[t]" their own board games ("Maker"). Going to the museum has even become a game: "Occupy White Walls," released free on STEAM in 2020, "allows users to design their own art gallery," using 2,200 architectural elements and "more than 6,000 artworks ranging from Old Master paintings to contemporary creations"—it even has a virtual AI curator "to help interpret users' collections and suggest works they might enjoy" (Machemer).

10. The Waterloo collection was established in 1971 and held public exhibitions until its closure in 2009, at which time the 5,000 physical objects were transferred to the Canadian Museum of Civilization in Ottawa, Canada (Elliot).

11. The interactive nature of the V&A exhibition (and its associated "What's Your Game Face?" test) asked participants to consider the sort of player they were: whether "cheater," "distracted gamer," "gloating winner," "goody two-shoes," "no gamer," and "sore loser." *Game Plan* toured a number of other British museums, including the Maidstone Museum and the Novium Museum.

12. We exclude from this discussion museum exhibitions of video games, such as the Smithsonian American Art Museum's 2011 "Art of Video Games" and others.

13. Some earlier books *describe* board games broadly across cultures and periods, particularly R. C. Bell's three volumes.

14. We must offer an important proviso here: the search engines of both databases produce results from scans of page images run through an optical-character recognition software (OCR). In neither case are those scans proofread against the original and corrected. Gale obscures this problem—as does Google—by displaying only the images of the original pages, not the uncorrected OCR. The *BNA* is far more honest. Though the *BNA*'s uncorrected transcriptions are searchable and users can provide corrections, the visible record of the OCR warns users that the search results generated cannot offer any degree of comprehensiveness. In both databases, OCR-transcriptions have particular difficulty with any formatted word, such as those in bold or italics. And in many cases, where the paper has browned, reducing the contrast between print and field, the OCR provides mostly gibberish. With both the *NCCO* and the *BNA*, one can know what one has found, but one cannot imagine all that one has missed. As a result, one must view any search results as only slightly better than dumb luck. Even so, both are still useful resources, though we prefer the more open approach of the *BNA*.

15. In some iterations this advertisement is contained in one frame; in others it is split, but they always appear together and in the same order, so we consider them as a unit.

16. Nineteenth-century discussions commonly position these games as "the forerunners" of the games of the Roman Circus Maximus. See "Royal" and "Influence."

17. An 1847 record of "Festivities at Knowsley" Park records a "variety of athletic games and old English sports such as village rustics might engage," including "cricket," and "football" "pig races, climbing, etc." and a "stout competition for a shoulder of mutton, a joint of beef, and a purse containing 10s., placed on an greasy pole" (7c–8a-c).

18. The relevance of this sort of advertisement to a range of middling aristocrats becomes more obvious when we remember that Austen's *Persuasion* opens with Sir Walter Elliot reading his entry in the *Baronetage*.

Works Cited

"$12 Billion Board Games Market—Global Outlook and Forecast 2018–2023." *Globe News Wire* 7 August 2018. http://globenewswire.com/news-release/2018/08/071548201/0/en/12-Billion-Board-Games-Market-Global-Outlook-and-Forecast-2018-2023.htm. Accessed 20 October 2020.

"2020 Essential Facts about the Video Game Industry." Entertainment Software Association. https://www.theesa.com/wp-content/uploads/2020/07/Final-Edited-2020-ESA_Essential_facts.pdf Accessed 13 September 2020.

Abella, Jennifer. "Game On. An Intro to Regency Games." 15 April 2015. Jane Austen Summer Program. https://janeaustensummer.org/2015/04/15/game-on-an-intro-to-regency-games/ Accessed 20 October 2020.

"Adult Night: Virtual Game Nights, Friday, May 22, 2020." Calendar. North Carolina Museum of Natural Sciences. https://naturalsciences.org/calendar/adult-nights/#:~:text=Adult%20Nights%20has%20gone%20virtual,21%20years%20old%20to%20attend. Accessed 20 October 2020.

[Advertisement for Hoyle's *Games* and other books]. *Manchester Mercury*. 22 March 1808. 2e. *BNA* Accessed 20 October 2020.

[Advertisement for Hoyle's *Games* and other books]. *[London] Star*. 2 February 1808. 1b. *BNA* Accessed 20 October 2020.

[Advertisement for Hoyle's *Games* and other books]. *Northampton Mercury*. 12 March 1808. 4c. *BNA* Accessed 20 October 2020.

Advertisement for Parke's Shew Room. *Derby Mercury*. 8 August 1805. D4. *BNA* Accessed 20 October 2020.

Anderson, Nancy Fix. *The Sporting Life: Victorian Sports and Games*. London: Praeger, 2010.

"Art of Video Games." Smithsonian American Art Museum. 2011. https://americanart.si.edu/exhibitions/games Accessed 20 October 2020.

Austen, Jane. *The Novels of Jane Austen*. 5 vols. Ed. R. W. Chapman. 3rd ed. Oxford: Oxford University Press, 1988.

———. *Persuasion*. Austen, *Novels* vol. 5.

———. *Pride and Prejudice*. Austen, *Novels* vol. 2.

———. *Sense and Sensibility*. Austen, *Novels* vol. 1.

———. To Cassandra Austen. Monday 24-Tuesday 25 October 1808. Letter 60. *Jane Austen's Letters*. Ed. Deirdre Le Faye. 3rd Ed. Oxford: Oxford University Press, 1995. 149–52.

Bell, R. C. *Board and Table Games from Many Civilizations*. 2 vols. Oxford: Oxford University Press, 1960.

———. *The Boardgame Book*. London: Knapp Press, 1979.

———. *Discovering Old Board Games*. London: Shire Publishing, 1973.

Benson, Mary Margaret. "Excellently Qualified to Shine at a Round Game." *Persuasions: the Journal of the Jane Austen Society* 8 (1986): 96–100.

Blake, Kathleen. *Play, Games, and Sport: The Literary Works of Lewis Carroll*. Ithaca: Cornell University Press, 1975.

BNA: The British Newspaper Archive. British Library in collaboration with findmypast.com. https://www.britishnewspaperarchive.co.uk/ Accessed 20 October 2020.

"Board Games and Bright Lights: Family Sundays." Rubin Museum of Art. October 2017. https://rubinmuseum.org/events/event/board-games-bright-lights-10-01-2017 Accessed 20 October 2020.

A book of games, or A history of juvenile sports, practised at a considerable academy near London. London, 1810.

Bracey, Robert. *Playing with Money*. London: Spink and Son Ltd, 2019.

Brewster, Paul. "Some comments regarding the Games depicted on the Tomb of Mereruka." *East and West* (Rome) 13.1 (1962): 27–31. Rpt. Elliott. https://healthy.uwaterloo.ca/museum/Archives/Brewster/mereruka.html Accessed 20 October 2020.

Bristol, Olivia. *Six Edwardian and Victorian Board Games*. London: Michael O'Mara Books, 1996.

———. *Victorian Board Games*. London: Michael O'Mara Books, 1995.

"British Out-Door Games." *Young Englishman's Journal*. 27 (October 1867): 421–22. NCCO Accessed 20 October 2020.

Brumit, M. W. "They both like Vingt-un better than Commerce: Characterization and Card Games in Pride and Prejudice." *Persuasions Online*. Jane Austen Society of North America. 34.1 (Winter 2013). Accessed 12 September 2020.

Butler, Sarah. "Sales of board games and jigsaws soar during coronavirus lockdown." *The Guardian* 1 April 2020. https://the guardian.com/business/2020/

apr/01/sales-of-board-games-and-jgsaws-soar-during-coronavirus-lockdown. htm Accessed 20 October 2020.

Carter, John. *ABC for Book Collectors*. 5th ed. New York: Knopf, 1987.

"Charades and Bullet Pudding." 20 June 2011. Jane Austen Centre. https://janeausten.co.uk/blogs/games-to-play/charades-and-bullet-pudding. Accessed 20 October 2020.

"Christmas! New Publications, For the Instruction and Amusement of Young Persons." *Kentish Chronicle*. 19 December 1809. 1c. *BNA* Accessed 20 October 2020.

"Christmas! New Publications, For the Instruction and Amusement of Young Persons." *Norfolk Chronicle* 23 December 1809. 4c. *BNA* Accessed 20 October 2020.

Cormack, Malcolm. *Country Pursuits: British, American, and French Sporting Art from the Mellon Collections in the Virginia Museum of Fine Arts*. Charlottesville: University of Virginia Press, 2007.

Dickens, Charles. *Hard Times*. London: Bradbury and Evans, 1854. Googlebooks. Accessed 20 October 2020. Book 1, Chapter 6.

Eckroth, Stephanie. "Walter Scott and the Authoress: Anonymity and the Nineteenth-century Novel Market." *Papers of the Bibliographical Society of America* 105 (2011): 503–30.

Elliot Avedon Virtual Museum of Games. University of Waterloo, Canada. https://healthy.uwaterloo.ca/museum. Accessed 20 October 2020.

"Festivities at Knowsley." *Illustrated London News*. 2 October 1847. 7c-8a-c. *BNA* Accessed 20 October 2020.

"Fun and Games Night at My Museum." The Monterey County Youth Museum in California. https://mymuseum.org/event/fun-games-2020/ Accessed 20 October 2020.

"The Game Book for 1808." *York Herald*. 17 September 1808. 1c. *BNA* Accessed 20 October 2020.

The Game-Book for 1808. *York Herald*. 17 September 1817. 1c. *BNA* Accessed 20 October 2020.

The Game-Book for 1812. *The Globe*. 2 September 1812. 1c. *BNA* Accessed 20 October 2020.

"Game Night." Amon Carter Museum of Art, Fort Worth, Texas. https://www.cartermuseum.org/events/public-programs/game-night Accessed 20 October 2020.

"A Game of Skill," *Bristol Magpie*. 25 November 1893. 17a. *BNA* Accessed 20 October 2020.

"Game Plan: Board Games Rediscovered." Victoria and Albert Museum of Childhood. 8 October 2016–23 April 2017. https://www.vam.ac.uk/moc/exhibitions/gameplan/ Accessed 20 October 2020.

"Games to Play." Jane Austen Centre. 20 June 2011. https://janeausten.co.uk/blogs/games-to-play/tagged/game. Accessed 20 October 2020.

The Games We Played: American Board and Table Games from the Liman Collection Gift. New York Historical Society Museum and Library. http://nyhistory.org/exhibitions/the-games-we-played Accessed 20 October 2020.

Glover, Anne. *The Regency Reader, Passionately Blogging about all things Regency*. http://regron.com Accessed 20 October 2020.

Guerra, Douglas A. *Slantwise Moves: Games, Literature and Social Invention in Nineteenth-Century America*. Philadelphia: University of Pennsylvania Press, 2018.

Gurevich, Eli. "Game of Hounds and Jackals found carved in stone in Gobustan National Park, Azerbaijan" *Ancient Games: Playing Board Games of the Ancient World* Ed. Eli Gurevich. http://ancientgames.org Accessed 12 September 2020.

Harrow, Sharon, ed. *British Sporting Literature and Culture in the Long Eighteenth Century*. British Literature in Context in the Long Eighteenth Century. Ser. ed. Jack Lynch. Aldershot: Ashgate, 2015.

Harvey, Adrian. *The Beginnings of a Commercial Sporting Culture in Britain 1793–1815*. Aldershot: Ashgate, 2005.

Hawkins, Ann R., and Erin N. Bistline, eds. Special issue on Games and Gaming. CEA *Critic* 79.1 (2017).

Hofer, Margaret, and Kenneth Jackson. *The Games We Played: The Golden Age of Board and Table Games*. New York: Princeton Architectural Press, 2003.

"Hot Cockles and other Christmas Pastimes." 20 June 2011. Jane Austen Centre. https://janeausten.co.uk/blogs/games-to-play/hot-cockles-and-other-christmas-pastimes. Accessed 20 October 2020.

Hoyle, Edmond. *Hoyle's Games improved consisting of practical treatises on Whist, Quadrille, Piquet, Chess, Backgammon, Draughts, Cricket, Tennis, Quinze, Vingt-Un, Hazard, Lansquenet, Billiards, Faro or Pharo, Rouge & Noir, Cribbage, Matrimony, Cassino, Goff or Golf, Connexions, Reversis, Put, All-Fours, and Speculation. With an essay on game cocks; wherein are comprised calculations for betting upon equal or advantageous Terms*. Rev. ed. Ed. Charles Jones. London: printed by M. Ritchie for R. Baldwin, T. Payne, W. Lowndes, G. Wilkie, J. Scatcherd, Longman and Rees, E. Newbery, W. Stewart, J. Lee, T. Hurst, and J. Mawman, 1800.

Huggins, Mike. *The Victorians and Sport*. London: Hambledon and London, 2004.

"Influence of National Song." *Herts Guardian, Agricultural Journal, and General Advertiser*. 9 May 1863): 7b. *BNA* Accessed 20 October 2020.

International Tabletop Day. Geek and Sundry. tabletopday.com Accessed 20 October 2020.

"Ireland." *The Derby Mercury*. 11 November 1748. 2c. *BNA* Accessed 20 October 2020.

Jane Austen Centre. Bath, England. https://janeausten.co.uk. Accessed 20 October 2020.

Jordan, Thomas E. *Victorian Childhood: Themes and Variations*. Albany, NY: State University of New York Press, 1987.

Kane, Kathryn. Regency Redingote Blog. http://regencyredingote.wordpress.co/tag/games/page/1/ Accessed 20 October 2020.

Kayyem, Marisa, and Paul Sternberger. *American Board and Table Games of the Nineteenth Century from the Liman Collection*. New York: Columbia University Wallach Art Gallery, 1991.

"LaughFest Game Night coming to Grand Rapids Museum." 13-on-your-side News. WZZM (ABC). 4 February 2020. https://www.wzzm13.com/article/entertainment/events/laughfest/laugh-fest-game-night-grand-rapids-museum/69-10963980-d304-4f60-8488-d704b3c418de Accessed 20 October 2020.

"Let's Play: 100 Years of Board Games." San Francisco Museum, San Francisco, CA. https://www.sfomuseum.org/exhibitions/lets-play-100-years-board-games" Accessed 20 October 2020.

Liman, Ellen. *Georgian and Victorian Board Games: The Liman Collection*. New York: Pointed Leaf Press, 2017.

Machemer, Theresa. "This Free Game Lets Users Build their Own Virtual Art Museums," *Smithsonian Magazine* 20 April 2020. smithsonianmag.com/smart-news/explore-virtual-galleries-or-create-your-own-occupy-white-walls-180974702/ Accessed 21 October 2020.

"Maker Day: Building Board Games." Museum of History and Industry, Seattle, WA. https://mohai.org/event/maker-day-building-board-games/ Accessed 20 October 2020.

"A Merry Christmas." Advertisement for Birley's. *Worcester Herald*. 3 January 1857. 3d. *BNA* Accessed 20 October 2020.

Miles, Rachael. *Jilting the Duke*. The Muses' Salon. New York: Kensington Zebra, 2016.

———. *Chasing the Heiress*. The Muses' Salon. New York: Kensington Zebra, 2016.

———. *Tempting the Earl*. The Muses' Salon. New York: Kensington Zebra, 2016.

———. *Charming Ophelia*. The Muses' Salon. New York: Kensington Zebra, 2017.

Modern Language Association. *MLA International Bibliography (MLA-IB)*. EBSCO Discovery Service.

NCCO: *Nineteenth-Century Collections Online*. Gale. https://gale.com/primary-sources/nineteenth-century-collections-online.

Norcia, Megan. *Gaming Empire in Children's British Board Games, 1836–1860*. Studies in Childhood, 1700 to Present. New York: Routledge, 2019.

Oriard, Michael. *Sporting with the Gods: The Rhetoric of Play and Game in American Culture*. Cambridge: Cambridge University Press, 1991.

Pierre. "Playing with Money: 2019 Board Games Exhibition at British Museum." Interview with Robert Bracey. *NumisMag* 12 September 2019. https://numismag.com/en/2019/09/12/playing-with-money-2019-board-games-exhibition-at-british-museum/ Accessed 20 October 2020.

Pope, S. W. *Patriotic Games: Sporting Traditions in the American Imagination, 1876–1926*. Oxford: Oxford University Press, 1997.

"Recollections of an Antiquarian." *La Belle Assemblée* (July 1821): 8–10. NCCO Accessed 20 October 2020.

"The Royal Society of Literature." *Morning Post*. 27 May 1886. 3f. *BNA* Accessed 20 October 2020.

Sanborn, Vic. "Games Regency People Played: Blind Man's Bluff." *Jane Austen's World* 20 April 2011. janaustensworld.wordpress.com/tag/regency-games/ Accessed 20 October 2020.

"Selected Works: Games On!" The Louvre. Paris, France. https://www.louvre.fr/en/selections/game's Accessed 20 October 2020.

Shakespeare, William. *Complete Works of Shakespeare*. Ed. David Bevington. 3rd ed. Dallas: Scott, Foresman, and Co., 1980.

———. *Henry V*. Shakespeare, *Complete* 872–912.

———. *King Lear*. Shakespeare, *Complete* 1168–1215.

Shefrin, Jill. *Ingenious Contrivances: Table Games and Puzzles for Children*. Osborne Collection of Early Children's Books. Toronto, Canada: Toronto Public Library, 1997.

"Snapdragon." 20 June 2011. Jane Austen Centre. https://janeausten.co.uk/blogs/games-to-play/snapdragon. Accessed 20 October 2020.

Social Sports; or Holiday Amusements. Boston: W. J. Reynolds, 1849.

"Special Events: Family Game Night." Stuhr Museum of the Prairie Pioneer in Grand Island, Nebraska. https://www.stuhrmuseum.org/special-events/calendar.html/event/2017/03/03/family-game-night Accessed 20 October 2020.

St. Clair, William. *The Reading Nation in the Romantic Period*. Cambridge: Cambridge University Press, 2007.

Strutt, Joseph. *Glig Gamena Angel Deod or Sports and Pastimes of the People of England*. 2nd ed. London: White and Co; Longman, Hurst, Rees, and Orme; Lackington, Allen and Co; John and Arthur Arch; John Murray; John Harding; Crosby and Co; and Charles and Robert Baldwin, 1810. Googlebooks. Accessed 20 October 2020.

"Then and Now: A Century of Education at the Museum." Cleveland Museum of Art. June 2016. https://www.clevelandart.org/magazine/cleveland-art-may-june-2016/then-and-now Accessed 20 October 2020.

"The Sporting or Game Book." *Norfolk Chronicle*. 28 July 1804. 4b. *BNA* Accessed 20 October 2020.

"To Sportsmen & Game Laws." [Advertisement for Longman, Hurst, Rees, and Orme.] *Bury and Norwich Post, or Suffolk, Norfolk, Essex, and Cambridge Advertiser*. 2 September 1807. 1e. *BNA* Accessed 20 October 2020.

"To Sportsmen & Game Laws." [Advertisement for Longman, Hurst, Rees, and Orme.] *York Herald*. 18 October 1806. 1e. *BNA* Accessed 20 October 2020.

Trollope, Anthony. *The Warden. The Warden* and *The Two Heroines of Plumplington.* Ed. Nicholas Shrimpton. Oxford: Oxford World's Classics, 2104. 1–170.

"U.S. Video Game Content Generated $35.4 billion in revenue for 2019." Entertainment Software Association. 23 January 2020. https://www.theesa.com/press-releases/u-s-video-game-content-generated-35-4-billion-in-revenue-for-2019/ Accessed 20 October 2020.

Victoria and Albert Museum of Childhood. Bethnal Green, London. https://www.vam.ac.uk/moc/ Accessed 20 October 2020.

Vignaux, Marianne. "Card Games in Jane Austen Novels." Jane Austen Society of New Zealand. 25 October 2018. https://janeaustensocietynz.wordpress.com/2018/10/25/regency-card-games-talk/ 20 Accessed 2020.

"What's your #GameFace?" Victoria and Albert Museum of Childhood. https://www.vam.ac.uk/moc/exhibitions/gameplan-whats-your-gameface/ Accessed 20 October 2020.

Williams, J. L. *The Boy's Own Book; A Compendium of all the Sorts and Recreations of Youth.* Paris: Baudry's European Library, 1843. https://www.google.com/books/edition/The_Boy_s_Own_Book/QfBdAAAAcAAJ?hl=en&gbpv=1&bsq=bear Accessed 20 October 2020.

Section I

Games in Motion

Chapter 1

Bodies in Play

Boxing, Dance, and the Science of Recreation

KRISTIN FLIEGER SAMUELIAN AND MARK SCHOENFIELD

True Ease in Writing comes from Art, not Chance,
As those move easiest who have learn'd to dance.

—Alexander Pope, "Essay on Criticism"[1]

Let boxing be the Briton's pride,
The Science of their schools

—Pierce Egan, "A Boxing we will go"[2]

Introduction: Bodies in Motion and *Caleb Williams*

As poetry emerged from a predominantly patronage system over the course of the eighteenth century, poets engaged heterogeneous markets that unevenly combined patronage and commercial exchange. This transformation allowed for—even required—differentiation between the professional and the amateur, and these two complementary categories then eclipsed the image of "the humble drudge left to wait in the anteroom" by the "noble lord" (Kernan 104).[3] Arts that were implicated in performance or spectacle, dancing and boxing developed a similarly consolidated professionalism, which depended on avid amateurs as both enthusiastic participants and knowledgeable observers—connoisseurs—and on professionals who competed or performed and who enacted public personalities available for consumption and imitation. An article in the 1838 *New Sporting Magazine*, "Lamb and Pitman's Racket Match," stresses this link between the spectacular body and the legitimating force of elite—even if unevenly professionalized—literature. The essay, subtitled "The Mind, The Eye, and the Muscle," declares "[t]here is always something of poetry in trained and active corporeal power" ("Lamb" 245). Citing perhaps the best-known professional amateur, the author elevates boxing by including it in this same legitimating project: "[George Gordon,] Lord Byron described dancing as 'the poetry of motion;' but other exercises may well come under this description. Some of the attitudes of the pugilist and the wrestler are the *Homeric* or the *Miltonic* poetry of motion—as dancing is the Spenserian."[4] While the article continues the conceit by pairing fencing, quoits, cricket, and "the Barclay match" (an arduous pedestrian event in which participants walked 1000 miles at an average of a mile per hour) with various literary genres, the initial focus on dancing and boxing acknowledges their cultural predominance.

Lord Byron was himself both a boxer and—despite or perhaps because of his own perceived incapacity—a writer about dancing. The theme of poetic motion, and the *New Sporting*'s variations on it, suggest that the linkage between visual aesthetic and bodily engagement is becoming central to the professionalization—as simultaneously science and art—of recreation. Adrian Harvey, drawing on the periodical record from 1793 to 1850, has charted the transformation in competitive sports and the public's spectatorial and pecuniary engagements with them. The configuration of these sports reflected economic and social shifts, which restructured class delineations through professionalization, urbanization, and industrialization and which codified leisure time as a commercial opportunity.[5] Further, like other forms of entertainment, sports relied on their representation within print to secure their popularity. Noting the rise of periodicals specifically devoted to sports, Harvey contends that, from 1793 to 1815, "the press transformed the sporting culture, effectively rendering it national" (31). Like Harvey, Sharon Harrow emphasizes the role of mass marketing in popularizing "a culture of sports" (1). While Daniel O'Quinn identifies multiple genres of distribution, including prints, broadside poetry, and drinking songs, both dancing and boxing were well enmeshed within British society prior to this explosion and so were positioned especially to capitalize on it (98). In particular, a scientific presentation of boxing and dancing served to balance the professional and the recreational, as it mediated, constrained, or directed—or failed to—impulses of violence and sexuality implicit in the mythos of the two activities. A discourse of science legitimizes them, regulates their engagements with both violence and sexuality by claiming them as the domain of the studious and the schooled—of those, in other words, with both leisure and means.

Throughout the long Romantic era, periodicals developed a discourse and theorization of the body in motion that included vocabularies for dance and boxing as sciences. This trend toward a schematic of that most natural and unnatural of objects, the human body, fit into the cultural phenomenon in which multiple subjects—education, chess, dueling, and even the history of amusements, for example—were rhetorically reformulated as scientific through a variety of presentational strategies. In the cases of dancing and boxing, this discourse enabled professionalization, providing audiences with standards of judgment and teachers with pedagogical precision that coincided with and colluded in the maintenance of a recreational amateur performance. Boxing studios and dance training provided spaces for gentlemen to improve their technique, and thereby their gentlemanliness. Identifying these activities as sciences was meant to displace their unsettling origins in unconstrained violence and unlicensed sexuality by sustainable, regulative aesthetic norms. Yet these displaced horizons re-emerged in complaints about the violence and sensuality of the activities, and in both subtle and overt representations in novels and essays. This configuration of recreation is legitimated by scientific discourse, which focuses on bodies: their coordinated movement, malleability, and trainability. Athletic training combines "general principles of disciplining the body and forms of highly individualized (and, as Foucault would point out, internalized) self-coercion" (Regier 288). But the cultivation of order that is the scientific project necessarily engages its inverse: disorder, disruption of norms, chaos.

William Godwin's *The Adventures of Caleb Williams* demonstrates a political valence to the discourse of order and disorder embedded in representations of recreation, and particularly the interplay between boxing, as a confrontation within masculinity, and dancing, as a display of differentiated genders. The series of contests in this novel engage both class and national identity institutionally in terms of the story's multiplying tribunals, but the backstory of contending squires, which occupies most of the first volume, locates contest in the space of public amusement:

assemblies of rural gentry, country fairs.[6] These confrontations are between contesting constructions of masculinity, the highly educated Ferdinando Falkland, "a man of small stature, with an extreme delicacy of form and appearance" and Barnabas Tyrrel, an adept in "the science of horse flesh" and in "the theory and practice of boxing, cudgel play, and quarter-staff" who could serve as a "model for that hero of antiquity, whose prowess consisted in felling an ox with his fist, and devouring him at a meal" (Godwin 75). These two compete for the admiration of the community, as Falkland's arrival displaces Tyrrel's dominance. Describing Falkland as an "outlandish foreign-made Englishman," Tyrrel insists that a "nation of such animals would have no chance with a single regiment of the old English votaries of beef and pudding," a contrast in the familiar terms of nationalism, armed superiority, and robust diet (Godwin 78). The first narrated conflict between the two begins when Miss Hardingham, Tyrrel's "fair inamorata," decides to "so adjus[t] her manoeuvres as to be engaged by Mr. Falkland as his partner for the dance of the evening"; just before the first dance, Mr. Tyrrel appears, ready to "lead her forward to the field" (Godwin 80). The combination of the militaristic metaphors and the scene of the country dance at the "village assembly" underscores the regulative social functions of dancing (only Falkland is unaware of Miss Hardingham's intentions, as he is "unpardonably deficient in the sciences of anecdote and match-making" [Godwin 80]). When Falkland asserts his claim to the first dance with Hardingham, Tyrrel objects, and a verbal altercation ensues:

> "Sir," interrupted Mr. Tyrrel abruptly, "that lady is my partner."—"I believe not, sir: that lady has been so obliging as to accept my invitation."—"I tell you, sir, no. Sir, I have an interest in that lady's affections; and I will suffer no man to intrude upon my claims."—"The lady's affections are not the subject of the present question."—"Sir, it is to no purpose to parley. Make room, sir!"—Mr. Falkland gently repelled his antagonist. "Mr. Tyrrel!" returned he, with some firmness, "let us have no altercation in this business: the master of the ceremonies is the proper person to decide in a difference of this sort, if we cannot adjust it: we can neither of us intend to exhibit our valour before the ladies, and shall therefore cheerfully submit to his verdict."—"Damn me, sir, if

> I understand."—"Softly, Mr. Tyrrel; I intended you no offence. But, sir, no man shall prevent my asserting that to which I have once acquired a claim!" (Godwin 81)

Like a field of battle, the dance floor is revealed as a controlled space, one in which the display of bodily prowess takes a specific form, not of "our valour before the ladies," but of the coordinated heterosexual display of courtship. Rather than the violence that such courtship always threatens (in his prior travels in Italy, Falkland, displaying a similar ostentatious obliviousness to female machinations, narrowly averts a duel because he appears to be courting), there is an application to "the master of the ceremonies." Dancing, here, temporarily displaces the martial heroics of violence, and aligns itself with legality. The contemplation of a juridical appeal to the master of the ceremonies sufficiently flusters Tyrrel that he flees, muttering "curses" that "the laws of honour did not oblige Mr. Falkland to overhear" and which, "indeed," the narrator continues, "it would have been no easy task to have overheard with accuracy" (Godwin 81). The implication is that he does actually hear them, or at least their tone, but the crowded room colludes with the laws of honor to allow him to pretend not to, by the same doubled regulation by which dance both is and is not courtship. Godwin offers this moment as a set-piece to emphasize these dynamics, and only as an incidental moment of the plot. Not only does Miss Hardingham never reappear, but the dance itself is never narrated; the point of view switches to Tyrrel's malignant thoughts for a few sentences, and then the chapter ends.

What follows in the novel is a series of confrontations between Falkland and Tyrrel, waged as a kind of cold war by proxy over the affections of Tyrrel's cousin and ward Emily. Her death and his culpability for it precipitates Tyrrel's exclusion from the assembly room, a communal space "conceived nostalgically in fiction as emblematic of a lost form of sociality" that lets Godwin's novel challenge "the ruling order in its politely civilized (Falkland) and brutally tyrannical (Tyrrel) typologies" (Russell 144). Despite having been "notified" of this decision "by letter by the master of the ceremonies," Tyrrel intrudes, whereupon Falkland declares, in language reminiscent of the dance, "Whatever were your rights, your infamous conduct has forfeited them" (Godwin 161–62). At first, Tyrrel, cowed by Falkland's language, retreats, but he soon returns, and an impromptu boxing match takes place. The setting is the same assembly space of the earlier dance and of Falkland's public success when Clare read his "Ode to Chivalry," an event which, like Falkland's rhetoric at the dance, also temporarily banished the confused Tyrrel:

> In a moment he was in a part of the room where Mr. Falkland was standing, and with one blow of his muscular arm levelled him with the earth. The blow however was not stunning, and Mr. Falkland rose again immediately. It is obvious to perceive how unequal he must have been in this species of contest. He was scarcely risen before Mr. Tyrrel repeated his blow. Mr. Falkland was now upon his guard, and did not fall. But the blows of his adversary were redoubled with a rapidity difficult to conceive, and Mr. Falkland was once again brought to the earth. In this situation Mr. Tyrrel kicked his prostrate enemy, and stooped apparently with the intention of dragging him along the floor. (Godwin 164)

While this final indignity, reminiscent of Achilles dragging the body of Hector, is prevented, the interpreting Caleb Williams observes, "The slightest breath of dishonour would have stung him to the very soul. What must it have been with this complication of ignominy, base, humiliating, and public?" (Godwin 164). The narrative of the fight itself implies some training on Falkland's part, as he stands "upon his guard," but he is no match for either Tyrrel's strength or his speed (Godwin 164). Like so many accounts of boxing matches in the period, this is posed as a competition between differences in style and differences in character. Offered as if an anticlimax to Falkland's loss of dignity, the chapter concludes with noting that "Mr. Tyrrel was found by some of the company dead in the street, having been murdered at the distance of a few yards from the assembly house" (Godwin 165). Godwin's decision to bookend the battles between Falkland and Tyrrel with a country dance and an impromptu boxing match signals the social importance of these events and exposes their continuity as organized social activities that are sites of both pleasure and risk, play and violence. Throughout this scene, the narrative voice emphasizes that Tyrrel and Falkland are public figures for specular consumption; when Tyrrel enters the assembly, "every eye was turned upon him" (Godwin 161). As he "advanc[es]" in his project of quelling dissent, "[t]he whole company were astonished. They felt the same abhorrence and condemnation of his character; but they could not help admiring the courage and resources he displayed upon the present occasion" (Godwin 162).

Later in the novel, after Caleb's suspicions about Falkland's murder of Tyrrel have taken hold, Falkland himself is placed in the double position of spectacle and spectator when, in a scene echoing Hamlet's Mousetrap, he listens to a peasant's description of a murder while Caleb observes him. The accused peasant describes being tormented in a way that parallels Tyrrel's tormenting Falkland. While Falkland, during his inquest, describes himself as having been deprived of appropriate justice—that of a duel—by Tyrrel's death, the peasant challenges his assailant, and the manner of the duel is class-appropriate: "The challenge was accepted; a ring was formed; he confided the care of his sweetheart to a bystander; and unfortunately the first blow he struck proved fatal" (Godwin 206). In *Between Men*, Eve Sedgwick demonstrated that the cultural dispositions of homosociality and heteronormativity are mutually constitutive. If dancing is the regulation of sexuality toward heteronormativity, boxing regulates violence in the service of (prosocial) homosociality; hence the generalized attention to bodies in motion throughout this novel, with particular reference to boxing and dancing. A fuller context of this dynamic emerges in the periodical discussion of the two activities, hinged between the scientific and the artistic, the professional and the amateur.

Dancing

Two years before the publication of *Caleb Williams*, in 1792, an essay appeared in the *Universal Magazine of Knowledge and Pleasure* that identified dance as art by way of its equivalence with logic. "Historical Observations on Dancing" claims that "[a]s Logic is termed the Art of Thinking, so Dancing may be called the Art of Gesture. Logic teaches us to order and arrange our thoughts, as to give them perspicuity and propriety of connection; and by Dancing we are taught to direct our motions in such a manner, as to give them gracefulness, harmony, and ease" (3). Logic and dance in this analogy are rhetorical structures that organize inchoate elements (thoughts, motions) to produce an appearance of symmetry (propriety of connection, harmony). What makes this work of cataloguing and arranging an art is that, in its expressiveness, it persuades us to believe that the perspicuity is our own, that the propriety of connection, the harmony and ease we perceive, inhere in the symbolic system—thinking or gesture—and that logic and dance illuminate order rather than impose it. And those means of illumination and expression are not unique to particular minds or bodies but are universally reproducible, thanks to the essential yet ineffable qualities all minds and bodies share. This commonality allows observers of dance to perform the illuminations in the theater of their own minds, in a fantasy of shared recognition.

Dancing particularly, although it seems "mechanical," is one of the "imitative arts" ("Historical" 3). Here imitation means the act of borrowing "from nature" that is "the province of genius alone," although imitation can also mean influence, a rendering of the relationship between performer and audience that leaves the audience vulnerable and that we will return to ("Historical" 3). The question of why the imitation and not the original—"Why is not nature left to itself?"—is addressed through the Burkean notion that the imitation of nature is not its contrary but its replication: in James Chandler's formulation, "a second nature which is at once within Nature yet parallel to it [. . .] at once metaphorical and metonymous with Nature" ("Historical" 3; Chandler 67). Dance's imitative properties are crucial to the process by which the art becomes a science: dance has "borrowed various graces from various forms; and . . . by combination, has reduced them to a systematic science" ("Historical" 3). In other words, the order is inherent and yet cultivated through the act of borrowing that is part of what makes dance an art. Further, the science of dance is congruent with the pleasures derived from both performance and spectatorship. An 1806 article in *La Belle Assemblée*, "On Dancing," calls dancing "that exhilirating [*sic*] science, which thaws the lingering juices, and wakes the soul while it excites the body" and includes it with poetry, music, "architecture, painting, and sculpture": those "arts which have contributed to the civilization, amusement, or fame of the nations in which they have been cultivated" (449).

Art for these authors means both practical skill and aesthetic value—artisanship and artistry—although arguably only the latter requires admiring or delighted spectatorship. Yet art can also mean showmanship designed to dazzle and fool the spectator: sleight of hand, conjuring, magic. The intricate relationship between art and science, theory and spectacle, is embedded in nineteenth-century discourse about professionalism, which presumes a historical progression from practice to theory even as pedagogy insists on the reverse. In explaining how medical practice can coexist with atheism, for instance, Robert Southey claims that "the medical profession [. . .] was an art in the worst sense of the word, before it became a science, and long after it pretended to be a science, was little better than a craft": doctors were first sorcerers and charlatans—artists in the worst sense—before they pretended to be scientists—that is, artists in the best sense—at which point and for a long time after they were "little better" than craftsmen: practitioners unversed in the theory of their calling (294). The merging of art and science common to dancers, poets, musicians, architects, sculptors, and painters identifies them as professionals. Whatever their plastic material may be—marble, paint, mortar, paper, instrument, or human body—they are working with their minds.

The *Universal Magazine's* "Historical Observations," although dated 1792, is drawn almost entirely from a contemporary review of Giovanni Gallini's *Treatise on the Art of Dancing*, published in London in 1762. Gallini was an expatriate Italian choreographer; his treatise, more influential than it was original, borrowed heavily from Enlightenment cultural theory, particularly the work of French choreographer and dance theorist Jean-Georges Noverre, whose 1760 manifesto *Lettres sur la danse* set out to reinvigorate ballet by reconnecting it with ancient pantomime. Noverre's goal, in Jennifer Homans's words, was to "strip away centuries of social veneer and rediscover the natural man hidden beneath" (76). Without actually disrupting established forms, Noverre composed *ballets d'action*, forerunners of modern story ballets, that reflected a "utopian desire to return to a presocial world and to rediscover a primitive and universal language that would speak directly to all human beings, from the lowliest peasants to kings" (Homans 76). In his Preface to the 1803 edition of *Lettres*, Noverre claimed to have "achieved a revolution in dancing, as striking and as lasting as that achieved by Christoph Willibald Gluck in the realm of music" by demanding "action and expression" of his dancers instead of mere "mechanical technique" (2). Between technique and theory, Noverre argued, there is an "immense distance," because theory—or "the genius which places dancing beside the imitative arts"—consists in "observations and principles drawn from nature," which "always end by conquering"—that is, overcoming irrelevant traditions and hide-bound prejudice (1, 2).

Noverre's insistence on "a faithful likeness of beautiful nature" in his ballets extended to a reform of what dancers should wear onstage (9). Ancient mimes had danced naked. Modern opera dancers, while not going this far, should avoid costumes that are "opposed to the liberty, speed, prompt and lively action of the dance"; this was particularly true for the "ridiculous paniers" [*sic*] worn by female dancers, or *danseuses* (Noverre 74). These "deprive the figure of the elegance and correct proportions which it should have" and "disguise [. . .] every grace" (Noverre 74). While Noverre was only for reducing "by three-quarters" the width of a *danseuse*'s panniers, others of his contemporaries carried costume reform further, doing away with panniers for both men and women in favor of lighter fabrics and filmy garments—especially for the women—that revealed the body's shape while allowing much more freedom of movement (74).

When Noverre's protégé Charles Didelot staged several ballets in London in the 1790s, both the choreography and the costuming caused a sensation. If Noverre's concern about panniers was that "they impede and trouble the *danseuse* to such a degree that the movement of her panier generally takes up far more of her attention than that of her arms and legs," Didelot's celebration of what legs can do, unimpeded by panniers, became the subject of much salacious attention, engendering numerous engravings that depicted *danseuses* in filmy garments with legs provocatively raised (74). The proliferation of (to all appearances) sexually available French opera dancers on English stages became the subject of a 1798 speech before the House of Lords by Bishop Shute Barrington, which put a nationalistic spin on the revolution and conquest that Noverre had named as intrinsic to his legitimating project. Barrington highlights not the dancers' imitation of nature but the imitation they inspire in English audiences. Their influence is corrupting and, in his estimation, to blame for a steep rise in immorality and particularly divorce within the aristocracy:

> The French rulers, while they despaired of making any impression on us by the force of arms, attempted a more subtle and alarming warfare, by endeavouring to enforce the influence of their example, in order to taint and undermine the morals of our ingenuous youth. They sent amongst us a number of female dancers, who, by the allurement of the most indecent attitudes, and most wanton theatrical exhibitions, succeeded but too effectually in loosening and corrupting the moral feelings of the people; and, indeed, if common report might be relied upon, the indecency of those appearances

> far out-shamed any thing of a similar nature that had ever been exhibited—he would not say, on any Christian theatre, but even upon the more licentious theatres of Athens and of Rome. (Barrington 1307)

What made dancing in filmy garments in the eighteenth century more shameful than dancing naked in the second was the emphasis these ballets put, not just on the body but also on the body's arrangement for the spectator. Both the Bishop's prudery and the dancers' sexual display are subjects of a 1798 engraving by James Gillray, titled "Operatical Reform, or la Dance a l'Eveque." This print shows Didelot's wife Rose and two other dancers in sheer costumes that reveal breasts and buttocks. Rose Didelot is on the right with her back to the audience. The dancer in the center has her right leg raised horizontally. On one plinth a satyr with a mask for a codpiece looks at the dancers and grins; on the other an updated Venus de' Medici in a relatively modest shift appears shocked. The caption reads as follows:

> 'Tis hard for such new fangled orthodox rules,
> That our OPERA-Troop should be blam'd,
> Since like our first parents, they only, poor fools,
> Danc'd Naked, & were not asham'd! ("Operatical")

Gillray's print satirizes and shares Barrington's Francophobia. The title includes the French word for Bishop (*eveque*), and the text seems to dismiss the Bishop's campaign by associating it with dissenting upstarts (reform, new-fangled) as well as rule-bound orthodoxy. At the same time, the dancers' bodies, particularly Mme Didelot, are objects of ridicule and salacious scrutiny. Didelot's famously sharp features—long nose and pointed chin—contrast with her rounded buttocks in a way that licenses both prurience and disgust.

In all of these representations, what raises the science of dance to the level of art is also what puts it outside the bounds of propriety and safety. Theorizing dance is in itself an un-English enterprise, whether one identifies the science with ancient paganism or with revolutionary France—and dance theorists as well as their detractors located it in both places. In *Lettres* Noverre had argued that, for dancing to "arrive at that degree of the sublime which I demand and hope for it, it is imperative for dancers to divide their time and studies between the mind and the body" (108.) Focus too much on the body and "[t]he man of intelligence disappears, there remains nothing but an ill-ordered machine given up to the sterile admiration of fools and the just contempt of connoisseurs" (Noverre 108). But, because one cannot separate the dancer from the dance, it is impossible not to focus too much on the body—impossible not to inhabit that indeterminate space between connoisseur and implicated voyeur that makes the observer as vulnerable as the dancer.

A scene from Jane Austen's *Pride and Prejudice* explores this vulnerability from several angles. As Kristin Samuelian has observed, when Lydia Bennet's "eager" dancing with militia officers causes Fitzwilliam Darcy to look on "in silent indignation at such a mode of passing the evening," the benignly vulgar Sir William Lucas observes him, remarking, "There is nothing like dancing after all.—I consider it as one of the first refinements of polished societies" (810; Austen 63). Both Sir William's comment and Darcy's sardonic, proto-anthropological rejoinder—"it has the advantage also of being in vogue amongst the less polished societies of the world.—Every savage can dance"—borrow language from current discussions on the proper function of dance (Austen 63). When Sir William continues, "Your friend performs delightfully [. . .] and I doubt not that you are an adept in the science yourself," he highlights a linkage whose focus is not so much the performance of science as the science of performance (Austen 63).

For Darcy, on the other hand, as for anti-dancing theorists throughout the period, nature is precisely the sticking point. As something any savage can do, dancing belongs equally, even properly, to cultures whose economies cannot support the kind of professionalism identified by Southey and the periodical writers. Natural man, in other words, cannot be an artist. Darcy and Sir William have their exchange in a drawing room, and their comments are occasioned by a spontaneous dance at the end of a dinner party, part of an effort to redirect the pedantic Mary Bennet's tedious piano playing into something more socially useful (Samuelian 810). Despite the attention it generates, the dance at the Lucases' is not a successful performance. In its self-centeredness and inward focus, it is the opposite of art. But it illustrates the uneasy position dance occupies. Like poetry, painting, or music, dance is an art that troubles distinctions between the professional and the amateur. Ordinary people enjoy watching professionals dance, but they also enjoy dancing themselves. And the extent to which they also, like Sir William, enjoy watching other ordinary people dance underscores that dancing is never a completely amateur activity. More precisely, because of its role in courtship practices, dancing's amateur status is professionalized within a marriage economy. In Austen, how a young woman behaves or is treated at a dance is directly connected to her courtship narrative, and inability or unwillingness tends to increase rather than decrease value. When Sir William, "struck with the notion of doing a very gallant thing," offers Elizabeth as a partner, despite Darcy's own secret wish to dance with her, his desire for *her* is increased by her "resistance" (Austen 63–64). For both Elizabeth and Darcy, stasis is the safest way to ensure propriety, and the correct arrangement of parts is correct only in imagination or theory. When it becomes embodied, it becomes uncontrollable, subjecting practitioners and watchers alike to insult and injury: unsafe.

The notion that mobility correlates with and produces instability—social, sexual, political—emerges also in a shift that began to take place in professional dancing in the later Romantic period. From the naturalism and athleticism of *ballets d'action* such as Noverre's 1763 *Médée et Jason* or Gasparo Angiolini's 1761 *Don Juan*, ballet especially moved toward an emphasis on female beauty and even fragility in the rise of the ballerina. The most obvious example of this is the enormous popularity of Marie Taglioni, the first danseuse to dance *en pointe* as an aesthetic, rather than an acrobatic, display. Taglioni's father, as Homans has pointed out, "belonged to the last generation of ballet masters with an aesthetic loyalty to the ancien regime" and insisted "on a certain old-fashioned composure in his daughter's otherwise iconoclastic dancing" (136). Although Taglioni was extremely strong, she used her powerful musculature largely to make physical feats such as dancing *en pointe* look effortless. Called by one critic "the perfect 'Restoration' ballerina," Taglioni nonetheless came to prominence with the end of the Bourbon restoration and the start of the "bourgeois monarchy" of Louis-Philippe I (quoted in Homans 142). She, thus, in Homans's words, "fused the elegance and refinement of a lost aristocratic past with a new and airy spirituality"—pre-Revolutionary stateliness married to bourgeois femininity (142). In Taglioni's signature ballet *La Sylphide*, first choreographed by her father in 1832, she figured as an ephemeral, seductive sprite who was nonetheless virginal and, in the end, self-sacrificial. Taglioni and *La Sylphide* created a sensation across Europe, inspiring everything from stage coaches to women's magazines to paper dolls (Homans 163). Taglioni was hardly immobile, and her fragility was carefully cultivated to obscure not only extremely powerful legs but also an oddly shaped body that included a curved spine. Her aesthetic, then, was at least partially in response to bodily constraints, making the emphasis of her dance not simply what the body can do (which, notably, no longer carried the sexual valence it had for Gillray and his contemporaries) but also what the body dictates. The science of her art is as much a solution as it is an invention.

Boxing

Just as dancing was a sublimation of sexuality that rendered it acceptable, at once visible and hidden, boxing was a reorientation of masculine aggression performed within bounds; and like dancing, boxing was always on the edge of failing in its sublimation. Cultural references to boxing, like those to dancing, have an ancient legacy. In William Cowper's translation of the *Odyssey*, when Odysseus is incognito among the Phaeacians, he is goaded into challenging the Phaeacian youths: "Then, come the man whose courage prompts him forth / To box, to wrestle with me, or to run" (8. 249–50). Perhaps chastened by the eloquence of his speech with its praise of hospitality, but more likely because he has just demonstrated enormous strength in hurling a heavy discus further than any of the youth, none steps forward to enter the ring (whether for boxing or wrestling; in both ancient Greece and late-eighteenth-century England, the sports were similarly dangerous, each allowing throws and punches). The king smooths over the situation by confessing that "[w]e boast not much the boxer's skill, nor yet / [t]he wrestler's" and instead substitutes a dance: "Come, ye Phaeacians, beyond others skill'd / To tread the circus with harmonious steps, / Come, play before us" (Cowper 8. 298–300).

The king represents the dancers' agility as carrying a high aesthetic value, and links it to their naval prowess and so imperial status. For historians of boxing, this moment validated the sport by associating it, like dancing, with the classical past. Yet, again like dancing, boxing in the eighteenth century was struggling to develop a legitimating discourse amid charges of immorality, brutality, and corruption. At once popular and illegal, the sport developed within a rising celebrity culture by constructing heroes with distinctive characters and national reputations (Downing 21–22 and n1). Kasia Boddy charts the development of boxing in England, which paralleled the reimagining of dancing; boxing "began to flourish in the early eighteenth century, at the expense of other sports such as quarterstaff and backsword," and 1743 saw the first "written rules" (29). Thus, the "great Enlightenment project of systemization and law-making" was "extended to pugilism" (Boddy 29). As an enlightenment project, boxing was a site of class consolidation and knowledge production; this process, however, was contentious and uneven, as the sport was simultaneously stigmatized as the locus of untrammeled aggression.

The *Gentleman's Magazine*, founded in 1733, first mentions a boxing match as such in 1750. In August 1754, *Gentleman's* reprints an essay, renamed "Battle in Norfolk; with Remarks," from *The Connoisseur* of the same month, that provides a detailed account of a "dreadful combat" between Pettit and Slack, the magazine's first sustained discussion of the sport (364). In a blend of slang and journalistic precision, the writer sets a heteroglossic tonality that would continue in writing about boxing through Lord Byron and Pierce Egan into the 1820s. Writing before the era of Daniel Mendoza and the scientific revolution of the sport, when agility and craft displaced strength as its primary aesthetic value, the author observes that Slack, the eventual winner and morally superior fighter, opposes Pettit's strategy of rushing around the stage and attempting to throw him off it by "oblig[ing] [Pettit] to stand to close fighting" ("Battle" 364). The final exchange becomes a parable of the confrontation, in which Slack allows Pettit to throw him "over the rails" in order to "fi[x] a blow under *Pettit's* ribs, that hurt him much" ("Battle" 364). Defeated by both Slack's stationary technique and his own fear, Pettit flees and Slack collects a prize of ten guineas.[7] Broughton, the champion before Slack, was similarly and frequently described as holding his ground: John Godfrey declared, "He [Broughton] steps not back, distrusting of himself to stop a blow, and piddle in the return" (56). Instead, he "steps bold and firmly in; bids a welcome to the coming blow" in order to set up a "pile-driving" counterpunch (Godfrey 56).[8]

After an extended metaphor (reminiscent of the Falkland/Tyrrel feud in *Caleb Williams*), connecting English pugilistic strength and their beef-centered diet in opposition to French bodily fragility and culinary delicacies, *Gentleman's* (following *The Connoisseur*) argues that the eventual failure of Broughton's boxing studio resulted from an aristocratic preference for "scented gloves" over "the gauntlet" and for "a more genteel employment for their hands, in shuffling a pack of cards and shaking the dice" ("Battle" 364–65). Recognizing that boxing functioned as a spectator sport because it participated in gambling, the writer concludes by imagining that boxing "would doubtless be reduced to a science; and *Broughton*, in imitation of that great genius *Hoyle*, might oblige the public with a Treatise on the Fist, and Calculations for laying the Odds at any Match of Boxing" ("Battle" 365). Throughout the article, an emphasis on the fists as the core of proper boxing invokes the image of the contestants standing toe to toe, hammering one another. Given that this approach had left Broughton beaten and blinded by Slack, this final vision recuperates Broughton in literary space, in compensation for his banishment from the pugilistic stage (Boddy 37). At the same time, it indicates something of the forlorn condition of boxing, less a science or sport than a subset of gambling.

The public unease about boxing is registered throughout the period. As Boddy notes, in Hogarth's 1751 series *The Four Stages of Cruelty*, James Field, a boxer recently "hanged for robbery," is mentioned twice, first in a notice of a championship fight, and then by name, "engraved above a skeleton which overlooks the dissection of an executed criminal" (38). This unease was bolstered in 1768 when Thomas Knight killed Robert Ball in a match arranged in consequence of a dispute over "a club reckoning at a public house" ("To the Editors" 271). Knight was acquitted by the jury, as was often the case in duels—and this match was so structured—despite the clear law on the question pointing to conviction. A "Letter Writer" to the *Oxford Magazine* directs his condemnation of the acquittal to "the fighting gentry of this metropolis," urging them to recognize the inherent deadliness of the sport (271). In 1773, a boxing match that results from a challenge issued in consequence of inappropriate staring at a lady in Vauxhall Gardens turns out to be a fraud, as one of the boxers, Capt. Miles, is revealed as "Mr. F—d's own livery servant, dressed *à la militaire*, to impose upon Mr. Bate" ("Monthly" 462). This fraud results in a further duel by class-appropriate gentlemen firing class-appropriate pistols, resulting in the "whole company" being "perfectly satisfied" ("Monthly" 462). The logic here is that boxing allows class impositions and frauds, and unsettles matters, escalating them to the potentially deadly force of the duel. The disrepair of the sport is evident in its categorization in the 1780 *Town and Country* as part of the "aera of fashionable disappointment in polite amusements": the pseudonymous Castigator describes an event that "began by a boxing match, was succeeded by prize-fighters, and it is said, if the just resentment of the spectators had not interrupted the continuance of such barbarous amusements, would have continued to bear and bull bating" (176).

Over against this unease was a growing discourse that, like the Enlightenment recuperation of dance earlier in the century, legitimated boxing as a science, the domain of professionals who employed intellect equally with force. Henry Lemoine's 1788 book on boxing, *Modern Manhood*, included a chapter on the "History of the Science of Natural Defence." Distinguishing the scientific style from gouging, blocking with elbows, and other "Creole manner of fighting," Lemoine insists that the "beauty of boxing is in *hitting clean*, guarding, fending, and keeping off blows with judgment, all of which depend on the eye" (87). In this way, he provides a continuity between practitioner and audience: each relies upon rapid, analytical observation to perfect his experience. Boddy points out that pugilism began to recover ground in the 1780s, as "the highest echelons of the aristocracy" became interested (38). Around the time of the publication of Lemoine's book, the public latched onto "a highly publicized series of fights between Richard Humphries and Daniel Mendoza" (Boddy 38). The third and last of these is described in an anonymous pamphlet which records that the betting odds suggested the crowd believed "it would be impossible to beat the Jew if blows were watched for, and the fight carried on in a regular scientific manner" ("Circumstantial" 45). The more scientific fighter is also the more gentlemanly: Mendoza "scorned to take some advantages, which were perfectly consistent with the fairest rules" ("Circumstantial" 46). For Mendoza, performing such refinement also managed his public Jewish identity.

Considerably smaller than most professional boxers and, like Marie Taglioni, cultivating an aesthetic that was compensatory, Mendoza had developed ways of moving to offset his size. This helped to produce his reputation (propagated by both himself and the press) as the first scientific boxer, who used motion and footwork to defeat larger and stronger opponents. Capitalizing on his fame, Mendoza produced his *Art of Boxing* in 1789, which offered "so regular a system" of boxing instruction "as to render it equal to fencing, in point of neatness, activity, and grace" and therefore available even to men "unwilling to risque any derangement of features," who can "venture to practice the Art from sportiveness" because "sparring is productive of health and spirits, as it is both an exercise and an amusement" (vii–viii). The text begins by outlining the "first principle to be declared in Boxing," which is "to be perfectly master of the equilibrium of the body, so as to be able to change from a right to a left-handed position; to advance or retreat striking or parrying; and to throw the body either forward or backwards without difficulty or embarrassment" (Mendoza 1). This notion of the body in equilibrium as being a body in motion not only serves to characterize

Mendoza's style, but also reverses "*The Connoisseur*'s" aesthetic assessment of the Pettit-Slack fight. It further allows Mendoza to suggest boxing as a graceful sport in which mastery was distinguishable from the brutality that, in his analysis, only incidentally accompanied the activity. In his first lesson, he describes a pas de deux between master and student, in which the former strikes and the latter parries. He further distinguishes the specific advantages of "long-armed" or "short-armed" boxers and the technical implications for each (Mendoza 25–26).

By taking an aesthetic that risked but evaded effeminacy, Mendoza participated in the production of a scientific discourse of boxing that was, as Karen Downing has argued, "the result of concentrated effort on the control and use of the body" (15). She notes that "many pamphlets" replicated Mendoza's approach, consolidating a notion of the "gentleman boxer" who exhibited the "necessary bodily control for effective boxing, for gentlemanly comportment, and for the preservation of personal and national health itself" (Downing 16). As John Whale has indicated, Pierce Egan would follow this trend of classifying boxing as a science to enhance its aesthetics and social acceptability (260).

With the prominence of the rivalry between Mendoza and Humphries, a varied market developed for boxing: the staging of actual professional bouts on which a great deal could be wagered, traveling boxers, and the training of gentlemen in the "art." Scientific discourse also allowed an aesthetic norm that permitted boxing to be a performance; celebrated boxers toured the countryside, sparring in pairs or with locals at fairs and other public arenas, on elevated platforms that served as stages for spectators. Expanding on an article in the November 1789 *Walker's Hibernian Magazine*, "A Knight of the Fist" wrote the "Editors of the Sporting Magazine" for the June 1795 issue. Noting his "elegant acquisition of pugilism," the Knight declares that the sport, "cultivated as it has been and, indeed, now is, by the higher orders of society, classes with the rest of the *fine arts*, and rates its practitioners with the men of *science*; nor have we found gentlemen performers less anxious to display their talents in a *boxing duet* than in a musical one" (137). Inclined "to encourage this great and noble science," the Knight hopes that "the lists of *Mendozian* practitioners" will add "noble names" to those of "Humphries, Ward, Ryan, Johnson, Perrins, Big Ben, the Bath butcher, &c, &c" (137). The Knight continues by particularly praising Mendoza "for establishing an academy at the *Lyceum*" (137). Journals that opposed boxing, by contrast, pointed to the rhetorical use of "science" in elevating what they viewed as brutality. In the 1811 *Scots Magazine* article "Thoughts on Pugilism," "Civis" compares watching a boxing match to observing a slave being whipped, and continues, "A band of idle and Herculean vagabonds are caressed by the rich and powerful, and their execrable trade is nominally elevated to the dignity of a science" (812).

Boxing, whether explicitly or implicitly, in praise or derision, relied on a scientific understanding—a connoisseur's appreciation of the sport. If the *Scots* article suggests the prevalence of the use of scientific discourse through its refutation, a comparison of two accounts, thirty years apart, of the same fight illustrates its solidification. Around the time of the first Mendoza-Humphries fight, in Birmingham, the local Isaac Perrins, seconded by his brother and "a Birmingham man," fought London star Tom Johnson, who was accompanied by Will and Joe Ward, both established fighters in their own right ("Domestic" 520). The contemporary account, in the *General Magazine and Impartial Review*, describes a bout between two unevenly matched boxers, the less trained Perrins at 6'2", 17 stone, and Johnson, at 5'8", 13 stone ("Domestic" 520). The reporter describes the setting; lists the "professors" who were present (including Banastre Tarleton, who served as an umpire), and describes the fight with relatively little commentary, as in "Second round—Perrins fell—received a blow. Third ditto—Johnson fell—received a blow" ("Domestic" 520). In one of the few places where commentary erupts as metaphor and even sentimentalism, the writer notes that, when the contestants stripped, it "called to idea the disparity described between David and Goliath, for Johnson absolutely appeared a dwarf by the side of his antagonist." In consequence of this inequality, "the mind was immediately interested in his fate" ("Domestic" 519). Having established suspense, the writer undercuts the sympathy for Johnson by noting that Ward, Johnson's second, "secretly" advises Johnson to "wait ten minutes at least for his antagonist; viz. not to make any effort, but to evade his adversary" ("Domestic" 520). Indeed, throughout the fight, Johnson "evaded and frequently ran round him," a technique at the time of dubious integrity ("Domestic" 520). Only in retrospect, following up on the implication that the scientific approach correlates with litheness—a concept echoed by both Mendoza and Godwin—the reporter rephrases this action as displaying "great science and judgment, as well as wonderful intrepidity," yet makes it clear that Perrins "reproached the conduct of Johnson, and said he fought like a coward" ("Domestic" 520). Johnson succeeds, as the larger man "failed much in wind" and could not master "the shifting mode of Johnson" ("Domestic" 520). The reporter summarizes in what amounts to a eulogy for both Perrins's career and his toe-to-toe style: "It is but justice, however, to say, that he discovered great courage and good bottom. What he had in weight, he wanted in professional science and activity" ("Domestic" 520).

Thirty years later, in *Blackwood's Magazine*, the December 1819 account in "Boxiana; or, Sketches of Pugilism" is more heavily steeped in scientific discourse. The author, identified as John Wilson by John Strachan, follows Pierce Egan's account of the fight in [the original] *Boxiana*, along with several others knitted into a historical progress (215). Beginning by locating boxing within a larger discussion of the law of supply and demand, the author asserts that the "axiom" of "political philosophy" (a discipline he assures his readers he despises) that "a demand for any article always produces a supply" applies "neither to poetry nor pugilism—nor indeed to any of the fine arts" ([Wilson] 279). In a typical *Blackwood's* move, he argues that "the growth of genius is not, in any department, caused by the same principles as the growth of corn" and follows this claim with a series of paired geniuses, classical and contemporary, who "did not come into the world, because the world demanded them." "Pollux and Belcher—Phidias and Chauntry—Homer and Walter Scott": genius occurs equally in boxers, sculptors, and poets and is sui generis, independent of economic principles, outside the economy altogether ([Wilson] 280). By extension into boxing, *Blackwood's* aphorism "The ring was formed by the champions—the champions were not begotten by the ring" echoes romantic notions of the poet creating the public by which s/he will be appreciated ([Wilson] 280).

Blackwood's makes this fight a turning point in the technical development of the sport, legitimating Johnson's movement—in contrast to Slack's earlier dashing about—and resolving the ambiguity about movement into a positive identification. An earlier recounted fight between Johnson and Ryan begins with "the science [. . .] displayed in all its perfection" in which "the parryings and faints were as well executed, as if they had been fencing-masters of the first reputation"; yet the second round "was terrible beyond description; science seemed forgotten, and they appeared like two blacksmiths at an anvil" ([Wilson] 281). By contrast, in the Perrins fight, Johnson's science grows throughout the match, a metonym of the sport's own development. The article dramatizes the transformation by coordinating the boxing with an argument between the two fighters about manhood and identity:

> Tom, finding he was over-matched, was obliged, for the first time in his life, to have recourse to shifting, to prevent his being beat straight forward; which conduct, occasioned some murmuring from the spectators, and Perrins began to treat him with contempt, by exclaiming, "*Why, what have you brought me here! this is not the valiant Johnson, the* champion *of England, you have imposed upon me with a mere boy.*"—Tom's manly heart felt most bitterly this keen sarcasm, and, bursting with indignation, instantly cried out, "By G-d! you shall soon know that Tom Johnson *is* here!" and directly made a *spring* at Perrins, and put in a lunge over the left eye, that closed it up in a twinkling. ([Wilson] 281)

Crucially, the narrative voice characterizes the feinting and moving that Perrins insults as strategy: "Johnson followed up this advantage for three more rounds with success, and his *science* was of great service, in puzzling his antagonist" ([Wilson] 281). It is this puzzlement that provokes Perrins's disparagement, and, as the fight drags on, Johnson's technique takes on an economic valence as storing strength, the boxer's capital: "Johnson's knowledge of the science was here displayed in fine style—in warding off the chopper, and back-handed strokes of his adversary; by which means Tom recruited his strength," while with each successive round, Perrins "appeared much the worse" and began falling "repeatedly from his exhausted state" ([Wilson] 281). Motion and technique triumph over size and strength, and critically for the sport, this method is attached to a complimentary, legitimating discourse.

Conclusion: Stepping Together

The discourses of boxing and dancing depend on marshaling a rhetoric of science—and consequently an aesthetic of motion—yet they proceed in this endeavor primarily as parallel play, largely without reference to each other. There are moments of intersection, often in which boxing annexes the cache of dancing to insist on the grace and legitimacy of the sport. Of the more than 25,000 references to dance and 1000 to boxing in the *British Periodicals* database from 1800–1839, roughly 275 articles reference both together.[9] As these numbers suggest, the greater prestige of dancing made it attractive cultural capital on which to borrow; an article by the pseudonymous Fibber on "Pugilism" for the 1821 *Literary Speculum* notes that Lord Chesterfield "advises people of quality to learn dancing, because it gives an air of gentility," adding, "how much superior in this respect is the science [of boxing] to all the steps and hops and distortions of the dancing-master?" (45). Occasionally, the two activities are brought together to characterize the age; Observator complains to *The Gentleman's Magazine* that the "degenerate age" identified by Sheridan in which "waltzing females, with unblushing face, / Disdain to dance but in a man's embrace" includes the current "disgraceful mania for boxing matches" (Observator 418). Expectedly, both forms of dancing and fighting appear in articles about foreign cultures, such as the *Annual Review*'s "The Stranger in America," which reads the character of Americans through their dances and, particularly in the South, their forms of boxing, which are at once particularly brutal and rule-bound, and associated with slavery (33–48). Similarly, L. de Bauclas's "Manners of the Belgians" in the 1835 *Court Magazine and Belle Assemblée* presents an anecdote about a fight breaking out at a dance to demonstrate that "in Belgium, a little pugilism spoils no friendship," and both activities serve to contain excesses of desire and emotions (196). The prolix but well-intended American who recorded his London experiences in the six-part "Jonathan Kentucky's Journal," published in the January 1821 issue of Henry Colburn's *New Monthly Magazine and Literary Journal*, describes attending a ball in which he is accosted by a "gallant and gay" Lothario, who teases, "in spite of your preaching you cannot keep out of the vortex" (IV 111). The centerpiece of the next excerpt is Jonathan's visit to a "pugilistic pasticcio at the Five Courts" ("Jonathan" VI 526). The exhibition begins with clumsy amateurs "so that the contest soon became a mere rivalry of hard hits" ("Jonathan" VI 526). By contrast, in the later fight "at last we had a rich scientific display of the whole art of attack and defense, by Spring and Harmer, and Belcher and Eales," displaying "the graceful variety of action and posture that arises out of the rapid succession of hitting, stopping, maneuvering, rallying, advancing, and retreating" ("Jonathan" VI 526). The emphasis on mobility that pervades both ball and exhibition, different as they are, coalesce to constitute urban vitality. Just before describing the ball, Kentucky states, "I have lately seen rather more than I wish of what is called *life* in London" ("Jonathan" IV 109); although explicitly he is complaining about the "overgrown metropolis," this may well also be a sly reference to a competing presentation of the city, Egan's *Life in London*, which began as a serial publication a few months prior to the beginning of the "Journal," and ended by eclipsing it as one of the most popular works of its kind (109).

Pierce Egan, in setting out to create a sense of motion, and consequently excitement about England's capitol metropolitan space, writes with a heteroglossic slang that gestures toward at once polite and dandified discourse and the jargon of the "fancy"—the connoisseurs of boxing. David Snowdon, building on Gregory Dart's analysis of "flash style," notes the theatricality shared by *Life in London* and Egan's boxing journalism (para 6). In explaining the effect of gin, Egan portrays the actions of dance through the language of boxing to create an aesthetic of energy: "Many new reels performed in the most lively manner by novices in the art of dancing, from this *moving* commodity [gin], and who *bar* nothing at their *cribs*, would beat De Hayes and D'Egville to a *stand-still*, with all their superlative knowledge of *pirouette* motions, either to describe or give *such* steps a name" (*Life* 319). In the articles that formed the basis of *Boxiana*, Egan built on Mendoza and the periodicals of the late eighteenth century to continue the popularization of boxing, both leveraging and enhancing the increase in sports writing and journalism of the spectacular (Cronin 220–22). Characterizing the world Tom and Jerry explore as the milieu of "the fashionable sciences," Egan predictably makes the former an adept at boxing, and particularly at deftness of movement (*Life* 71). "Distinguishing himself by superior science," he "prevent[s] himself from being *floored* by those of a more athletic nature" (Egan 73). Egan describes Tom's pugilistic evasive maneuvers using the slang of the fancy, concluding the paragraph by noting that "it was the opinion [of the 'first-rate professors of the gymnastic art'] that, had TOM entered the ring as a public candidate for boxing fame, he would have proved himself nothing but a *good one!*" (*Life* 73). As his complement, Jerry was "in all the sports and pastimes" of Hawthorn Hall, "the hero of the tale"; in particular, "At a harvest-home, or a merry-making at Christmas, JERRY exhibited as much, perhaps more, natural taste and agility in his dancing than those persons who could boast of the advantages of having had Opera teachers to instruct them. In short, he was the very *double*, or *counterpart*, of CORINTHIAN TOM; making an allowance for the different spheres in which their various talents were exercised" (Egan 135–36). Egan's "strategic representation of boxing culture as guided by rules, principles of fair play, and a righteous resistance to prejudice" is displayed, transgressed, and extended into ballrooms, dancehalls, and alleyways (Wright 503).

Though their meanderings through the various strata of London are filled with sports, entertainments, antics, and skirmishes of a variety of sorts, boxing and dancing maintain not equal dominance—that belongs to pugilism alone—but a kinship that parallels that of Tom and his second both in the text and in Cruikshank's illustrations. In "The Highest Life in London" and "Lowest 'Life in London'" Cruikshank features dancing as maintaining the collegiality and peace that the pugilistic attitude so often threatens, even while both represent a mode of arraying and regulating energies and excitement (Egan 343, 320). For Godwin, the failure of such regulation, in Falkland's murder of Tyrrel and discovery by Caleb, inaugurates his plot of paranoia, surveillance, and pursuit that critiques the English counterrevolutionary systems of social control. In *Caleb Williams*, as with the scientization of dance and boxing in contemporary public discourse, a generalized attention to bodies in motion positions recreation as a mediating social organization, one that privileges privilege. A "little pugilism," as elsewhere, here signals that the display and deployment of individual bodies in motion are forms of play at once entertaining and deadly.

Notes

1. See Pope ll. 362–63.

2. See Egan ll. 19–20.

3. Alvin Kernan argues that print "created the conditions that eventually separated the writer from the patron, and the social order he represented, by providing writers with a new way of earning a living—writing for a reading public" (102–103). More recently, Dustin Griffin emphasizes the persistence of patronage into the nineteenth century (222).

4. The August 1837 *Court Magazine* correctly attributes the phrase "poetry of motion" to Lady Morgan, noting in the same paragraph that Byron called the stars "the poetry of heaven" in *Childe Harold* ("Bird's" 101). The *New Sporting Magazine* may be combining these attributions to capitalize on Byron's authority.

5. While recreational forms of fighting and dancing occurred throughout regional and rural spaces, the locus of their professional presentation was London. Of the 485 pugilistic events Harvey categorizes, 182 were in London (37.5 percent), while, by contrast, of the 2608 competitions involving horses, 88 were in London (4 percent); of the total 6736 sporting events Harvey identified, 1127 (17 percent) were in London.

6. Kenneth Graham identifies "at least ten tribunals in *Caleb Williams*, varying in importance, formality, and corruption" (221).

7. In Paul Whitehead's 1744 *Gymnasiad*, the boxers "sweat" and "heave, each tugging Nerve they strain, / Both fix'd as Oaks, their sturdy Trunks sustain" (2. 25–26). Like the *Connoisseur*, Whitehead emphasizes an aesthetic of toe-to-toe confrontation.

8. This assessment of Broughton was reprinted frequently in 1788 as part of the debate about the efficacy and aesthetic of standing toe-to-toe in contrast to the newer, more mobile approach of Mendoza: see "Characters" 55; "Continuation" 127–28; "History" 173; and Mendoza, *Art* 34.

9. Three of the 32 articles with "pugilism" or "boxing" in the title mention dancing, while none of the 305 articles with "dance" or "dancing" in the title mentions boxing or pugilism.

Works Cited

An Amateur of Eminence. *The Complete Art of Boxing, According to the Modern Method*. London: M. Follingsby, 1788.

Austen, Jane. *Pride and Prejudice*. 1813. Ed. Robert Irvine. Peterboro, Ontario: Broadview Press, 2002.

"Battle in Norfolk." *The Gentleman's Magazine: and Historical Chronicle*. August 1754: 364–65.

Barrington, Shute. Speech on Esten's Divorce Bill, March 2, 1798. *The Parliamentary History of England*. Ed. T. C. Hansard. Vol. 33. London: Longman, 1818.

"Bird's Eye Papers for September." *The Court Magazine, and Monthly Critic*. 11.2 (August 1837): 97–104.

Boddy, Kasia. *Boxing: A Cultural History*. London: Reaktion Books, 2009.

Castigator. "Account of some Fashionable Amusements." *The Town and Country Magazine; Or, Universal Repository of Knowledge, Instruction, and Entertainment* (April 1780): 176.

Chandler, James. *Wordsworth's Second Nature: A Study of the Poetry and Politics*. Chicago: University of Chicago Press, 1984.

"Character of Boxers." *The Scots Magazine*. 50.2 (February 1788): 55–58.

"A Circumstantial Detail of the Final Contest between Mendoza and Humphries at Doncaster." Mendoza, Chapter 8. 44–48.

Civis. "Thoughts on Pugilism." *The Scots Magazine and Edinburgh Literary Miscellany*. 73 (November 1811): 811–12.

"Continuation of the History of Boxing." *The Edinburgh Magazine, or Literary Miscellany*. 7.2 (February 1788): 127–32.

Cowper, William, trans. *The Iliad and Odyssey of Homer, Translated into English Blank Verse*. 2 vols. London, 1791.

Cronin, Richard. *Paper Pellets: British Literary Culture after Waterloo*. New York: Oxford University Press, 2010.

Dart, Gregory. " 'Flash Style': Pierce Egan and Literary London 1820–28." *History Workshop Journal* 51 (2001): 180–205.

De Bauclas, L. "Manners of the Belgians." *The Court Magazine and Belle Assemblée*. 6.5 (May 1835): 194–98.

"Domestic Intelligence: Boxing." *The General Magazine and Impartial Review* 3 (November 1789): 519–21.

Downing, Karen. "The Gentleman Boxer: Boxing, Manners, and Masculinity in Eighteenth-Century England." *Men and Masculinities* 10 (2008): 1–25.

Egan, Pierce. "A Boxing we will go." *The Sporting Magazine*. 38 (September 1811): 295.

———. *Life in London*. London: Chatto and Windus, 1900.

Fibber. "On Pugilism." *A Literary Speculum*. 1. 1 (November 1821): 43–47.

Gillray, James. "Operatical reform;—or—la dance a l'eveque." 14 March 1798. National Portrait Gallery: NPG D12562.

Gilmartin, Kevin, ed. *Sociable Places: Locating Culture in Romantic-Period Britain*. Cambridge: Cambridge University Press, 2017.

Godfrey, John. *A Treatise Upon the Useful Science of Defence*. London: T. Gardner, 1747.

Godwin, William. *Things as they Are; Or, the Adventures of Caleb Williams*. 1794. Ed. Gary Handwerk and A.A. Markley. Peterborough, Ontario: Broadview Press, 2000.

Graham, Kenneth. "Narrative and Ideology in Godwin's *Caleb Williams*." *Eighteenth-Century Fiction* 2. 3 (April 1990): 215–28.

Griffin, Dustin. *Literary Patronage in England, 1650–1800*. New York: Cambridge University Press, 1996.

Harrow, Sharon. "Playing by the Rules." *British Sporting Literature and Culture in the Long Eighteenth Century*. Ed. Sharon Harrow. Burlington, VT: Ashgate, 2015.

Harvey, Adrian. *The Beginnings of a Commercial Sporting Culture in Britain: 1793–1850*. Burlington, VT: Ashgate, 2004.

"HISTORICAL OBSERVATIONS on DANCING: Illustrative of the Frontispiece to this Volume, representing the Muse TERPSICHORE." *Universal Magazine of Knowledge and Pleasure*. 91 (1792): 3–5.

"History of Boxing, by an Amateur." *The Gentleman's and London Magazine*. April 1788: 172–74.

Homans, Jennifer. *Apollo's Angels: A History of Ballet*. New York: Random House, 2010.

"Jonathan Kentucky's Journal, No. IV." *The New Monthly Magazine and Literary Journal*. 2. 7 (January 1821): 104–12.

"Jonathan Kentucky's Journal, No. VI." *The New Monthly Magazine and Literary Journal*. 2. 11 (November 1821): 522–32.

Kernan, Alvin. *Samuel Johnson and the Impact of Print*. Princeton, NJ: Princeton University Press, 1987.

Knight of the Fist. "On Pugilism. To the Editors of the *Sporting Magazine*." *The Sporting Magazine*. 6. 1 (April 1795): 137–38.

"Lamb and Pitman's Racquet Match.—Van Amburgh the Lion Tamer; The Mind, the Eye, and the Muscle" *The New Sporting Magazine*. 15. 90 (October 1823–28): 245–60.

Lemoine, Henry. *Modern Manhood or, the Art and Practice of English Boxing. Including the History of the Science of Natural Defence and Memoirs of the Most Celebrated Practitioners of that Manly Exercise*. London: H. Lemoine, 1788.

Mendoza, Daniel. *Art of Boxing*. 1789. *The Modern Art of Boxing, as Practised by Mendoza, Humphreys, Ryan, Ward, Watson, Johnson, and Other Eminent Pugilists*. 2nd ed. London: Daniel Mendoza, 1789.

"Monthly Chronologer: London." *London Magazine, or, Gentleman's Monthly Intelligencer*. 42 (September 1773): 461–65.

Noverre, Jean Georges. *Letters on Dancing and Ballets*. 1803. Trans. Cyril W. Beaumont. New York: Dance Horizons, 1966.

O'Quinn, Daniel. "Proxy Israelites." Gilmartin 97–121.

Observator. "Letter." *The Gentleman's Magazine: and Historical Chronicle* (May 1812): 417–18.

"On Dancing." *La Belle Assemblée: or Court and Fashionable Magazine* 1. 9 (1806): 449–52.

Pope, Alexander. "Essay on Criticism." *Poems of Alexander Pope*. Ed. John Butt. New Haven: Yale University Press, 1963. 143–68.

Regier, Alexander. "What is training?" *Sporting Cultures, 1650–1850*. Ed. Daniel O'Quinn. University of Toronto Press, 2018. 272–93.

Reid, J. C. *Bucks and Bruisers: Pierce Egan and Regency England*. London: Routledge and Kegan Paul, 1971.

Russell, Gillian. "The Place is Not Free to You." Gilmartin 143–162.

Samuelian, Kristin. "Dancing in Time and Place: Figuring Englishness in Romantic Periodicals." *ELH* 83. 3 (2016): 795–819.

Sedgwick, Eve. *Between Men: English Literature and Male Homosocial Desire*. New York, NY: Columbia University Press, 1985.

Snowdon, David. "Drama Boxiana: Spectacle and Theatricality in Pierce Egan's Pugilistic Writing." *Romanticism on the Net*. 46 (May 2007).

Southey, Robert. *The Doctor, &c*. 7 vol. New York: Harper, 1836. Vol. 4.

Strachan, John. "John Wilson and Sport." *Romanticism and* Blackwood's Magazine*: 'An Unprecedented Phenomenon.'* Ed. Robert Morrison and Daniel Roberts. New York: Palgrave, 2013.

"The Stranger in America; containing Observations made during a long Residence in that Country, on the Genius, Manners, and Customs of the People of the United States [. . .]" *The Annual Review and History of Literature*. 6 (January 1807): 33–48.

"To the Editors of the *Oxford Magazine*." *The Oxford Magazine*. Supplement to Volume One (December 1768): 271–72.

T[own], Mr. [George Colman and Bonnel Thornton]. *The Connoisseur*. No. 30 (22 August 1754): 230–38. Rpt. *The British Essayists*. vol. 18. Ed. Alexander Chalmers. London and Edinburgh, 1802. viii–ix.

Whale, John. "Daniel Mendoza's Contests of Identity: Masculinity, Ethnicity and Nation in Georgian Prize-fighting." *Romanticism* 14 (2008): 259–71.

Whitehead, Paul. *The Gymnasiad, or Boxing Match. A very short, but very curious Epic Poem*. London: M Cooper, 1744.

[Wilson, John]. "Boxiana; or, Sketches of Pugilism." *Blackwood's Edinburgh Magazine*. 6. 33 (December 1819): 279–84.

Wright, Julia. "Cosmopugilism: Thomas Moore's Boxing Satires and the Post-Napoleonic Congresses." *Studies in Romanticism* 56 (Winter 2017): 599–23.

Chapter 2

Baseball in the Frame of Gilded-Age America

MATTHEW VON VOGT

Within the annals of U.S. baseball history, 1886 and 1887 carry little canonical significance. While the particularities surrounding the "invention" of baseball have long been contested, the sport was firmly entrenched by that time in the United States, even spreading well beyond its initial anchoring within New York State.[1] Organized baseball leagues enjoyed modest tenure, and while the American League would not materialize until early in the twentieth century (although ancestral incarnations existed), the National League began in 1876 and remains.

Yet if these years fail to resonate as a landmark period within the history of organized baseball, they enjoy a pole position within the visual and material cultural histories of the sport. A pair of salient events emerged during the two years: the culmination of Eadweard Muybridge's *Animal Locomotion* (begun several years earlier), and the first year of the inaugural grand-scale baseball card set, a photographic collection released by Old Judge and Gypsy Queen cigarettes (by their parent company, Goodwin & Co.) between 1887 and 1890.[2] Muybridge's collection of stop-motion plates, of course, extends well beyond baseball, including men, women, and zoo animals, engaged in various activities and depicted via a grid that throws into spatial relief the granular temporal activity of the subjects depicted. Still, plates 273–288 feature baseball players from the University of Pennsylvania, and Muybridge's comments suggest more than a passing interest in the sport; in reference to one of the plates, he noted: "See how curiously [. . .] and yet how perfectly, this plate illustrates the occurrence of an error in catching" (qtd.in Edelman 68). Hailed as a scientific breakthrough—the University of Pennsylvania student newspaper remarked, "The work is absolutely unique in its way. Nothing of its style and magnitude has hitherto been attempted, and many of its analyses of motion will be revelations to the scientific world"—Muybridge's stop-motion images share motifs with the baseball card set, specifically through the uniform representation of the athlete against an ascetic backdrop, reflecting a Gilded-Age impulse to visually and materially document the sport (qtd. in "Muybridge").

The documentation of baseball began well before 1887, evidenced by newspaper coverage (*Sporting Life*, a dedicated sports publication, having started in 1883), as well as the writings of Henry Chadwick and other "fathers" of the sport. My interest however lies with the baseball cards' photographic framing of the players, specifically within the sociohistorical context of the Muybridge stop-motion plates. The focus is not to speculate whether the cards drew influence from Muybridge's photographs, but rather to excavate the shared implementation of photography and print in documenting the nineteenth-century baseball player. Two questions guide this analysis: First, if we follow Bill Brown and grant baseball cards the "narrativity of material objects," which cultural images of baseball may we glean from the photographic representation of the baseball player? (*Sense* 103). And second, how do these images of baseball change when we view the baseball cards not only as visual but also as material (cardboard) objects? In reading the baseball cards in the orbit of Muybridge, I argue that the photographic cards modernized the sport through imbuing it with the visual vocabulary of the pictorial archive. Alongside this theme, I posit that the mass cultural anchoring of the cards in cigarette packages demonstrates the inseparability of baseball from the consumer economy.

These themes surface in the representation of Hall of Fame slugger King Kelly. A veteran player by 1887, Kelly began his career with Cincinnati in 1878, shifting to the Chicago White Stockings two years later, making the team the best in the country. On 14 February 1887, he was traded from Chicago to Boston for $10,000, an act that complicated attempts to represent him (as they were in the process of completing the set). As with the rest of the Old Judge set, the photographic cards were shot in the Joseph Hall Studio in Brooklyn, New York.[3] Each card stands 1½ x 2½ inches. Two cards from 1887 still depict Kelly in a Chicago uniform, while the majority represent him with Boston, referring to "$10,000 Kelly." In one of the 1887 Boston Gypsy Queen cards, Kelly appears ready to catch a baseball ("$10,000" [hands aloft]). The suggestion of arrested motion recalls Muybridge (even if close inspection reveals that the ball hangs from a string in the photographic studio). Not only does the documentation of Kelly's name and body categorize the individual baseball player, but in such cards, the player appears athletic, engaged in physical activity.

Other Old Judge and Gypsy Queen cards from 1887–1890 appear less dynamic. In another of the Chicago Gypsy Queen cards, Kelly appears against a nature backdrop. He clutches a baseball bat, choking up on the handle, but his gaze meets the photographer, alluding to portraiture rather than evoking an event captured in media res ("$10,000" [parallel bat]). Other cards make even less effort to simulate a game, clothing the players in formal attire. Here it is notable that Hall of Famer Cap Anson, an elitist figure who had eschewed being represented by the initial 1887 cards, acquiesced to the stiffer representation of later editions.[4] In the 1888 Goodwin & Co. card he appears without uniform, instead clad in a suit coat ("Capt."; see Figure 2.1). His name is listed in upper-case

Figure 2.1. Captain Adrian C. Anson of the Chicago White Stockings appears in a suit rather than a uniform. Old Judge Cigarettes, Goodwin & Co. New York, 1888. Courtesy of the Benjamin K. Edwards Collection of Baseball Cards at the Library of Congress. Washington, D.C.

letters as "Capt. Anson Chicago's," with the cigarette label positioned below the photograph. The written text of the caption alone indicates his profession (although, as was common practice, this same photograph was recycled for multiple years). Such cards confer genteel respectability toward the game, but achieve this through clothing removed from uniform, equipment, or ball field.

Within the Old Judge and Gypsy Queen series, a network of representations thus emerges, with the (evoked) stop-motion aesthetic juxtaposed against more formal representations. In each case, the documentation of the player's name purports to individualize the athlete, in turn professionalizing the sport. This is true even if the cards are relatively impersonal, as the players appear against an amorphous backdrop, with the same studio setting recycled for myriad players.

Across the cards, however, the photographic representation of the baseball player contends with the label of the cigarette manufacturer. In the early set, the inscription of "Old Judge" at top and "Goodwin & Co." at bottom flanks the photograph. Later cards, as in the Anson example, list "Old Judge" and "Goodwin & Co." together at bottom. In each instance, photographic and verbal (commercial and biographical) registers remain inextricably intertwined. If the verbal and photographic documentation professionalizes the player, the documentation of the cigarette manufacturer—not to mention the material properties of the cigarette package housing the cards—embeds the sport within the consumer economy. Baseball's Janus face surfaces, as the photographic documentation of the player coexists with a commercial imperative to sell consumer goods.

The inseparability of baseball player and cigarette manufacturer reflects the parallel emergence, and ultimate convergence, of baseball cards and tobacco. Baseball cards existed well before the first large-scale set; over the preceding decade, cards were released sporadically, primarily tied to a specific team. However, these were regionally specific and hardly the kind of event that would launch an entire industry. The baseball card industry instead gained traction through the development of the tobacco industry, which saw rapid progress following the Civil War. Based in New York (still the national epicenter for baseball), Goodwin & Co. was a logical candidate to release the first large-scale baseball card set.[5] Thus, rather than a visual aberration, we may read the documentation of the cigarette manufacturer as emblematizing the eventual imbrication of baseball and cigarettes.

While it is easy see where the cigarette company might benefit from courting baseball—obscuring the health consequences of cigarette consumption—one may also see why the cigarette logos bear no place in Muybridge's baseball plates. By contrast, Muybridge's study was completed within an academic context, subsidized by the University of Pennsylvania, under the auspices of professors from the Pennsylvania Academy of Fine Arts (Edward A. Coates and artist Thomas Eakins), as well as professors from the physiology, physics, civil engineering, and dynamical engineering departments. Previously residing in California, where *Horse in Motion* was completed, Muybridge's relationship with the University of Pennsylvania began through his relationship with Fairman Rogers, a trustee of both the university and the Academy of Fine Arts. Rogers invited Muybridge to the university to conduct a series of lectures, which eventually led the faculty to fund Muybridge's *Animal Locomotion*. Begun in 1884, the project took three years to complete, but its institutional grounding at the University of Pennsylvania anchored the project within a scientific framework.[6]

If the baseball cards purport to legitimize the sport through professionalizing it via photographic portraiture and verbal documentation, Muybridge's efforts legitimize baseball through a more explicitly scientific lens. As with the cards, Muybridge documents the player, but rather than recording team or uniform, he noted such details as the phases of movement, time intervals, and quantity of movement (Plate 275). Basic descriptions of the activity conducted were recorded; thus, plate 275 shows "Base-ball; batting (low ball)" takes place, with model number 30 shown (Rabinowitz 12). One completed movement is registered (hitting), and the nude body of the player not only contrasts with the pristine uniforms of the Old Judge cards but also relies on its scientific context to dispel charges of indecency (although the plates still aroused controversy when exhibited) (Gordon).

Muybridge's statistical documentation was not recorded on the plates, but rather catalogued in an accompanying abstract. Still, while his statistics bear no relation to the actual accomplishments of professional athletes, it is worth noting that *Animal Locomotion* statistically documented the sport prior to the baseball cards proper (the recording of statistics on the reverse of the baseball card did not become common until the twentieth century). If the Old Judge cards professionalized the sport, however, the subjects of *Animal Locomotion* were amateurs, albeit talented ones. His three subjects were Thomas Love Latta, catcher and captain for the University of Pennsylvania team, as well as teammates Robert Edward Glendinning and Morris Hacker Jr (Muybridge). While the project might have been funded by the players' parent institution, their nudity visually distances them from their academic affiliations, even if Muybridge notes in his prospectus that his subjects were exemplary athletes, "young men aged from eighteen to twenty-four,—each one of whom has a well-earned record in the particular feat selected for illustration" (12).

Honorific though the plates may be, the statistics recorded by Muybridge and the grid background obliquely affiliate the plates with the physiognomic aesthetics of the "pictorial [anatomical] statistics" recorded by Francis Galton, Alphonse Bertillon, Thomas Henry Huxley, and John Lamprey, among others (Galton qtd. in Sekula 47). Infamous for their documentation of racial minorities (in the case of Lamprey and Huxley) and the criminal body (Galton and Bertillon), these photographers coalesce around an anthropological intent to objectively categorize the body, in the process lending photography "a proper role within a new hierarchy of taste" (Rabinowitz 6). The photographers position the minority or criminal subject against a grid, in the process *scientifically* measuring the subject's features, with the motivation that personality traits could be gleaned through one's proportions (a long forehead, for example, signified intelligence). Anthropometric photography privileged the *heightened* gaze of the viewer against a photographic subject literally measured under scrutiny.

Muybridge's adoption of the grid participates in this cultural moment, as well as the Darwinian-Spencerian positivism undergirding such anthropometric initiatives. The iconographic affinities between Muybridge and these photographers have not gone unnoticed, and Muybridge was familiar with their work (Gordon). The positioning of the photographic subject against a uniform, grid background suggests an implied scientific gaze across the Muybridge photographs, a hierarchical view privileging the white male doctor as assumed viewer (that the Muybridge plates were primarily marketed within a scientific context bear this out). And if the photographic grid suggests an exclusionary politics of documentation, this was the case with *Animal Locomotion*, in which, as Sarah Gordon notes, the set begins with male athletes and progresses to women, pathological human subjects, and finally animals (ending with a chicken).[7] Placed in the first half of the stop-motion set, the baseball players enjoyed a rather lofty, even if not pristine, position within Muybridge's hierarchy.

While nineteenth-century baseball cards did not implement a grid per se, we may perhaps read the uniform backdrop of the photographic studio, as well as the exhaustive impulse to visually document the players, as a kind of grid—or at least, a documentary aesthetic that stressed not only the commemoration of the sport but also its photographic archiving against a uniform backdrop. The documentation of names, positions, and teams further underscores the scientific rigor of the baseball cards' documentation of the sport. If Muybridge and the physiognomic legacy is exclusionary, the baseball cards are no less so, documenting a sport from which women, as well as racial and ethnic minorities, were excluded (although where the oppressed subject for Galton, Bertillon, Huxley, and Lamprey is *represented*, the baseball cards manifest oppression through *absence*). The systematic recording of baseball players against a uniform backdrop suggests that the baseball cards posit a kind of physiognomy of the sport, one which positions the sport as professional, urbane, and performed by upstanding gentlemen.

The temporal arrest of the stop-motion photographs also coheres with a modernist impulse to arrest time. In his landmark study of physiognomic photography, Allan Sekula notes that anthropometric photographs helped catalyze photographic modernism, and Muybridge's photographs are installed in modern art museums. In his abstract, Muybridge stresses the appeal of *Animal Locomotion* for artists, and Thomas Eakins (himself a sponsor of *Animal Locomotion*) utilized stop-motion aesthetics toward his own work. Furthermore, the "grid" comprises a prime keyword within the high modernist vocabulary, referring to the serial patterns of avant-garde painters (even if, as Rosalind Krauss argues, the modernist grid bears a more abstract aesthetic than the anthropometric photographic grid—exemplified by Kasimir Malevich, Piet Mondrian, and others—and purports to isolate opticality, eschewing the numerical thrust of the grids deployed by Muybridge and anthropometric photography).[8] In borrowing from the Muybridgean aesthetic, however loosely, the Old Judge baseball cards not only solicit an educated gaze but also position baseball as a modern/ist sport.

This essay has read the Old Judge set alongside Muybridge to elucidate a physiognomy of baseball premised on modernity and professionalization. Yet a different view of the cards—and baseball—emerges when we account for their cardboard materiality. If the photograph imbues the cards with a scientific, modern urge to pictorially archive the body, viewing the cards as material objects stresses their ephemeral position as objects of unregulated circulation, handled by the consumer rather than the more local scientific public solicited by Muybridge. If the stop-motion plates represented the fruit of several years of hard work and institutional funding, the relatively inexpensive materiality of the cardboard object facilitates the creation of a fashionable item that could be released anew each passing year. Put differently, if viewing the Old Judge cards through Muybridge stresses their position as archival objects, viewing them as cardboard stresses their position as collectors' items. Considered as photographic archive, the baseball cards confer a systematic, modern, professional image of the sport; considered as material collection, the baseball cards become objects of use, not only mass cultural ephemera but also handled by a consumer subject liable to organize the collection as she saw fit.

In viewing the cards as pop cultural objects, we may constellate the cards alongside other photographic genres that were viewed as consumable items, distinct from stop-motion iconography. The miniature size of the cards, for example, recalls the mid-nineteenth-century *carte-de-visite* portraits popularized by Eugene Disderi, the small, pictorial photographs that became popular collector's items and, as Elizabeth Siegel notes, "the most popular form of photographic portraiture throughout the 1860s" (17). The later Old Judge cards, specifically those conveying the face or still body rather than evoking arrested movement, register as particularly acute facsimiles of the *carte-de-visite*. As a hybrid medium, part photograph and part cardboard, part scientific archive and part mass cultural collectors' item, the differential materiality of the baseball cards correlates with a heterogeneous image of a sport that is both object of rigorous, modern documentation and object of modern consumption.

Both the cards' photographic documentation and their cardboard substrate position baseball as a modern sport—the former through evoking modern science and modernist aesthetics, the latter through embedding the sport within material culture of industrial-capitalist America. Yet late-nineteenth-century baseball cards were not only avatars for a modern sport, but also gesture at baseball's essential pastorality. Apropos of this topos, one of the recurrent photographic backdrops for the Old Judge cards, including that deployed in the 1887 King Kelly Gypsy Queen card depicting him holding a bat aloft, conveys a nature setting, in many cases a rural field. Such pastoral motifs surface with particular intensity in chromolithograph cards: if the photographs modernize the sport, chromolithographs evoke the premodern. We may observe this with the Goodwin Champions series, a fifty-card set featuring notable figures from across American popular culture (only eight baseball players, each of them world-class, were included). In their cards from this set, King Kelly and Cap Anson appear against a brilliant sky and the proximity of their faces to the sky, as well as the general groundlessness of the image (their legs are absent) lends a mythical connotation, almost anointing them as secular gods. The backs of the cards indicate the other "Champions" in the series (see Figures 2.2–2.5). (The richly saturated colors also could only have seemed more acute to a public accustomed to black and white photographic cards.)

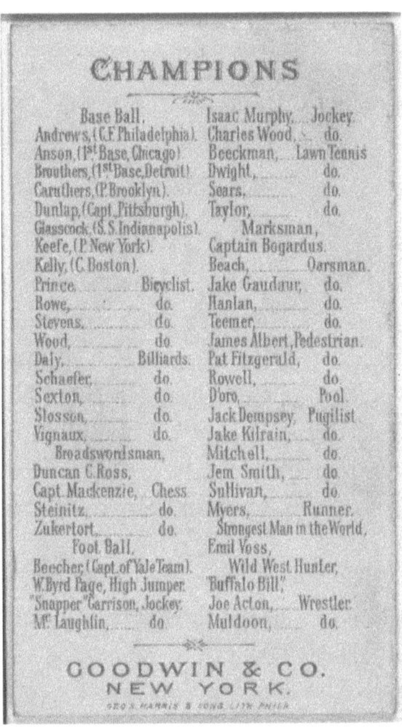

Figure 2.2. In Goodwin's chromolithograph, Captain Anson, wearing a brilliant blue shirt, is identified by his position (1st base) and his team, Chicago White Stockings. Old Judge and Gypsy Queen Cigarettes. Goodwin & Co. New York, 1888. Courtesy of the Benjamin K. Edwards Collection of Baseball Cards at the Library of Congress. Washington, D.C.

Figure 2.3. The reverse of Goodwin's card shows Anson among other "Champions" from baseball and other sports. Old Judge and Gypsy Queen Cigarettes. Goodwin & Co. New York, 1888. Courtesy of the Benjamin K. Edwards Collection of Baseball Cards at the Library of Congress. Washington, D.C.

Figure 2.4. In Goodwin's chromolithograph, King Kelly against a bright blue sky and wearing a red tie, is identified by his position (center field) and his team, the Boston Beaneaters. Old Judge and Gypsy Queen Cigarettes. Goodwin & Co. New York, 1888. Courtesy of the Benjamin K. Edwards Collection of Baseball Cards at the Library of Congress. Washington, D.C.

Figure 2.5. The reverse of Goodwin's card shows Kelly among other "Champions" from baseball and other sports. Old Judge and Gypsy Queen Cigarettes. Goodwin & Co. New York, 1888. Courtesy of the Benjamin K. Edwards Collection of Baseball Cards at the Library of Congress. Washington, D.C.

Other chromolithograph sets, including the 1887 Allen & Ginter set and the 1889 Goodwin Round Albums, contain similarly vibrant colors and seem altogether displaced from industrial modernity, a theme reinforced by the absence of the cigarette logo on the front of the cards[9] (see Figure 2.6). Here again, the back of the card shows the other "World's Champions" (see Figure 2.7). Most chromolithograph sets were especially exclusive—reserved for premier athletes—with checklists on the back listing each card within the set; emphasis lay not on scientific documentation, but on celebrating the best players the sport had to

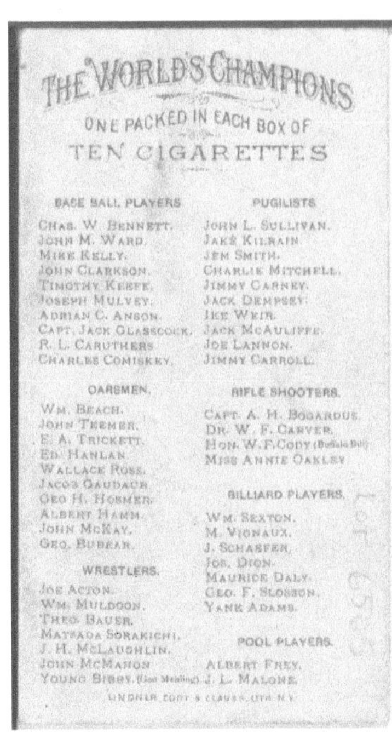

Figure 2.6. Captain Adrian C. Anson holds a bat aloft in Allen & Ginter's card. Allen & Ginter's Cigarettes, Richmond, VA, 1887. Courtesy of the Benjamin K. Edwards Collection of Baseball Cards at the Library of Congress. Washington, D.C.

Figure 2.7. The reverse of Allen & Ginter's card shows Anson among other "World's Champions" from baseball and other sports. Allen & Ginter's Cigarettes, Richmond, VA, 1887. Courtesy of the Benjamin K. Edwards Collection of Baseball Cards at the Library of Congress. Washington, D.C.

offer. However, not all chromolithograph sets were so rarified, and the 1889 Buchner Gold Coin set documented nearly 150 players, each set within a pastoral baseball diamond more or less abstracted from an actual baseball contest—indeed, the rural baseball *landscapes* evoke the tranquil nature settings of contemporaneous Gilded-Age painters (see Figures 2.8 and 2.9). For the most part, however, black-and-white photographic sets comprised a more inclusive alternative to the rural exclusivity of the chromolithographs.

Through prioritizing the pastoral, the chromolithographs strive toward a premodern ideal that had long defined the sport in the United States. The decades antedating the first wide-scale baseball card set saw

Figure 2.8. King Kelly is presented here against the pastoral baseball diamond common in the Gold Coin card set. Gold Coin Chewing Tobacco, 1887. Courtesy of the Benjamin K. Edwards Collection of Baseball Cards at the Library of Congress. Washington, D.C.

Figure 2.9. The reverse of Buchner's Gold Coin image of Kelly reminds purchasers to "[c]ontinue to save the wrappers. They are valuable." Gold Coin Chewing Tobacco, 1887. Courtesy of the Benjamin K. Edwards Collection of Baseball Cards at the Library of Congress. Washington, D.C.

baseball concretize its mythical status as America's pastime and achieve widespread awareness of the rules and etiquette surrounding the sport. These efforts were due in large part to the persistence of Henry Chadwick, perhaps the leading baseball journalist of the nineteenth century, whose landmark book *The Game of Baseball* was published in 1868. In that volume, Chadwick recounts his first encounter with baseball in characteristically colorful prose:

> It was in 1856, I think, when on returning from the early close of a cricket match on Fox Hill, I chanced to go through the Elysian Fields during the progress of a contest between the

> noted Eagle and Gotham Clubs. The game was being sharply played on both sides, and I watched it with deeper interest than any previous [cricket or rounders] match between clubs that I had seen. It was not long before I was struck with the idea that base ball was just the game for a national sport for Americans, and reflecting on the subject, it occurred to me, on my return home, that from this game of ball a powerful lever might be made by which our people could be lifted in a position of more devotion to physical exercise and healthful out-door recreation than they had hitherto, as a people been known for. (10)

Mythical connotations abound, from the fact that the game was played at Elysian Fields to the metaphorical "lever" that baseball was to assume in a narrative of progress relating to national health. While Chadwick writes colorfully, his language was not purely ornamental: he was also a persistent documenter and prescriptively articulated a vision for the sport and its attendant standards for purity and honor. A taste of his abstemious views can be grasped in what follows:

> Secondly, we have avowed ourselves on all occasions the open foe to all those evil influences which of late years, we regret to say, have only too surely crept in as a drawback to the permanent establishment of the game as a pastime thoroughly unobjectionable in every point of view. We claim to rank among our enemies every low-minded, vicious "rough," whether clad in broad-cloth or homespun, every professional gambler who aims to make rival clubs his tools, and every foul-mouthed blaspheming "sport," whose only idea of enjoyment, connected with any game or trial of skill, consists of the amount of animal gratification it can afford him, either as a means of gambling, of vicious excitement, or of intemperance. (Chadwick 162–63)

Given their manufacture at the hands of cigarette companies, both the photographic sets and the chromolithograph ones challenge the puritanical myth of America's pastime presented by Chadwick. Yet the heightened rurality of the chromolithographs still goes farther in upholding the Chadwickian image of baseball as a "pure," mythical celebration of Edenic America.[10] Rather different images of baseball emerge through the material and visual cultures of late-nineteenth-century America: if the Goodwin & Co. sets situate baseball within a context of archival documentation associated with Muybridge, the chromolithographs assent to a premodern ideal. Cardboard proves a most flexible material, promoting divergent narratives for the constitution of the sport.

Ultimately, the photographic framing of baseball demonstrates that photography and baseball were mutually reliant. For baseball (and baseball cards), Muybridge's stop-motion photographs legitimized the sport, imbuing it within a theretofore underrecognized scientific context. The photographic cards throw into relief how baseball cards marshaled photography to more rigorously document baseball and endow the sport with a modern physiognomy. Meanwhile, for Muybridge, baseball's all-American character (evidenced by Chadwick and Albert Spalding) made the sport a ripe subject for the stop-motion lens. At the same time, photographic documentation of the sport existed alongside the premodern myth of America's pastime, which persists to this day; in this sense, the photographic framing of the baseball player carries a tension between tradition and modernity that continues to inform the sport.

As photographic objects, the baseball cards borrow from Muybridge's contemporaneous aesthetic. As material objects, however, the baseball cards throw into relief what is kept out of view by both Chadwick's rhetoric of purity and that of Muybridge: namely, baseball's inextricable ties to mass culture and its consumer products. If the cards render baseball a "material game," this is a more honest and complex view of the sport than emerges through Muybridge or Chadwick alone, a view that does justice to the rich layers of the sport's identity. As a heterogeneous medium, photography comprised one ingredient within the cultural and ideological melting pot of late-nineteenth-century baseball.

Notes

1. The most common of baseball's "creation narratives," effected in 1907 by Albert Spalding, is that baseball was founded by Abner Doubleday in Cooperstown, N.Y. A Civil War general, Doubleday's history as a Civil War general made him, in the eyes of Spalding, the ideal patriarch for the sport—a man who could synthesize the emergence of baseball with the consolidation of the nation, thereby crystallizing baseball's status as quintessential American sporting activity. Spalding's conclusion came as the result of the Mills Commission, a lengthy search committee formed in 1905 to determine the identity of the

"father" of baseball. These creation myths have long since been dispelled, most systematically by John Thorn and David Block.

2. A smaller set was released a year prior.

3. The Old Cardboard website and its eponymous journal offer a thorough production history of baseball cards (from both the nineteenth and twentieth centuries).

4. For more on Anson's animosity toward photographic baseball cards, see Miller, Gonsowski, and Masson. Anson was one of the primary figures responsible for excluding African Americans from the sport, and his principal role in that now outshines his fame as an athlete. Anson forms a clear counterpart to Kelly in this regard, who was recognized as a fan favorite.

5. Peter Devereaux and Dave Jamieson document the rise of baseball cards in relation to that of cigarettes. Devereaux's analysis, which takes as its departure point the baseball card collection at the Library of Congress, provides an especially comprehensive elucidation of the development of the baseball card industry during its cigarette era. For Devereaux, the emergence of Babe Ruth signaled a sea change in baseball's identity that necessitated a shift from cigarette cards to more wholesome conduits. (There is a certain irony here, given Ruth's legendary penchant for self-destructive consumption.)

6. Over time, however, Muybridge's work assumed a much broader, vernacular context, as evidenced by the exhibition of his lecture slides by his Zoopraxiscope during the 1893 World's Fair in Chicago. According to Lauren Rabinowitz, after his Zoopraxiscope failed to attract adequate public attention, his slides were transposed into souvenirs.

7. Nancy Mowll Mathews also discusses the hierarchical layout of *Animal Locomotion*, while Marta Braun addresses Muybridge's work in the context of anthropometric photography.

8. For Krauss, intent on treating modernism as a psychoanalytic subject, patterns such as the grid mask a repressed threat to modernist rationality.

9. For further examples, see "Capt. Anson, Chicago"; "Mike Kelly. Boston"; and "Mike Kelly."

10. Chadwick's image of baseball comports with what has come to be recognized as the myth of America's pastime, premised on, in the words of Bill Brown, "freedom, myth, and pastorality." Brown's aim is not to promote this myth; rather, a central project of his essay works to disprove it, arguing instead that baseball's identity is inextricably linked to capitalism.

Works Cited

"$10,000 Kelly." [hands aloft]. Gypsy Queen Cigarettes (N175). Goodwin & Co, NY. https://www.tcdb.com/ViewCard.cfm/sid/62053/cid/5253341/1887-Gypsy-Queen-(N175)-NNO-King-Kelly. Accessed 3 October 2020.

"$10,000 Kelly." [parallel bat] Gypsy Queen Cigarettes (N175). Goodwin & Co, NY. https://www.tcdb.com/ViewCard.cfm/sid/62053/cid/5253341/1887-Gypsy-Queen-(N175)-NNO-King-Kelly. Accessed 3 October 2020.

"1887 N28 Allen & Ginter Gallery of Cards," Gallery of Cards. N-Cards List. *Old Cardboard* Accessed 17 April 2021.

"1887 N284 Buchner Gold Coin Gallery of Cards," Gallery of Cards. N-Cards List. *Old Cardboard* Accessed 17 April 2021.

"1888 N162 Goodwins Champions Gallery of Cards." Gallery of Cards. N-Cards List. *Old Cardboard* Accessed 17 April 2021.

"1889 A35 Goodwin Round Album Gallery of Cards." Gallery of Cards. N-Cards List. *Old Cardboard* Accessed 17 April 2021.

"Adrian C. Anson." The World's Champions (N28). Allen & Ginter's Cigarettes. Richmond, VA. 1887. Benjamin K. Edwards. https://www.loc.gov/item/2007680751/. Accessed 3 September 2020.

"Anson." Old Judge & Gypsy Queen Cigarettes. Champions (N162). Goodwin & Co. New York, 1888. Benjamin K. Edwards. https://www.loc.gov/item/2007686400/. Accessed 3 October 2020.

Benjamin K. Edwards Collection of Baseball Cards. Prints and Photographs Division. Library of Congress. Washington, D. C.

Block, David. *Baseball Before We Knew It: A Search for the Roots of the Game.* Lincoln and London: University of Nebraska Press, 2005.

Bloom, John. *House of Cards: Baseball Card Collecting and Popular Culture*. Minneapolis: University of Minnesota Press, 1997.

Brown, Bill. *A Sense of Things: The Object Matter of American Literature*. Chicago: University of Chicago Press, 2003.

———. "The Meaning of Baseball in 1992 (with Notes on the Post-American)." *Public Culture* 4.1 (1992): 43–69.

Braun, Marta. *Eadweard Muybridge*. London, UK: Reaktion Books, 2012.

Capt. Anson, Chicago." Goodwin Round Album, 1889. *Old Cardboard* https://oldcardboard.com/n/albums/a35/a35.asp?cardsetID=1267. Accessed 3 October 2020.

"Capt. Anson, Chicago's." Old Judge Cigarettes. Goodwin & Co. (N172). New York, 1888. Benjamin K. Edwards. https://www.loc.gov/item/2007686400/. Accessed 3 October 2020.

Chadwick, Henry. *The Game of Baseball*. 1868. Columbia: Camden House Library of Baseball Classics, 1983.

Devereaux, Peter. *Game Faces: Early Baseball Cards from the Library of Congress*. Washington, D. C.: Library of Congress, 2018.

Edelman, Rob. "Eadweard Muybridge and Baseball-in-Motion." *Baseball: A Journal of the Early Game*. Ed. John Thorne. 7. 2 (Fall 2013): 62–70.

Gordon, Sarah. *Indecent Exposures: Eadweard Muybridge's Animal Locomotion Nudes*. New Haven: Yale University Press, 2015.

Jamieson, Dave. *Mint Condition: How Baseball Cards Became an American Obsession*. New York: Grove Press, 2010.

"Kelly." Old Judge & Gypsy Queen Cigarettes. Champions. Goodwin & Co. New York. 1888. (N162) Benjamin K. Edwards. https://www.loc.gov/item/2007686400/. Accessed 3 October 2020.

Krauss, Rosalind. *The Optical Unconscious*. Cambridge, MA: MIT Press, 1994.

———. *The Originality of the Avant-Garde: And Other Modernist Myths*. Cambridge, MA: MIT Press, 1986.

"Mike Kelly." Goodwin Round Album, 1889. http://vintagecardprices.com/card/basebal-card-values/1889-Goodwin-Co-Baseball-Album-Mike-King-Kelly-4/367047. Accessed 3 October 2020.

"Mike Kelly. Boston." Allen & Ginter's World's Champions (N28). 1887. https://www.tcdb.com/ViewCard.cfm/sid/62051/cid/3848244/1887-Allen-&-Ginter-World's-Champions-(N28)-NNO-Mike-Kelly. Accessed 3 October 2020.

Miller, Jay, Joe Gonsowski, and Richard Masson. *The Photographic Baseball Cards of Goodwin & Company (1886–1890)*. Privately printed, 2008.

Mowll Mathews, Nancy. "Art and Film: Interactions." *Moving Pictures: American Art and Early Film, Volume 1, 1880–1910*. Manchester: Hudson Hills, 2005. 145–58.

"Muybridge and the Athletes." Penn Libraries University Libraries Digital Image Collection. http://hdl.library.upenn.edu/1017/d/archives/20050208003. Accessed 11 October 2020.

Muybridge, Eadweard. *Animal Locomotion: an electro-photographic investigation of consecutive phases of animal movements, 1872–1885*. Vol. 1: Males (nude). Plate 275. Philadelphia: J. B. Linscott, 1887. Digital Commonwealth: Massachusetts Collections Online. Boston Public Library. https://ark.digitalcommonwealth.org/ark:/50959/70795v784. Accessed 3 October 2020.

Old Cardboard http://oldcardboard.com/ Accessed 12 March 2021.

"Old Judge Cabinets." *Cap Chronicled* http://www. capanson. com/baseball_cards.html Accessed 11 October 2020.

"The Original Gypsy Queen N175 set." *Lifetime Topps project* https://lifetime-topps.wordpress.com/2011/05/09/the-original-gypsy-queen-1887-n175-set/ Accessed 11 October 2020.

Rabinowitz, Lauren. "The Fair View: Female Spectators and the 1893 Chicago World's Columbian Exposition." *The Image in Dispute: Art and Cinema in the Age of Photography*. Ed. Dudley Andrew. Austin: University of Texas Press, 1997. 87–116.

Sekula, Allan. "The Body and the Archive." *October* 39 (Winter 1986): 3–64.

Siegel, Elizabeth. *Playing with Pictures: The Art of Victorian Photocollage*. Chicago: Art Institute of Chicago, 2009.

Thorn, John. *Baseball in the Garden of Eden: The Secret History of the Early Game*. New York: Simon & Schuster, 2011.

Chapter 3

"We are only horses and don't know"

Sport and Danger in Fox Hunting

ERIN N. BISTLINE

Imagine a nineteenth-century English fox hunt: men in bright red coats and black hats, glossy-coated horses, caught mid-stride or while leaping over fences, brush, ravines, streams, and the hounds, muscular in white, black, and brown, running in packs, noses to the ground, tails pointing out. All this set amid the English countryside, verdantly green, with stone outcroppings and hedgerows. It is a magnificent game played out over acres of field, valley, hill, and stream. Eighteenth- and nineteenth-century painters such as George Stubbs, Henry Thomas Alken, James Pollard, Francis Calcraft Turner, and Sir Alfred Munnings were fascinated with such scenes, painting them over and again, until the hunt became synonymous with a kind of Englishness. We find this sunny stereotype even as late as 1929, when Siegfried Sassoon's narrator in *Memoirs of a Fox-Hunting Man* contrasts his childhood reading of Robert Smith Surtees's comic presentation of the hunt with his own experience: my "first reaction to the 'field' was one of mute astonishment [. . .] these enormous confident strangers overwhelmed [my] mind with the visible authenticity of their brick-red coats" (23).

Of course, these images and recollections overlook the cruelty of the game. The moment of the kill is rarely portrayed: it's the hunt that matters, the men and animals working in concert. This awkward contrast didn't go unnoticed by the burgeoning animal welfare movement, which worked to change the rhetoric of the hunt. Nor did it dissuade Anna Sewell from calling attention to the dangers of the hunt in her bestselling novel *Black Beauty*. There, in the early, happy chapters of Black Beauty's foal-hood, a tragic hunting accident results in the deaths of both man and horse. Some young colts watching in a nearby field blame the foolhardiness of the rider, asserting his death "serves him right, too" (Sewell 8). Black Beauty's mother however, quickly admonishes the colts for their attitudes: "Though I am an old horse, and have seen and heard a great deal, I never yet could make out why men are so fond of this sport; they often hurt themselves, often spoil good horses, and tear up the fields, and all for a hare or a fox, or a stag, that they could get more easily some other way; but we are only horses and don't know" (Sewell 8). We, the readers, however, do know, and, despite what Black Beauty's mother says, so, too, do those colts. They had just experienced not only the death of a human—their owner's son—but also of his horse; both were victims of what the horses saw as a ridiculous practice. Why, with death as a possible or even probable outcome, would humans race after animals over dangerous terrain? Why would anyone engage in such a dangerous game?

In this volume, we consider nineteenth-century games broadly, and in that context, this essay examines the ways that the fox-as-game and the hunt-as-game permeated nineteenth-century print culture. Across the nineteenth century in Britain, as Allyson N. May notes, the fox hunt always occupied a contested space, and in this essay I trace the contours of the English obsession with the game, as it appears in periodicals and other ephemera.

The Hunt as Game: William Spooner's *Funnyshire Fox Chase*

To begin, then, I start with the hunt as an actual board game. In 1839, popular game maker William Spooner advertised a "droll and amusing game of adventure": *The Funnyshire Fox Chase*, subtitled either "a new game" or "an interesting game" ("New" 990). Spooner was known for games that "adopted a humorous or satirical take" on real adult pastimes, such as the "Royal Race Course [and] Comic Steeplechase" or the others published in the same series with the *Funnyshire Fox* (Norcia 52). Essentially centering on wealth and social status, Spooner's series of games gently mocks the class whose expensive gaming pursuits often resulted in embarrassment, financial loss, or worse: as such, Spooner's *Funnyshire Fox* reveals fox hunting's social position. As in the actual hunts, the "gentry chase their prey up and down the board, losing mounts, leaping fences, and contending with landscape challenges like ditches and cliffs" (52). The 12 January 1839 *Literary Gazette and Journal of Belles Lettres* describes *The Funnyshire Fox* as "a new tee-totum game, like the game of goose, &c., which Mr. Spooner has ingeniously invented as a change of amusements for the juveniles at this season. It seems well devised to interest them, and the sport is full of incidents to retard or throw out the keenest hand" ("Varieties" 30). Spooner's *Funnyshire Fox* enjoyed at least modest success, with editions in 1830, 1841, 1842, and in the 1880s, with English, German, and Italian versions. The novelty set included a hand-colored game board printed on canvas or linen, a rule book, a "Totum" that players would spin to determine the "Fox's" move as well as their own, and so on (Funnyshire). Beautifully rendered, the game board is organized as a map: its complicated path winds its way through a representative fox country replete with typical hunting scenes, hounds, spectators, diversions, and pitfalls. The available images of the few extant games show only the board and the rule book, not the Totum, character tokens, or monetary "counters" described in the instructions.

As play begins, the Huntsmen and the Fox alike occupy the "Going Out" space in the lower left corner. The rule book clearly directs players ("Huntsmen") to move the Fox before pursuing him and indicates that they may occasionally offset bad luck by tendering counters to a "Pool" (Funnyshire). Players direct the Fox by spinning the Totum, turning up either "S." for "Scent" and "F." for "Fault." Moving to a corresponding "S" or "F" circle, the Fox leads the way while the Huntsmen take turns moving him (and themselves) farther as successive Totum spins direct. Players hope to follow the Fox's "scent" steadily toward the upper right corner's final game space. As luck dictates, however, Huntsmen's spins may send them in unhelpful directions and land them in such obstacles as "Cold Bath Corner," "Tickle Nose Gorse," or even "Catch the Nag Gammon." Each of these locations is depicted with a cartoon: "Catch the Nag Gammon" shows a red coated rider sitting on the ground, hat beside him, while a panicked groom chases his horse (who races toward the edge of the game board). In "Frighten 'em Common," bulls chase a rider whose horse is nowhere to be seen, and at "Small Beer Hill," a woman in an apron offers a rider a tankard of beer. These locations (corresponding to real-life obstacles) may delay or even end play for some Huntsmen, but they only temporarily reprieve the Fox and thus prolong the game for the rest.

The successful Huntsman evades all or most pitfalls to arrive triumphantly at the game's final space, cornering the Fox before the remaining competitors arrive. Less fortunate players are ejected when they land in such traps as the "Thrown Out" space at "Despair Ditch," or they may be forced off the scent by an unlucky spin at the "Hope Turning" space. According to the rules, though, Huntsmen may improve their odds by exchanging counters for at least one additional chance at this important juncture. It almost seems that the Fox could reach safety, particularly as he can evade Huntsmen in the obstacles that slow players or force them out of play. Game design prevents this, however. The Huntsmen outnumber the Fox, and their spins dictate both his moves and their own. Play inevitably drives the fox to the sole game location bearing a bleak rather than humorous name: "Kill him Wood." Although the rule book indicates that all players may find themselves "thrown out," such an event simply requires that each Huntsman pay a "forfeit" into the Pool so that "the game is recommenced." The hapless Fox, like most of his living counterparts, survives only if the Huntsmen become bored with the chase. Notably, the game includes no silly illustrations of the wounded Fox or his ultimate death throes, bloodied hounds, or severely injured horses or riders. Instead, a Huntsman holds the dead fox triumphantly over a pack of hounds.

Spooner's game both indicates the cultural significance of fox hunting as well as points to the complicated discourse surrounding it. *Funnyshire Fox* was marketed as a simple entertainment designed for children, but it tacitly comments on the "game" of hunting foxes in the far more literal sense. Beyond merely entertaining youthful participants, *Funnyshire Fox* may well have helped prepare children for a more adult—and more serious—"game"—the actual hunt. Or, it may have allowed adult players to experience the thrill of a virtual chase without incurring steep expenses, risking physical danger, or witnessing brutal slaughter. But though the huntsmen (and at least one huntswoman) ride out in hopeful glory, *Funnyshire Fox*'s illustrations highlight that they may ultimately humiliate themselves. A field of elegantly attired riders surrounded by dozens of straining hounds may lose the fox as often as catch it. *Funnyshire Fox Chase* makes clear that the hunt on the board and in the field are equally arbitrary, relying not on skill but on chance.

This ambivalence in the options for reading (and playing) *Funnyshire Fox Chase* appears as well across the nineteenth century in periodical articles and other ephemera. I consider periodicals both for sportsmen and for a more general readership to trace the patterns of discourse relating to the game. Review of the periodicals doesn't reveal a growing opposition to the hunt as the antivivisectionist movement became more prominent—instead, from the very beginning of the century, positive depictions existed alongside the negative, showing—as is common with most cultural phenomena—the embedded nature of the practice of the hunt for nineteenth-century society. Below, then, I draw on representative moments to catalog the ways that the hunt received attention in the periodical press.

The Game at Play in the Nineteenth Century

Surprisingly only a handful of (long) nineteenth-century books devoted themselves to the fox hunt. Peter Beckford's 1781 *Thoughts on Hunting, in a Series of Familiar Letters to a Friend*, considered the first book to focus on hunting as a sport, laid out the practices and rules for the sport, thus establishing the origin of modern fox hunting in England (May 1). Beckford himself asks "Is it not strange, in a country [. . .] so famous for the best hounds and the best horses to follow them [. . .] that only the practical part of hunting should be known? There is, however, no doubt, that the practical part of it would be improved, were it accompanied by theory" (3). Often reprinted, Beckford's work remained the "standard work on the subject" for "[m]ore than a hundred years" (ix). The editor of the 1840 edition found that before "Mr. Beckford's book appeared, no work on the subject of Hunting had been published, except an anonymous publication in 1733" (vii). At the opposite end of the long nineteenth century and across the pond, Joseph Thomas's 1928 *Hounds and Hunting through the Ages*, offered what is still considered the comprehensive study of hunting in America.

But in the nineteenth century proper, the terrain of the fox hunt falls primarily to comic and anecdotal writers, such as William Chafin's *Anecdotes respecting Cranbourn Chase, with a very concise account of it: together with the rural amusements it afforded our ancestors in the days of yore* (1818); Nimrod's [Charles Apperley] *The Chace, the Turf, and The Road* (1837) and *Nimrod's hunting tour in Scotland and the north of England: with the table-talk of distinguished sporting characters and anecdotes of masters of hounds, crack riders, and celebrated amateur dragsmen* (1874); Surtees's comic *Jorrocks' Jaunts and Jollities* (1838) and nonfiction *The Analysis of the Hunting Field: being a series of sketches of the principal characters that compose one: the whole forming a slight souvenir of the season, 1845–46* (1847); John Mills's works, including *The Old English Gentleman, or the Fields and the Woods* (1841); Harry Hieover's [Charles Bindley] *The Hunting-field* (1850); James Edward Austen Leigh's *Recollections of the early days of the Vine hunt: and of its founder William John Chute* (1865); and Edward Pennell Elmhurst's *The Cream of Leicestershire: eleven seasons' skimmings, notable runs and incidents of the chase, selected and republished from "The Field"* (1883). In works such as these, (armchair) hunters could explore the game, tracing actual "Funnyshire fox chases" from the safety and comfort of their homes.

But works on the hunt also garnered an appeal beyond the wealthy aristocrat or the country squire. In 1858, for example, *The Sporting Magazine* carried a series by Mills, entitled "Hounds and Hunting: The Past and Present," which traced the history of fox hunting particularly in "Merrie England in the olden time" (143). Mills—author of *Christmas in the Olden Time: or the Wassail Bowl* (1838); *The Old English Gentleman, or the Fields and the Woods* (1841); *The Stage Coach: or the Road of Life* (1843); *The English Fireside: a tale of the Past* (1844); *Life of a Foxhound, and Flyers of the Hunt* ([1859]), *Stable Secrets: The Life of a Racehouse* (1861)—was known for his stories of England's past and particularly of her countryside. According to Mills, fox hunting's origin story begins with a Yorkshire Knight, hungry for his dinner. As he and his hounds make their way across the fields after an unsuccessful hunt, one of his hounds leads him on a chase after a fox. He proclaims, "[w]e shall hunt fox, fitchew, marten cat, and hare before long," but the adrenaline rush that the Yorkshire Knights feels in the hours-long chase distracts him from his hunger (174). The hunt ends when the Yorkshire Knight, on the verge of giving up, watches the fox collapse in exhaustion. The extract concerning the hunt circulated in March 1858 in at least six regional magazines: the *Leicester Mercury* (Leicestershire), *Sherborne Mercury* (Dorset), the *Taunton Courier, and Western Advertiser* (Somerset); the *Carlisle Journal* (Cumberland), and *Cheltenham Examiner* (Gloucestershire), and the *Wiltshire Independent* (Wiltshire). General readers may have found appealing the tying of the hunt's origin to the determination and adaptability of the rural gentry.

While late-nineteenth-century hunters might have thought their practice originated with a Yorkshire Knight, modern commentator Ben Johnson places fox hunting's first appearance in Norfolk with a "farmer's attempt to catch a fox using farm dogs in 1534." Others such as Raymond Carr and David C. Itzkowitz trace the origin of the modern fox hunt to Leicestershire, where farmer and politician Hugo Meynell served as Master of the Hounds of the Quorn Hunt (named after his home) for forty-seven years. But since the hunt itself remained largely unchanged since its medieval origins, calling Meynell or anyone the father of modern fox hunting seems unjustified (see Middleton, "Fox" and "Origins").

But however the English sport emerged, hunting certainly changed in at least one way across the nineteenth century: more people participated in it. The increasing popularity of the hunt appears clearly in the increasing number of hunts: from "72 packs in 1821" up to "84 by 1850" (Anderson 37). A 14 percent increase over 30 years may seem minor, but each pack includes a large number of riders. In the Quorn Hunt, still in operation today, around 100–150 riders participate in a single hunt (Quorn).

The Sporting Magazine: Lists, Notices, and Descriptions

As the number of hunts increased across the nineteenth century, British periodicals carried increasing numbers of notices of the people, places, and results of the game. Further, the period between 1780 and the 1890s saw exponential increases in the number of periodicals published. In the 1780s fewer than 100 periodical titles were in print, but by the 1890s, approximately 3,400 new magazine and newspaper titles were being produced (Rose 31). In keeping with this explosion, the number of periodicals devoted to sports and sporting increased substantially, including such long-running titles as *The Sporting Magazine* (1793–1870), *Sporting Times* (1865–1931), and *Horse and Hound* (1884–present). Given the audience of these magazines—sportsmen themselves—the references to and discussion of fox hunting in them remained almost exclusively positive.

The first and most robust of these specialized periodicals, *The Sporting Magazine* offered a broad discussion of all things related to sports from its first issue in 1793 to its final volume in 1870. In fact, Tony Mason considers *The Sporting Magazine* to be "certainly one of the most important of nineteenth-century sporting periodicals" (293–94). Over its eight decades in print, *The Sporting Magazine* set the bar for what sort of content and tone readers could expect from a sporting magazine. Though its format and proportion of content shifted over time, several features remained constant (and were inherited by later periodicals of the genre). Each issue included lists of upcoming events, important weather information (such as the phases of the moon), and descriptions of outcomes for major events. Often, as with Mills's "Hounds and Hunting," the magazine offered serialized extracts of longer works. Additionally, the magazine offered profiles of award-winning horses. In July 1857, for example, *The Sporting Magazine* highlighted Blink Bonny, who won the Derby and Oaks in 1857, and her jockey, opening the eight-page article overviewing the lives and careers of both horse and man with a reproduction of Harry Hall's engraving of the two. This interest in horseflesh extends to the fox hunt as well, and especially during fox hunting season, the contents of the periodical included two or three articles per issue devoted to the sport and additional references in passim. Although medical discussions were not common, the April 1835 issue of the *London Medical and Surgical Journal* advises how to treat a common—and deadly—injury: Dr. E. Harrison's "Dislocations of the Neck from Hunting Accidents, and their Reductions," advice which we know would do more damage than good.

Most commonly *The Sporting Magazine* and its competitors featured lists of upcoming and past hunts. These notices offer varying levels of detail. Some simply list places and times of future hunts; others provide brief reports of various hunts, providing details about who attended, what roles they played, how they performed, and what the ultimate outcome of the hunt was. In *The New Sporting Magazine*, for example, Charnwood, who observed a 27 December 1850, hunt, sings the praises of Sir Richard Sutton and the Quorn Hunt. This run—of more than forty miles in a little over four hours—Charnwood, a frequent contributor to the magazine, called "unparalleled [. . .] in distance, in duration, in speed, and all the various points which constitute the perfection of sport" (93).

Some of the content related to fox hunting focused on the hounds themselves or to those who followed them (and the sport) enthusiastically. For instance, the January 1845 issue of *The Sporting Magazine* included a "Diary of Sport with her Majesty's Hounds" which records several occasions during which the hounds hunted deer. The writer highlights how frequently this may have happened, indicating that the Queen's warden, "Mr. Brown [. . .] never loses an opportunity when it is possible to have a start" ("Diary" 1).

As one would expect, sporting magazines tended to be almost exclusively positive in their portrayal of fox hunting. As late as 1878, magazines praised its benefits. *The Illustrated Sporting and Dramatic Times* extolled the virtues of the sport in "Fox Hunting" in the 9 November 1878 issue, stating that "[p]robably there is no happier moment in the existence of any man who really means going [on a hunt] than the first find of the season" ("Fox Hunting" 186). But as Mason notes, *The Sporting Magazine* was fairly early in its denunciation of the crueler sports such as bear baiting and cock fighting (293–94). In 1823, Parliament attempted to outlaw some blood sports (bull baiting and cock fighting), largely considered to be entertainments of the working class, but they excluded fox hunting from the proposed legislation. *The Sporting Magazine*—in "highly emotional language"—responded by pointing out the "horrors" of fox hunting (Anderson). Like the nineteenth-century author of the original article, Anderson attributed this distinction between the hunt and other blood sports to socioeconomic factors. This recognition that fox hunting held its horrors, though a minor strain, still appears across the life of the magazines.

Hunting and Hunters in General Magazines

Magazines for general audiences also included the hunt in their pages, but they included a wider range of perspectives, both positive and negative. The general magazines, for example, were far more likely to provide notices of individuals hurt or killed in hunting accidents. One such instance appeared in the 28 November 1857, issue of *The Leader and Saturday Analyst*'s article "Accidents and Sudden Deaths," which described in detail the death of Martin Hawke while fox hunting. During a jump, Hawke's horse fell, "threw his rider off headforemost, and then turned over upon him" ("Accidents" 1130). Later in the same column, Cornet Richard Charles Echalaz's death is described as "a repetition of that of Mr. Hawke" (1130). Though fox hunting accidents appear frequently in lists, the presence of two deadly accidents in a single column highlighted the stakes of the game.

General periodicals also featured profiles of individuals well known in fox hunting circles and their obituaries (whether or not they died in hunting accidents). While both maintain a somber tone, the profiles, much longer than an obituary, provide much more detail about the individual's life than the obituaries. The optimistic "Future of Fox-Hunting" from the 2 October 1858, issue of the *Saturday Review* celebrates the life of Assheton Smith, a Master of Hounds: "Fox-hunting is a great

British institution, and this man gave himself up to it, heart and soul, and was the first in his generation in its service. Let him have his due place of honor" ("Future" 320). Despite praising Smith, the article questions the purpose and future place of fox hunting in English life. This rhetorical shift—from praise to more sober critique—doesn't appear in such treatments in the sporting magazines, particularly as it detracts from Smith's legacy.

This more complicated response appears in the January 1852 *Leader and Saturday Analyst* overviewed an awards dinner during which Henry John Coyners was honored for his work on the hunt. Unlike the somber tone of the obituaries and profiles, "Fox Hunting Glories" begins by recording the hearty good cheer of the participants. The article offers snippets of the speeches along with audience responses such as "(loud laughter)" or "(cheers)" sprinkled throughout ("Fox Hunting Glories" 53). Following the last snippet, which highlights the great "blessings" of fox hunting, the author shifts focus ("Fox Hunting Glories" 53). While the speaker commented on the way that fox hunting "encourages bravery, courage, and enterprise in a people, and above all things [. . .] promotes kind feeling and good fellowship," the author believes that "[e]very man not a fox-hunter must blush in his shoes. This extravagant praise is laughable enough, but what a basis of pluck, good nature, and energy it discloses! Applied to rural sanitary reform, for instance" ("Fox Hunting Glories" 53). The shift from "extravagant praise" to the problems of a lack of water (and clean water) in the fox hunting countryside—an issue only undertaken the last quarter of the nineteenth century—carries an intentional barb. As with the *Saturday Review* article about Smith's legacy, the author for *The Leader and Saturday Analyst* ends by questioning the purpose and benefit of the sport, when the local citizens don't even have reliable access to water, clean or dirty, thus signaling the cultural tensions surrounding it.

These same tensions appear in contemporary reviews of books about fox hunting. *The Critic*'s review of Scrutator's *The Master of the Hounds*, titled "Fox Hunters Painted by a Friendly Brush," questions both the mind and authenticity of the novel's author and of people who argue against the sport. Though the reviewer acknowledges that most arguments against fox hunting are trite ("loss of time, risk of neck, worthlessness of fox, and damage to fields and fences")—he still posits that "any one who has given himself the trouble to understand anything about the true state of the case" needs no "refutation of the absurd outcry" ("Fox-hunters" 873).

This position—so positive to the hunt despite its dangers—is explained in part by Scrutator's own relation to the hunt: according to Peep-out, author of "Harriers and Fox Hounds," Scrutator was a Mr. Horlock, a Master of Harriers (766).

Hounds, Horses, and Riders: Images of the Hunt

The hunt became a popular locus for illustration as well. As soon as the technology would allow, periodicals supplemented their articles with visual representations of hunts, first as engravings and later as photographs. For the most part these illustrations offered views of the triumphant hunters returning, highlighting the success of the hunt. Across the nineteenth century, these illustrations tended to focus on the hunters (primarily men), their hounds, and horses. Erica Munkwitz, who studied the hunt from 1897 forward, finds the omission of women from representations of the hunt glaring. As early as 1900, Munkwitz shows, women held the position of Master of Hounds, a position they would not have been able to achieve without significant time actively involved in a hunting group. For Munkwitz, "[r]iding and hunting in the late 1800s and early 1900s have much to tell us about sporting, gender and social advances. Equestrian sports, as exemplified by fox hunting, provided new and radical possibilities for female emancipation" (396). Rob Boddice dates women's participation in the hunt to 1870, though the hunt was still considered to be a site of manliness, establishing and strengthening characteristics of upper-class, British masculinity (8). For Boddice, the idea of hunting as a manly activity was tied to the belief that men were the hunters in early human society and to religious interpretations giving men dominion over animals.

Throughout periodicals, the quality and types of the images of fox hunting varied considerably. Some, such as those included in *The Illustrated Sporting and Dramatic News* for 9 January 1909, offered detailed recreations of paintings or engravings. In that issue, Lionel Edwards illustrated Peep-out's article about dogs in the fox hunt (Peep-out 766). Edwards depicted the Master of Hounds in action and included a close-up illustration of the hounds at rest. More detailed and of higher quality than images from other artists, Edwards's illustrations still present an idealized, safe version of the sport. No danger is to be seen.

The 1838 issue of *The New Sporting Magazine* features an engraving of a specific person: William Pinney, Esq., a Member of Parliament from

Lyme-Regis. The accompanying article praises the image's quality: "It is not often that we see a better hunting picture than the original from which our engraving is taken" ("Fox Hunting Portrait" 138). But what is of particular note is not Pinney's upright bearing, but the "remarkably fine and spirited" action of the horse ("Fox Hunting Portrait" 138). Unlike many of the images from periodicals, this illustration provides the name of both the original artist—well-known animal painter, Abraham Cooper, R. A.—and the engraver, frequent *New Sporting Magazine* contributor, T. E. Nicholson (Cormack 449).

The shift to photographs continued to focus on fox hunting scenes, presenting participants waiting at the lodge or the stables before or after the hunt. Others—such as those in the 1919 issue of *The Bystander*—show a more active moment, with the participants mounted on their horses in the field. A. W. C's "By Field, Stream & Covert" highlights the royal participation of the King of Denmark and the King of Sweden. Though most of the figures (as is typical) are men, the presence of women about to participate in the hunt is noteworthy. Women also appear in other illustrations in the issue, but in those they are identified by their relationship with the men: "Chatelaines of the Old Berkeley Hunt," for instance, shows two women talking, one holding the leash of a terrier; both are identified as the wives of the previous and current Masters of the Hunt (1003).

Images of the hunt also served a purely illustrative function, particularly when they were appended to stories, poetry, and serialized novels. For example, the 1859 Christmas Eve issue of *Reynold's Miscellany of Romance, General Literature, Science and Art* provides an extract from William Watkins's *British Sports and Pastimes*, under the title "Chapter XIV—Fox Hunting." The accompanying image, "Full Cry," opens the extract. Though much less detailed than Edwards's illustrations from *The Illustrated Sporting and Dramatic News*, Watkins's image does maintain the idealized representation of the hunt. Watkins builds up the excitement of the hunt while diminishing the possible threats to hunters. His description begins mid-hunt, with the hounds giving chase; "some [riders] get over" a fence in the field, but "others get part over, and then find themselves turning somersaults into the ploughed ground" (Watkins 413). Despite Watkins's lighthearted description, riders jumping and falling was a common moment for injury and death, as was the case for the dead rider in *Black Beauty*. Another purely illustrative example occurs in the 1867 issue of *Once a Week*, where J. P. T.'s essay on fox hunting depicts a single rider and a single hound racing across the countryside. Images of individual riders typically depict a specific hunter, which is not the case here. The layout of the article makes the enlarged initial T appear to be part of the horizon, more fully integrating the image and the accompanying text.

The market for illustrations of fox hunting ranged far beyond the periodicals, including collections of prints related to the game. An advertisement in *The Illustrated and Sporting News* records The Fine Art Union offering a "set of (4) fox hunts coloured in oil" for 8s, 6d with the coupon included in the advertisement or for four guineas without it ("Advertisement" 267). This advertisement offers brief descriptions of the images for sale, including one titled "Full Cry," which, despite the title, is not the same as the illustration for Watkins's chapter. Instead, this "Full Cry" shows "Dogs, horses, and their rider well up, except one who is down" in a "picture [that] finely illustrates the excitement and peril of English foxhunting, and is more than worthy of the artist's great reputation" (267). The artist, however, is unnamed, limiting the reader's ability to gauge the truth of the description.

Visual representations of fox hunting found in periodicals most often present an idealized version of the sport, ignoring its dangers and ethical issues. And the bent of these illustrations tends to be consistent whether the publication catered to the sportsman or to a more general audience.

Stories of the Hunt in the Magazines

General periodicals frequently included brief references or representations of fox hunting, some as short as a sentence or phrase. In these, the hunt quickly characterizes a place or character. For example, in the Christmas issue for 1869, Charles Dickens's *All the Year Round* included "Lady Macnamara's Story" which uses an interest in the hunt as indicative of an idle mind. The narrator's husband "had no immediate employment afloat, so his mind naturally turned to the occupation he loved best, next to his profession—fox-hunting" ("Lady" 84). Similarly, in the serialized novel *A Bitter Bondage*, published in the 1877 *London Journal*, fox hunting becomes a shorthand for a type of undesirable man, even when used comically. There, the main character Agnes rejects a whole range of suitors: "Amongst the fox-hunting squires, or billiard-playing, flirting, military men from the neighbouring garrison town, or the croquet-loving curates who formed the staple of Mrs. Garrison's society as regarded the stronger sex, she had met none whose attentions she would not have repelled had they been offered" (*A Bitter* 395). Though the men in these groups are not obviously similar, none of them, Agnes complains, can evoke "the fiery passion of which the poets discourse so eloquently" (*A Bitter* 395). Fox hunters, it seems, were not much desired as husbands or lovers.

Likewise, from the very first installments of Hawley Smart's *Sunshine and Snow*, published in *The St. James's Magazine* beginning in 1877, knowledge of fox hunting (or the lack of it) becomes a shorthand for a fine (or mean) character. While the January 1878 issue seems to value the Reverend Roberts for his engagement with the sport—"Nobody ever questioned the Rev. Roberts's knowledge about fox-hunting in the Cottleston county"—by the second volume, that knowledge, and by extension the Reverend's intelligence, is undercut (Smart 83). In the middle of the hunt, Rev. Roberts and his niece follow a doctor across the country instead of the hounds.

While Smart's story calls into question the intelligence of a follower of the hunt, H. S. Salt's 1893 essay "Cruel Sports" explicitly argues that the sport "is not only cruel to the victims of the chase, but ruinous to the mental capacity of the gentlemen who indulge in it" (546). While the Reverend Roberts ultimately can't tell the difference between man and fox, Salt's fox hunter is morally and mentally deficient, neither "manly" nor "gentle" (546).

While the hunt unmans its male participants, it masculinizes its female. As Erica Munkwitz shows in her analysis of literary depictions of women fox hunters, quoting *The Young Ladies' Equestrian Manual*, female hunters are depicted as behaving outside the bounds of social propriety. Prior to 1860, women were dissuaded from not only fox hunting itself, but also the activities related to a successful hunt (Munkwitz, "Vixens"). Indeed, the *Young Ladies' Equestrian Manual* warns that "[n]o lady of taste ever gallops on the road" and "not above one among a thousand" would "attempt the following of hounds" (qtd. in Munkwitz, "Vixens" 76).

But while the periodicals and specialty publications acknowledged the danger fox hunting posed to one's character, the hunt itself remained a locus for celebration of Englishness. In 1865, the *New Sporting Magazine* published Bob Bullfinch's poem "Fox-Hunting," a bucolic celebration of the joy and excitement of the hunt. From start to finish, Bullfinch focuses on the hounds themselves, opening with "Hark to that challenge! 'tis a well-known hound" and closing with the following:

The pack in joy around the dead fox bay
The echoing horn proclaims the stirring news
The sun bursts forth, and from the heavens a ray
Of light streams on us and the rocks repeat
Our merry loud who'ops and death halloos! (355, 356)

Though Bullfinch offers a grim depiction of the dead fox, his poem overall celebrates the hunt, finding it a sort of metaphor for life in the English countryside. And this heady praise is characteristic of the literary pieces published across the century in the sporting magazines.

Jobs, Income, and Damages from Fox Hunting

Though the beginnings of the pastime may have been humble or at least practical, by the mid- and late nineteenth century, fox hunting was largely a rich man's sport. But the idea that the hunt was the province of the wealthy was fairly new, E. S. argues in "The Democratic Fox Hunt," published in *The Graphic* in October 1889. E. S. points to the pervasiveness of the hunt across the century—in the past fifty years, "there was scarcely an able-bodied man in the rural districts of Yorkshire who had not, at one time or another in his life, followed the hounds" (498)—to argue that the hunt was a sport for every man. Despite E. S.'s enthusiasm, most discussions accepted that the costs of the hunt made it prohibitive for most. Mike Huggins, in his historiographic overview of British upper-class sport, estimates that starting a hunting stable in 1899 would have cost approximately one to two thousand pounds. The yearly upkeep would be at least that much and would include "pay for huntsman, whippers-in, kennel boys and other staff," as well as for farmers in the area (Huggins 369).

For the most part, discussions of the cost of participation in fox hunting appear in passing references in texts focused on other issues or even in literary texts. An article about dogs might mention the cost of a terrier or pack of hounds as a comparison to other trained dogs. A narrator may reference the price a character paid for a horse or a riding habit. However, Aniseed, in the 1910 *Illustrated Sporting and Dramatic News* article "The Poor Man in the Hunting Field," provides a more focused look at the topic, acknowledging the long struggle participants had with the cost of the sport. Along with acknowledging that "[m]uch has been written on the subject of this article, but the theme is one of such perennial interest that perhaps no apology is need for making a few remarks," Aniseed provides a possible budget for hunting affordably, using as little as thirty-three pounds (502). Aniseed does not indicate how much using his method would save from the average cost of a hunting season, nor do other discussions offer any clear estimate, but he claims that followers would make a significant saving.

Those in favor of the hunt pointed to the positive effect on local economies created by the increased number of visitors to the region. A hunt on private lands would still bring people to the region—people who might stay in local inns. And if they lodged at the manor house, the host might hire more people to work on the estate for the event. Whether at the inns or the manor, visitors would consume food and drink during the event. Others argued for the benefit to the fields themselves. A reviewer in an 1858 issue of *The Critic* stipulated that any concerns about the fox hunt, even if they were valid, would be outweighed by the benefits of fox hunting, including the necessity of controlling fox populations.

Those opposed to the hunt pointed to the economic damage caused by the hunters, their horses, and their hounds. For example, in an 1815 letter in *Cobbett's Political Register*, A Kent Farmer estimated that with a season of 120 days, the hunters caused approximately 3,000 pounds' worth of damage in the region. This included hurting animals such as sheep—not including the horses that the hunters ride—and damaging crops and fences (A Kent).

Horses, Hounds, and Foxes: Concerns for the Rights and Well-being of Animals

Legislation in Great Britain to protect animals from ill treatment began in the late 1700s (see Beers and Kean). But the first legislation—The Cruel Treatment of Cattle Act, or Martin's Act (after Richard Martin who advocated for it and later created what would become the Royal Society for the Prevention of Cruelty to Animals)—did not pass until 1822. The legislation allowed for fines and imprisonment to people who were found to "beat, abuse, or ill-treat any horse, mare, gelding, mule, ass, ox, cow, heifer, steer, sheep, or other cattle" (qtd. in Kean 34).

As legislation about the treatment of animals increased across the century, the ethical aspects of the hunt garnered more pages. These discussions varied in focus, including sporting, hunting in general, and fox hunting specifically. However, while many of the laws addressed the treatment of farm animals, the horses were not the only—or even the main—topic of discussion in terms of fox hunting. Periodicals included discussions of animal rights in fox hunting most often in terms of the fox, and much less regularly in terms of the dogs and horses participating.

From early in the century (and even before), both general and sporting magazines considered bull baiting and cock fighting cruel sports. In fact, in the 1820s, *The Sporting Magazine* and other similar periodicals condemned these "blood" sports. Some—like the Archbishop of York—distinguished between the cruelty of pigeon hunting in particular, denouncing "the men who make a pastime, and the women a holiday, over the trapped bird, released without a chance, wounded again and again" and the sports like fox hunting that occurred in "natural spaces" (qtd in Cox 480). This distinction determines whether a sport is cruel, not by its inherent practices, but by the location of the hunt. J. Charles Cox's "Sports and Pastimes" published in an 1874 issue of *The Examiner* rejects this distinction: "[T]he fox is an animal whose whole characteristics and mode of life are alien to the enclosed and highly cultivated lands where the pursuit of it most abounds" (480).

Ultimately, this question of whether the fox hunt is a natural part of agricultural life or a cruel blood sport shifted (mostly) to the side of the fox. The complicated nature of this debate appears in a 1919 exchange in *The Saturday Review*, prompted by the The Dog Protection Act of 1919 introduced by Sir Hamar Greenwood as a means to limit vivisection, but which was actively opposed by doctors and others in the medical field ("Dog's" 613). In a letter to the editor, George Greenwood objected to a previous writer's definition of cruelty as inflicting unnecessary pain, since by that definition, fox hunting would also be cruel. Fox hunts, George Greenwood asserted, are not by any argument necessary, nor is any harm to the fox justified. The ethical questions of the hunt—like those of vivisection—call upon men to sympathize with the animals: "If man desires to be above 'the ape and the tiger,' let him learn to bear suffering rather than seek to escape it through the sufferings of his humbler and helpless kindred" (Greenwood 397). E. James of East Haddon's letter to the editor of *The Northampton Mercury*, addressed similar concerns, but in reference to the Royal Society for the Prevention of Cruelty to Animals. In "Cruelty to Animals and Fox Hunting," James advocates for Mrs. Prender, the leader of the local chapter of the group, to "turn her attention to the fox-hunting squires, parsons, and farmers, and amongst them a 'Band of Mercy' for the suppression of fox torture."

Despite strong evidence of the dangers for the hunt, most articles assumed that well-bred dogs, horses, and humans were somehow safe. In 1871, the *Western Daily Press*'s article "Fox Hunting and Cruelty to Animals" contradicts this belief, outlining a devastating hunt after which two horses, Nailor and Spectre, died from running more than thirty miles in a day for a hunt. The Royal Society for the Prevention of Cruelty to Animals later prosecuted this case, although it is unclear whether the blame being placed on the individuals came from a condemnation of the sport itself or from the behavior of the riders individually. *The Western Daily Press* article emphasizes the fact that the riders brought their horses from fourteen miles away and then, despite the horses showing signs of exhaustion and needing to be "supplied with gin and water to revive them," the riders rode their mounts an additional nine miles ("Fox-hunting and Cruelty"). This focus on the extra miles makes clear that the riders were responsible for any damages, not the sport itself.

While it's impossible to tease out a growing trajectory against the hunt from the periodical coverage—articles critical of the hunt appeared in the early years of the century as well as the later—the pervasive references to the hunt itself, both explicit and more oblique, reveal the complicated position the hunt held across the century. As a game, a practice, and a cultural interest, fox hunting runs through the nineteenth century as a sort of Funnyshire Fox Hunt, leaving traces through the periodicals, hiding behind allusions, bursting out into the fields of discussion, then disappearing again. And we—the players—are left with thousands of pages revealing the disappearing body of the fox.

Works Cited

"Accidents and Sudden Deaths." *Leader and Saturday Analyst*. 8. 401 (28 November 1858): 1130.

"Advertisement." *The Illustrated Sporting and Dramatic News*. 7. 173 (30 May 1877): 267.

A Kent Farmer. "Fox Hunting." *Cobbett's Political Register*. 29. 7 (18 November 1815): 222.

Anderson, Nancy Fix. *The Sporting Life: Victorian Sports and Games*. London: Praeger, 2010.

Aniseed. "The Poor Man in the Hunting Field." *Illustrated Sporting and Dramatic News*. 74. 1940 (19 November 1910): 502–503.

A. W. C. "By Field, Stream & Covert: Hunting by Air." *The Bystander*. 64. 837 (17 December 1919): 1003.

Beckford, Peter. *Thoughts upon Hunting: In a Series of Familiar Letters to a Friend*. 4th ed. London: J. Debrett, 1802.

———. *Thoughts upon Hunting: In a Series of Familiar Letters to a Friend*. London: Cowie, Jolland, and Co., 1840.

Beers, Diane L. *For the Prevention of Cruelty: The History and Legacy of Animal Rights Activism in the United States*. Ohio: Ohio University Press, 2006.

"A Bitter Bondage." *The London Journal, and Weekly Record of Literature, Science, and Art*. 69. 1689 (1877): 393–96.

Boddice, Rob. "Manliness and the 'Morality of Field Sport': E. A. Freeman and Anthony Trollope, 1869–1871." *The Historian* 70.1 (2008): 1–29.

British Newspaper Archive (*BNA*). Findmypast Newspaper Archive in partnership with the British Library, 2020. https://britishnewspaperarchive.co.uk

Bullfinch, Bob. "Fox-Hunting." *New Sporting Magazine*. 185 (May 1856): 355–56.

Carr, Raymond. *English Fox Hunting: A History*. Weidenfeld & Nicolson, 1986.

Charnwood. "A Memorable Day with the Quorn." *New Sporting Magazine*. 21 (February 1851): 90–93.

"Chatelaines of the Old Berkeley Hunt." *The Bystander*. 64. 837 (17 December 1919): 1003. http://hathitrust.org. Accessed 18 October 2020.

Cole, Lucinda. *Imperfect Creatures: Vermin, Literature, and the Sciences of Life, 1600–1740*. Ann Arbor: University of Michigan Press, 2016.

Cormack, Malcom. *Country Pursuits: British, American, and French Sporting Art from the Mellon Collections in the Virginia Museum of Fine Arts*. Virginia Museum of Fine Arts, 2007.

Cox, J. Charles. "Sports and Pastimes." *The Examiner*. 3458 (9 May 1874): 480–81.

"Diary of Sport with Her Majesty's Hounds." *The Sporting Magazine*. 5.25 (January 1845): 1–2.

"The Dogs' Protection Bill." *The British Medical Journal*. 1 (17 May 1919): 613.

E. S. "A Democratic Fox-Hunt." *The Graphic*. 40. 1038 (18 October 1889): 498.

"Fox-hunters Painted by a Friendly Brush." *The Critic*. 17. 440 (11 December 1858): 873.

"Fox Hunting." *Illustrated Sporting and Dramatic News* 10. 249 (9 November 1878): 186.

"Fox Hunting and Cruelty to Animals." *Western Daily Press*. 12 January 1871.

"Fox Hunting: Facts, History and the Law." *Countryfile Magazine*. 10 May 2017. http://www.countryfile.com/explore-countryside/wildlife/foxhunting-facts. Accessed 10 Oct. 2020.

"Fox Hunting Glories." *Leader and Saturday Analyst*. 3. 95 (17 January 1852): 53.

"Fox-Hunting Portrait of William Pinney, Esq., MP." *New Sporting Magazine*. 14. 83 (March 1838): 138.

"The Future of Fox-hunting." *Saturday Review of Politics, Literature, Science and Art*. 6. 153 (2 October 1858): 320–21.

Greenwood, George. "The Dog's Bill." *The Saturday Review of Politics, Literature, Science and Art*. 127. 3313 (26 April 1919): 397.

Harrison, E. "Dislocations of the Neck from Hunting Accidents, and their Reductions." *London Medical and Surgical Journal*. 8. 157 (31 January 1835): 18–19.

HathiTrust Digital Library. http//:hathitrust.org.

"Henry Thomas Alken." Tate Museum. https://www.tate.org.uk/art/artists/henry-thomas-alken-3. Accessed 20 January 2020.

Horse & Hound Magazine. TI Media Limited, 2018. https://www.horseandhound.co.uk/. Accessed 14 October 2020.

Huggins, Mike. "Sport and the British Upper Classes c. 1500–2000: A Historiographic Overview." *Sport in History* 28. 3 (2008): 364–88.

"Hunting." *Horse & Hound Magazine*. TI Media Limited, 2018. https://www.horseandhound.co.uk/hunting. Accessed 18 October 2020.

Itzkowitz, David C. *Peculiar Privilege: A Social History of English Foxhunting, 1753–1885*. Hemel Hempstead: Harvester Press, 1977.

James, E. "Animal Cruelty and Fox Hunting." *The Northhampton Mercury* (1893): 5. *BNA*. Accessed 18 October 2020.

Johnson, Ben. "Fox Hunting in Britain." *Historic UK: The History and Heritage Accommodation Guide*. 2015. https://www.historic-uk.com/CultureUK/Fox-Hunting-in-Britain/. Accessed 18 October 2020.

J.P.T. "Fox-Hunting." *Once a Week*. 4. 97 (9 Nov 1867): 551. http://Hathitrust.org. Accessed 18 October 2020.

Kean, Hilda. *Animal Rights: Political and Social Change in Britain since 1800*. London: Reaktion, 1998.

"Lady Macnamara's Story." *All the Year Round*. 3. 56 (25 December 1869): 84–93.

Mason, Tony. "Sport." *Victorian Periodicals and Victorian Society*. Ed. J. Don Vann and Rosemary T. VanArsdel. University of Toronto Press, 1994. 291–97.

May, Allyson N. *The Fox-Hunting Controversy, 1781–2004: Class and Cruelty*. London: Routledge, 2016.

Middleton, Iris. "Fox Hunting Traditions: Fact or Fantasy?" *Sport History Review* 28.1 (1997): 19–32.

———. "The Origins of English Fox Hunting and the Myth of Hugo Meynell and the Quorn." *Sport in History* 25.1 (2005): 1–16.

Mills, John. "Hounds and Hunting." *New Sporting Magazine*. 212 (Aug. 1858): 100.

Munkwitz, Erica. "'The Master is Mistress': Women and Fox Hunting as Sports Coaching in Britain." *Sport in History* 37. 4 (2017): 395–422.

———. "Vixens of Venery: Women, Sport, and Fox-hunting in Britain, 1860–1914." *Critical Survey* 24. 1 (2012): 74–87.

"New Games for the Holidays." *The Athenaeum*. 639 (December 1839): 990.

"New Novels." *The Academy*. 917 (30 November 1889): 351–53.

Nimrod [Charles James Apperley]. *The Chase, the Turf, and the Road*. London: Edward Arnold, 1898.

Norcia, Megan. *Gaming Empire in Children's British Board Games*. London: Taylor and Francis, 2019.

Peep Out. "Harriers and Foxhounds." *Illustrated Sporting and Dramatic News*. 70. 1843 (9 January 1909): 766–67. *BNA*. Accessed 20 October 2020.

The Quorn Hunt. The Quorn Hunt. 2018. https://www.quorn-hunt.co.uk. Accessed 13 October 2020.

Rose, Jonathan. "Education, Literacy, and the Victorian Reader." *A Companion to the Victorian Novel*. Ed. Patrick Brantlinger and William B. Thesing. Malden, MA: Blackwell Publishers, Ltd., 2002. 31–47.

Salt, H. S. "Cruel Sports." *The Westminster Review*. 140. 1 (July 1893): 545–53.

Sassoon, Siegfried. *Memoirs of a Fox-Hunting Man*. Ed. Paul Fussell. London: Penguin Books, 2013.

Sewell, Anna. *Black Beauty*. Peterborough, Canada: Broadview Press, 2016.

Smart, Hawley. *Sunshine and Snow*, vol. II. *St. James's Magazine*. 4. 33 (1878): 71–93.

Spooner, William. *The Funnyshire Fox Chase*. 1842. *Worthpoint*. https://www.worthpoint.com/worthopedia/antique-board-game-funnyshire-fox-1900474918. Accessed 18 October 2020.

Surtees, Robert Smith. *Jorrock's Jaunts and Jollities*. London: George Routledge and Sons, 1874.

"Varieties." *The Literary Gazette and Journal of the Belles Lettres*. 23. 1147 (12 January 1839): 29–30.

Watkins, William. "British Sports and Pastimes. No. XIV—Fox Hunting." *Reynold's Miscellany of Romance, General Literature, Science and Art*. 23. 603 (1859): 413. *BNA* Accessed 20 October 2020.

Section II

Communal Games

Chapter 4

"The Memory Game"

Play, Trauma, and *Great Expectations*

SEAN GRASS

Late in December 1869 Charles Dickens's family descended on Gad's Hill Place to celebrate the holiday season—not his wife, Catherine, from whom he had separated a decade earlier, but his eldest daughter and son, Katey and Charley, their spouses and the latter's children, his son Henry fresh from earning honors at Cambridge, and his daughter Mamie and sister-in-law Georgina Hogarth, both of whom lived at Gad's Hill all the year round.[1] But "the man who invented Christmas," as Lee Standiford has recently called him, described this particular holiday to his friend George Dolby as "one of great pain and misery to him" owing to renewed problems with his left foot and hand (441). Each day he kept to his bed until evening, when he would rouse himself to come join in the merriment and games. Years later, Henry recalled one such evening in particular, when his father threw "all his energy" into a round of "The Memory Game," which required players to remember and repeat a growing string of proper nouns, then add a new one to the chain (Dickens, "Memories" 1. 24). As Henry wrote,

> My father, after many turns, had successfully gone through the long string of words, and finished up with his own contribution, "Warren's Blacking, 30, Strand." He gave this with an odd twinkle in his eye and a strange inflection in his voice which at once forcibly arrested my attention and left a vivid

> impression on my mind for some time afterwards. Why, I could not, for the life of me, understand. (1. 24)

Only in 1872, when John Forster published the first volume of his *Life of Charles Dickens*, did Henry finally understand his father's odd excitement that night. Adding "Warren's Blacking, 30, Strand" to the chain of nouns had been a game-within-the-game for Dickens, a nominally playful insertion of his ferociously traumatic early memories into the circle of holiday cheer and familial affection.

The story of Dickens's miserable childhood has been told often enough, most recently and thoroughly by Michael Allen in *Charles Dickens and the Blacking Factory*, that it need not be rehearsed fully here. His father's imprisonment for "the Deed," his time living apart from his family, his feelings of degradation when he was taken from school and forced instead to work in the front window at Warren's—these things have been familiar since Forster published in his biography the autobiographical "fragment" that Dickens wrote in 1846 and/or 1847 before abandoning it in favor of *David Copperfield*. In the fragment Dickens describes his "secret agony of [. . .] soul" as his "early hopes of growing up to be a learned and distinguished man, [were] crushed in [his] breast," and he recalls the gnawing anxiety of parceling out his six weekly shillings into penny loaves and morsels of cheese (qtd in Forster 26). "I know," Dickens wrote, "that I have lounged about the streets, insufficiently and unsatisfactorily fed. I know that, but for the mercy of God, I might easily have been, for any care that was taken of me, a little robber or a little vagabond" (qtd in Forster 28). Moreover, Dickens claimed, he had kept these experiences a profound secret, never having "in any burst of confidence with any one, [his] own wife not excepted, raised the curtain [he] then dropped, thank God" (qtd in Forster 35). Dickens may in fact have told Catherine of his past, or at least allowed her to read the fragment after he set it aside (Slater 424). But Dickens's fiction had always carried coded allusions to his early trials, which had hovered playfully in the liminal space between secrecy and disclosure. By inserting Warren's Blacking into "The Memory Game," Michael Slater writes, Dickens was "playing with his unwitting family the private game that he had so long played with his wider family of unwitting readers" (607). That game allowed Dickens simultaneously to express and contain trauma by subduing its potential excesses to the orderly requirements of play.

The idea of "orderly" play may seem misplaced in a discussion of Dickens, since play—especially if taken to mean not just games and recreations but also imaginative fancy, linguistic invention, clowning, and play-acting—appears so often in his fiction, most memorably when, as in the famous opening of *Hard Times*, it provides a ludic antidote to the "Facts" of a rigid and objectivizing industrial culture. Gail Turley Houston argues that Dickens's novels advance a theory of play "as the restorative force for a society embedded in Utilitarian facts," a society epitomized most obviously in mentally inflexible teachers such as Thomas Gradgrind and Bradley Headstone (267). At age seven, Dickens went with his father to London to see the famous clown Joseph Grimaldi, whose antics delighted him so much that two decades later, in the late 1830s, he agreed to edit the *Life of Grimaldi* for Richard Bentley, though he was already committed simultaneously to editing *Bentley's Miscellany* and writing *Oliver Twist* (Slater 8, 111–12). He was also prone to clowning himself, even near the end of his life when, during his 1866 reading tour, he took advantage of a deserted street in Southsea to climb the steps of a house, knock, and lie down "on the upper step, clown fashion," where he was discovered by the woman who opened the door (Dolby 40).[2] Spontaneous fun of this kind appears throughout his fiction, in Sam Weller and Trabb's boy, Sloppy and Charley Bates. As Mark Hennelly has noted in his extensive work on play in Dickens, *The Pickwick Papers* alone mentions "popular games and antic forms like bagatelle, rackets, ice-sliding, marbles, dancing the frog hornpipe, boxing, blindman's bluff, riddle and slanging matches, gambling, drinking bouts, *écarté*, snapdragon, Saint Joan, rook-hunting, forfeits, skittles, whist, cracking, dueling, and Dickens's personal favorite 'leapfrog'" ("Dickens's" 28). For Hennelly as for Houston, Dickensian play signifies possibility and liminality, originating in the dynamic uncertainty Freud attributes to the *fort-da* game in *Beyond the Pleasure Principle*, or in what Jacques Derrida calls "the disruption of presence" ("Deep" 165; 292). Above all, such readings suggest, play in Dickens disrupts order—even if, as Hennelly argues of *Little Dorrit*, it fails sometimes to provide a durable ludic alternative to a stultifying culture ("Games" 187).

But play is not always ludic or liberating. On the contrary, as Johan Huizinga explains in *Homo Ludens*, it often consists of elaborate rules and prescribes limits of location and duration. "Inside the play-ground," Huizinga writes, "an absolute and peculiar order reigns. [. . . Play] creates order, *is* order. Into an imperfect world and into the confusion of life it brings a temporary, limited perfection" (10). Rather than disrupt order, play can impose it, substituting for the unruliness of life an unmerited faith in the possibility of arranging and containing the disorder of lived experience. In this respect, as Gregory Colón-Semenza argues in his study of Renaissance sport, the appeal of play parallels Pierre Bourdieu's discussion of the *habitus* and the way in which "formal models" reduce complexity to the more appealing proposition "that we are in control of our own lives" (Bourdieu 47; Colón-Semenza 19). This is particularly true of sports and games, which not only establish a comprehensible hierarchy of winners and losers but also abide by strict rules that may not correspond with social codes. Whist players may play cards only when it is their turn, and the trick's winner depends upon rules of trump suits and face values; opponents in a boxing match pummel one another in ways that would expose them to criminal prosecution outside of the sacred space and time of play. The aim of many sports and games, Colón-Semenza argues, is in fact to *promote* "orderly violence" by sanctioning the interplay of control and excess (14). Rather than offer pure ludic release, then, games can function to permit and regulate forms of physical, emotional, and psychological violence that might otherwise be suppressed.

Among Dickens's novels, *Great Expectations* in particular illustrates the capacity of games to function in this way, and it does so especially in two extended scenes—when Pip plays Beggar My Neighbour with Estella and when he boxes with "the pale young gentleman"—that illustrate the relation between play and Pip's attempts to understand, and eventually narrate, the psychological and discursive effects of his childhood trauma (71). Both scenes might be read as sites of trauma themselves. In playing cards with Estella, Pip feels shame for the first time at being "coarse and common," and in fighting the pale young gentleman, he discovers an inner savagery that frightens him and affirms his guilty relation to the convict on the marshes (*Great* 102). But these scenes, I will argue, activate trauma rather than inflict it. They serve as conduits through which the young Pip experiences traumatic recurrence and comes to grips with older sources of anguish and shame. Above all, these instances of play provide the discursive vehicle by which the older Pip comes to narrate trauma without allowing its violent excesses to overwhelm the text. In her essay on the representation of trauma in Dickens's short story "The Signalman," Jill Matus explains that for Freud "[t]he hallmark of trauma [. . .] was the inability to possess memory, to make the event the subject of narrative" (419). Instead, she observes, the traumatic memory possesses the sufferer, recurring intensely when it is not wanted and upsetting the role of memory in the formation of a coherent self. But making trauma the subject of narration is very much the point of *Great Expectations*, so Pip must find an antidote to this "'disease of time' in which the events of the past continually obtrude on the present" (*Great* 430).[3] He does so in part by using games to undo this temporal disruption, exploiting their capacity to regulate trauma by subjecting it to the time- and rule-boundedness of play.

Play appears in many forms in *Great Expectations* and signifies in several ways. The novel describes Trabb's boy's ludic antics and Uncle Pumblechook's running sums, the friendly contest between Pip and Joe to see who can eat his bread and butter the fastest, and the less friendly one between the boys at Mr. Wopsle's great-aunt's school, who conduct a "competitive examination on the subject of Boots, with a view of ascertaining who could tread the hardest on whose toes" (*Great* 61). Dickens told Forster early in his work on *Great Expectations* that he had deliberately made its beginning chapters "exceedingly droll" by putting "a child and a good-natured foolish man, in relations that seem[ed] to [him] very funny"; and in the *Times* E. S. Dallas assured readers who had lamented the seriousness of *Bleak House*, *Hard Times*, and *Little Dorrit* that they would find Dickens returning in *Great Expectations* to his "old *Pickwick* style" (*Letters* 9. 325; 6). But much of the novel's play also touches forms of violence and pain—cannibalism, cruelty, guilt, and shame, among others—that bear heavily upon darker matters. *Great Expectations* begins with a macabre joke, when Magwitch observes that Pip has got "fat cheeks" and adds, "Darn me if I couldn't eat 'em," before terrifying Pip with the claim that he is hiding on the marshes with another "young man" who has "a secret way, pecooliar to himself, of getting at a boy, and at his heart, and at his liver" (10–11). Orlick, too, threatens to consume the young Pip—and nearly does so later in the novel—telling him that "it was necessary to make up the fire [at the forge] once in every seven years, with a live boy" (*Great* 91). Even late in the novel, play often wears this sinister aspect, as when the returned Magwitch plays "a complicated kind of Patience with a ragged pack of cards" and keeps score by thrusting "his jack-knife into the table," and when Pip remarks that the death casts on the shelf in Jaggers's office seem to be "playing a diabolical game of bo-peep" (*Great* 253, 290).

But it is particularly the scenes in which Pip plays cards with Estella and fights with the pale young gentleman that develop and complicate this relation between games, trauma, and violence and illustrate their necessary convergence in Pip's narrative. When Pip first visits Satis House, Miss Havisham tells him frankly why she has summoned him there: "I sometimes have sick fancies [. . .] and I have a sick fancy that I want to see some play" (*Great* 51). Her desire to see play appears from the start as a product of, and perhaps an antidote to, her own trauma. But her use of play in this fashion undoes its capacity to ameliorate trauma since it ignores play's typical rules of duration and location, robbing it of its regulatory power. Having shut out the sun, stopped the clocks, and arrested even the progress of her wedding toilette—Pip notes, "She had not quite finished dressing, for she had but one shoe on"—Miss Havisham lives in perpetual recurrence, granting trauma continual free rein in the present rather than envisioning play as a means of limiting its duration (*Great* 50). She also tries to make Pip play to order, commanding him to "play, play, play!" with "an impatient movement of [her] fingers" (*Great* 51). As Ella Kusnetz points out, the command is preposterous since "[p]lay cannot be performed on demand" (1512). But the point for Miss Havisham is not really play, anyway. She wants, rather, to create a theater of cruelty in which Pip must suffer as a proxy for the men whom she is rearing Estella to punish in the outside world. Since Pip only knows how to play Beggar My Neighbour, it is within the rules of the game that Estella beggars him as she does, and also that Pip's losses imply the economic humiliation he feels when she ridicules his "coarse hands" and "thick boots" (*Great* 51–52).[4] But even as a boy Pip can scarcely believe his ears when Miss Havisham encourages Estella to play by telling her, "Well? You can break his heart" (*Great* 51). Miss Havisham also violates the rules of play, in other words, by treating the game as a training ground for inflicting trauma in the real world rather than as a privileged space for containing and mitigating trauma's excesses.

For Pip, conversely, the card game serves precisely this regulatory function by imposing rule-boundedness on the alienating phantasmagoria of Satis House, with its decayed wedding feast, stopped clocks, and spectral bride. His arrival to Miss Havisham might best be understood as a descent into not only terror but also the temporal disruption characteristic of trauma. Left at the gate by Pumblechook, Pip follows Estella through the desolate grounds and the darkened passages of the house until they arrive at what he calls "the strangest lady I have ever seen, or ever shall see":

> I saw that the bride within the bridal dress had withered like the dress, and like the flowers, and had no brightness left but the brightness of her sunken eyes. . . . Once, I had been taken to see some ghastly wax-work at the Fair, representing I know not what impossible personage lying in state. Once, I had been taken to one of our old marsh churches to see a skeleton in the ashes of a rich dress, that had been dug out of a vault under the church pavement. Now, wax-work and skeleton seemed to have dark eyes that moved and looked at me. I should have cried out, if I could. (*Great* 49–50)

The house is more like a crypt, its alienating power intensified by Estella persistently calling him "boy" rather than Pip and by his growing sense that he has arrived at a place outside of natural time (*Great* 49). Having noted first that "[n]o glimpse of daylight was to be seen" in the house, Pip soon realizes, too, that all the clocks "had stopped at twenty minutes to nine" (*Great* 49–50). When Estella discharges him into the brewery grounds again, he is disoriented. "The rush of daylight quite confounded me," he writes, "and made me feel as if I had been in the candle-light of the strange room many hours" (*Great* 53). As Pip stammers out to Miss Havisham when he cannot play at first, "it's so new here, and so strange, and so fine—and melancholy—" trailing off into uncertainty whether he "might say too much, or had already said it" (*Great* 51). Even before the card game, then, he illustrates the temporal disorder and narrative failure that characterize the traumatic event.

In this context, playing Beggar My Neighbour offers a kind of reprieve, a return to familiarity amid Pip's feelings of fear and alienation and a release from the vague demand that he play. The choice of game obviously suits the novel's broader portrayal of Pip's economic humiliation, and in this sense both the game and the vicious dialogue that accompanies it help to underscore Satis House's traumatic effect. Still, it is worth remembering that Pip and Estella play Beggar My Neighbour for the simple reason that it is the only card game he knows how to play, and its very familiarity allows Pip to begin to process the nature of his pain. While playing cards, he realizes for the first time that "everything in the room had stopped, like the watch and the clock, a long time ago," and he notes a few sentences later that Miss Havisham "sat, corpse-like, as we played" (*Great* 52–53). It is during the card game, too, that Estella's abuse first makes Pip so "ashamed of [his] hands" that—though he knows how to play—he "misdeal[s]," as is "only natural" when he knows that she expects him to blunder (*Great* 52). The card game drives Pip implicitly toward a conscious recognition of temporal disorder and deeply felt shame, which culminates in his first faltering attempt to give voice to trauma. After Estella denounces him "for a stupid, clumsy laboring-boy," Miss Havisham invites him to tell her privately what he thinks of Estella, coaxing from him the declarations, "I think she is very proud. [. . .] I think she is very pretty. [. . .] I think she is very insulting. [. . .] I think I should like to go home" (*Great* 52). His controlled responses show him working through in language, for the first time, his humiliation, budding desire, and growing alienation. They index the traumatic feelings evoked by the game, arriving finally at something like autobiographical disclosure and a longing for home.

But the trauma that Pip indexes here has origins that predate Satis House, as the novel suggests in his reaction to being left in the courtyard after he has finished playing. Estella appears with a tray of food and leaves it on the ground, looking at him, he writes, "as insolently as if I were a dog in disgrace":

> I was so humiliated, hurt, spurned, offended, angry, sorry—I cannot hit upon the right name for the smart—God knows what its name was—that tears started to my eyes. [. . .]
>
> [. . .] Within myself, I had sustained, from my babyhood, a perpetual conflict with injustice. I had known, from the time when I could speak, that my sister, in her capricious and violent coercion, was unjust to me. I had cherished a profound conviction that her bringing me up by hand, gave her no right to bring me up by jerks. Through all my punishments, disgraces, fasts and vigils, and other penitential performances, I had nursed this assurance. (*Great* 53–54)

This return to memories of his sister's abusive rearing implies that playing cards has activated trauma rather than inflicted it, driving Pip back upon a primal scene of fear and abjection that precedes the novel's beginning in the churchyard, since it is rooted instead in the anguish of his orphanhood and the longing for coherent identity that drives him in the first place to seek out his parents' tombstones and try to read what they were like "[f]rom the character and turn of the inscription[s]" (*Great* 9). Pip's response to Satis House thus reprises David Copperfield's first return from school, when he comes home to find a new baby nestled at his mother's breast. Like David's bewilderment, Pip's cathartic weeping maps what Robert Lougy calls "the contours left behind by ancient separation trauma" in order "to register the scars that an inescapable tragedy leaves behind" (418). Only after leaving the rule-boundedness of the card game does Pip experience his trauma as excessive, giving way to the unruliness of crying, kicking the wall, and tearing his hair. Even for the older, narrating Pip, passing from the card game to the courtyard seems to make trauma unavailable to discourse, as his index of humiliation, desire, and alienation becomes instead "the smart without a name" (*Great* 53).

Narrative disorder seems, in fact, to be a primary effect of Pip's traumatic day at Satis House, which ends in his return to the forge and the explicit demand that he account for himself. His sister and Pumblechook interrogate him closely, shoving his face "ignominiously [. . .] against the kitchen wall" because he does not answer their questions "at sufficient length" (*Great* 56). Pip's refusal to answer them stems partly from his aggressive desire to frustrate their curiosity. But he also blames his childish "dread of not being understood," remarking, "I felt convinced that Miss Havisham [. . .] would not be understood; and although she was perfectly incomprehensible to me, I entertained an impression that there would be something coarse and treacherous in my dragging her as she really was (to say nothing of Estella) before the contemplation of Mrs. Joe" (*Great* 56). What Pip does not say is that any such narrative would also involve dragging Mrs. Joe before her own eyes by disclosing his sense of her injustice, the way in which Miss Havisham's and Estella's treatment have forced upon his conscious thoughts "the smart without a name" that originates in Mrs. Joe's callous treatment (*Great* 53). Made almost frantic by their questioning, Pip tells them instead an absurd story about playing with flags aboard a "black velvet coach" while four immense dogs "fought for veal cutlets out of a silver basket" (*Great* 57). The lies silence Mrs. Joe and Pumblechook, but they do so, tellingly, by substituting ludic play for the orderly card game that permitted Pip's recognition and expression of trauma. He cannot come to grips with Satis House's disruptions by telling the story in this way. Thus, when he goes to Joe, penitent, to tell him that he has lied to the others, he still fails to articulate the connection between Miss Havisham's and Estella's treatment of him and the tale he has told, only observing confusedly "that the lies had come of it somehow, though I didn't know how" (*Great* 59). And he falls asleep still mired in temporal disruption, "recalling what 'I used to do' when I was at Miss Havisham's; as though I had been there weeks or months, instead of hours: and as though it were quite an old subject of remembrance, instead of one that had risen only that day" (*Great* 60).

Pip's card game with Estella thus matters for not only what it reveals of Pip's psychological development but also what it signifies regarding his eventual arrival to the capacity for self-narration. As Pip's lies to Mrs. Joe and Pumblechook suggest, eliding trauma leaves one still at its mercy, still lost in its temporal and discursive effects. Achieving a coherent identity requires Pip instead to overcome trauma's resistance to narration by finding a discursive or symbolic mode for representing it, accounting for its recurrences while containing its excesses. Play becomes a dominant trope in *Great Expectations* because it serves this very function, for both the young Pip who is forged by trauma and the older one who must narrate it and subdue it to psychological, temporal, and discursive order. After his first day with Miss Havisham and Estella, Pip's visits to Satis House become regular and more frequent, and his duties expand to include the *work* of pushing Miss Havisham around in her garden-chair while the trio sings "Old Clem." But the visits never cease to include play. On the contrary, Pip recalls play as part of their collective routine, noting how "when we played at cards Miss Havisham would look on, with a miserly relish of Estella's moods" (*Great* 77). Though the young Pip cannot articulate his trauma outside the sacred space of play, the older Pip seems to recognize Satis House retrospectively as a site of his psychological and narrative formation. "That was a memorable day to me," he writes of his first visit, "for it made great changes in me. [. . .] Pause you who read this, and think for a moment of the long chain of iron or gold, of thorns or flowers, that would never have bound you, but for the formation of the first link on one memorable day" (*Great* 60). The boy who played has become, in middle age, the narrator who sees causality and connection, the "long chain" of events, experiences, and sensations—some of them traumatic—that converged at Satis House and permitted the formation of a coherent identity scarred by neglect and shame (*Great* 60).

Pip's boxing match with the pale young gentleman illustrates from another perspective this development toward the capacity to narrate trauma. The fight occurs during Pip's second visit to Satis House, which begins with Pip meeting Miss Havisham's grasping relations but then mostly repeats his first: he and Estella play Beggar My Neighbour, she beggars him repeatedly, and Miss Havisham appoints a day for his return. But this time, after Estella discharges Pip and feeds him "in the former dog-like manner," he prowls about until he finds himself unexpectedly face to face "with a pale young gentleman with red eyelids and light hair" who approaches him and says, "Come and fight" (*Great* 73–74). What the other boy has in mind, though, is not a fight but a boxing match characterized by elaborate techniques and what he calls the "Laws of the game!" (*Great* 74). Pip knows nothing of those laws, so the other boy provokes him into fighting by butting his head into Pip's stomach, which causes Pip to "hit out at him" (*Great* 74). Having elicited Pip's anger, the other boy cordons it off, leading him to "a retired nook of the garden"—an appropriate ground for play—and then "dancing backwards and forwards in a manner quite unparalleled within [Pip's] limited experience" (*Great* 74). Though the adult Pip claims to have been frightened of his dexterous opponent, he pummels the pale young gentleman, an outcome that Hennelly argues "redress[es] the foul play" that Pip has experienced with Estella by providing him with a game that "he can 'morally and physically' master" ("Mysterious" 163). More to the point, the game permits violence that would not be sanctioned outside of the sacred ground. In retrospect, Pip writes, "I am sorry to record that the more I hit him, the harder I hit him . . . I go so far as to hope that I regarded myself while dressing as a species of savage young wolf" (*Great* 75). The simile revives Pip's kinship with the convict on the marshes, whom he has described as eating like a dog, taking "strong sharp sudden bites [. . .] as if he thought there was danger in every direction" and might "chop with his jaws" at anyone foolish enough to disturb him (*Great* 21).

But as a boy Pip does not understand how the "Laws of the game" function to permit and contain his savagery. After the fight, Pip writes, "My mind grew very uneasy on the subject of the pale young gentleman. [. . .] I felt that the pale young gentleman's blood was on my head, and that the Law would avenge it" (*Great* 75). For the next several days he thinks of himself as liable to punishment, as a ravager of "the studious youth of England" and proper object for the officers of "the County Jail"

(*Great* 76). He tries to wash the pale young gentleman's blood from his trousers "in the dead of night," and he invents incredible alibis for the cuts on his knuckles, much as Jaggers has done years earlier at Molly's criminal trial (*Great* 76). When the appointed day comes for his return to Satis House, he approaches the gate wondering "[w]hether myrmidons of Justice, specially sent from London," might be waiting to take him into custody, or whether Miss Havisham "might rise in those grave-clothes of hers, draw a pistol, and shoot [him] dead" for the outrage committed against her house (*Great* 76). These fears reflect partly the overwrought anxieties of a child who knows he has done wrong, magnified in this case by Pip's ancient sense of guilt, his sister's neglect, and his accidental association with the convict on the marshes. When Pip returns to the site of his combat with the pale young gentleman, he spies "traces of his gore" and, in an echo of Cain, even tries to "cover them with garden-mould from the eyes of man" (*Great* 76). That no punishment follows his bloody combat teaches Pip an important lesson about the function of games in permitting and containing violent excess, about their ability to sequester violence spatially, temporally, and ontologically from the real world. It teaches him, too, to avoid Miss Havisham's error of mistaking the playground for real life, and of treating trauma as identity rather than as a recurrence that can be mitigated and regulated by play.

The beginning of Pip's apprenticeship to Joe ends, for the most part, his visits to Satis House and childish playing of games. But the novel continues to stress the way in which games, recreations, contests, and other forms of play bear meanings that would otherwise struggle to find suitable expression in the world that the novel describes. Jaggers in particular underscores the significance of play, appearing repeatedly in Pip's telling as the consummate gamester, especially when he can use games to express and contain traumatic or violent excess. At Little Britain, he plays games with witnesses and juries—games the system, so to speak—while at home he goads Pip and his friends into "baring and spanning [their] arms in a ridiculous manner" to compare their muscles, a hypermasculine contest that is only a pretext for displaying the strength of Molly's wrists and so hinting at murder, legal deception, and the other guilty excesses that first brought Estella to Satis House (*Great* 166). A few chapters later, Pip describes playing whist with Jaggers, Miss Havisham, and Estella after the latter has returned from France, noting how Jaggers "took our trumps into custody, and came out with mean little cards at the ends of hands, before which the glory of our Kings and Queens was utterly abased" (*Great* 186). The passage renders symbolically the way that Jaggers has orchestrated the relationships that shape the novel while also disrupting social class, since he is the one who gives the genteel Miss Havisham a pauper murderess's daughter to raise and affirms Pip's relation to the convict of his early remembrance. Jaggers uses a game metaphor, too, to query Pip on the painful subject of Estella's engagement, remarking, "So, Pip! Our friend the Spider [. . .] has played his cards. He has won the pool" (*Great* 291). By novel's end, even Herbert Pocket recognizes how play gives cover for things that would otherwise violate laws and codes. Helping Pip to plan Magwitch's escape, Herbert suggests that they use their recreation, rowing, to get Magwitch out to sea. "You fall into the habit," he tells Pip, "and then who notices or minds? Do it twenty or fifty times, and there is nothing special in your doing it the twenty-first or fifty-first" (*Great* 283). The orderly routine of sport, Herbert surmises, will simultaneously permit and conceal their illicit conduct.

In her study of writing and play in *Great Expectations*, Kusnetz concludes that Pip's is a case of arrested development, for he cannot ever leave his childhood behind and remains, even at the end, "Mr. Pip" (2. 148). Certainly the closing chapters suggest that Pip may have learned little by novel's end. Like David Copperfield, who foolishly marries Dora before returning to Agnes, Pip tries to shift his misguided affection from Estella to Biddy only to find that she has already married Joe, and his prayer over the dying Magwitch—"O Lord, be merciful to him, a sinner!"—might hint that he remains blind to his own need for merciful judgment (*Great* 342).[5] Above all, the novel's published ending implies that Pip has never quite relinquished his feelings for Estella, even though he has become a hard-working middle-class man rather than the effete gentleman he once hoped to be. But it is unreasonable to expect Pip to outgrow his childhood if by *outgrow* we mean escape and elide utterly his past traumas. The novel suggests instead that maturing means arriving at a sense of identity that acknowledges the significance of childhood trauma in forming the adult subject, and that succeeds at breaking down trauma's resistance to narration. As Miss Havisham tells Pip when he first departs for London, "You will always keep the name of Pip, you know" (*Great* 123). Pip's goal, then, is never really to leave his self-given name behind but rather to bring his traumatic experiences into that same realm of discourse, to open trauma, too, to the possibility of naming. This seems to have been Dickens's secret aim for the novel, too. Twice *Great Expectations* alludes to his old association with Warren's Blacking: first when Pip fears "that in some unlucky hour I, being at my grimiest and commonest, should lift up my eyes and see Estella looking in at one of the wooden windows of the forge"; and again when Joe tells Pip that, upon arriving to London, he and Wopsle "went straight off to the Blacking Ware'us" but found that it "didn't come up to its likeness in the red bills at the shop doors" (*Great* 87, 171). Both scenes offer fantasies of display that recall Dickens's shame at being placed in the front window at Warren's while he labeled bottles of blacking, and both remain embedded in the privileged space of the narrative game that Dickens played so incessantly, for so long, with his readers.

This treatment of play as a vehicle for expressing and containing trauma provides a powerful connection between *Great Expectations* and the novels that followed it—particularly *Our Mutual Friend*, which returns repeatedly to instances of play that harbor violence, desire, and pain. *Our Mutual Friend* begins by turning *Great Expectations*' rowing into both a grisly occupation and, for Lizzie Hexam, a site of intense shame, and it ends by making Lizzie's rowing into a cathartic expression of her love for Eugene Wrayburn. Jenny Wren, meanwhile, covers over the traumas of her physical debilities and alcoholic father by imagining "long bright rows" of beautiful children inviting her to "Come and play," and also by playing at being the mother of a "bad child," the latter an implicit attempt to make narrative sense of the temporal disruption thrust upon her by her father's failings (*Our* 240, 239). But the best illustration of the traumatic freight that games carry in *Our Mutual Friend* comes in Eugene's nocturnal play with Bradley Headstone—"the pleasures of the chase"—which he designs deliberately to "goad the schoolmaster to madness" by leading him on aimless and endless walks all over the City:

> I tempt him on, all over London. One night I go east, another night north, in a few nights I go all round the compass. Sometimes, I walk; sometimes, I proceed in cabs, draining the pocket of the schoolmaster, who then follows in cabs. I study and get up abstruse No Thoroughfares in the course of the day . . . glide into them by means of dark courts, tempt the schoolmaster to follow, turn suddenly, and catch him

> before he can retreat. Then we face one another, and I pass him as unaware of his existence, and he undergoes grinding torments. (*Our* 542–43)

Developing elaborate strategies and unwritten rules, Eugene creates a game that has no object *but* expressing and containing his contempt for the schoolmaster, heightening Bradley's shame at his pauper roots, and inflaming the aggressive desire that each man has for Lizzie. He creates, in other words, a game that epitomizes what *Great Expectations* suggests is the truest function of play: providing a privileged space for violent or traumatic feeling that has no other point of entry into the novel. For Eugene, the game ends when he travels upriver to find Lizzie, unaware that he is still being followed; for Headstone, liberation from the ritualized order of the game permits him to erupt in violence.

When Dickens puzzled his family by adding "Warren's Blacking, 30, Strand" to "The Memory Game" in December 1869, he was already deep in the writing of *The Mystery of Edwin Drood*—the very novel, of all his works, which he designed as an elaborate game with his readers. In his "Postscript: In lieu of a Preface" for *Our Mutual Friend*, he wrote that he had worried that "a class of readers and commentators would suppose that I was at great pains to conceal exactly what I was at great pains to suggest: namely, that Mr. John Harmon was not slain, and that Mr. John Rokesmith was he" (*Our* 821). But in the case of *Edwin Drood* his anxieties ran the other way. During his last walk with his father, Charley Dickens recalled, "[O]ur talk [. . .] presently drifting to *Edwin Drood*, my father asked me if I did not think that he had let out too much of his story too soon" (*Mystery* xxvi–xxvii). That he did not is evidenced in the endless speculations on how it might have ended, despite the straightforward declarations by Charley, Forster, the novel's illustrator Luke Fildes, and others that Edwin has been murdered by his uncle and that, in Forster's words, "[t]he last chapters were to be written in the condemned cell, to which [John Jasper's] wickedness, all elaborately elicited from him as if told by another, had brought him" (808). What is particularly striking in this account of the prospective denouement is that Dickens appears to have envisioned the elaborately wrought narrative game of *Edwin Drood* as reaching its culmination in an act of traumatic memory and self-narrative disclosure, as if he understood that such memory and disclosure were only possible at the end of such a novel. It is as if he understood, that is, that such a haunting, violent confession as Jasper's could only emerge into narrative through the regulating power inherent in the orderly space of play.

Notes

1. For accounts of Dickens's Christmas activities in 1869, see Henry Dickens, 23–24; Forster, 845; Slater, 607; and Claire Tomalin, 383.

2. Edward Wagenknecht includes several such anecdotes. See 59–65.

3. Matus draws this idea of trauma as a "disease of time" from Allan Young. See especially 7.

4. Kristen Parkinson notes that "Dickens chooses to call the game beggar-my-neighbor [*sic*], although it is also known as beat your neighbor out of doors and strip jack naked. While all three names imply humiliation of one's opponent, only beggar-my-neighbor puts that humiliation in explicitly economic terms" (123).

5. Edgar Rosenberg discusses this passage in detail in the "Writing *Great Expectations*" section of the Norton edition, where he argues that Dickens intended Pip's piety sincerely (432–33).

Works Cited

Allen, Michael. *Charles Dickens and the Blacking Factory*. St. Leonards: Oxford-Stockley, 2011.

Bourdieu, Pierre. *The Logic of Practice*. 1980. Trans. Richard Nice. Cambridge: Polity Press, 1990.

Colón-Semenza, Gregory M. *Sport, Politics, and Literature in the English Renaissance*. Newark: University of Delaware Press, 2003.

[Dallas, Eneas Sweetland]. "*Great Expectations*." *Times* (17 October 1861): 6.

Derrida, Jacques. *Writing and Difference*. 1967. Trans. Alan Bass. Chicago: University of Chicago Press, 1978.

Dickens, Charles. *David Copperfield*. 1850. Ed. Jerome H. Buckley. New York and London: Norton, 1989.

———. *Great Expectations*. 1861. Ed. Edgar Rosenberg. New York and London: Norton, 1999.

———. *Hard Times*. 1854. Ed. Fred Kaplan. New York and London: Norton, 2000.

———. *The Letters of Charles Dickens*. 12 vols. Ed. Madeline House, Graham Storey, and Kathleen Tillotson. Oxford: Clarendon Press, 1974–2002.

———. *The Mystery of Edwin Drood*. 1870. Ed. Margaret Cardwell. Oxford: Clarendon, 1972.

———. *Our Mutual Friend*. 1864–65. Ed. Michael Cotsell. Oxford: Oxford University Press, 2008.

Dickens, Henry F. "Memories of My Father." 1928. Page vol. 1.

Dolby, George. *Charles Dickens as I Knew Him: The Story of the Reading Tours*. 1885. Page vol. 4.

Forster, John. *The Life of Charles Dickens*. Ed. J. W. T. Ley. London: Cecil Palmer, 1928.

Freud, Sigmund. *Beyond the Pleasure Principle*. 1920. Ed. James Strachey. New York and London: Norton, 1990.

Hennelly, Mark M. "'Deep play' and 'women's ridicules' in *Oliver Twist*, Part IV." *Journal of Evolutionary Psychology* 20.1–2 (1999): 165–74.

———. "Dickens's Praise of Folly: Play in *The Pickwick Papers*." *Dickens Quarterly* 3.1 (1986): 27–45.

———. "The Games of the Prison Children in Dickens's *Little Dorrit*." *Nineteenth-Century Contexts* 20.2 (1997): 187–213.

———. "The 'mysterious portal': Liminal Play in *David Copperfield*, *Bleak House*, and *Great Expectations* (Part One)." *Dickens Quarterly* 15.3 (1998): 155–66.

Houston, Gail Turley. "'Pretend[ing] a little': The Play of Musement in Dickens's *Little Dorrit*." *Dickens Studies Annual* 41 (2010): 265–80.

Huizinga, Johan. *Homo Ludens: A Study of the Play-Element in Culture*. Boston: Beacon Press, 1955.

Kusnetz, Ella. "'This leaf of my life': Writing and Play in *Great Expectations* (Part Two)." *Dickens Quarterly* 10.3 (1993): 146–60.

Lougy, Robert E. "Dickens and the Wolf Man: Childhood Memory and Fantasy in *David Copperfield*." *PMLA: Papers of the Modern Language Association* 124.2 (2009): 406–20.

Matus, Jill. "Trauma, Memory, and Railway Disaster: The Dickensian Connection." *Victorian Studies* 43.3 (2001): 413–36.

Page, Norman, ed. *Charles Dickens: Family History*. 5 Vols. London: Routledge, 1999.

Parkinson, Kristen L. "'What do you play, boy?': Card Games in *Great Expectations*." *Dickens Quarterly* 27.2 (2010): 119–38.

Rosenberg, Edgar, ed. *Great Expectations*. 1861. New York and London: Norton, 1999.

Slater, Michael. *Charles Dickens*. New Haven and London: Yale University Press, 2009.

Standiford, Les. *The Man Who Invented Christmas: How Charles Dickens's* A Christmas Carol *Rescued His Career and Revived Our Holiday Spirits*. New York: Crown, 2008.

Tomalin, Claire. *Charles Dickens: A Life*. New York: Penguin, 2011.

Wagenknecht, Edward. *The Man Charles Dickens: A Victorian Portrait*. Norman: University of Oklahoma Press, 1966.

Young, Allan. *The Harmony of Illusions: Inventing Post-Traumatic Stress Disorder*. Princeton: Princeton University Press, 1995.

Chapter 5

Seeing Victorian Culture through Croquet's "Treacherous Wire Portal"[1]

CATHERINE S. BLACKWELL

In February 1865, British readers may well have been stunned by the latest installment of Charlotte Yonge's *The Clever Woman of the Family*, published in parts in *The Churchman's Family Magazine*. Character Bessie Keith, impelled by "the infection of croquet fever," indulges her passions for croquet and flirtation despite her advanced pregnancy (Yonge 258). Wearing a "mass of pretty, fresh, fluttering blue and white muslin, ribbon, and lace," she engages in a *tête-à-tête* with an amorous croquet partner; but when threatened with discovery, she dashes from the pair's semi-secluded bench (Yonge 461). Panic deafens her to her sister-in-law's called warning about the croquet wicket in her path, and Bessie trips and falls, "entangled in her dress" (Yonge 464). Her tumble causes the premature birth of her son, after which Bessie herself succumbs to her injuries, victim of a quite literal croquet trap. American readers of *The Clever Woman* remained unaware of Bessie's strange demise until *The Living Age* finally published chapter 26 in late March. Oddly, none of the British or American contemporary reviews of the novel make any reference to Bessie's death by croquet.

However bizarre its treatment of the croquet plot, *The Clever Woman of the Family* neither introduced nor ushered out nineteenth-century literary discussions of the game. At least three other 1860s novels incorporate croquet scenes to teach their readers something of appropriate social behavior: Anthony Trollope's 1862–64 *The Small House at Allington*; Lewis Carroll's 1865 *Alice's Adventures in Wonderland*; and Louisa May

Alcott's 1868–69 *Little Women.* During the same period, satirists and other short-fiction writers embraced the game so warmly that it permeates mid-nineteenth-century press. Croquet afforded writers a perfect vehicle, in fact, because it circumvented rigid period gender roles by allowing the sexes to compete directly against one another.[2] Interestingly, press writers often depicted croquet's social impacts quite differently than did novelists. We cannot know how accurately either reflects public opinion, although we do know the sport enjoyed immense popularity. In this chapter, I first examine how the periodicals of the 1860s reflect a historical moment newly obsessed with all things croquet. Using the continuing popular-press coverage to supply context, I then explore how four Victorian novels manipulate this passion in their treatment of the game.

Croquet, anyone?

It's hard to trace the exact moment when croquet became a transatlantic obsession. But by the 1850s in Britain and America, a range of periodicals eagerly described male and female aristocrats playing the game together at lawn parties. Fueling public enthusiasm, such publications boosted the burgeoning sporting goods industry.[3] The earliest advertisements seem to be those for John Jaques's croquet sets, available in a variety of models. For example, in May 1857, Jaques capitalized on the game "so much in vogue among the higher circles" by marketing both standard croquet sets for 25d. and "superior" models for 45d. ("New," *Morning* 1). Jaques's subsequent advertisements underscore how thoroughly he understood trends and his customers' specific tastes. In 1858, he expanded his line to include a £3 "polished hard wood" set, and in 1860, he added an economical 21d. version ("New," *Illustrated* 21; "Game," *Morning* 1). By 1859, each set Jaques sold included "the laws of the game" ("Game," *Illustrated* 15). Based on the frequency and regularity of his advertisements, Jaques appears to have gained a substantial part of the market by catering to buyers' income brackets as well as their need for clear-cut regulations.

But the paraphernalia available for those playing croquet went far beyond the sets themselves. Retailers began to market croquet attire, at first competing primarily to sell the boots women could wear on the lawns. According to a 1 January 1864, *Waterford News* advertisement, shoppers at "William Burrowes' Glasgow Boot and Shoe House" could purchase Balmorals for between 4s. 6d. and 5s. 6d. or "Kid Side Lace Boots" for 5s.

9d. (1). Other advertisements show that these prices represented standard rates reasonably well, with noticeable variations likely being tied to the place of the sale. On 2 January 1864, *The Leicester Mercury* also advertised ladies' Balmorals, although the upper price limit at "R. and J. Dick's in the Haymarket" exceeded Burrowes's by a full shilling (1). For those who preferred "Alex B. Clark's Family Boot and Shoe Manufacturer" in the Marylebone district, prices rose even more steeply: ladies could purchase "Imperial Balmoral boots for 6s. 6d. to 8s. 6d." but, according to the 9 January 1864, *Marylebone Mercury*, would pay between 6s. 6d. and 10s. 6d for "Paris Kid Boots" (1). Women might wear such boots in multiple settings, of course, but many period illustrations reveal their popularity on the lawns (see Figure 5.1). As the 23 September 1865, *London Review* noted, croquet provided eager artists "a good chance for drawing neat boots and ankles" because "the looped petticoat and attitudes place a great deal at their disposal" ("Croquet" 327).

Like Jaques, boot manufacturers soon recognized they could manipulate the increasing demand for all things croquet in profitable ways. A

CROQUET.

Chorus of Offended Maidens. "WELL! IF CLARA AND CAPTAIN DE HOLSTER ARE GOING ON IN THAT RIDICULOUS MANNER—WE MAY AS WELL LEAVE OFF PLAYING."

Figure 5.1. "Croquet," from 1863 *Punch's Almanack*, depicts several "offended maidens" condemning a flirtatious couple even as their own lifted skirts showcase their ankles. Collection of Catherine S. Blackwell.

single enterprising craftsman tested the market first, apparently determined to displace Balmorals as the female croquet players' footwear of choice. On 15 June 1864, *The Evening Freeman* briefly described the "artistic boot-making" of one Mr. Butler, whose "croquet boot of patent leather, beautifully picked out in handsome colours and tracery, extends to the knee and is buttoned and laced up the front" ("Skilled" 3). Other papers picked up the story, which notably did not tell readers whether Mr. Butler personally retailed his wares or, if not, where ladies might purchase them. However, the 30 June 1864, *Irish Times* reported that Butler, "of 28 Nassau street," had "furnished a very handsome case" throughout the ongoing Dublin International Exhibition of Arts and Manufactures ("Irish" 3). Three weeks later, in the *Dublin Weekly Nation*, James Butler himself announced that "[having] completed the Manufacture of Goods for the Exhibition, [he would] give his undivided attention to the execution of all Orders entrusted to him" (2). His gamble on croquet and other ladies' sporting boots, it seems, had proven quite successful.

Utilitarian or ornate, ankle- or knee-high, feminine croquet boots fascinated men, and women knew it. Periodicals had begun claiming that young ladies used the game—and their boots—to excite male chivalry and libido, and such cries reached a fever pitch as the sport's popularity grew. For example, the 15 October 1864 *Reader* tied croquet's "strong influence [upon] the matrimonial market" firmly to ladies' bootlaces: "Ah! we might name more than one fair owner [of] provoking feet who could send you—*per croquet*—to Hongkong or 'up the country'" ("Literature" 469). The 29 November 1864, *Kentish Gazette* took matters a step farther by observing that the male player who prostrates himself as a "little hussy" croquets[4] "is looking [not at her] ball all that time [but at] the prettiest little foot and ankle in all the world" ("Ladies" 2). Nor were such rhapsodies uncommon. Even if female players failed to notice men ogling their feet and ankles on the croquet lawn, they could hardly have overlooked the popular press's many candid accounts of such behavior.

Within approximately one year after his unqualified triumph, the innovative bootmaker James Butler had relocated and begun advertising his shop as the "only house in Dublin that can supply the [. . .] Croquet Boot [and others] as they ought to be" ("James" 3). Nevertheless, competing retailers simultaneously began marketing ladies' croquet boots of their own, always at unspecified prices. Negotiations would presumably have been conducted at the point of sale. This pattern altered temporarily on 18 April 1867, when the *Liverpool Daily Post* advertised J. and

W. Jeffery and Co.'s "cheap lot" of "Ladies' Elastic side Diamond Croquet Boots" for 5s. 6d. per pair ([J.] 1). As a review of advertisements reveals that Jeffery and Co. routinely purchased bankrupt or retiring businesses' stock for resale at dramatically reduced rates, however, such boots' original retail prices may be lost forever.

Meanwhile, a rainy climate and the porous nature of Balmorals or other croquet boots combined to supply even more satirical fodder. Despite having accused women of boldly displaying their feet and ankles, the periodicals also taunted ladies who did not. *Punch* led the charge, its 1 July 1865 "Oh, How Kind!!" article simultaneously poking fun at unattractive "goloshes" and ladies' hesitation to don them before stepping onto wet croquet grounds (261; see Figure 5.2). Nor could women escape ridicule by simply waiting for the grass to dry. On 15 December 1866, *Punch* mocked a fictive "Miss Cumbermould" whose fear of "damp boots from exposure to the atmosphere, &c." revealed a hopeless anti-croquet "hereditary complaint" ("Society" 241). Others followed suit, pointedly

Figure 5.2. In "Oh, How Kind!!" from 1865 *Punch, or the London Charivari*, jealous "Miss Spriggs" seeks to weaken "Flora's" feminine allure by urging her to don "goloshes." Collection of Catherine S. Blackwell.

cautioning that women had far more at stake than wet feet or ruined boots. The 20 July 1867 *Saturday Review*, for instance, resoundingly condemned the "atmosphere of vulgarity and ugliness" surrounding a lady wearing "two big black boats" on her feet: she might "escape a catarrh, but she loses her lovers. [. . .] A pretty face counts for less than nothing to the man [subjected to] the ghastliness of goloshes" ("Croquet" 77). At least one canny retailer perceived the jests' lucrative potential and seized it. On 26 July 1867, the *Derbyshire Advertiser* announced that C. E. Martin, Dublin, was now marketing the "new registered croquet boot for the lawn or the sea-side [. . .] of elegant design, and so made as to be perfectly waterproof" ([C.] 4). The advertisement does not indicate prices, but its regular repetition—together with an abrupt end to published "goloshes" humor—suggests that the new impermeable boots resolved this particular feminine dilemma.

Even so, the popular press and its readers had yet another feminine croquet garment in their sights: the crinoline. Railing against the "feeble game," a 17 September 1864, letter to the *London Evening Standard*'s editor asserts that female croquet players "determined no longer to be 'wanderers'" snare unwitting male partners by flaunting "otherwise uselessly ornamental petticoats, and tidy Balmorals" ("To" 6). Professional satirists concurred but devoted much closer attention to the "useless" garments' appearance. The mallet-wielding "hussy" whose partner only pretends to watch her ball, for example, further tempts him by "fring[ing her pretty feet] with a rare petticoat of divers colours" ("Ladies" 2). As such female caricatures became ever more predatory, their male counterparts correspondingly grew more naive and helpless against feminine wiles. In *Every Saturday*'s 21 July 1866 short story "Married in Spite of Himself," a twenty-three-year-old curate finds himself drawn "bitter, disgusted, dissatisfied" to the altar by wicked "Lizzie," who has lured him with *Punch* croquet cartoons featuring "striped petticoats" and visible ankles (70). This escalation of a now-familiar refrain suggests that innocent men could find themselves matrimonially trapped by the seductive power of croquet artwork alone. Husband-hunters need not risk their own modesty at all!

Perhaps nothing rationalized the press's insinuations quite as noticeably as Alexander and Macnab's tantalizing croquet petticoat advertisements. The 1 April 1865 *Scotsman* announced that this purveyor "embrac[ed] all the Latest Novelties in Croquet Petticoats," which it would sell at deeply discounted prices: among other items, "bordered petticoats" four yards wide and forty-four inches long were marked down from 5s. 11d. to 2s. 9-1/2d., while the "Very New Mohair Petticoatings, in [one-inch] Stripes," could be had for 1s. 11-1/2d. rather than the "regularly charged 2s. 6d." (6). Pointedly capitalizing the many "PETTICOATS" and "PETTICOATINGS," Alexander and Macnab compensated for their advertisements' lack of artwork with eye-catching, titillating repetition. Further, their detailed and alluring descriptions appear to have inspired contemporary periodical fiction illustrators. In its October 1865 number, for example, *The Peterson Magazine* accompanied its first installment of Frank Lee Benedict's "Coquette vs. Croquet" with "The Game of Croquet," a woodcut featuring striped, bordered, *and* embroidered petticoats (see figure 5.3). Alexander and Macnab's low April prices may have attracted early buyers, but naturally the bargains did not last. On 19 February 1866, the *Edinburgh Evening Courant* noted that the firm had discounted its four-yards-wide "Rich Light Ground Embroidered Croquet

Figure 5.3. "The Game of Croquet," from the 1865 *Peterson's Magazine* first installment of Frank Lee Benedict's "Coquette vs. Croquet," features female players' tempting array of petticoats. Collection of Catherine S. Blackwell.

Petticoats" from 12s 9d. to 6s 11-1/2d. ("Alexander" 3). While prices fluctuated seasonally and likely reflected available stock, the days of buying striped and otherwise fancy croquet "petticoatings" for less than 2s. were a distant memory by early 1866.

Such goods seem laughably affordable today, especially in the absence of appropriate fiscal context. Their cost becomes much more sobering when compared to a routine nineteenth-century budget component: servant's wages. Petticoat and croquet boot prices rose swiftly and steadily, but the period's most popular household management guide still advocated the same serving-class wages in 1863 it had recommended two years earlier. According to the redoubtable Mrs. Isabella Beeton, a woman making "no extra allowance [. . .] for Tea, Sugar, and Beer" should pay her lady's maid a yearly wage of between £12 and £25; her "maid-of-all-work" between £9 and £14 per year; and her scullery maid between £5 and £9 annually (8). Various factors affected these recommendations, of course, including a house's location and an employee's length of service. Nevertheless, the implications are clear. A lady opting for one good pair of Balmorals and a single embroidered petticoat might spend almost as much *for those two items alone* as she paid her entry-level lady's maid for approximately three weeks' work and almost twice her inexperienced scullery maid's monthly wage.

The prices commanded by the most highly sexualized female croquet attire and the staggering number of relevant advertisements strongly suggest that the popular press had been at least partly right all along: ladies *did* actively vie for lustful male attention on the croquet-lawns. Additionally, they were willing to pay handsomely for the privilege of publicly testing modesty's limits. While some women doubtless wished only to set or follow prevailing fashion trends—and, of course, flirt—many more almost certainly viewed their costly boot-and-petticoat expenses as canny investments toward securing appropriate spouses. Nor should this concept shock modern readers' sensibilities, given nineteenth-century attitudes about fiscally advantageous matrimony and society's tireless focus on the marriage market. That newspapers so often satirized these aspects of the game merely reflects its prevalence and popularity. Notwithstanding periodicals' sly allusions, both sexes likely deemed croquet a perfectly acceptable forum for both modern mixed-gender competition and preliminary romantic overtures. And it was novelists who advanced this brave new world's most important discussions about rules and gendered social codes.

Flirts and Cheats: Anthony Trollope's *Small House at Allington*

By the time *The Cornhill Magazine* published the first installment of Trollope's *Small House at Allington* in September 1862, croquet mania had moved well beyond its infancy. Given such a robust sporting culture, it seems reasonable for Trollope to make his heroine Lily Dale meet future love interest Adolphus Crosbie on the croquet-ground and then promptly debate the rules with him. Although Crosbie initially lacks skill, his previous experience and the game's simplicity soon embolden him to challenge Lily, its acknowledged "queen" (Trollope 20). Contemporary accounts suggest that limited rules frequently prompted such interpretive quarrels, even among players who were not well acquainted with one another. In his study of nineteenth-century croquet and gendered cheating, Jon Sterngrass calls Lily's and Crosbie's disputes the "inevitable" result of competition (402). This assessment neatly reflects human nature while tacitly acknowledging the awkwardness with which young men and women gradually adapted to the new mixed-gender sport. Yet for Crosbie and Lily, competition swiftly develops first into romance and then engagement, a shift that R. M. Lewis says reveals the couple's regulatory squabbles as "part of [their] larger war of hearts and minds" (370). Some couples presumably build successful relationships on such foundations, but Trollope's lovers fail miserably, probably for several reasons. As Deborah Denenholz Morse notes, their courtship unfolds exclusively at Allington—Lily's natural habitat and Crosbie's very occasional rustic holiday destination (18). This fact underscores the young couple's fundamental philosophical differences and their physical separation. The country lass honors her commitment and by extension societal rules whereas the city lad swiftly breaks them, abandoning Lily for an aristocratic bride he wrongly assumes will enrich him. In discussing *The Small House*, nineteenth-century critics focused particularly on Lily's steadfastness, Crosbie's perfidy, and the pair's ill-fated match. Summing up the reviewers' collective disgust, the 2 April 1864 *Illustrated Times* book critic "[wondered] how the poor child contrived to become so much attached to this snob in a few weeks; [and] how the snob came to jilt her" for another penniless woman (Review 14). No period review comments either on croquet or its rules, suggesting that contemporary critics found the motif unimportant, unconvincing, or completely unnoticeable given croquet's sheer ubiquity.

Although Lily Dale does not overtly set her cap at Crosbie, *The Small House* trades heavily on both the game's pervasiveness and its well-recognized ties to casual flirtation. These qualities jointly frame the Dale-Crosbie romance and predetermine its fate: croquet throws Lily and Crosbie together but, as an artificial construct, reflects the inherent fictionality of steadfast true love blooming from a mere six-weeks acquaintanceship. Whether or not such affairs actually occurred, the period's newspapers and journals increasingly portrayed them almost as everyday events. The *Punch Almanack for 1863* cartoon in Figure 5.1, for instance, features six mallet-wielding "Offended Maidens" eyeing a flirtatious couple in the background ("Croquet" 1). Ranging from disgust to anger to sly knowingness, the Maidens' expressions suggest that the ladies (like their illustrator) have grown all too accustomed to such behavior on the lawns. For the gibe to provoke laughter, the scene had to ring true with *Punch*'s readership, a probability reinforced by the magazine's rich and regularly deployed repertoire of croquet-related satire.

On 25 July 1864, however, *The Belfast News-Letter* took a more ripped-from-the-headlines approach, breathlessly reiterating the *Queen's* report that Lady Florence Paget (the beautiful "rage of the park, the ball-room, the opera, and the croquet lawn") had thrown over her intended and eloped with the Marquis of Hastings ("Recent" 4). The piece does not place the errant couple together on the lawn, but arguably it did not *need* to do so. Given croquet's reputation for encouraging public flirtations and the press's constant allusions to it, readers might easily have associated the game with far more serious indiscretions than gentle romantic banter. Newspapers played along, portraying croquet-grounds as iniquitous honey traps. "Like the Pharisee of old," the 3 September 1864 *Saturday Review* warned, "young ladies want to be more seen of men. The cry is for more freedom, a wider field for flirting operations" ("Croquet" 298). In this description, the lawn becomes a battlefield dominated by women. Worse, the game transforms female players from enthusiasts to audacious minxes boldly flaunting their physical assets, a depiction many periodicals happily reinforced and embellished. On 1 July 1865, *London Society*'s "A History of Croquêt"—slyly attributing its barbs to "[c]ynical old bachelors and misogynists"—asserted that "men like the game [because] girls show their ankles [while] women like it [because] it fosters their conceit" (60). Here, women's sins are expanded to include vanity as well as immodesty and aggression. Modern readers cannot know how seriously the public took such printed claims and innuendos, but their sheer volume suggests a willing audience for such critique.

Worse yet, the press repeatedly alleged that young ladies routinely cheated at croquet. We see these charges in drawings and cartoons, many with no title or caption. For example, the March 1869 *Girl of the Period Miscellany*,[5] depicts a flirtatious "Mai[d] of the Mallet" who, feeling her male partner's gaze upon her lovely face, surreptitiously taps his ball with her toe (215; see Figure 5.4). Although errant Balmoral boots frequently took the blame for such maneuvers, many critics argued that expertly whisked skirts, improper mallet touches, or even weaponized rules altered

Figure 5.4. In this untitled image from 1869 *Girl of the Period Miscellany*, a coy "Maid of the Mallet" disadvantages her smitten male partner by slyly nudging his ball with her toe. Collection of Catherine S. Blackwell.

games' outcomes every bit as effectively. *London Society*'s July 1865 "History" baldly announced that cheating "has always been allowed, [and] is the prerogative of ladies," further complaining that "now any person can defend any [ill-gotten] position in the game [by] quoting some rule of the printed authorities" (62). In fact, the initial argument between Adolphus Crosbie and Lily Dale seemingly reflects a variant of this tactic. When Crosbie casually observes that his Shropshire friends play the game differently than do the Allington folk, Lily sarcastically retorts that "they don't play the game [legitimately . . .] in Shropshire" (Trollope 20; my addition). This taut exchange might signal Crosbie's attempt to bend rules, yet it might also reveal Lily herself as the bad actor.

In this scene, Trollope simultaneously reflects contemporary game tactics and demonstrates a kind of prescience. United Kingdom publishers released eleven competing croquet manuals between 1866 and 1870, a period that commenced well after the final *Small House* installment. Varying widely as to length and content, the competing manuals allowed individuals to claim protection under systems unfamiliar to their fellow players. Captain Mayne Reid's 1863 *Croquet*, for instance—the first serious challenge to Jaques's "laws"—sets forth 129 rules (and numerous explanatory notes) compared to Jaques's thirty-nine. Ironically, Reid's volume triggered rule breaking of a most serious and public variety. Several periodicals in 1864 and 1865 covered Reid's infringement suit against the Earl of Essex and his publisher Emily Faithfull for illegally reproducing *Croquet*, a case that peripherally involved Edmund Routledge because his *Manual of British Rural Sport* also propounded rules (see, e.g., "Croquet," *London* 256; "Croquet," *Athenaæum* 290; *American* 5). The 17 September 1864 *London Review* took Essex's case, vigorously defending the respondents and casting aspersions on Reid's "vigilance [in having] hunted down his *feminine* plagiarist" even as it rather grudgingly reported Reid's victory ("Croquet" 310; my emphasis). Reid's new compendium may have owed its success as much to notoriety as to its merits, but it encouraged the publication of a host of rule manuals, starting with Jaques's own enhanced 1865 *Croquet: The Laws and Regulations of the Game*.

Fair Play and the Fairer Sex: Lewis Carroll's *Alice's Adventures in Wonderland*

The Essex/Reid case might even have influenced Lewis Carroll's bizarrely violent flamingos-and-hedgehogs croquet match in *Alice's Adventures in*

Wonderland. A skilled player in his own right, Carroll had undoubtedly witnessed heated rules disputes; and he firmly believed that women cheated to win without experiencing remorse (Sterngrass 406). He even suspected young Alice Liddell of playing unfairly on occasion, describing her *Wonderland* namesake as a "curious child" who "once [tried] to box her own ears for having cheated herself in a game of croquet" (Carroll 12–13). Carroll may therefore have desired a single, universally accepted volume of stringent official rules, not trusting Alice (or others) to self-regulate. He also enjoyed a long friendship with John Jaques, his frequent companion on the lawns (Joe Jaques). Given their familiarity and the latter's extensive ties to the game, moreover, Carroll may have esteemed him as croquet's most knowledgeable and trustworthy arbiter.

Perhaps more to the point, Carroll's ideologies about conduct and duty rendered overly competitive female play wholly unacceptable to him. Michelle Beissel Heath notes that while Carroll disliked imagining Alice caught in a "never-ending tea party [or] badly played croquet," he deemed combatting "rudeness and violence" with genteel ritual an inviolable feminine duty (54). Well-conceived rules for a most popular pastime ensured honest, congenial play *and* reinforced womanly behavior and responsibility. Yet Jan Susina argues that Carroll's *Wonderland* promotes not rigidity but "a happy balance" between the dullness of a game with "[e]xcessive rules" and the "randomness" of one with few or none (424). In other words, players enjoy croquet games involving simple universal laws, wooden implements, and stable wickets. They do *not* enjoy struggling against rules that constantly mutate according to players' whims—not to mention flamingos, hedgehogs, and live "jacks" with minds of their own. Ladies who played nicely would presumably enjoy themselves without becoming angry or indulging unwomanly competitive urges.

Carroll's loyalty to Jaques and complex relationship to croquet may help explain *Wonderland*'s evolution from manuscript to published edition. Carroll gave his young friend the handwritten *Alice's Adventures Underground* as an early Christmas gift in November 1864, having already expanded his own copy while readying it for publication (Susina 422). Despite its many similarities to *Wonderland*'s murderous croquet match, the *Underground* version conspicuously omits Alice's cross observation that her fellow players "quarrel so dreadfully one can't hear one's-self speak [and] don't seem to have any rules in particular; at least, if there are, nobody attends to them" (Carroll, *Wonderland* 124). The line clearly reminds Alice, and her readers, to play congenially and follow the rules.

Carroll added that reminder even as Reid's infringement suit press coverage intensified. By doing so, Carroll likely sought to memorialize his own complaints: Jaques's intellectual rights were being cavalierly disregarded, and nobody *could* properly adhere to contradictory rulebooks. If nineteenth-century reviewers noticed this subtext, however, they did not mention it in their *Wonderland* reviews.

The Feminine Art of Winning: Louisa May Alcott's *Little Women*

By the time Louisa May Alcott published the first *Little Women* volume in 1868, the debate over whether rules were fundamentally necessary divided America from England and, theoretically, women from men. In April 1865, for example, *Godey's Lady's Book and Magazine* established sound and motion as a way of distinguishing between fair play and foul: "A ball is considered to be fairly hit when the sound of the stroke is heard [but unfairly] 'pushed' when the face of the mallet is allowed to rest against it, and [propels the ball without] being drawn back" ("Croquet" 377). This description renders cheating gender-neutral, but the magazine's predominantly American female readership would have understood the warning that women—allegedly the most prolific cheaters—should avoid suspicion by hitting their croquet balls smartly and making their movements as noticeable as possible.

British men seemingly disdained such guidelines, however. The 23 September 1865 *London Review* argued against enforcing "rules 'according to Hoyle' in croquet," noting that the "majority" preferred their games "diluted with gossip and chat and love-making" ("Croquet" 327). This writer goes on to offer rather tongue-in-cheek support for the wholesome conversational opportunities a more relaxed, friendly game afforded to even the most bashful or socially awkward male players. Undaunted and unrelenting, *The Lady's Almanac for the Year 1866*, published in Boston, redirected readers' attention from flirtation to fairness, underscoring the point that a legitimate "hit" involved an audible blow rather than "a shove" ("Game" 123). This sound-based distinction between licit and illicit play neatly but tacitly vilified as unladylike the practice of "shoving" the ball with toe or skirt. *Godey's* then expanded upon its own earlier explanations, detailing rules and game layouts in a three-part "Croquet: Its Implements and Laws" series published in its February through April

1867 numbers. By summer's end, British men mockingly suggested that serious *female* approaches lent the game an unwarranted gravitas potentially at odds with *male* players' true objectives. On 20 July 1867, the *Saturday Review* critiqued Edmund Routledge's "New Handbook," challenging its claim that croquet had acquired a scientific dignity "unless the author proposes to add to inductive and deductive a new class of *seductive* sciences" ("Croquet" 77; my emphasis). The reviewer then shifts his attention from the "Handbook" to the game itself, aggressively urging ladies to stop worrying about rules and focus instead on dressing to attract male attention.

As a nineteenth-century woman of stout moral reputation, Louisa May Alcott ignored such masculine taunts and aligned herself with rule-abiding ladies' periodicals. At the same time, she followed Carroll in manipulating the croquet motif's flexible capacity for illustrating accepted conduct codes. The 1868 first volume of *Little Women* engages croquet's inherent violence and patterns much differently than Carroll's *Wonderland* does. Alcott makes her players divide into teams, label themselves "Englishers" and "Americans," and prepare for battle (135). In this way, she acknowledges the children's respective national allegiances, affording the "Americans" a chance to reinforce their Revolutionary War victory and the "Englishers" an opportunity to unofficially revise history. Thus, Alcott echoes the periodical press's croquet-battle allusions just as she flexes her patriotic military vocabulary: the Americans "skirmish" determinedly, "contest[ing] every inch of the ground as strongly as if the spirit of '76 inspire[s] them" (135). Alcott safely distances her adolescent characters from youthful aggression and the game's violence by locating both in the by-then-distant American Revolution. Instead of avoiding expected gender differences, however, Alcott wisely turns them to her advantage. Her players have a cheater in their ranks, but he is neither a "little woman" nor an American. Tellingly, a *British boy* commits the sin: thinking to check Jo's progress, Fred Vaughn gives his ball "a sly nudge with his toe, which put it just an inch on the right side" (Alcott 136). This phrase neatly rewrites the widely accepted "history" of cheating while reinforcing American superiority. At the same time, Alcott slyly nudges the British male periodical writers who consistently made such transgressions a strictly female undertaking.

Like Carroll, Alcott incorporates traditional lessons about women's duty and appropriate behavior, but *Little Women* showcases the "value of female citizenship and sport" in ways *Wonderland* does not (Beissel Heath

53). Jo, famous for losing her temper, realizes she must now demonstrate patience as well as technical obedience. Yet she does not sacrifice her inherent competitiveness, and Alcott does not treat this quality as unladylike. After confronting Fred with his misdeed, Jo scrupulously avoids a quarrel by redoubling her efforts to win fairly. Her sister Meg likewise exhibits feminine virtue by resisting Ned Moffat's persistent flirting (Philips 410; Beissel Heath 53). Here, too, Alcott turns the tables on male writers' tendency to identify ladies as flirts and men as innocent targets. Her "little women" thus properly fulfill their feminine responsibilities, merging them neatly with natural competitiveness and national pride. With these simple shifts in narrative, Alcott reshapes the ways young girls might imagine themselves on the croquet-ground. The little women's conduct, in fact, illustrates the patient feminine virtue Carroll hoped to foster in Alice without undermining a very human desire to win. Despite praising *Little Women* as wholesome literature for girls, though, nineteenth-century reviewers completely disregarded Alcott's subtle insights about mixed-gender croquet.

The Wages of Sin: Charlotte Yonge's *The Clever Woman of the Family*

Charlotte Yonge's *The Clever Woman*, which debuted in the January 1864 issue of *The Churchman's Family Magazine*, seems to have appeared at a moment when the periodical press's treatment of croquet became increasingly hysterical. Prior to her book's first installment, coverage had focused on the tame: occasional descriptions of society or church croquet parties; *Punch*'s few relatively mild croquet-related cartoons and verses, and Trollope's *The Small House* installments in *Cornhill Magazine* (for British readers) and *Harper's New Monthly Magazine* (for Americans). Though notices of croquet gradually increased during the spring, particularly as papers advertised the season's latest croquet sets, most popular press coverage remained comparatively benign. This changed in the late summer of 1864, when the 25 July *Belfast News-Letter* reported Lady Paget's elopement ("Recent" 4). By September, however, papers had started publishing some of the racier pieces I have already discussed.

But by the time these titillating croquet stories began appearing in the periodical press, Yonge had already committed some of Bessie's worst sins to print. The overtly moralistic *Clever Woman* comfortably coexisted with published innuendo and, perhaps, Yonge herself helped fuel the unchecked obsession her novel deplores. For example, chapter 9—in which Bessie encourages curate Mr. Touchett to become the "most fervent [croquet player] of all"—predates Lady Paget's elopement by some three weeks (Yonge 219). Chapter 15—in which she resolves to marry the aging Lord Keith not for love but for his money—appears just two days before the 3 September 1864 *Saturday Review* accuses young ladies of seeking "fresh outlets for the exercise of their powers of fascination" ("Croquet" 298). In the same chapter, Bessie casually announces that she intends to throw over Charles Carleton, whom she has long tormented and with whom her brother will later catch her, thus precipitating her calamitous tumble. The numerous croquet boot and croquet petticoat advertisements published contemporaneously or nearly so with these installments coincide with Bessie's tastes, but they do not foretell her rise and very literal fall.

Yonge's novel engages many of the same questions about womanly duty and conduct explored in *The Small House*, *Wonderland*, and *Little Women*. Bessie Keith exhibits scant fidelity and devotion compared to these other novels' heroines, though, and she makes little effort to behave responsibly. By nineteenth-century standards, wholesome literature could not allow such an unrepentant female character to escape unscathed. Kim Wheatley describes Bessie as "beyond redemption," observing that Yonge banishes her to "hell" for incurring extravagant debts, coldly wedding and then neglecting the wealthy Lord Keith, and spreading the "contagion" of her croquet addiction (906). Yet so harsh a judgment seemingly disregards the other characters' heartfelt grief and their assessments of Bessie's guilt. Sister-in-law Rachel, the novel's heroine, blames Carleton for Bessie's death; Rachel's husband Alick agrees, adding that "it was not thanks to [Carleton] that there was nothing worse" (Yonge 487–88). When pressed, the bereft husband admits that Bessie's character had disappointed him. Nevertheless, he too attributes accountability to others by pointing out that reckless spending is "not uncommon in the set she was too much thrown against" (Yonge 510). Even considering the fateful hoop, then, Wheatley's analysis overemphasizes croquet's relationship to Bessie's deeply flawed character, at least as the novel portrays it.

Beissel Heath diverges from Wheatley, arguing that *The Clever Woman*'s noncondemnation of croquet itself and Yonge's positive portrayal of it elsewhere firmly tie Bessie's "moral lapses" not to the game but to the "lack of moderation" her obsession for it reveals (51). In this elegantly succinct assessment, Bessie's croquet passion neatly dovetails with her penchant for compulsive spending and flirting. Conversely, Livia Arndal Woods's more recent analysis identifies the "mallet and hoop [as] crudely obvious sexual symbols," pointing to the "croquet field [as] the site of a promiscuous mixing of the sexes, avoidance of feminine duty, [and the female body's threat to] modesty, morality, and future wellbeing" (47). From this perspective, croquet emblematizes not only Bessie's errant sexuality and irresponsibility but *all* women's innate immorality. Woods's theory thus coincides with Wheatley's by magnifying Bessie and her croquet addiction while minimizing Yonge's other characters, including the clever women whose association with the game remains irreproachable. That croquet could simultaneously represent female innocence and damnation-worthy vice seems troubling at best.

Moreover, Yonge's contemporaries would almost certainly have wondered why these modern critics would bother arguing over the game or this character at all. Neither Bessie's flawed nature nor her absurdly dangerous wicket garners a single comment in *The Athenæum*'s 8 April 1865 review (Review 489). As if to explain these omissions, the 10 April 1865 *Pall Mall Gazette* describes her as a tiresomely instructive "impersonation" whose "gay, giddy [and flirtatious]" personality makes her "a not very dutiful or affectionate wife [who] neglects her husband in his illness" (Review 11). Bessie possesses few or no redeeming qualities, in other words, but she does not behave egregiously enough to shock or even interest contemporary readers. Further, the review suggests that she probably did not promote the feminine soul-searching Yonge hoped to inspire. Touching on the novel in its brief 1868 omnibus review of "Our Heroines," finally, *The Ladies' Cabinet of Fashion* merely comments that "[p]retty bright Bessie appeals to our sympathies" ("Our" 89). This remark does little more than raise a few mildly thought-provoking questions, such as why readers—or at least this reviewer—sympathized with the thoughtless, immoral character at all and whether such a response ultimately undermined her power as a cautionary example. Additionally, reviews of this novel share with those of Trollope's *The Small House* a non-acknowledgment of croquet itself. Simply put, neither Bessie Keith's addiction to the game nor croquet's role in her death particularly concerned nineteenth-century reviewers, who theoretically reflected the average reader's reactions to her.

"Croquet! Seductive, sweet game!"[6]

Nineteenth-century literature's rich croquet imagery sensually immerses modern readers in the forgotten pleasures of lush, fragrant lawns echoing with youthful laughter and the sharp report of wooden mallets striking balls. As we visualize colorful petticoats and tidy ankles, we can almost see young people eagerly striding across the pitch toward new, less restrictive gender roles. We vicariously experience the game's unique challenges and the sheer fun its players enjoyed. These sensations easily explain Victorian-era Britons' and Americans' obsession with croquet. As I conclude this chapter, however, I find myself both perplexed and seduced by the many questions my research has raised but has not fully answered. Nineteenth-century writers and reviewers could not have anticipated our modern confusion, of course, but they left behind them inexplicably conflicting descriptions of croquet culture.

In studying this phenomenon, I have carefully reviewed the limited available modern criticism as well as thousands of pages published between 1858 and 1898: seventeen rule books; the four novels examined here; numerous issues of *Punch*, *Godey's*, *Cornhill Magazine*, *The Churchman's Family*, *Harper's New Monthly*, *Liddell's Living Age*, *The Saturday Review*, and other periodicals; many contemporary reviews; and the *British Newspaper Archive*'s entire collection for the forty-year period. Nevertheless, I cannot definitively prove whether or not any serious injuries (let alone deaths) occurred on croquet lawns or quantify female (or male) cheating. Nor can I confidently estimate the average woman's annual croquet-specific crinoline and boot expenditures or assess the game's true place in the Victorian marriage market and mores. Evolving concepts of "news" media only enhance my uncertainty. Today's hefty multipage daily or weekly papers and websites bear almost no resemblance to the nineteenth century's very short, advertisement-centric newspapers. Simply put, the scarcity of meaningful facts requires the modern scholar to take somewhat speculative analytical leaps.

From our twenty-first-century perspective, moreover, the 1860s popular press seemingly answers such questions quite differently than do 1860s novels. That comes as no surprise, at least not at first blush. We should expect the era's periodicals to explore issues lightly or even satirically, one might argue, and its novels to probe more deeply or with greater seriousness. After all, today's sports-related magazines, ezine light fiction, and situation comedies entertain while serious novels and films provoke thought, shared subject matter notwithstanding. But here the analogy ends. Whereas we can evaluate *modern* fiction by exploring reception and the factual bases of fictionalized events, the same cannot be said of Victorian-era croquet literature. The novels discussed here drew contemporary reviews focused primarily on plot synopsis, brief character descriptions, and very limited critical assessment. Period news coverage, meanwhile, rarely extends beyond the topics of politics and crime.

Perhaps more importantly, many nineteenth-century book reviews evaluate even serious novels from the pages of lighthearted periodical press. This placement necessarily affects their tone and quality, as sharp criticism and factual correction would chime harshly against neighboring columns' playful satire and fashion news. Still, both novels and the press obviously showcase croquet—a game society and entrepreneurs alike clearly adored. Why, then, did period reviewers *alone* completely disregard it when evaluating tales that so painstakingly use the game to teach important social lessons? Here I must speculate, especially as this question relates to Bessie's overtly ludicrous death: croquet's complete absence from nineteenth-century criticism suggests a tacit (or perhaps even explicit) agreement to ignore the motif. We see it with our modern eyes, of course, but that almost certainly stems from croquet's absence from our own lives. Yet I suspect nineteenth-century readers noticed the gap as well. Although they might not have associated *Small House*, *Wonderland*, or *Little Women* with croquet-rulebook publishing wars, they probably internalized those novels' lessons about rules and proper social interaction. And while Yonge's bizarre death scene may not have inspired readers' earnest introspection, it surely forced them to weigh Bessie's fatal weaknesses against the prevailing croquet mania playing out around them and in the press. Without the periodical press, finally, novelists might never have made Lily, Alice, Jo, and Bessie play the popular game at all. Had they not, they would have deprived us of intriguing nineteenth-century cultural insights and ultimately left us much the poorer.

Notes

1. The title's "treacherous wire portal" quote is borrowed from "Immorality."

2. As Erin N. Bistline notes in chapter 3, Erica Munkwitz has identified fox hunting as one of the period's only other socially acceptable mixed-gender sports and games (97).

3. Maurice Suckling's quantitative analysis (chapter 11) demonstrates croquet's substantial presence in the Games Research Database's nineteenth-century games listings (265).

4. A "croquet" is a maneuver by which a player can legitimately move an opponent's ball. To execute the move, she positions her ball against the other, places her foot upon her own ball, and then strikes it sharply ("Croquet, v.," *OED Online*).

5. Edited by "Miss Echo," variously identified as Letitia Elizabeth Landon (who died in 1838) and Eliza Lynn Linton. Drawing in part from Linton biographer George Somes Layard's account, Kristine Moruzi describes the *Miscellany* as a lightly satirical response to Linton's anonymous and damning March 1868 *Saturday Review* article, "The Girl of the Period" (9). Layard quotes *Punch* contributor Joseph Ashby-Sterry's claim that the journal was edited by Frank Vizetelly, an *Illustrated London News* artist and correspondent (143; Stephen 386). For her part, Moruzi agrees that most *Miscellany* contributors were male but limits Vizetelly's role to that of illustrator (12).

6. See "Awfully Nice" 31.

Works Cited

Alcott, Louisa May. *Little Women*. New York: Library of America, 2005.

"Alex B. Clark's Family Boot and Shoe Manufacturer." *Marylebone Mercury*. 7. 334 (9 January 1864): 1.

"Alexander and Macnab's Grand Opening, Edinburgh." *The Scotsman*. 3056 (1 April 1865): 6.

"Alexander & Macnab's Great Sale." *Edinburgh Evening Courant*. 24102 (19 February 1866): 3.

American Literary Gazette and Publisher's Circular. 4. 5 (2 January 1865): 5.

"Awfully Nice." *The Girl of the Period Miscellany*. 1 (March 1869): 31.

Beeton, Mrs. Isabella. *The Book of Household Management*. London: S. O. Beeton, 1863.

Beissel Heath, Michelle. "Not 'All Ridges and Furrows' and 'Uncroquetable Lawns': Croquet, Female Citizenship, and 1860s Domestic Chronicles." *Critical Survey* 24. 1 (2012): 43–56.

Carroll, Lewis. *Alice's Adventures in Wonderland*. Boston: Lee and Shepard, 1869.

———. *Alice's Adventures Underground: Being a Facsimile of the Original MS. Book Afterwards Developed into "Alice's Adventures in Wonderland."* London: Macmillan and Company, 1886.

"Croquet." *The Athenæum*. 1923 (3 September 1864): 290.

"Croquet." *The London Review*. 9. 218 (3 September 1864): 256.

"Croquet." *The London Review*. 9. 220 (17 September 1864): 310.

"Croquet." *The London Review*. 11. 273 (23 September 1865): 326–28.
"Croquet." *Punch's Almanack for 1863*.
"Croquet." *The Saturday Review*. 18. 462 (3 September 1864): 297–98.
"Croquet: Its Implements and Laws." *Godey's Lady's Book and Magazine*. 74. 440 (February 1867): 141–43; 441 (March 1867): 235–36; 442 (April 1867): 235–36.
"Croquet. The Rules of the Game of Croquet." *Godey's Lady's Book and Magazine*. 70. 30 (April 1865): 377.
"Croquet, v." *OED Online*. Oxford University Press. December 2018. www.oed.com/view/Entry/44799.
"The Croquet Season." *The Saturday Review*. 24. 612 (20 July 1867): 77–78.
"The Game of Croquet." *The Illustrated London News*. 35. 986 (6 August 1859): 15.
"The Game of Croquet." *The Morning Post*. 26966 (22 May 1860): 1.
"The Game of Croquet." *Peterson's Magazine*. 48. 4 (October 1865): n.p.
"The Game of Croquet. Written for the Lady's Almanac." *The Lady's Almanac for the Year 1866*. Boston: George Coolidge, 1865. 112–28.
"A History of Croquêt." *London Society. An Illustrated Magazine of Light and Amusing Literature for the Hours of Relaxation*. 8 (July 1865): 58–64.
"The Immorality of Croquet." *The Saturday Review*. Rpt. *Littell's Living Age*. 7th ser. 1. 2832 (15 October 1898): 199–200.
"The Irish Exhibition." *The Irish Times, and Daily Advertiser*. 6. 2401 (30 June 1864): 3.
[J. and W. Jeffery and Co.] *Liverpool Daily Post*. 12. 3672 (18 April 1867): 1.
"James Butler, Boot and Shoe Manufacturer, 28 Nassau-Street." *Dublin Weekly Nation*. 21. 48 (23 July 1864): 2.
"James Butler, (late Nassau street, Now 5 Upper Sackville street." *The Irish Times and Daily Advertiser*. 7. 2689 (3 June 1865): 3.
Jaques, Joe. "Jaques of London, the Company that Invented Croquet, Ping Pong and Happy Families." *The Telegraph*. 19 June 2014.
Jaques, John. *Croquet: The Laws and Regulations of the Game, with a Description of the Implements, Etc. Etc. Illustrated with Diagrams and Engravings*. London: Jaques and Son, 1862.
———. *Croquet: The Laws and Regulations of the Game, with a Description of the Implements, Etc. Etc. Illustrated with Diagrams and Engravings*. London: Jaques and Son, 1865.
"The Ladies' Corner." *Chambers's Journal*. Rpt. *Kentish Gazette*. 177. 48 (29 November 1864): 2.
Layard, George Somes. *Mrs. Lynn Linton: Her Life, Letters, and Opinions*. London: Bethune & Co., 1901. 142–43.
Lewis, R. M. "American Croquet in the 1860s: Playing the Game and Winning." *Journal of Sport History* 18. 3 (Winter 1991): 365–86.
"The Literature of Croquet." *The Reader*. 4. 94 (15 October 1864): 469–70.

"Maid of the Mallet." *The Girl of the Period Miscellany*. 1 (March 1869): 212–16. Image at 215.
"Married in Spite of Himself." *Every Saturday*. 2. 29 (July 21, 1866): 69–70.
[Martin, C. E.] "The New Registered Croquet Boot for the Lawn or the Sea-side." *The Derbyshire Advertiser and Journal*. 22. 1122 (26 July 1867): 4.
Morse, Deborah Denenholz. "Broken English Pastoral: *The Small House at Allington* 1864." *Reforming Trollope: Race, Gender, and Englishness in the Novels of Anthony Trollope*. Burlington: Ashgate, 2013. 13–38.
Moruzi, Kristine. "Fast and Fashionable: The Girls in *The Girl of the Period Miscellany*." *Australasian Journal of Victorian Studies* 14. 1 (2009): 9–18.
"New Out-Door Game—Croquet." *The Illustrated London News*. 33. 929 (31 July 1858): 21.
"The New Out-Door Game, Croquêt." *The Morning Post*. 26013 (15 May 1857): 1.
"Oh, How Kind!!" *Punch, or the London Charivari*. 48 (1 July 1865): 261.
"Our Croquet Party." *North Wales Chronicle*. 38. 1915 (18 June 1864): 3.
"Our Heroines." *The Ladies' Cabinet of Fashion*. Vol. 33. 2nd Ser. 1868. 89–90.
Philips, Anne K. " 'Fun Forever'? Toys, Games, and Play in Louisa May Alcott's *Little Women*." *American Journal of Play* 2. 4 (Spring 2010): 401–18.
"R. and J. Dick's, Haymarket." *Leicester Mercury*. 29. 1451 (2 January 1864): 1.
"The Recent Elopement and Marriage in High Life." *Belfast News-Letter*. 126. 32,838 (25 July 1864): 4.
Reid, Captain Mayne. *Croquet*. London: Charles James Skeet, 1863.
Review of *The Clever Woman of the Family*. *The Athenæum*. 1944 (8 April 1865): 489.
Review of *The Clever Woman of the Family*. *Pall Mall Gazette*. 1. 54 (10 April 1865): 11.
Review of *The Small House at Allington*. *The Illustrated Times*. 4. 472 (2 April 1864): 14.
Routledge, Edmund. *Routledge's New Handbook of Croquet*. London: Routledge & Sons, 1867.
"Section 8.—Croquet." *Manual of British Rural Sports; Comprising Shooting, Hunting, Coursing, Fishing, Hawking, Racing, Boating, Pedestrianism, and the Various Rural Games and Amusements of Great Britain*. 4th ed. London and New York: Routledge, Warne, & Routledge, 1859. 504–505.
"Skilled Native Labour." *The Evening Freeman*. n.s. 1352 (16 June 1864): 3.
"Society for the Relief of the Wilfully Blind." *Punch, or the London Charivari* 51. 15 (December 1866): 241.
Sterngrass, Jon. "Cheating, Gender Roles, and the Nineteenth-Century Croquet Craze." *Journal of Sport History* 25. 3 (Fall 1998): 398–418.
Susina, Jan. "Playing Around in Lewis Carroll's *Alice* Books." *American Journal of Play* 2. 4 (Spring 2010): 419–28.
"To the Editor." *The London Evening Standard*. 12517 (17 September 1864): 6.

Trollope, Anthony. *The Small House at Allington*. Ed. Dinah Birch. Oxford: Oxford University Press, 2015.

Wheatley, Kim. "Death and Domestication in Charlotte M. Yonge's *The Clever Woman of the Family*." *Studies in English Literature, 1500–1900*: The Nineteenth Century 36. 4 (Autumn 1996): 895–915.

"William Burrowes' Glasgow Boot and Shoe House." *Waterford News*. 15. 793 (1 January 1864): 1.

Woods, Livia Arndal. "Now You See It: Concealing and Revealing Pregnant Bodies in *Wuthering Heights* and *The Clever Woman of the Family*." *Victorian Network* 6. 1 (Summer 2015): 32–54.

Yonge, Charlotte. *The Clever Woman of the Family*. Ed. Clare A. Simmons. Ontario: Broadview Press, 2001.

Chapter 6

Acting Charades in 1873

Girls and the Stakes of the Game

HEATHER FITZSIMMONS FREY

In February 1873, following the festive Christmas holiday season, Grace MacDonald, age nineteen, created a home newspaper—*The Hastings Gazette*—with her siblings and cousins. Included in the *Gazette* is MacDonald's "[e]xperience at a tea party in a country town," an entertaining report of a January country party she and her sister attended. Her essay candidly comments on the clothes, company, conversation, and activities of the country party, including their evening charades: "After tea, charades were proposed and those who were to act soon being chosen retired to the fire lit bedroom to consult and arrange." MacDonald's account of the charades offers a glimpse of her experience of this popular but ephemeral game, but it also reveals how Victorians played the game, what the conditions of playing could be like, and what the stakes were for participants and audiences, particularly girls.

Playing the Game

Charades in the nineteenth century were quite different from the solo-pantomime guessing games we play today. The word *charade* likely originated in the Occitan word for "chatter or gossip," though when charades made their way from France to Britain in the 1780s, they were exclusively a solitary reader-based word game (Bryan x). Usually written in rhyme, charades were riddles that presented clues to each of a word's syllables as if each syllable were a separate word, then concluded the riddle with a clue to the word as a whole.[1] By the 1830s, although people continued to write, publish, and solve riddle-charades, some people were enthusiastically promoting "acting charades" (also called "charades in action" or "charade dramas") for social events in England, the United States, and France where the acting games supposedly originated.[2] These charades were not individual affairs, but instead group activities, where teams chose a word in secret, divided it into syllables, then played it out in scenes for the party as a whole. If, for example, the actors chose the word *fortune*, they would perform scenes illustrating *for*, *tune*, and the word as a whole, then they would invite the audience to solve the charade by guessing the word.

Beyond this general structure, how the game was played and the player's attitudes toward it varied considerably, as MacDonald's essay highlights. Positioned somewhere between a riddle, a participatory game, and a private theatrical performance, acting charades were usually performed indoors, typically in a drawing room where the furniture was rearranged to create a small performance space. As with home theatricals, the ideal space had folding doors or at least a single door that could be used to enter and exit the stage space. Rigging up curtains was desirable, but not essential: as guidebook writers explain, charades can be successful if the performers merely walk on and off the performance space. In practice, acting charades could be somewhat spontaneous or carefully rehearsed. Props could be whimsical or parodic, gathered opportunistically, or purpose-built. Costumes might be made from repurposed household items or rented. The intention might be to dazzle and entertain the audience of family and friends, to stump them, or to ensure that they guessed the word.

Grace MacDonald and the Country House Party

In 1873, at nineteen, Grace MacDonald was, by Victorian standards, a middle-class "girl": a female person, unmarried but still perceived as marriageable, and financially dependent on her father (Dyhouse).[3] Grace's father George was the well-known author of *The Light Princess* and *The Princess and The Goblin*, and his wife Louisa Powell MacDonald wrote plays for family to perform, sometimes for fun, sometimes for charity, and sometimes to raise money to bring the MacDonald family to Italy's healthful climate that she believed would help her family members suffering from consumption.[4]

The MacDonalds and their eleven children were also known for their amateur theatrical entertainments, charades, and *tableaux vivants*. In issues of their family newspapers like *The Hastings Gazette* and *The Reculver Record*, the young people often refer to their family productions, and in MacDonald's 1870 diary (at age sixteen), she makes it clear that she and her siblings were involved in all aspects of creating theatricals, from getting costumes and makeup ready to acting. MacDonald records in her diary that she loved such theatricals: when one particular performance of "Cinderella" ended, with no new ones to look forward to for at least a month, she complained, "all acting is over now so it will be hum drum now for a long time" (3.15.408).

An Unmarried Girl at a Country-House Party

In the essay she wrote for February 1873 *Hastings Gazette*, MacDonald presented herself eager to be sociable, to make a good impression, to meet eligible young men, and to make friends, but as also somewhat awkward and out of place. She recorded that she and W (her sister Winifred), wore "substantial dresses" appropriate for walking in winter weather because their hostess insisted "it was not a party." But the rest of the company wore muslins, with the exception of "the vicar and three boys aged twelve to fifteen who constituted the male portion of the few friends." Finding no one to talk with, MacDonald ruefully related that she "tried to make friends with [a] baby," only to make him cry. After returning the baby to his mother, MacDonald examined a photograph of a girl in an elaborate dress for as long as she was able, noting that she "was not very sorry when they were called down to tea." Not wearing a party dress, she was probably simultaneously disappointed and relieved that there were not more eligible young men in attendance. Her social situation was clearly not off to an auspicious start.

MacDonald records little of the tea itself: "Tea progressed as most teas do I suppose & though everybody seemed to find plenty to laugh at in the smallest jokes I am not aware that anyone said anything worth recording." Instead, she focused on what was to be the highlight of the evening: performing charades. MacDonald's wry tone and astute observations point to some significant performance markers that help illuminate the potential significance of the game of charades for young participants.

Preparing to Play

MacDonald's statement that "charades were proposed" reveals that the party guests had not already planned and rehearsed the riddles. Had the guests wanted to do so, they would have found ample materials to guide them. By the 1850s, the home theatrical publishing industry had created a range of niche markets, including home recitations, *tableaux vivants*, and full plays (Newey 97). And by the 1870s numerous charade-advice manuals suggested words, costumes, set design, and even how to make curtains for an at-home theatre.[5] Written for ladies only, or for children, or for mixed company, these books, intended to inspire young thespians, were part of a rapidly expanding market of books to support families, and especially women, who were increasingly expected to entertain at home, and who as Mrs. Valentine also noted in her 1869 *Games for Family Parties and Children*, "generally prefer[red] written ones [models]" (121). Even so, as Mrs. Valentine observed, "*[i]mpromptu* acted charades are very improving, and often quite as amusing as those learned and prepared before representation" (121).

The attitude toward preparation with charades was one way in which playing charades varied by the occasion and the hosts. The Brothers Mayhew in *Acting Charades: Deeds not Words* value limited preparation time, under which circumstances, "the mind must be exerted with high pressure-ingenuity" (x). Some books even try to combine both instincts. George Bellew's collection *The Art of Amusing* gives detailed descriptions of how to get up simple, brief, visual charades, stating that "our mission is not to deal much with the costly or complicated" but to provide "charades to be got up on the spur of the moment, which are not less entertaining than the more elaborate performances" (271). As Bellew points out, the nearly improvised charade-game could still draw from a published model. We see preference for written models as well in Annemina de Younge's *Joy; or, New Dramatical Charades for Home Performance* where she explains that her charades

> were originally written to enliven the winter evenings of a residence in the country. So much amusement was derived from learning and rehearsing the parts, and preparing the dresses, and the representation being very successful, the authoress was induced to think of sending forth her various characters to seek their fortunes in the world, hoping they might cause similar amusement in other families of charade-loving boys and girls. (v)

Like the hostess at MacDonald's country house party, de Younge hoped her charades would enliven the winter evening. But unlike MacDonald's hostess, de Younge believed that preparation and rehearsal formed a large part of the pleasure of the entertainment, and she treated her charades much more like an at-home theatrical than an ingenious guessing game.

Whether the charades were drawn from written models or imagined on the spot, these sorts of social and leisure activities were typically overseen by middle-class women who were trying to imitate aristocratic behaviors (Bryan 38). But because theatricals were often the purview of children, juveniles, and young people, I argue that a feminized element of childcare and education was frequently involved in this kind of entertainment. For example, Mrs. Pullan's 1855 collection of riddles includes acting charades specifically intended for the schoolroom; Mrs. Valentine's collection assumes the performers will be young; de Younge notes that improvised charades could be "improving," and the 1899 *What Boys and Girls Like* notes that not only do charades require "plenty of good temper" but since there are a limited number of principal parts, some children must take turns taking larger parts, and "if elder children are kind and thoughtful, they will try to make some easy little parts, so that their younger brothers and sisters may also join in the fun." Certainly, Juliana Horatia Ewing notes in her 1855 diary that she acted charades to "amuse the others" or that she "settled about the charades with the girls," demonstrating that preparation and caring for her younger siblings happened simultaneously.

The elements of care and creating easy social situations were both significant women's responsibilities, and as a result, Katherine Newey argues that producing home theatrical entertainments should even be considered women's work. Mary Isbell also discusses the significance of women stage managers and notes that whether men or women took on home entertainment leadership roles, they were given entirely different kinds of advice on how to manage and arrange theatricals, women being encouraged to emphasize the congenial social occasion, and the importance of rendering one's leadership invisible, while male theatrical leadership emphasized strong vision and authoritarian execution (24, 111). As women increasingly became responsible for organizing social occasions, parlor-room theatrical activity was a space where female leadership was welcome and often desperately needed. Female leadership and at-home theatrical activities were not synonymous in the 1870s, yet what would have been called "stage management," rather than stage-direction, was a popular activity among girls and women.

Since MacDonald's country house charades seem to have been decided upon somewhat spontaneously, the teams had little advance preparation and no written guidebooks to direct them. MacDonald and the other willing thespians left the drawing room to make a plan, and she notes admiringly that "Miss G—a tall young [*sic* . . .] seemed quite upto [*sic*] everything and planned the charade very well." Whether Miss G had already thought about the possibility of charades and had a word ready in her mind or not is uncertain, but based on the ease with which the charade was organized, Miss G may have had an idea that she was eager to try out, either from reading advice manuals, from witnessing previous charades, or from musings of her own in advance of the party. MacDonald, whose previous theatrical experience allowed her to judge whether the acting charade was well planned, notes that Miss G was in charge. At the country party, someone needed to facilitate a congenial social occasion, so having Miss G as the leader makes sense.

When MacDonald introduces Miss G, she puts in brackets "(who we had met at larger parties in this town at which she had neither acted herself nor allowed her brother Gus aged 15 to do so)." This statement is important for several reasons. First, although there was a significant consumer market for books about private entertainments and home theatrical activities, many middle-class Victorians viewed commercial theatrical activities with suspicion, and, as Newey puts it, "withdrew into the refuge of the domestic family home, [where] home performance became an alternate to public entertainments" (93). Yet, middle-class wariness and anti-theatrical prejudice manifested itself in multiple and inconsistent ways. MacDonald and her family might have played acting charades, performed plays for their own enjoyment, and even raised money through private home performances of *Pilgrim's Progress*. But MacDonald's older sister Lilia and her fiancé broke off their engagement because her fiancé's aunt refused to give him his inheritance if Lilia would not promise to stop amateur acting (Saintsbury 123). Even acting at home was considered unacceptable by his aunt, and many at-home advice manuals include a justification for the morality and educational benefits of taking part in at-home theatrical activities, no doubt directed at people like Lilia's fiancé's aunt.[6] Second, the fact that Miss G and her brother had not previously acted, but now Miss G organized the charade, demonstrates that some families' beliefs about home entertainments were not necessarily fixed. Third, since Miss G had not previously allowed her *brother* to act demonstrates that the concern about the appropriateness of theatrical performance, in their family at least, was not a gendered one. MacDonald's observations point to a shifting social landscape: how acting charades were played and performed could vary from home to home, indicating as much about those who played them and their communities as it does about how they understood the rules.

Kissing, Charades, and Mistletoe

Miss G and the young people at the party agreed that the word they would perform was to be Mistletoe, with three syllables, meaning four scenes. A drawing-room game of acting charades might include performances in pantomime, those briefly rehearsed with improvised spoken word, or scripts that were memorized and rehearsed. Guidebooks often emphatically suggest that one of these methods is to be preferred, and fictional accounts seem to suggest that there were different conventions among different social circles.[7]

MacDonald, however, and her fellow actors had no ideas for charades already and no written models: they left the drawing room to make a rapid plan. MacDonald was left with "two boys who were of course not much use," bringing to mind Charlotte Yonge's descriptions of parlor theatricals in which boys were either difficult to encourage to participate, or challenging to manage (*Historical*). In some detail, MacDonald describes the melodramatic storyline they decided upon and, in so doing, she makes clear that their performance was not pantomime, but semi-improvised. But in connecting the scenes into a single narrative rather than having three distinct stories, MacDonald and the guests adhere to Anne Bowman's notion of "the original and genuine Charade, of which the ideas or scenes employed suggest the several syllables and the complete word should naturally arise out of the other, and thus give harmony and point to the whole" (5). Their tale begins with lovers (Dora and Captain Smith) planning to elope and ends with an unexpected inheritance for Captain Smith, resulting in family support for the previously secret engagement to Dora. He celebrates first by kissing his lover, and then everyone else under the mistletoe, "but this scene was chiefly a jumble of kisses, Captain Smith kissing everyone all round in a rather wild and wholesale manner."

The stakes of this public display of kissing and affection are difficult to pin down. Mrs. Pullan's 1855 *Book of Riddles* gives some advice for pantomime acting including "affection may be denoted by energetic kissing and shaking of hands; unalterable love by wild glances at the ceiling and slapping the side with the hand" (98). The Brothers Mayhew suggest in their merry book of advice that "[i]f any embracing should be required in the course of the piece, it is—under the present arbitrary laws of society and mothers—better to leave this interesting process to husbands and wives" (ix). Yet the young people at this party were all unmarried. Were the boys too young to be considered consequential? Marah Gubar discusses the very complex and often conflicting views Victorians held regarding children, innocence, sexuality, and precociousness. She argues that Victorian creative cultural productions explored tension between childhood innocence and "otherness from adults," which clashed with a "vision of the child as a competent collaborator, capable of working and playing alongside adults" (Gubar 9). This unease encompassed childhood precociousness and sexuality, leading writers to represent "young people as complex, highly socialized individuals who (like adults) had to struggle with thorny issues of pressing contemporary relevance" (Gubar 181). Ambivalence and uncertainty about children and heteronormative romance may have given Captain Smith some license to kiss in a "wild and wholesale manner."

Games involving kissing (such as the game of forfeits) were also popular in Victorian drawing rooms, and of course, the mistletoe itself encouraged kissing. In a short story published in February 1876, Sir Luke (a rich and elderly uncle who invites his estranged family for the holiday) exclaims, "I want you young people to have an old-fashioned Christmas evening—blind-man's buff, forfeits, acted charades, puss in the corner, kissing under the mistletoe—and lots of it" ([Braddon] 332). Although one niece declares Sir Luke "vulgar," the youngest, Lucy, plays the games with enthusiasm, and in spite of her sisters' disapproval, she is the story's intended heroine. Placing kissing within the context of a game seems to have made crossing ordinary behavior boundaries possible, while increasing possible excitement for playing participants. Yet, if Lucy's sisters disapproved, and the Brothers Mayhew advise caution, young people would have to be careful about how they played and in front of whom. At the country party that MacDonald attended, there were no elderly women in attendance to cast judgment on the young people—as Gus kissed all the girls around him wildly, did that matter?

Emily Bryan, Pamela Cobrin, Shanan Custer, Emma Dassori, Ann Mazur, Megan Norcia all discuss ways that the subject of private theatricals could be used to promote conversation about particular ideas in the drawing room: perhaps reinforcing or subverting notions about Empire, appropriate girls' and boys' activities, women's suffrage, women's education, or alcohol consumption. In charades in particular, Bryan notes that writers such as Anne Bowman use the structure of the charade riddle to subvert expected narratives about marriage, such as how women negotiated their own desires for independence, the requirements of society, and beliefs about the general desirability of married life. However, at the party MacDonald attended, the way Miss G organized the charades meant "mistletoe" did not attempt to be subversive or radical. While charades certainly could perform the function of bringing complex ideas and conversations into the drawing room, just as they could bring professional theatrical styles and concerns into a private space, they could also operate in comparatively benign, conventional ways, reinforcing status quo ideas about what a "good" narrative might be, what constitutes a happy ending for the characters, and what women should desire. And, perhaps, these lower-stakes performances were socially valuable and easier to manage: MacDonald indicates that the audience enjoyed the charade and wanted more when this one ended.

Costumes, Props, and Performing the Charade

Even in a relatively impromptu charade like the one MacDonald describes, costume mattered. MacDonald tells us that she was to play Dora, the lover, while fifteen-year-old Gus played Captain Smith. One girl[8] played the sister although she was initially going to play the part of the mamma, but "she would have to put something on her head and was only allowed to act if she did not dress up." Here we can see the complex negotiations of at-home theatrical performance that young people needed to address if they were going to play the game, and particularly, we can see that ideas about "dressing up" may have been connected to "lying" in ways that merely acting may or may not be.

Even if a girl did not have to negotiate her family's anti-theatrical prejudices, costumes were associated with high stakes. While De Younge concedes that the tastes of participants might be otherwise, she notes very seriously, "as so much depends upon costume, it was thought that a few hints might be acceptable":

> The two Ladies might be dressed in the old style; dresses opening down the front to display a stomacher and underskirt, elbow-sleeves, rich lace, jewels, and a light, graceful looking mantle would also be appropriate for the garden scene. For the Count, cavalier style—short cloak, hat and feathers, ruffles &c., as gay as possible, and Alonzo must look as much like a gallant knight as he can. Both should have a moustache, either put on or corked. Very good feathers may be cut in paper and curled with the scissors. The colours worn by the different performers should contrast as much as possible. (*Joy* Act 1, first syllable, 3)

De Younge's very specific suggestions, reminiscent of advice for a home theatrical performance, are connected to ideas about "correctness" and fashion, championed by writers such as Mrs. Aria, Ardern Holt, and the writers in *Myra's Fashion*, all of whom provided ideas for middle-class women wanting to dress up, but also to make a good impression and to ensure that they did not appear foolish or awkward. Ardern Holt explains that fancy dress (or costume) gives a woman an excellent opportunity to show her charms to advantage but also explains that there are only certain ways of dressing that are correct, and some characters will only suit certain women—a fair woman, for example, must never dress as Cleopatra (*Fancy* 1, 2).

Girls and young ladies faced with the necessity of looking correct, appropriate, and charming may have been anxious about fancy dress parties, but advance planning could ensure that they made satisfying choices (Holt, *Fancy* 6). These notions contrast with those of The Brothers Mayhew who recommend innovation over exactness:

> We have known Louis XIV, called for in a full court dress, and only five minutes allowed for the toilet. [. . .] The most prominent characteristic of the costume must be seized and represented. In the Roman, a sheet will do for a toga; in the knight, the coal scuttle for helmet, and the dish-cover for breast-plate, make capital armour; and in Louis XIV, the ermine victorine wig for the well powdered peruke, and the dressing-gown for embroidered coat, would express pretty well, the desired costume. (x)

The Brothers Mayhew may, as men, be less attuned to the concerns women might have about the presentation of self even in games. Likewise, the jolly and fun-loving tone of the book diminishes the significance of being well-dressed and effectively on display for the game of charades. In this introduction, interestingly, the Brothers do not dare to describe how one might costume the ladies except to tease that "no expense should be spared, and every sacrifice be made, even though the incidents of the piece should include the upsetting of a tray of tea-things, or the blacking all the young ladies' faces" (10).[9]

Another male writer, Frank Bellew also supports less elaborate, costly, and planned charades, stating, "[c]harades of this kind, we are inclined to think, give more real pleasure after all, than the studied costly elaborations. They are perhaps not so pretty; but, gracious goodness! Where there are charming young ladies—in fact, pretty ladies of any age—what else could mortal man desire in the way of beauty?" (269). Yet regardless of whether costumes were elaborate or not, they appear to be central to the enjoyment and the playing of acting charades. Anne Bowman does not actually describe costumes, explicitly leaving them up to the good taste of the actors. The guest at the country party MacDonald describes (who was only permitted to act if she didn't dress up) was caught precariously between the notion that costumes could be fun and the anti-theatrical prejudice shared by some middle-class families, and she found a way to participate in spite of her family's particular interpretation of morality.

MacDonald does not describe the set or any props they used to act their charade, but the range of published advice about sets and props is as disparate as advice on how to act. Some, such as the Brothers Mayhew, suggest using placards that simply inform the audience where they are:

"There is also this advantage,—as each spectator with be his own scene painter, the views are sure of giving general satisfaction" (vii). Others suggest hastily painted backdrops are good enough, and others seem to indicate that the most important thing is that backdrops must be able to be changed quickly, since the game works best if there isn't a long lull between scenes. In G. E. Wyatt's novel *Archie Digby*, the boys rig up a green room and a curtain, but restrict themselves to a key piece of furniture to represent a scene (for example, a lounge chair for the lady (played by a boy) to sit on, while another boy tries to woo her. In the *Art of Amusing*, Frank Bellew praises the ingenuity of "a steam fire-engine to be manufactured out of a baby's crib and a tea-kettle; and Mont Blanc from two chairs, a fishing-rod and a sheet" (275). Though MacDonald writes that her team had a separate room as a "green room" or room to rehearse in, the performances probably took place in the drawing room itself, without any special effects or curtains.

Rules of the Game: Guessing and Performing

After the successful presentation of "mistletoe," MacDonald records a rare thing in a home journal or diary: a description of theatrical failure. Aspects of charades and theatricals that do not work out as intended are often the subject of fiction (*Archie Digby*, *Vanity Fair*, Charlotte Yonge's "The Strayed Falcon," for example), but most frequently in the diaries and letters I have read, the participants say that they "went off well" or were a "success" without elaborating. Avoiding recording congratulations and compliments, like many others reflecting on the aftermath of a theatrical performance, MacDonald seems to suggest that their charade was completely successful: "No sooner was the charade over, than on our return to the drawing room they (the audience) wanted another & after the necessary amount of talk we left the room."

Who will guess and who will perform is also one of the rules that must be established in the game of acting charades. For their impromptu charades, the Brothers Mayhew explain that in detail how everyone playing should be involved in both guessing and performing:

> The two most celebrated performers of the party choose "their sides," and whilst the one group enacts the charade, the other plays the part of the audience. A word is then fixed upon by

> the *corps dramatique*; and "my first, my second, and my whole" is gone through as puzzlingly as possible in dumb show, each division, making a separate and entire act. At the conclusion of the drama, the guessing begins on the part of the audience. If they are successful, they in their turn perform: if not, they still remain as audience. (vi)

Phebe Westcott Humphreys, who permits spoken word, but also encourages planned improvisation, does not necessarily insist that everyone should take turns acting and writes in *What Boys and Girls Like*:

> The great thing in a charade is to try to puzzle your audience as much as you can. You must choose a word of two or more syllables, such as "Bagpipe." First you must act the word "Bag," and be sure that the word is mentioned, though you must be careful to introduce it in such a way that the audience shall not guess it is the word you are acting. [. . .] You must be quick as ever you can between the acts, for all the fun will be spoiled if you keep your audience waiting. (n. pag.)

Annemina de Younge's dramatic charades are quite long and much more like miniature plays. Rather than trying to confuse her audience, she writes that her charades could be considered a success because "it is supposed that the 'Words' are sufficiently prominent, as those which have been performed were guessed at the original representation" (de Younge v). When charades are rehearsed extensively, only those who have prepared in advance perform. But if charades are impromptu, anyone might be asked to participate, depending on the way that social event is arranged. In fact, the country party MacDonald attended may have suffered from a lack of social arrangement because the actors were simply those who were willing to act. In the second attempt at a charade, Gus and Miss G abandoned the acting team and joined the audience, but somehow, MacDonald remained. Her family experience with charades and private theatricals might lead one to believe that she could lead a group through a charade, but it does not appear that MacDonald was an able stage manager.

First, MacDonald attempts to blame the other young people with whom she must work: "I found that the other actors had deserted us and left me with only two other girls and two boys who of course were not of much assistance." Boys, as I've mentioned before, were often viewed as not very helpful in theatricals, but MacDonald also criticizes the remaining girls: "One of the girls was as flabby & simpering & soft as a girl could be (perhaps in consequence of having passed her Cambridge examination), and the other, though she did her best at trying to think of words & how to act them did succeed no better than myself." MacDonald's own obviously conservative viewpoint about women's education, clearly in contrast to her family's views about participating in theatrical activities, reminds us that families could be liberal-thinking in some ways, but not others. Unlike Miss G, who probably had a word ready to try, MacDonald seems not to have had an idea for a charade, and her group did not receive "much help from the hymn books which were the only books on the table." Many guidebooks profess to solve this very problem, as the editor's introduction to the new edition of Frank Bellew's *Art of Amusing* indicates:

> [H]as the reader ever been present at a social gathering, when a general awkwardness was experienced by all present, from the mere fact that no one knew any little game or pastime *sufficiently well* to direct its performance? The editor candidly confesses that such has been his experience very often; and when, last Christmas, he provided himself with some of Mr. Bellew's instructions, and performed sundry tricks and assisted in several games to the great joy of a party of young people, he determined upon re-editing the work for a circle somewhat larger than that of his own home. ([vii])

As an antidote to a lack of ideas, the published guides could be used as inspiration or actually consulted in the moment. Anne Bowman even advises tearing out the page of the book with the charade solutions on it so that the answers may not be available if several different groups of charade performers are working from the same book.

MacDonald laments that "after spending what seemed a long time in trying without success to think of something that would [. . .] & having received one or two deputies from the fast-becoming-impatient-audience, we made up our minds to give it up and return to the drawing-room which we accordingly did, feeling very small indeed." An experience of failure was compounded, no doubt, by the social expectations that MacDonald would be able to act as a leader, supporting the younger and less experienced guests in an amusing activity. The embarrassment, however, did not ruin MacDonald's evening, which included more games, snacks, sherry, before bundling up to go home in the cold. She concludes her essay with a question: "What degree of thinness must the dresses of the fairer sex be, and how many people must there be assembled before an evening ceases to be a few friends, and becomes an evening party?"[10] The charades were MacDonald's major interest at the country party, but anxiety about dresses and guests may have ultimately overshadowed her concern.

Naming the Stakes: Acting Charades for Victorian Girls

Playing a game of acting charades in mid- to late-Victorian England is difficult to describe definitively because it might, in fact, have been a range of different experiences. MacDonald reminds us that playing the game was influenced by issues about preparation, leadership, and guests who chose to be in the audience. The subject matter could be provocative and political, increasing the stakes for players, but it might just as easily reinforce status quo ideas about gender roles, the imperial project, and social institutions like marriage. Even when the subject was not provocative, while men and boys might be willing to dress in foolish ways, girls might worry about how they looked when they put themselves on display, thinking about issues such as "correctness," as well as showing off their own specific charms to advantage.

Hostesses may have used charades as a way to create a pleasant and amusing evening at home, but if the charades were unsuccessful, guests might be made to feel uncomfortable, awkward, and even partially responsible for an event that went less than smoothly. Gender roles and gender expectations further influenced playing charades: MacDonald comments that boys cannot be relied upon to be clever and innovative, and girls must lead in ways that offer social lubrication but without strident theatrical vision. Finally, even as home entertainment encouraged families to turn away from professional theatrical and musical events, charades and private theatricals were directly connected to these public experiences, which means that their moral baggage manifested itself in multiple ways in the drawing room. While charades and theatricals might make experimenting with some behaviors (such as kissing or even cross-dressing) more acceptable within the context of the game, families who were suspicious of the professional theatre might not be willing to participate in theatrical performances at home.

The fact that the young people MacDonald describes were negotiating their family beliefs about theatricals, acting, and costume confirms that these games were not uniformly received across the middle classes, nor were the responses static. Acting charades put individuals on display: participants needed to appear attractive and clever, socially appropriate and morally acceptable, all in front of an audience who might not only judge the success of the charade, but the performing participant. For an unmarried girl like Grace MacDonald and her community, a great deal was at stake in an evening of frivolity, and the significance of acting charades, especially for girls who needed to look good and correct, successfully manage social situations, and appear to be well-mannered and morally upright, could be weightier than even male contemporaries writing amusing advice might realize. Whether silent or spoken, impromptu or rehearsed, and whether they featured carefully chosen props and painted backdrops or the imaginations of the audience, acting charades had the potential to be an amusing part of an evening's entertainment, but they were also serious business for hostesses, participants, and audience alike.

Notes

1. Many of these charades-as-riddles are very puzzling, especially to modern readers unfamiliar with contemporary words. The following riddle is typical (and quite solvable): "My first descends from yon eternal skies; / A winged weapon from my second flies; / And in my whole these colors may be seen, / Yellow and blue, as well as red and green." Answer: Rainbow.

2. Emily Bryan asserts that "[t]he earliest example of the acted charade" appears in volume five of Mary Russell Mitford's 1832 *Our Village* (34). However, this form of entertainment and game circulated well before it found its way into print. Also in 1832 in the third edition of *The Little Girl's Own Book*, Lydia Maria Child includes one detailed example and describes Charades in Action, writing, "I think these plays are generally too difficult to be interesting to children; however, I will mention them that they may have an idea what they are" (170).

3. Victorians used the word *girl* differently whether it was to describe a middle-class or lower-class person. In a middle-class context, a girl could be a female person as young as five, or into her mid-twenties, unmarried but still

perceived as marriageable. In this cultural ideal, a girl was dependent on her father, while a woman was dependent on her husband. Of course, some girls needed to work outside the home as governesses or companions, but a state of dependence was the desirable norm (See Dyhouse).

4. Caroline Grace MacDonald (1854–1884) contracted tuberculosis in 1880, married in 1881, gave birth to a daughter, Octavia, in 1882, and died three years later. Octavia died of tuberculosis at the age of nine.

5. Katherine Newey describes the range of niche markets the home theatrical publishing industry was either creating or exploiting by the 1850s, some of which were written for ladies only, others for children, and others mixed company (97).

6. Charlotte Yonge and Christabel Coleridge's joint novel 1893 *Strolling Players* uses a range of characters to explore various middle-class ideas about amateur theatrical and semi-amateur theatrical activities. Yonge and Coleridge both participated in theatrical activities in their own homes, but Yonge almost never attended the professional theatre, believing that ballet was actually "disgusting" (*Womankind* 123).

7. Frank Bellew extends this invitation "to those who are fond of charades, and indeed to all those good people who love to be merry, we commend what the French call *charades en action*, or pantomime charades. These charades, as the name indicates, are acted, not spoken. The great rule to be observed is silence, nothing more than an exclamation being allowed" (274). The Brothers Mayhew similarly suggest that the charades must be done in "dumb-show" while Anne Bowman, Annemina de Younge, Mrs. Pullan, and Mrs. Valentine believe that scripts should be memorized to the purpose. In *Archie Digby*, the boys plan their scene, and improvise the wooing, which is clearly spoken word.

8. The journal is difficult to read. It might say Miss P. G., who may be the same Miss G who organized the charade, or may, in fact, be someone different.

9. Private theatricals and dramatic charades do include instances requiring blackface performance, but I have only found male blackface characters. Presumably most ladies would not allow anyone to put black cork on their faces—not for any kind of moral reasons, but because the look would be perceived as unflattering and/or comical.

10. The question was probably shared by many girls, and Ardern Holt published one answer, differentiating between various gatherings and the etiquette expected at each ("Etiquette").

Works Cited

Aria, Mrs. *Costume, Fanciful, Historical, Theatrical*. London: Macmillan, 1906.

Bellew, Frank. *The Art of Amusing: A Collection of Graceful Arts, Games, Tricks,*

Puzzles and Charades Intended to Amuse Everybody, and Enable All to Amuse Everybody Else. Edinburgh: John Grant, 1875.

Bowman, Anne, and other writers. *Acting Charades and Proverbs Arranged for Representation in the Drawing Room*. London: George Routledge and Sons, 1891.

[Braddon, Mary Elizabeth] "Sir Luke's Return." *Australian Journal*. 129 (1 February 1876): 328–34.

Bryan, Emily. "Nineteenth-Century Charade Dramas: Syllables of Gentility and Sociability." *Nineteenth-Century Theatre and Film*. 29.1 (2002): 32–48.

Child, Mrs. Lydia. *The Little Girl's Own Book*. 3rd Ed. London: Thomas Tegg, 1832.

Cobrin, Pamela. "Dangerous Flirtations: Politics, the Parlor, and the Nineteenth-Century Victorian Amateur Actress." *Women and Performance: A Journal of Feminist Theory* 16.3 (November 2006): 385–402.

Custer, Shanan Wexler. "Little Mothers, Mischievous Boys, and Good Little Christians: Characters in Children's Parlor Plays in American, 1858–1903." *Catholic Theatre and Drama: Critical Essays*. Edited by Kevin J. Wetmore Jr. Jefferson, NC: McFarland & Co, 2010.

Dassori, Emma. "Performing the Woman Question: The Emergence of Anti-Suffrage Drama." *ATQ: American Transcendental Quarterly* 19.4 (2005): 301–17.

De Younge, Annemina. *Joy; or, New Dramatical Charades for Home Performance*. London: James Blackwood & Co. [1860].

Dyhouse, Carol. *Girls Growing Up in Late Victorian and Edwardian England*. London: Routledge, 1981.

Ewing, Juliana Horatia. *Diaries*.1855–1866. MS. HAS 41. Sheffield Archives, Sheffield.

Gubar, Marah. *Artful Dodgers: Reconceiving the Golden Age of Children's Literature*. New York: Oxford University Press, 2009.

Holt, Ardern. "Etiquette for Ladies and Girls—II." *The Girl's Own Paper* (26 June 1880): 407.

———. *Fancy Dress Described; or, what to wear at Fancy Dress Balls*. 5th Ed. London: Debenham and Freebody, 1887.

Humphreys, Phebe Westcott. *What Boys and Girls Like: Indoor Games, Outdoor Games, Charades, and Tableau*. Printed for the Author, 1899.

Isbell, Mary. *Amateurs: Home, Shipboard, and Public Theatricals in the Nineteenth Century*. Dissertation. University of Connecticut, 2013.

MacDonald, Caroline Grace. *Diary*. 1870. MS. III Box 15 Folder 408. MacDonald Collection, Beinecke Library, Yale.

———. "Experience at a tea party in a country town." *Hastings Gazette*. February 1873. MacDonald Juvenilia. Beinecke Collection, Yale.

MacDonald Children. *Hastings Gazette*. December 1873. MS III/ 14/402. MacDonald Collection, Beinecke. Yale.

Mayhew, Augustus and Henry (The Brothers Mayhew). *Acting Charades or Deeds not Works: A Christmas Game to Make a Long Evening Short*. London: D Bogue, [1850].

Mazur, Ann. "Victorian Women, the Home Theatre and the Cultural Potency of *A Doll's House*." *Victorian Institute Journal* (2012): 1–24.

Newey, Katherine. *Home Plays for Ladies: Women's Work in Home Theatricals. Nineteenth Century Theatre* 26.2 (1998): 93–111.

Norcia, Megan. "Performing Victorian Womanhood: Elsie Fogerty Stages Tennyson's *Princess* in Girls' Schools." *Victorian Literature and Culture*. 40 (2013): 1–20.

———. "Playing Empire: Children's Parlor Games, Home Theatricals, and Improvisational Play." *Children's Literature Association Quarterly* 29.4 (2004): 294–314.

Pullan, Mrs. *Book of Riddles, containing charades, enigmas, conundrums, rebuses, puzzles, anagrams, acting charades, acting proverbs &c*. Pastimes for the Parlour series. London: Darton and Co., 1855.

Saintsbury, Elizabeth. *George MacDonald: A Short Life*. London: Canonsgate Books, 1987.

"The Stage at Home." *Myra's Journal of Dress and Fashion*. 12 (1 December 1887): 658.

Thackeray, William Makepeace. *Vanity Fair*. London, 1848.

Valentine, Mrs., ed. *Games for Family Parties and Children*. London: Frederick Warne and Co., [1869].

Wyatt, G. E. *Archie Digby, an Eton Boy's Holidays*. London: Thomas Nelson and Sons, 1917.

Yonge, Charlotte. *Historical Dramas*. London: Groombridge and Sons, 1864.

———. *Womankind*. New York: Macmillan and Co, 1877.

———, and Christabel Coleridge. *The Strolling Players*. London and New York: Macmillan and Co, 1893.

Section III

Playing the World

Chapter 7

Dangerous Games

The Advent of Wargaming in the Nineteenth Century

ANDREW BYERS

While most games are designed for entertainment or pedagogical purposes, games can also be deadly serious business. Modern militaries, beginning in the nineteenth century and continuing into the present, have increasingly come to embrace the use of wargames for training and concept development. Wargames have a long history: created at least 2,500 years ago, the Chinese game now known under its Japanese name *Go* is the oldest surviving game intended to teach nobles, rulers, and military leaders the fundamentals of strategic problem solving. The Indian game *Chaturanga* is another ancient strategy game, and the likely ancestor of chess and other related games (Vego 116–17). Having rapidly spread across Europe during the Middle Ages, chess became a popular pastime, and "war chess" variants were developed in the early modern era to better reflect military developments and teach the rudiments of military strategy (Young 6–13). These early wargames, as with later, more complex ones, shared several traits: they attempted to simulate military problems that could be encountered by military commanders, encouraging players to attempt to solve them through gameplay; they codified the risks and tradeoffs that real-world commanders would also face in making their decisions; and they allowed players' decisions to be evaluated for pedagogical purposes during and after gameplay (Loper and Turnitsa 333; McHugh 2). Unlike most civilian games, wargames are intended to simulate or model the kinds of problems that military officers face in real-life situations for explicitly pedagogical, analytical, and professional-development purposes. This modeling or simulation element of wargames is one of the key differences between military and civilian games. As one recent text written for the modeling and simulation community in the defense industry defined it,

> Modeling is the purposeful abstraction and simplification of the perception of a real or imagined system with the intention to solve a sponsor's problem or to answer a research question. Combat modeling therefore purposely abstracts and simplifies combat entities, their behaviors, activities, and interrelations to answer defense-related research questions. (Tolk 7)

Wargames as models of war to be explored by their players thus serve a kind of bridge between purely theoretical classroom training, which, by necessity, cannot possibly simulate the actual experience of leading soldiers into battle, and practical experience, which is mostly available only during war or, to a lesser extent, resource-intensive field exercises involving hundreds or thousands of participants (Sayre 1–2). As Western militaries began to professionalize and systematize their bodies of knowledge in the early nineteenth century, wargames came to play an increasingly prominent role in how these militaries trained officers and developed new strategic and operational concepts in a rapidly changing environment.

Following the Napoleonic wars, the art of war was embraced as a science; the work of military strategists like Antoine-Henri Jomini received widespread attention, and the Prussian military's early-nineteenth-century reforms came to be regarded as heralding a new era of modern warfare throughout Europe and the United States. It is little surprise then that the early-nineteenth-century Prussian wargame *Kriegsspiel* (literally meaning "wargame") received so much attention outside Prussia. It offered the possibility of systematizing military science in tabletop exercises—rather than engaging in expensive and elaborate field exercises—that could be used to train military officers and develop new military tactics, operational concepts, and strategies. Austria-Hungary, Great Britain, Italy, France, and Russia would all adopt tabletop wargames, usually modified versions of *Kriegsspiel* in the 1860s and 1870s. The U.S. Army and Navy also came to embrace wargames, in fits and starts, in the decades following the Civil War.

This chapter will discuss the history of wargaming in Europe, centering on developments in Prussia, the global innovator in wargaming, leading up to the creation of the influential Prussian wargame *Kriegsspiel*; the transnational transmission and reception of *Kriegsspiel* (and related wargames) among the major powers and the United States; unique American developments in wargaming design and innovation; the institutional adoption, application, and resistance to wargaming in the U.S. Army and Navy; and some of the longer-term effects of wargaming on militaries.

The Birth of Nineteenth-Century Wargaming

The origins of *Kriegsspiel*—and modern wargaming—began in Prussia in 1811. The advent of tabletop wargaming came at a time in which the Prussian military was undergoing a long period of internal reform following its disastrous defeat at the hands of Napoleon. Among other reforms, Prussia began to restructure its officer corps to emphasize professionalism and open it up to the middle class; it also created the General Staff, a small, elite body dedicated to systematically studying war and designing military mobilization and campaign plans (Wawro). In an effort to better train Prussian officers for the conduct of war, the General Staff would later come to embrace the use of tabletop wargames. The creator of the original *Kriegsspiel*, George Leopold Baron von Reiswitz, invented a game to teach the rudiments of war at a time in which the Prussians were struggling to respond to the changing tactics of Napoleonic warfare (Hilgers 43). Von Reiswitz's game was soon adopted as a favorite pastime by Prussian princes, who demonstrated the game to their father (King Friedrich Wilhelm III) and helped popularize the game among the Prussian high nobility (Hilgers 43–44). Von Reiswitz's original game required an elaborate wooden chest of drawers whose top surface served as a space for gameplay (Hilgers 44–46). The game used wooden playing pieces to depict terrain features and military units, as well as an umpire, who would resolve the effects of combat and movement (Vego 108–109). Players would provide their orders to the umpire, who would then adjudicate the results of the players' decisions, updating the location and status of units on the table and providing information to each player based only on the information available to that player's units. The movement of units was not restricted to chessboard-like squares, but was designed to reflect accurate movement rates for what would be possible for actual military units on various types of terrain on a board (and later, maps), a key innovation of the game that made movement much more realistic than had been attempted in earlier games. *Kriegsspiel* included a set of complex tables for resolving combat: when units came into contact with each other, the tables would be consulted to determine combat attrition, based on range and terrain. These combat-results tables would also form the foundation for most later wargames. Dice were rolled to add an element of chance to the combat encounters.

Kriegsspiel and other wargames diverged sharply from civilian games and even quasi-strategic games like chess in terms of the object of the game. To be sure, each wargame player (or side, if multiple players were involved) sought to win the game by defeating the opponent on the simulated field of battle; however, the purpose of the game was not simply to win, but to develop and exercise professional skills and the kind of decision making required by military officers commanding real troops. As one Prussian observer put it,

> The well grounded decisions of the umpire and approbation of one's comrades are the only possible rewards. Whoever best follows up his movement, adopts the simplest and most natural means to the end, and departs least from the general idea of the operation will have won the match, even though he may have lost a few more pawns than his adversary. [. . .] The advantages they will derive from it will be to acquire skill in reading maps, in the selection of movements best suited to the different arms of the service, in the choice of positions, etc. The interesting discussions which are sure to follow a match will be of incontestable value in the study of the military art. (qtd. in Young 20)

These fundamental features of *Kriegsspiel* would form the basis for almost all subsequent wargames in the nineteenth century. In many ways, von Reiswitz's game would encompass some of the core attributes of war—the "fog of war" (uncertainty and information asymmetry in military operations) and "friction" (the disparity between a unit's optimal performance and their real-world performance in battle due to chance events)—later articulated by Prussian strategic theorist Carl von Clausewitz in his influential work *Vom Kriege* [*On War*]. The fog of war and the effects of friction (chance) on military performance would become two of the key features of almost every wargame from Reiswitz's early work to the present, sharply differentiating them from earlier strategic games like chess and Go, which contained no elements of chance or imperfect information for either player.

Von Reiswitz's son, Georg Heinrich Rudolf von Reiswitz, a lieutenant in the Prussian army, developed the original game further in 1824 by eliminating the need to use elaborate tabletop terrain structures and modifying the game to use standard topographical maps (Caffrey). Reiswitz the Younger demonstrated his revised version of the game to General Karl von Müffling, Chief of the Prussian General Staff (1821–29), who became an enthusiastic proponent of tabletop wargaming, purportedly exclaiming, "This is no ordinary game, this is a war academy. I must and will recommend this to the army most warmly" (qtd. in Hilgers 52). Müffling was true to his word, ordering that all army garrisons procure copies of *Kriegsspiel* and begin using it. A wide variety of wargaming societies, mostly composed of junior army officers, emerged over the next several decades; from these societies sprang many of Prussia's wargame innovators, including Julius von Verdy du Vernois and Jakob von Meckel, whose enthusiasm for wargaming spread as junior wargaming enthusiasts advanced in the ranks of the Prussian army (Wilson 6).

If von Müffling was the earliest major Prussian promoter of tabletop wargaming, then Helmuth von Moltke the Elder was the next. Von Moltke had been interested in wargames as a young lieutenant as early as 1828, even founding a wargaming club in Magdeburg (Caffrey). By 1857, von Moltke had attained the rank of general and had been appointed the Chief of the Prussian General Staff (1857–88); almost immediately, he began implementing a series of policies to increase the use of wargaming throughout the Prussian army. He required applicants to the Prussian War College—which trained officers for the General Staff—to include a letter from the applicant's commanding officer attesting to his ability to serve as a senior wargame umpire. Prussian General Kraft later wrote: "The ability to quickly arrive at decisions and the cheerful assumption of responsibility which characterized our officers in the Franco-Prussian War of 1870–71 was in no small measure due to the war games" (qtd in Vego 110).

After Prussia's dramatic successes in the German Wars of Unification—under the direction of von Moltke the Elder—led to the creation of modern Germany in 1871, the other great powers looked to the

Prussian military reforms in an effort to emulate Prussia's successes on the battlefield. Prussian wargames became an important element to be emulated by other militaries. Immediately after its defeat at the hands of Prussia in 1866, Austria-Hungary began to adopt Prussian wargames, without much modification or independent innovation, ultimately making weekly wargaming training sessions mandatory for officers and cadets (Young 28). Great Britain began to adopt Prussian wargaming for its own army in 1872, with the publication of *Aldershot*, a lightly edited English-language translation of *Kriegsspiel*, and a second set of wargame rules by British Captain Evelyn Baring based on the work of Prussian wargame designer Wilhelm von Tschischwitz. This latter game's preface reads, in part, "The increased importance which is now attached to [the game] may be, in some measure, due to the feeling that the great tactical skill displayed by the Prussian officers in the late war [the Franco-Prussian War of 1870–71] had been, at least partially, acquired by means of the instruction which the game affords" (Baring iv). Baring's game was officially introduced to the British army in 1883 by the Duke of Cambridge, with official publication of the rules in 1896 and 1899, and was adopted by U.S. Army Captain C. W. Raymond at West Point, who formed a wargaming society there (Young 27–28, 31). The Italian army first introduced wargaming in 1873, using a modified set of rules based on Prussian wargame designer Thilo von Trotha's work, which mainly emphasized training officers to maneuver hypothetical units of troops on maps. These map-maneuver games were incorporated into the education of staff and logistics officers at the Italian War College (Young 28–29). The Russian army began to incorporate wargaming into its training regimen in 1875 and 1876 to teach officers map reading, maneuvers, and logistics (Young 29). The Japanese fundamentally reorganized their army along Prussian lines during the Meiji period, following the Prussian defeat of France in the Franco-Prussian War. Handpicked by von Moltke the Elder, Prussian Major (later General) Jakob von Meckel introduced wargaming, among many other elements of Prussian military philosophy and strategy, to the Japanese army during his time as the Prussian liaison (1885–88) (Young 30). The French were late and unenthusiastic adopters of wargames: *Kriegsspiel* was introduced to some French army units in 1874 but not officially incorporated into the French War College's curriculum until 1899 (Young 29).

The Germans continued to innovate wargames in the late nineteenth century, and because of the German reputation for military prowess, these game developments also came to dramatically influence the wargames of other nations. In 1877, German Captain Julius Naumann published a new set of rules to address an artificiality of most wargames at the time: military units would generally fight at full capability until they were destroyed. Naumann's revised game mechanics raised the possibility of a unit's ceasing to function effectively after it had received some casualties but before it was utterly destroyed (Caffrey; Perla 30). This was an attempt to introduce more realistic morale effects of combat to wargaming, reflecting the common experience of combat units becoming "broken" and combat-ineffective long before every soldier in the unit had been killed.

Another, even more important, innovation was the development of what came to be called "Free" *Kriegsspiel* in a series of publications between 1873–76 (Vego 110–11). By the early 1870s, one of the limitations of *Kriegsspiel* had become apparent: some umpires tended to issue game rulings based on rigid interpretations of the rules, refusing to modify them based on common sense, which limited the acceptance of wargames among a broader audience. In response, other umpires began to unofficially modify their game rulings based on their own experience. As one German wargame designer put it, "[i]f after the wars of 1866 and 1870, the game enjoyed an upsurge, it was not due to the rules but rather in spite of them. It is doubtful if there was a single war game in the Prussian Army that was played according to the rules" (von Meckel qtd. in Wilson 8). Von Meckel advocated dispensing with dice altogether; while they were useful in generating random factors in gameplay—unexpectedly poor performance on a given day, the death of a unit's commander, misinterpreted orders—their use sometimes produced illogical results and complicated later analysis of individual game outcomes. Using some of von Meckel's ideas for streamlining *Kriegsspiel* gameplay, Prussian Colonel (later General and Minister of War) Julius von Verdy du Vernois published *Contribution to the Wargame* (*Beitrag zum Kriegsspiel*) in 1876, establishing Free *Kriegsspiel* as a new mode for playing the game (Vego 111; Perla 31–32). Though von Verdy's game provides a single, detailed scenario and set of opposing forces for gameplay, it also lays out an entirely new way of playing a wargame that does not rely on extensive use of tables, but rather presents the game as a kind of narrative thought-exercise worked through by the players, with the umpire adjudicating the results of the players' decisions based on his own judgment (von Verdy). After the widespread adoption of

Free *Kriegsspiel*, the older types of games were called "Rigid" or "Strict" *Kriegsspiel*, which continued to require extensive consultation of complex rules sets, a time-consuming activity that proved unpopular with many players and made frequent or casual gameplay difficult. In Free *Kriegsspiel*, players with combat experience were explicitly invited to ignore many of the game's rules, substituting their own professional judgment. While this made game adjudication more subjective, and therefore opened the possibility for contentious debates, it also made games less cumbersome and quicker. These rule changes also inadvertently introduced the problem of "command influence," which might occur when a player outranked the umpire, who would be likelier to defer to the higher-ranking player's judgment. These limitations aside, Free *Kriegsspiel* proved popular in Germany and abroad—for example, von Verdy's rules would be later translated from the French by U.S. Army Captain (later Major General) Eben Swift in 1897 (von Verdy).

Regardless of which set of rules were used, the German army employed wargames to train and test the effectiveness of various sizes of military units, from the smallest games that might involve a handful of infantry companies, a few cavalry squadrons, and a few artillery pieces per side to larger games that would involve a whole army division on a side (Vego 111–12). Even larger, strategic games were used by the General Staff and senior officers to plan whole operational plans starting in 1848 (the first strategic wargame used a scenario involving a war between Prussia and Austria, not unlike the actual war in 1866) (Vego 112). As Chief of the General Staff (1891–1906), Field Marshal Alfred von Schlieffen used wargames extensively, in conjunction with staff rides and field exercises, to design what would become the Schlieffen Plan, Germany's plan to defeat the Triple Entente in World War I (Vego 112–13). While invaluable for training officers and developing new operational plans, the German experience with wargaming helps highlight some of the limitations of wargames. For example, all wargame scenarios must be constructed using particular assumptions—e.g., enemy force compositions or level of resistance—that might not hold true in an actual war. Additionally, nineteenth-century German wargames did not attempt to simulate political or diplomatic aspects of war, such as the likelihood of British intervention if the German army violated the neutrality of Belgium (as happened in 1914). Thus, despite their long development, wargames remained decidedly imperfect simulations of complex political-military scenarios.

The American *Kriegsspiel*

Following the American Civil War, several U.S. military officers also became increasingly interested in the possibility of adopting a Prussian-style wargame in the United States. In 1866, Colonel Charles Richardson published the first of these, called *War-Chess, or the Game of Battle*, and Reverend Wilhelm of Pittsburgh published *Militaire* in 1876; both of these early American wargames were modeled on earlier European chess variants, which provided new types of chess pieces and board layouts, but beyond instilling a rudimentary sense of strategic planning, were not suitable for wargaming purposes (Young 31; Richardson). These war-chess games had limited utility for training officers and had already been supplanted in European military circles by *Kriegsspiel* and its variants by the 1870s because of their artificiality and inflexibility.

Many within the U.S. Army, including the army's commanding general William T. Sherman, opposed the adoption of wargaming by the army altogether. Sherman objected because the wargames of the day tended to rely on simple attrition-based models of warfare rather than incorporating rules for morale and leadership, as many later wargames would. Sherman's address to the 1869 graduating class at West Point makes this clear:

> I know that there exist many good men who honestly believe that one may, by the aid of modern science, sit in comfort and ease in his office chair, and with little blocks of wood to represent men, or even with figures and algebraic symbols, master the great game of war. I think this an insidious and most dangerous mistake. Science may test to a pound the strain on every chord, and brace, and rod of the most complicated structure, or it may separate the component parts of every mineral; but it cannot penetrate the hearts of men. The soldier in the ranks is not a block of wood or a mere unit; he is a man like yourselves, full of feeling and passion, varying in size, and strength, and all the attributes of manhood. As one man varies from another, so bodies of men vary still more, whilst certain characteristics pervade them all. The only schools where war and its kindred sciences can be popularly learned are in the camp, in the field, on the plains, in the mountains, or at the regular forts where the army is. You

> must understand *men*, without which your past knowledge were vain. (8–9; emphasis in original)

Sherman's opposition would set the tone for the U.S. Army's official position on wargames for the next two decades, limiting its adoption by the Americans, though there was very little other development in army operational art in the decades following the Civil War, which featured a massive demobilization and return to a miniscule peacetime standing army mostly stationed in small garrisons and far-flung outposts on the Western frontier.

Wargaming languished in the U.S. Army for the next decade, though development and wider adoption continued throughout Europe. The next American wargame would come from a junior officer, Lieutenant Charles A. L. Totten, who published his own wargame, *Strategos*, in 1880 (Totten; Perla 57–58; Young 3–5, 56–61). *Strategos* was unusual in that it was developed mostly independently of the dominant German wargames, offering what its author claimed was a new, unique way to simulate war. Compared with other wargames of the time, Totten's game featured two modes of gameplay: the "Battle Game" and the "Advanced Game." The Battle Game simplified gameplay, offering less detail—and less of an attempt to simulate the realism of actual combat—and was intended to introduce novice players to the concept of wargaming, gradually helping them increase their skill level as they moved into more complex games (using the Advanced Game) that involved larger numbers and types of units over time, with more complicated maneuvers. Though Totten claimed to have originated his game independently, *Strategos*' Advanced Game is actually similar in gameplay to *Kriegsspiel* and does not diverge significantly from the *Kriegsspiel* family of games. Despite (or perhaps because of) its independent origin, *Strategos* was ultimately eclipsed by German-derived games, and represented a dead end of game design that was not adopted and modified over time.

Two years later, building on the modifications to *Kriegsspiel* made by Naumann, von Trotha, Tschischwitz, and Baring, Captain W. R. Livermore published a translated and lightly modified *American Kriegsspiel*, a Strict *Kriegsspeil* game, which came to be the most influential wargame in the United States in the nineteenth century. Livermore's contribution to the game rules included an update to the original game's attrition tables for battle casualties based on actual casualty statistics from the German

Wars of Unification (1866 and 1870–71) and the American Civil War (Caffrey). (The original *Kriegsspiel* rules produced fewer casualties than the results of these new modern wars.) In addition to attempting to more accurately reflect the combat casualties produced in recent wars, Livermore also physically modified the game pieces to streamline gameplay and eliminate some of the calculations and paperwork generated during play by introducing new wooden block pieces representing different units that could be flipped to indicate casualties—some twentieth-century wargames using cardboard unit counters would include a similar feature—along with other blocks to indicate ammunition usage, unit fatigue, and field fortifications, as well as physical pointers shaped like arrows and swords to indicate the direction and volume of fire and direction and fire of movement, respectively (Perla 55).

Livermore acknowledged that these innovations did not speed gameplay as much as he would have liked, so he urged umpires to sometimes rely on their own judgment in order to streamline gameplay, as in Free *Kriegsspiel*:

> It cannot be too strongly stated that all these computations not only need not, but must not, be made in every case, after the players and umpire have had a little practice, especially if they are at all familiar with military operations. They are intended to facilitate and hasten the game and should not be so perverted as to retard it. (26)

Despite these technical modifications, broader adoption of Livermore's game continued to meet institutional opposition within the army, mostly due to its perceived complexity and the need to consult a variety of complicated tables and engage in mathematical calculations during gameplay. Regarding this complexity, one early-twentieth-century U.S. Army officer commented that

> Livermore's system is the best of its class; but it can not be readily and intelligently used by any one who is not a mathematician, and it requires, in order to be able to use it readily, an amount of special instruction, study and practice about equivalent to that necessary to acquire a speaking knowledge of a foreign language. (Sayre 20)

This is undoubtedly an exaggeration, though it seems to reflect a common sentiment among U.S. Army officers at the time that represented a considerable impediment to the wider adoption of *American Kriegsspiel*. Nor did Free *Kriegsspiel*, with its discarding of most rules calculations in favor of the judgment of individual umpires, seem to offer a better way forward for American wargamers, owing to the general lack of skilled and combat-experienced umpires available in the U.S. Army. One army officer highlighted this problem in an 1881 talk on wargaming at West Point:

> However possible such an exercise [Free *Kriegsspiel*] may be in Germany, it will certainly be found generally impracticable in our own country. In Berlin, where there are always many officers of the General Staff, who devote their undivided attention to the study of the art of war, it may be quite possible to obtain competent directors [umpires]. [. . .] In this country [. . .] [o]nly in a few exceptional cases would it be possible to obtain a director the superiority of whose experience and attainments would be so undoubted that his decisions would receive unhesitating acceptance. (Raymond 4–5)

The problem of experienced and respected umpires needed for a Free *Kriegsspiel*–style American wargame does not appear to have improved over the next two decades, with one army major complaining in 1900 that "[w]here competent umpires can be obtained, this system [Free *Kriegsspiel*] will do passably well. But, to fill the position acceptably, the umpire should have had extensive experience in modern war and should have mastered its teachings" (qtd. in Sayre 22). With the massive demobilization of the U.S. Army following the Civil War, the lack of other major military conflicts involving the army over the next several decades, and the engineering-heavy curriculum of the U.S. Military Academy at West Point in the nineteenth century, such combat-experienced officers who had made a systematic study of strategy and operations were in short supply for many decades in the U.S. Army, hampering the adoption of Free *Kriegsspiel*–style wargames in the United States.

Despite resistance to the wider adoption of wargaming by his fellow army officers, Livermore found an ally in U.S. Navy Lieutenant William McCarty Little at the Naval War College, one of the foremost early advocates of naval wargaming. While most nineteenth-century wargames were designed for armies, McCarty Little developed a naval wargame based on his conversations with Livermore and the work of British Captain Philip H. Colomb, Royal Navy, who designed *The Duel*, the first naval wargame, in 1878 (McHugh 27). Livermore and McCarty Little co-hosted the first joint U.S. Army-Navy wargame in 1887 (Caffrey). Opposition from senior officers in the army ended further participation by the army, though McCarty Little and other wargaming proponents in the navy continued to conduct naval wargames. These games took on three forms: a single ship versus ship combat (inspired by *The Duel*); a fleet engagement game composed of two rival fleets engaged in combat with each other; and a strategic game involving the entire navies of two large naval powers stationed around the globe (often representing the navies of the United States and Great Britain) (McCarty Little; Perla 66; Wilson 18–19). By 1894, naval wargaming was well established at the Naval War College in Newport, Rhode Island, under McCarty Little's direction (Perla 65–66; Barber). Secretary of the Navy Hilary A. Herbert (1893–97) visited the Naval War College in 1895, spending the bulk of his time there observing gameplay, and announced that he was "well pleased by what [he] saw" (qtd. in Perla 66). Throughout this period, McCarty Little and other proponents of wargaming remained convinced of its potential, as well as its limitations; in his address to the 1897 graduating class of the Naval War College, college president Captain Caspar F. Goodrich (1889–92 and 1896–98) captured both sentiments:

> I am confident [. . .] that you have derived much benefit from the tactical games. [. . .] Experience and study will improve this as well as the other games, so that they may more nearly represent the conditions of actual warfare. It should be borne in mind, however, that a reasonable approximation is the best we can hope for [. . .] because of the imperfections that must necessarily exist in this mimic warfare, its results can not be accepted in their entirety, but must be analyzed and digested before they can be made the basis of future campaigns. (qtd. in McHugh 48)

Despite its continued resistance to institutionalized adoption of wargaming, the U.S. Army did not entirely discard wargaming, and when it established the Army War College in 1901, it included wargaming on the curriculum of the new school for senior officers. Officers at the Army War College continued to develop new wargaming practices in the early twentieth century, including moving from the use of wooden blocks to represent military units to transparent overlays so that records of games played could be maintained for further study, and devising a standardized format for submitting moves to a game umpire, which became the predecessor for operations orders in the U.S. Army today (Caffrey). In the twentieth century, the military services would increasingly come to rely on wargaming for military training, education, and concept development, perhaps to an even greater degree than other Western militaries.

By the beginning of the twentieth century, some American army officers—while acknowledging the value of wargames—sought to downplay their "game" aspects (Perla 33–34). One such officer, Captain (later Brigadier General) Farrand Sayre wrote that

> [t]he idea that a map maneuver [Sayre's preferred term for wargames] is a kind of game has always been harmful to this class of military exercises. As already pointed out it leads to a multiplicity of technical rules which obscure the real purpose. The term of "war game" probably has something to do with this misconception and has led many to believe that it is a form of amusement. (31–32)

While the "game" elements of wargames remained intact in military circles despite these concerns, this view highlights some of the tensions inherent in wargaming for military planners. As Peter Perla has pointed out, however, the elimination of the game elements of wargames would run the very real possibility of increasing the bias and subjectivity of the wargame's direction, potentially leading to individual officers and the military as a whole learning the wrong lessons from a wargame, and thereby lessening its value tremendously (33).

Conclusion: Wargames in the Nineteenth Century

Over the course of the nineteenth century and into the early twentieth century, all the major Western armies (and eventually, navies) adopted wargames as a means of training officers and developing new ways of using military force in battle. The primary driver of this adoption was the trend toward modernization in militaries during this period, which required finding new ways of managing institutional change. The nineteenth century was a time of transformation for militaries, in terms of the increasing professionalism within the discipline and the conceptualization of military science as a "science," the industrialization of warfare, the growth in the size of militaries and the creation of mass armies (in Europe, though not the United States after the Civil War), and the array of technological changes that came to affect how wars would be fought (first with the revolutionary new military capabilities offered by mass industrial production, the railroad, the telegraph, and rifling, and later with the adoption of steamships and armored warships and technologies of mass firepower, including the machine gun and heavy artillery).

Wargames were one of the ways that militaries interested in capitalizing on these changes and competing with other military powers could do so in a cost-effective way. Wargames offered militaries a venue for training officers—junior officers at the start of their careers as well as mid-career and senior officers—to think seriously about how they would command military units in the field, especially during war, and a means of practicing these ideas via repetition, experimentation, and analysis in ways that would be impractical or prohibitively resource-intensive during peacetime field training exercises. To an even greater degree, strategic wargames that involved entire armies or the complete military forces of an entire nation allowed militaries not only to engage in planning exercises that could never be attempted with actual forces in peacetime but also to develop entire war plans for hypothetical (or likely) conflicts. Wargames, especially naval versions, also allowed militaries to consider how conflicts might play out if specific new technologies or warship capabilities were introduced; these types of wargames began to influence research, development, and acquisition of naval technologies in the early twentieth century.

Despite the many benefits of wargaming, they were not a panacea in an age of profound military change. They were always, at best, rough approximations of reality, and misleading ones at worst, limiting the extent to which the lessons of wargames might be applied to real-world situations. Twentieth-century wargames became increasingly complex in an effort to address the crudeness of earlier wargames, though they never became ideal reflections of reality, despite wargame designers' and computer modelers' best efforts. Simulating the complexities of war remains elusive. By their very nature, wargames remained artificial and failed to capture the changing nature of nineteenth-century warfare. Though wargamers attempted to alter their games' mechanics to reflect, for example, the morale effects of battle and the casualty rates of the mid-century wars in Europe and North America, wargames could never really demonstrate how soldiers and officers might experience modern war and its destructive effects on the human body. War planners from all the major powers were unprepared for the horrors of modern, mass warfare when it would finally come in 1914, having failed to understand the incredible lethality of this new kind of war, despite the examples of the American Civil War and the Russo-Japanese War (Howard).

In many ways, wargames may have even heightened strategists' conviction that they could command multimillion-men armies in a strictly rational way, marshalling them from across an entire nation, then dispatching them to the front lines in just a few weeks' time, according to elaborate timetables created during peacetime and tested via wargames and field exercises. Real armies, composed of flesh-and-blood soldiers, cannot be commanded as perfectly as armies of wooden blocks. Orders can be misunderstood. Officers make mistakes. Units can crumple under the strain of battle while others fight on, long past the point of sensibility, all in unpredictable fashion. Clausewitz's fog and friction in war can shape—and often do—the course of battle in ways that no wargame can predict. New applications of technologies can be tested and experimented with in wargames, but military planners can never truly understand how these systems will function and the cascading effects their introduction may have until they see them tested against an actual adversary. Wargames are always attempts to simulate reality; wargames approximate the conditions of war, to varying degrees of success and imperfection, but they can never represent reality itself, despite wargaming advocates' hopes.

It was not just the art of war itself that changed during the nineteenth century; wargaming also changed tremendously. From the initial games like war-chess and its many variants that abstracted unit movement in entirely artificial ways emerged *Kriegsspiel* and similar games that attempted to simulate realistic movement and effects of warfare on military units according to elaborate rules sets. The very complexity of these games prevented easy use, hampering wider adoption, which eventually spurred the adoption of wargames that deemphasized rules complexity in favor of subjective rulings by umpires who would ideally rely on their own combat experience. While these less rules-bound wargames were easier and quicker to use, they introduced a greater degree of subjectivity, which sparked disagreements over game rulings and made analysis of game results much more challenging. Understanding that military units do not fight to the last man and often collapse or retreat in the face of withering fire, wargame designers also sought to introduce the morale effects of combat into wargames, though never satisfactorily because of the abstract factors involved. Naval officers increasingly came to realize that wargames might offer value for planning for war at sea as well as on land.

Aware of wargames' limitations, wargaming initially met institutional resistance from many military officials, though it eventually grew in influence in the late nineteenth century, ultimately coming to shape national policy and defense acquisition programs. The adoption of wargames by Western militaries also serves as a case study of the kind of transnational flows of military "best practices" that frequently took place in the mid- and late nineteenth century: beginning in Prussia—often idealized by other militaries during this period as being at the forefront of military innovation—but eventually spreading across Europe and the United States to take on new forms and influences. Wargames would not long remain the sole domain of military professionals. The nineteenth-century history of wargaming also presages growing civilian interest in wargaming: Fred Jane created the first civilian naval wargame in 1898 and H. G. Wells the first land-based civilian wargames in 1911 and 1913; a significant civilian wargaming hobby and industry would arise following World War II (Perla). Ultimately, wargames—for military practitioners and civilian hobbyists alike—represent an attempt to simulate an aspect of reality via gameplay. As games, wargames appeal to players in part because of their apparent ability to both simulate a complex phenomenon and area of human endeavor—war—and to offer military players a sense of mastery of this phenomenon, the ability to translate gameplay into professional expertise, and, perhaps, win a war.

Works Cited

Barber, James A. Jr. "The School of Naval Warfare." *Naval War College Review* 21 (April 1969): 89–96.

Baring, Evelyn. *Rules for the Conduct of the War-Game*. London: Topographical and Statistical Department of the War Office, 1872.

Caffrey, Matthew Jr. "Toward a History Based Doctrine for Wargaming." *Air and Space Power Journal* (Fall 2000): n. pag. http://www.au.af.mil/au/afri/aspj/airchronicles/apj/apj00/fal00/caffrey.htm; Accessed 3 June 2016.

von Clausewitz, Carl. *On War*. Trans. Michael Howard and Peter Paret. Princeton: Princeton University Press, 1976.

von Hilgers, Philipp. *War Games: A History of War on Paper*. Trans. Ross Benjamin. Cambridge and London: The MIT Press, 2012.

Howard, Michael. "Men Against Fire: The Doctrine of the Offensive in 1914." *Makers of Modern Strategy: From Machiavelli to the Nuclear Age*. Ed. Peter Paret. Princeton: Princeton University Press, 1986. 510–26.

Livermore, W. R. *The American Kriegsspiel: A Game For Practicing the Art of War upon a Topographical Map*. Boston: Houghton, Mifflin, 1882.

Loper, Margaret L. and Charles Turnitsa. "History of Combat Modeling and Distributed Simulation." *Engineering Principles of Combat Modeling and Simulation*. Ed. Andreas Tolk. Hoboken, NJ: John Wiley and Sons, 2012. 331–55.

McCarty Little, William. *The Strategic Naval War Game or Chart Maneuver*. Rpt. United States Naval *Proceedings* 38.4. No. 144. Annapolis, MD: U. S. Naval Institute, 1912.

McHugh, Francis J. *Fundamentals of War Gaming*. 3rd ed. Newport, RI: U. S. Naval War College, 1966.

Perla, Peter P. *The Art of Wargaming: A Guide for Professionals and Hobbyists*. Annapolis, MD: Naval Institute Press, 1990.

Raymond, Charles W. "Kriegsspiel, A Paper Read Before the United States Military Service Institute at West Point, N.Y., February 17, 1881." Fort Monroe, VA: United States Artillery School, 1881.

Richardson, Charles. *War-Chess, or the Game of Battle*. New York: C. B. Richardson, 1866.

Sayre, Farrand. *Map Maneuvers*. Fort Leavenworth, KS: Staff College Press, 1907.

Sherman, William T. *Address to the Graduating Class of the U. S. Military Academy, West Point, June 15, 1869*. New York: D. Van Nostrand, 1869.

Tolk, Andreas. "Challenges of Combat Modeling and Distributed Simulation." *Engineering Principles of Combat Modeling and Simulation*. Ed. Andreas Tolk. Hoboken, NJ: John Wiley and Sons, 2012. 1–22.

Totten, Charles A. L. *Strategos*. 2 vols. New York: D. Appleton, 1880.

Vego, Milan. "German War Gaming." *Naval War College Review* 65.4 (Autumn 2012): 106–47.

von Verdy du Vernois, Julius. *A Simplified War Game*. Trans. Eben Swift. Kansas City, MO: Hudson-Kimberley, 1897.

Wawro, Geoffrey. *Warfare and Society in Europe, 1792–1914*. London and New York: Routledge, 2000.

Wilson, Andrew. *The Bomb and the Computer: Wargaming from Ancient Chinese Mapboard to Atomic Computer*. New York: Delacorte Press, 1968.

Young, John P. A *Survey of Historical Developments in War Games*. Bethesda, MD: Operations Research Office, The Johns Hopkins University, 1959.

Chapter 8

The United States as Wonderland

British Literature, U.S. Nationalism, and Nineteenth-Century Children's and Family Board and Card Games

MICHELLE BEISSEL HEATH

In 1844, nearing the midpoint of the nineteenth century, Anne Abbot, a clergyman's daughter, published *Doctor Busby and His Neighbors: A Story*. The tale itself was not particularly successful, as is perhaps evident by the carelessness of its publication. In her preface, Abbot finds herself apologizing to her readers in blunt terms:

> Whoever may chance to take up this book, ought to have fair warning of certain shocks he will meet with, from an abrupt transition of subject. Should he get out of patience and toss the book aside as a clumsy production, we cannot blame him. It is unjustifiable and disrespectful for an author thus to take an unsuspicious reader off his feet, and set him down in a new place, where he stares about him, wondering where, in the name of common sense, he may be. (*Doctor* 1)

Though she believes her "contrite apology" will cajole the reader into a "forgiving spirit" enabling the narrative to be got through, she is forced to admit significant writerly fault: "No scribbler impressed with a proper idea of the responsibility of authorship, considers his work done when he has covered the prescribed number of sheets. If he leave them to take their chance in the press, it is meet that such ostrich-like indifference should have its reward" (Abbot, *Doctor* 2). Her own such "reward," the final frank sentence of the preface—and the published manuscript itself—reveals, is an embarrassingly nearly unreadable work created through negligence: "The manuscript was sent off in haste, without any caption to the chapters, in consequence of which neglect, the blank spaces between were disregarded, and the proofs not passing under the eye of the author, who was rambling about the country, the mistake passed uncorrected" (Abbot, *Doctor* 3).

The omission of chapter headings, breaks, and transitions throughout *Doctor Busby and His Neighbors* can likely be attributed to the most notable feature of the tale: its production due to game origin. In 1843, Abbot invented the card game of "Dr. Busby," a game so popular throughout the nineteenth century it inspired many knock-offs (e.g., "Dr. Fusby") and may have influenced the creation of the still-played British card game of "Happy Families," generally attributed to John Jaques and John Tenniel just before the 1851 Great Exhibition.[1] "Dr. Busby" is one of the first—if not the first—home-grown games to be tremendously successful in the United States, which may be one reason Abbot is also often (and probably incorrectly) attributed with inventing the also popular 1861 card game of "Authors." Abbot's invention of the "Dr. Busby" card game and of her 1844 lesser-selling card game "Master Rodbury" directly led to the publication of the *Doctor Busby and His Neighbors* literary work. As Abbot explains in her preface to the narrative, "Messrs Ives, having a set of wood engravings of the personages in 'Dr. Busby,' employed the author of the game to write a story thereto. It was presumed that no one was so well able to satisfy the curiosity of the juvenile public about Dr. B. and his neighbors" (Abbot, *Doctor* 1). The story, readers are further told, "would have been more communicative on the subject of Henry," one of the primary characters based on a figure in the card game, "but assigned limits brought the tale to an untimely end" (Abbot, *Doctor* 1). In other words, the story was solicited to take advantage of the tremendous popularity of the "Dr. Busby" card game and was presumed to have a youthful, "juvenile," audience, features likely deemed not requiring of much in the way of quality, as far as the story itself went, a fact seemingly attested to by the haste of its production, the "assigned limits" of its form (not lengthy as the tale is fewer than 200 pages), and its missing chapter divisions.

Abbot's hasty melding together of games and literature to take advantage of commercial popularity emblematizes the history and trajectory of card, board, and parlor games on both sides of the Atlantic. As I note elsewhere, rising in tandem with the growth of children's literature by the end of the century was what Roger Tilley observes as "perhaps the main feature of [the "last quarter" of the nineteenth century] in England": "the great output of children's games" (168).[2] This "output" was no less impressive in the United States where by the end of the century, Margaret K. Hofer discerns, "improvements in printing and paper making enabled the large-scale commercial production of board games" (14). This dual rise was not coincidental: as Hofer's comments about printing and paper indicate, games, cards, and books share a history. Game manufacturers frequently started out also as book publishers and in their attempts to win over youthful audiences (and their parents) published not only games and toys but picture and toy books, as well as other works for the young, just as W. & S. B. Ives did in publishing both Abbot's story and games.[3] As Abbot illustrates as well, authors themselves also forged literary connections. Prominent children's writers such as Mark Twain and Lewis Carroll took stabs at creating games, as did, as we will see, individuals such as Mary Mapes Dodge, editor of *St. Nicholas Magazine*. Abbot herself published other works for the young and was even at one point editor of *The Children's Friend*. Game playing, too, featured prominently throughout literature for both children and adults throughout the nineteenth century (and earlier), as even a cursory glance at Carroll's *Alice* texts or the works of Charles Dickens indicates, and literature formed a primary focus for topics for games as well.[4] Indeed, as this essay will show through an examination of period games alongside an initial consideration of Abbot's works, paralleling Abbot's seeming goals in the literary narrative drawn from her card games were United States games' simultaneous deployment to cleanse negative associations (e.g., gambling), in particular to encourage standards of morality and "good behavior" among youth, and to promote educated, loyal patriotism. In the process, games were aimed at transforming the United States—through its youthful inhabitants and their families and a re-casting of "good," "civilizing" British literature—into an idealized fantasy: a land of particular promise, a reinvented "wonderland," as one game even bluntly suggests (Hill). As games were recouped to render them "appropriate" for youth and families, so the United States was (re-) imagined as especially fitting for those same audiences.

Abbot's literary productions consistently reveal her personal and political inclinations. Desultory ways, drink and gambling prominent among them, lead to the blemishing or downfall of her characters (who are sometimes rescued by the love of idealized, worthy women), temperance leagues are openly advocated, and pacifism is repeatedly called for—indeed, it is at the heart of one tale, unsubtly titled "How to Spoil a Good Citizen," wherein "camp life" and having been "drawn as a soldier" precipitate the ruin of the main character through drink, gambling, violence, and poor health (Abbot 13). He is "saved from scenes of bloodshed and rapine, and [therefore has] not the hardened ferocity of the soldier," but nevertheless he has been destroyed by his brief service in "the bloodless war," seemingly the 1838–39 Aroostook War (Abbot, "How" 13–14). The danger of war—and of filling young "head[s] full of glory, and patriotism, and all that" through war stories—is reinforced in other tales, such as the obviously didactic "Edward's Cap and Edward's Grandfather: Or, Playground Peace and the Peace of Nations" where a playground spat and a Peace Society visitor reveal the hypocrisy of a former soldier grandfather (Abbot 14).

Overtones of pacifism are missing, but otherwise the plot of *Doctor Busby and His Neighbors* follows a pattern similar to these other stories in its focus on discouraging activities such as drinking and gambling among youth, in this case through tellingly public morality as well as "good behavior." *Doctor Busby and His Neighbors* is essentially the tale of two young men, Robert Ninicumtwich and Harry Manly, drawn from the original card game's caricatures.[5] As we are told, "The one had a rich father, who chose his son should do just as he had a mind to do; the other had a poor one, who did not allow his son to follow the bent of his inclination" (Abbot, *Doctor* 80). Harry, the son of the poor farmer, is a model pupil and teacher, encouraged by the benevolent Dr. Busby but held back initially by his father's reservations that he is succumbing to "notions of rising above your condition, of despising the way of life which was good enough for your father, and his father before him" (Abbot, *Doctor* 38). Robert, the son of "people of fashion" yet who has "inherent in his nature a certain good taste," is idle and heading down a lazy, immoral path, but association with Harry at the good Mr. Rodbury's school completely alters his life and he strives to be better (Abbot, *Doctor* 8–9). The two eventually set off for college where, foreshadowed and predictably, they fall into bad company led by the revealingly named Blackford, who by degrees taints them. If Harry "took one step, Ninicumtwich always took two. He thought it enough for him to be half as good as Harry; so if he sipped a glass of wine, young Ninny drank a bumper or a bottle. If Harry played a game of cards without betting, Ninny played with stakes" (Abbot, *Doctor* 138). Once Harry realizes what has happened he tries to convince his companions of the error of their ways, to little avail. It is only when Rodbury falls ill and Robert is induced to visit that his love for Rodbury's daughter, Grace, is renewed and her refusal to marry him due to his bad ways spurs his final transformation.

Robert's ultimate transformation and Harry's overall worthiness—their appropriateness as model citizenry and the "rewards" the text confers upon them—are established not only with private displays of goodness but with multiple instances of public attention and repentance. The characters' use as public models is perhaps most obvious in the text's acknowledgment of the characters' origins: not only are illustrations from the cards interspersed throughout the narrative, the text openly acknowledges the connection when Harry's sister discusses playing a game with her suitor and he asks her, "Did you hear that some wag has put out a game, called Dr. Busby, with pictures, real likenesses of you and myself and Harry besides, and your father, pipe and all, &c?" (Abbot, *Doctor* 33). Early on in the narrative, Harry must demonstrate his mettle when the village school he has become master of faces public ridicule. As Busby explains to the young Harry, he needs to learn to "stand firmly on [his] own feet, and not expect to be bolstered up by the sympathy and admiration of the public. On the contrary, you may generally expect the said public to give you a thrust, or a hard shove, occasionally, by way of test of your manliness, and they will like you the better for standing your ground" (Abbot, *Doctor* 57). After weathering his bout of public exposure, Harry proves his worth and finally manages to achieve his desire, securing the approval of his father to continue his education.

Similarly, Robert only proves his worthiness and secures his desire—Grace's hand—through humbling public exposure. When he discovers that actions, not words, are the only way to convince Grace to marry him, Robert begins in earnest by joining Harry's temperance club, an act to which Harry admits, "there are advantages certainly, in publicly pledging one's self to a right course, which a private resolution, however strong, would not possess" (Abbot, *Doctor* 173). Abstaining from drink alone is not enough, however, and to win over his love Robert adopts "a plan of improvement" and "self-denial," aided by the maintaining of "a private journal, wherein he noted down his resolves, and all his failures and short comings" (Abbot, *Doctor* 177). Foiling Blackford in an attempt to seduce a young girl, Robert returns to his room to discover that "in his absence, [Blackford and his associates] broke and defaced everything in it [. . .] and took away his diary to make sport of at the club" (180). When he realizes what has happened and "he and Harry were convinced that it had been stolen on purpose to make it public," readers are assured that "this was the most genuine trial of patience Robert had ever had, yet he bore it like a hero," ultimately finding it fitting that the theft has forced his "proud heart" into "humbling myself before men" (Abbot, *Doctor* 181). Publicly revealed, Robert becomes a suitable partner for Grace, a compatibility the text tritely underlines by ending with what a few decades later would be a Horatio Alger-esque bootstrap scenario: the farm boy Harry is put in charge of a successful academy founded by Busby while Robert's family experiences a sudden series of financial misfortunes that forces them to go into lodgings and that yet proves their salvation. Their financial reversal "awake[ns]" his parents with purpose and convinces Grace, in what may be one of the text's most radical passages, that she can now be an "equal" with Robert rather than "an appendage to a rich man's fortune, a mere ornament" so that she not only accepts his hand but persuades him of the appropriateness of asking her father for it (Abbot, *Doctor* 186–87, 190–91).

The narrative cliché of the ending, however, also underscores the United States' literary reliance on Britain—a reliance, we will see, that is made evident time and again in games of the period—even as it aims to paint the United States, notably in opposition to Britain, as the most promising space for its youthful characters. Sporadically throughout the tale are comparisons between Grace and the Rodburys' adopted daughter Alice, who Mrs. Rodbury at times seems to prefer. Not much of substance is told of Alice until the very end of the tale when readers are unexpectedly informed of "a remarkable event" and given Alice's romantic back story: "She was about three years old when she was found drifting on a piece of wreck, and taken on board, by a pleasure party among whom was Mrs. Rodbury" who "clasped the shivering orphan to her warm heart, and well did she fulfill the vow internally made, that she would be to her a mother" (Abbot, *Doctor* 183). Alice's Uncle Alfred finally finds her years later as a young adult, whereupon "it was like being made a second time an orphan, to be carried away to England" (Abbot, *Doctor* 183). Tellingly, "her uncle was so far moved by her grief, that he promised that she should be at full liberty to return, if after visiting her relatives and her inheritance, she still wished it" (Abbot, *Doctor* 183). Return she does—to marry Harry and join him in the future in a house in "his favorite grove," an act that seems to confirm the promise of the United States as opposed to Britain, despite the allures of biological relatives and, perhaps especially notably, an inheritance (Abbot, *Doctor* 188).

"Edward's Cap and Edward's Grandfather" similarly alludes to a conflicted reliance on, and even an admiration for, Britain, with the specter of the Revolutionary War brought forth to highlight national pride, supposed forgiveness, and grudging respect, with readers informed by the former soldier grandfather that, "in fighting with England, we should be at least respectable, were we even beaten at last" (Abbot, "Edward's" 113). The Peace Society visitor also admits that "the English are a noble nation, were it not for their war spirit" and "I love the English, and am thankful that the principles of peace and justice prevailed over their roused military pride in our late dispute [over Oregon's boundaries] with them. It is one of the most encouraging signs of the times" (113–14). Even when it is disparaged, with the United States depicted as a promised land, particularly for youth, the might and legacy of England for the United States cannot be denied in these tales.

Nor can it be denied a few decades later, when in 1886 the Anglo-American Frances Hodgson Burnett introduced the phenomenally popular *Little Lord Fauntleroy*. Burnett's text shares with Abbot's works tie-ins with card games, a riches-to-rags-to-riches (-to-rags-to-riches) plot, the transformation of a dissolute character (though more cantankerous than drunken or debauched), the wish to bridge the Revolutionary War, and the potential of a youthful, entrepreneurial United States. A cattle ranch in the West (California) offers hopes for a young, hardworking father, the brother of an honest, energetic, young New York City bootblack, and his son, saved from the clutches of the son's unscrupulous mother.[6] As one of the elderly characters says, in the text's concluding paragraph, "It's [the United States] a good enough country for them that's young an' stirrin'" (Burnett 238).[7] The importance of these two themes—the transformation of the Old World and the hope of the properly civilized New or young—is tellingly captured in the distillation of text into game, into a set of playing cards, the very theme of which would seem to encourage that the cards be used among children and families rather than for adult gambling, an association with which games and playing cards were still tainted throughout the century. As the "Publisher's Announcement" from C. L. B.'s 1876 "Tyche: The Fireside Oracle" game indicates, "many object to games of chance in which something is won or lost, as calculated to stimulate a taste for gambling" (2–3).

The Russell Morgan Printing Company circa-1890 "Fauntleroy" playing cards notably feature only three scenes from the Reginald Birch illustrations for *Little Lord Fauntleroy*, one repeated on the back of each card, one on a special "Ace" title card, and one on the box container for the cards. The cards were issued in at least two decks, one red and one black, and on these decks the image on the Ace card is the same: Fauntleroy (Cecil Errol) showing his energetic, "manly" sporting capability through his mastering of horse riding (the image is of his little figure on a galloping horse). The cover box image of Fauntleroy's head and face is also the same between the red and black decks of cards. The other image, however, shifts between decks and hints at what game designers, if not the general public, also considered essential about the text. On the back of the black card deck, labeled "The Earl," is the "shall I be your boy" image of Fauntleroy and his grandfather exchanging caresses; on the red card deck is the image of the bootblack Dick giving Fauntleroy the gift of the red silk handkerchief, with the name "Dick" prominently and repeatedly displayed in the image, alongside pictorial representations of shoes and bootblacking, to leave players without doubt as to what the image is meant to represent. In other words, the two images repeatedly highlighted in the cards, in addition to the promise of young Fauntleroy himself, are those alluding to the transformation of the elderly British aristocrat through his democratically minded young New York grandson and the potential of youth of even the lower classes, if they have good hearts and are provided with means (including, the text itself indicates, not only money and physical equipment but education). Britain may be the land of traditions and a legacy of education and money, but the future for youth of the masses shines brightly in the United States in both text and game.

The bright potential and patriotic, glorious might of the United States (and unlike with Abbot's texts, a patriotism often celebrating war) are themes called forth time and again in games of the period, particularly after the Civil War and as the United States' centennial approached and was celebrated. Surrounding the centennial were a plethora of historical and patriotic games, including "Centennial Games" (1874), "The National Game of '76" (1881), "One Hundred Events of US Colonial History" (1876), "The Signers of America's Independence" (1877), "The Lion and the Eagle, or the Days of '76" (1883), and "Centennial, Seventy-Six" (1876). As with the likely goal of the "Fauntleroy" playing cards, many of these games aim to mitigate negative associations of playing cards. This was sometimes done by replacing the standard cards with supposedly more acceptable alternatives for, as the "Publisher's Announcement" for "Tyche" observes, "many people refuse to keep the common playing cards, because they think the associations to which such cards tend are below the proper standard" (C. L. B. 3). Hence, "The Lion and the Eagle" is a standard trick-taking card game played with partners, with one side as "American" and one "British," with supposedly more "acceptable" patriotic suits of lions, eagles, crowns, and bells. In the 1860s, during or just after the Civil War, the American Card Company, "confident that the introduction of national emblems in the place of foreign in playing cards [. . .] would be hailed with delight by the people of the American Republic, introduced the Union Playing Cards" (box cover). These playing cards offered "Goddess of Liberty in place of Queen, Colonel for King, Major for Jack" along with suits of "Eagles, Shields, Stars and Flags" (box cover). In what would seem to be outright advertising bravado, the company proclaimed the cards "the first and only genuine American cards ever produced. The success of these cards bearing national emblems [. . .] is unprecedented in the card trade. They have already become the leading cards in the American market" (box cover). Similar patriotism—with an overt "civilizing" didactic purpose—is on display in W. C. Smith's "Centennial, Seventy-Six," which advertises both on the game's box cover and in its introductory material its intentions for its presumed youth audience:

> In presenting this game to the American public, if one or both of two things are attained—first, the furnishing of an innocent and instructive home amusement, thereby enhancing the attractions of the home circle; secondly, but not least, introducing the subject of American History in an attractive manner, thus inspiring the minds of the young to the further study of the history of their country, to emulate the example and revere the memory of their patriot ancestors, for the precious dowry of freedom bequeathed them, to be preserved and handed down to posterity, the object of the author will have been accomplished.

While encouraging civilizing patriotism and combating the disreputable associations of playing cards, these historical and patriotic games envision the United States as a fantastic, mythic place, a land of soaring promise symbolized by such things as eagles and stars with a "dowry of freedom" presided over by a "Goddess of Liberty."

Political, patriotic, "civilizing," and historical games remained popular through the 1880s and even later, with a narrative of envisioned progress—and especially the United States' advancement if not mythic status—commonplace. Just as games of the time celebrate the United States' achievements and victory over Britain in the Revolutionary War, they emphasize equality and competition with Britain in areas such as exploration, colonization, and Western notions of progress.[8] At the end of the century, for instance, game creators produced various editions of games marking the race for the North Pole—a race notable primarily for its attempts at national glory. In the "Game of the Mariner's Compass" (circa 1890) players compete by beginning the trek to the North Pole from two different "centers"—London and New York—while both the 1896 "Race for the Pole" and 1907 "North Pole Game" highlight different countries' representatives' attempts to reach the pole, prominent among them of course explorers from the United States and Britain. Versions of the "Game of Nations" illustrate Eurocentric and often racist notions of progress, with stereotyped European and Asian style clothing and dress contrasted alongside stereotyped Native American and African teepees and huts, while historical games frequently made explicit European and Western perspectives, defining history, for example, as Richard G. Boone does in a "General Statement to Teachers" for "The Game of United States History," as

> a study of the abiding forms of human conduct as they appear in the various social institutions. The state is only one of these institutions, in many respects the most important one, but only one. The theme of them all is human life as it progresses, together with the machinery of government and home and school and church and social codes, as the means of its advance. (1–2)

Charles A. Gaskell, in the "Prefatory" material for his "Gaskell's Popular Historical Game," revealingly expresses pride in his game's efforts to mark "the progress of thought and social life" as "men like Kepler, Newton, Galileo, da Vinci, etc."

> are the true heroes and demigods of history. To such as these we owe almost everything we possess—the clothes we wear, the houses we live in, the books we read, the songs we sing, the railroads and telegraphs we use—indeed, even much of the food we eat, and in short, everything which distinguishes us from the savages of Africa or of the South Sea Islands. (2–3)

Unsurprisingly, of course, several statesmen and two authors from the United States are elevated to mythic status in Gaskell's list of "true heroes and demigods of history."

Indeed, for game producers, often what "distinguishes" the United States "from the savages" and makes it an exceptional and exceptionally promising space is "great" literature. Even in otherwise straightforward historical and exploration or imperial games, literary themes and allusions abound and these themes and allusions just as consistently reveal patriotic "civilizing" impulses and a tendency to comparison with Britain, a competitive desire to be viewed as equal to (and probably surpassing) the United States' former motherland. In a likely not coincidental trajectory, for instance, the explanatory booklet for F. A. Colwell's "The Race for the Pole" game prominently begins with the famous "best-laid plans" quotation from the British (Scottish) poet Robert Burns's "To a Mouse" and ends with a passage from United States author Francis Bret Harte's "An Arctic Vision," stipulating "all ye icebergs make salaam/ You belong to Uncle Sam" (lines 38–39). With the language choice of "salaam," the poem calls up the specter of British imperial prowess only to substitute figuration of the United States ("Uncle Sam")—imperial prowess, in this way, has been passed on, with the United States seemingly equal to or exceeding Britain in new realms of exploration and conquest. While commenting in its conclusion on the challenges of reaching the pole, the game's booklet even notes, "the reader will watch with interest for the one who shall proclaim to the world 'I have reached the pole.' Shall it be Scandinavia or Great Britain? Or shall it be the American eagle which shall swoop down upon that object and screech: 'I am here; America's ahead!'" With closing lines from Harte, the game's own position is clear.

A result of this sense of the importance of literature as an indicator of civilization, national achievement, and ultimate potential is a consistent reconsidering of "Authors." Like and perhaps surpassing "Dr. Busby," the game of "Authors" ran through edition after edition after its mid-century introduction and was, through both its design and associations, also strongly connected to literature and both sides of the Atlantic. In a section of the 1868 *Little Women* that overtly references refighting the United States' Revolutionary War on the game field between groups of youth from Britain and the United States, Louisa May Alcott pointedly has her characters turn to a "sensible game of Authors" (156, 163). Her praise of the game was not limited to the use of Jo as a mouthpiece for it: Alcott provided a testimonial for A. B. Carroll's 1889 edition of the game and is one of the few women—if not at times the only one—to be featured in many versions of the game.[9] The game itself was often a mini-battleground for United States versus British pride: most editions strove for a balance between United States and British authors, sometimes having to stretch the notion of author to include politicians and other public figures, generally with strongly patriotic associations, such as Henry Clay and John Quincy Adams. Though this stretching could result in the inclusion of minor writers or public figures of the day, the end result, as Lara Langer Cohen and Meredith L. McGill observe, was that

> the game condensed the field of authorship by equating "Authors" writ large with the particular writers it assembled. The selective elevation of these authors to "Authors" helped reinforce what we have come to know as a national literary canon, while demonstrating how canons can be formed through mass cultural phenomena as well as through more familiar, top-down, critical or institutional fiat. (210)

Ultimately, the game of "Authors" helped establish the United States' literary foundation, if not reputation, the solidifying of which game designers were keen to induce, promote, reinforce, and take advantage of in a repetitive cycle as literary underpinnings could be seen as providing games with "civilizing" if not moral veneers (and definitely an improvement on card games otherwise associated with gambling) and therefore incentives for purchase.

That a literary focus helped wrest the game of "Authors" and other games away from the negative connotations so often associated with gambling and playing cards is perhaps most apparent in the success of "Authors" in paving the way for many other games. Later card games frequently followed the same structure for play, with players trying to obtain a full set of (often four) cards, frequently referred to (after "Authors") as "books." Thus, W. C. Smith's "Centennial, Seventy-Six" specifically instructs in its "Directions for Playing" that "it may be played in the same manner as the popular game of Authors." The presumed power of literature to remove negative gambling stigma is also evident in the *Little Lord Fauntleroy* theme for the Russell Morgan playing cards and emphasized in E. G. Selchow and Company's "Carnival of Characters from Dickens" game. The game, which notably features British texts, was introduced in 1876 as the United States celebrated its centennial and was designed for playing a Dickens-specific version of the game of "Authors" even as "all games (without exception) that can be played with common playing cards can be played with Carnival."[10] The game's explanatory card describes "Carnival" as "suppl[ying] a want long felt in society. It is a high toned, literary game, combining all of the attraction, fascination, and skill required in the various games that can be played with the common playing cards." In other words, the Dickens-themed cards can be used as standard playing cards for standard playing card games (Cribbage, Euchre, and Whist are listed specifically), but supposedly as a result of its British "high toned" literary connection and further connection with the game of "Authors," "the unpleasant associations that attach to playing cards are, in this game, entirely dispensed with" (explanatory card).

As "Carnival of Characters from Dickens," if not Russell Morgan's *Little Lord Fauntleroy* playing cards demonstrate, too, in their efforts to elevate games from low-brow associations and make them acceptable for families, children, and United States homes, game producers in the United States repeatedly turned to British literature. In doing so, the games draw heavily from a British literary tradition and yet alter or interpret that tradition to reflect the United States' own concerns and interests: in this way, Fauntleroy and Dick are emphasized as epitomes of United States youth and even "greats" such as Dickens and his works are viewed through a seemingly "Americanized" lens favoring upstarts, underdogs, and even villainous characters generally opposed to British heroes and legends. George S. Parker and Company's circa-1900 "The Good Old Game of Oliver Twist" offers as its cover image—replete with famous quotation and a version of George Cruikshank's illustration—Dickens's well-known passage of "Please, Sir, I want some more." This cover image sets up well an underdog/David and Goliath tone, strikingly contrasting the slight figure of Oliver with the robust form of the master. This tone is maintained in the cards, which offer their own bit of a twist as the rogue Artful Dodger is nearly as valuable as Oliver Twist. The goal of the game is to be the last holding the Oliver Twist card, with players taking turns picking a card from each other and making matches. The player who holds the Oliver card has the advantage of not having to make matches, of retaining as many cards as received; whenever the Oliver card is drawn, the player receiving it also gets to call out "more" and receive an additional card from each player (direction booklet). The Artful Dodger card, meanwhile, entitles its owner at every turn to draw two cards from other players if that owner doesn't already possess the Oliver Twist card. Dickens himself gets (re-)evaluated by comparison in the 1887 game of "Literary Whist, or Games of Great Men," "compiled" by N. O. Wilhelm (instructions cover). While one of the games of "great men" possible to be played, "Children's Great People," is a version of "Authors," another, "Great Men's Casino," involves giving extra points at the end of the game to those who hold cards representing writers (Wilhelm 13). While "each great American Poet" garners a point, only two "great men" are called out specifically by name: the holder of the card of Charles Dickens gets a point while that of Benjamin Franklin receives two (Wilhelm 9). Other "great" British literary figures repeatedly portrayed and essentially demoted in games of the period are Robin Hood and Sherlock Holmes. Despite its title, Parker Brothers' 1893 "The Game of Robin Hood" centers around the Sheriff of Nottingham as "the game represents the attempt of the Sheriff to pass from the town of Nottingham to one of the King's Castles" and it is the Sheriff who seeks to evade capture by Robin Hood or one of his "merry men," Little John and Friar Tuck, otherwise described simply as "robbers" in the game (box cover interior).[11] Players therefore play either the Sheriff or one or more "robbers" and "it cannot be easily stated who stands a better show of winning the game, one of the robbers or the Sheriff" (box cover interior). In the multiple editions of Parker Brothers' 1904 "Sherlock Holmes" game, Holmes maintains his value (being worth five points at the end of the game when cards depicting criminals are worth but one) but the complexity of his persona and deductions are diminished, if not eliminated. He is reduced to a card that conducts "sweeps," taking other players' piles of cards. Notably, too, though they can help in gaining cards, cards such as "clue" cards are ultimately worth nothing (no points in the final tally).

The re-casting of "A(a)uthors" and literary tradition to promote the United States as on par with or above Britain and to render games more acceptable revealingly offered other simplifications and privileged other underdogs. The "Centennial, Seventy-Six" game gives as its initial goal the "furnishing of an innocent and instructive home amusement, thereby enhancing the attractions of the home circle" while the "Publishers' Preface" for the 1879 "Protean Cards" by the "Editor of *St. Nicholas*" (Mary Mapes Dodge) suggests the aim of the "Protean Cards" is "the greatest good of all," "innocent and profitable enjoyment for the home circle" (5). Such emphases on "home circle" reflect game manufacturers' desire to enter the domestic market as well as games' successful connection with the femininity so often conflated with domesticity in the nineteenth century. By 1901, Edith Nesbit could mock the cliché of "the refining touch of a woman's hand" in her satiric fairy tale "Fortunatus Rex & Co." in *Nine Unlikely Tales for Children*, but a connection with female authorship and the supposed "softening" and "refining" qualities of feminine influence is one of the means by which games were rendered fitting for youth and family audiences, as gambling was commonly associated with masculine adult games and sports (200). Indeed, one of the most prolific games manual writers of the period, George Frederick Pardon, published his not-betting-shy games manuals under the pseudonym of Captain Rawdon Crawley (William Makepeace Thackeray's sporting and gambling, card-playing soldier from the 1848 *Vanity Fair*) and notably titled his 1860 work *The Handy Book of Games for Gentlemen*, which he further dedicated to "His Royal Highness Albert Edward, Prince of Wales, The First Gentleman in England." Indeed, in justifying their games as appropriate for family and child audiences, game publishers relied on associations with children's texts such as *Little Lord Fauntleroy* and the children's periodical *St. Nicholas* and emphasized female authorship to such an extent that games based on nursery rhymes and fairy tales—often perceived as the purview of women and childhood—proliferated.[12] Female authorship was also emphasized specifically in many games. In its "Publisher's Announcement," for example, "Tyche" insists that it is "superior to all other domestic games in," among other things, "adaptation to the hopes, desires, and fancies of young people" by asserting that the game "is the work of a Literary Lady of Chicago" (C. L. B. 3). In shedding the stigma of playing cards, "Authors," too, took up the mantle of female authorship. The bulk of writers portrayed through various editions of "Authors" were men; however female authors such as Alcott made appearances, such as in the 1887 McLoughlin Brothers' "Improved Star Authors" which includes not only Alcott but Elizabeth Barrett Browning, Charlotte Brontë, Felicia Hemans, Jean Ingelow, George Eliot, and Harriet Beecher Stowe. Several versions of the game, including McLoughlin Brothers' "Queens of Literature," even featured female authors entirely. Female authorship, though, wasn't confined to writers portrayed on "Authors" cards. When Parker Brothers issued a "new edition" of "Authors" in 1897, the company crafted a slightly misleading and loose-date history for it, one that emphasizes its feminine origin and connects it to "Dr. Busby" (then acquired by the company), a game also created by a woman, of course: "The Game of 'Authors' was invented in Salem, many years ago by a number of young ladies, and was first published in Salem. It was elaborated from the old game of 'Dr. Busby,' which was invented and published in Salem in 1840" (instruction booklet 1).

Similar to other games of the period and Abbot's narrative use of the transformative, inspiring potential of good, "worthy" women, then, Parker Brothers' history of "Authors" privileges "underdog" female authorship in its attempts to transform the perception of games and cards. At the same time, the Parker Brothers' game stakes out a claim for place, repeating the name of its hometown and finally boasting, "Salem was therefore the home of the first famous American Games, as well as the place of publication of the two hundred later games now issued by Parker Brothers" ("Rules" 1). In this way, Parker Brothers essentially crafts a fairy tale surrounding the origins of United States games and its place in that fairy tale, re-casting or replacing British connections in the development of United States games. In this, too, it was not alone: Albert A. Hill, in the 1876 game "Right and Wrong, or The Princess Belinda," seeks to create a fairy tale that "promises to become as popular as the famous story of '*Cinderella; or, the Glass Slipper*' " and re-cast "wonderland," most famous in Lewis Carroll's British *Alice's Adventures in Wonderland* (1865) (directions card). Designed entirely as a narrative to be disrupted at key times by players, the story the game tells is of Belinda undertaking a world (and really universe) tour, the culmination of which is her leaving England to cross "the Atlantic in a cockle-shell, the sails of which were the wings of THE AMERICAN EAGLE. Strange as had been the adventures of Belinda, she was glad to reach once more her HOME IN WONDERLAND" (directions card; emphases in the original). Such a reimagining of Wonderland as the United States would likely be unrecognizable to Carroll's Alice, but it resonates well with views of the United States, literature, and history portrayed in United States games of the period.

Indeed, with its patriotic language and imagery as well as its transformation of British literary tradition, Hill's "Right and Wrong, or the Princess Belinda," like Abbot in her early game and literary text of "Dr. Busby," sought to conjure up images of the United States as a place of fantastic potential for youth. Like them, too, it sought to cast inhabitants of the United States as moral, good, patriotic-minded citizens unafraid of adventures and exploration or the public eye. In the process, the game and its predecessors, peers, and heirs insisted that United States literary creations, like their creators, were in every way equal to or better than their British peers and predecessors. How much their playing and reading publics agreed can only be speculated, but as nineteenth-century game creators sought to sanitize card and other games for families and youth in the United States, literary themes, nationalism, and competition ran rampant, rendering games, play, and literature battlegrounds in a (cultural) revolutionary war.

Acknowledgments

Many thanks to this book's editors and to the anonymous reviewers of this essay. Many thanks, too, to the Lilly Library for providing me with an Everett Helm Visiting Fellowship, The Strong National Museum of Play for giving me a Mary Valentine and Andrew Cosman Research Fellowship, the Children's Literature Association for providing me with a Faculty Research Grant, and the Research Services Council of the University of Nebraska, Kearney, for giving me a seed grant. The generous financial support afforded me by these fellowships and grants made the archival research for this essay possible. Especial thanks, too, to the librarians, archivists, and curators at the Lilly Library and The Strong National Museum of Play, without whose generous assistance this essay would not be possible. My thanks also go to Tanya Woodward for her kind assistance with the index.

Notes

1. Both games are played similarly, with, after the cards have been dealt, one player asking another player for a particular card. The goal is to collect all

the cards in each "family" (for example, the wife, husband, son, and daughter in Dr. Busby's family). The player with the most "families" at the end of the game wins. For more analysis of the "Happy Families" game and its aftermath, see my "Oh Golly."

2. For an extended consideration of the presumed connections between games, play, literature, aestheticism, and citizenship during the period, see my *Nineteenth-Century Fictions*.

3. As Hofer emphasizes, some games were even designed to look like books when stored and "the earliest game known to have been produced in America, *Traveller's Tour through the United States*, was made by a New York City bookseller in 1822" (19, 16). As one of this essay's anonymous reviewers points out, too, cards might be considered to "emulate the pages of texts [. . .] remaining new and unpredictable until they are turned."

4. As Robin Bernstein recently argues, "the history of children's literature exists not in opposition to, but in integration with, the histories of children's material culture and children's play," so much so that we need to "stop erecting arbitrary barriers between children's literature and play with material culture" (459–60).

5. As these names suggest, the cards and story are based on caricatured figures, with "Manly" Harry and "Ninny" Robert appropriately named, at least at the outset. As the game of "Dr. Busby" was reproduced throughout the century, the illustrations for its cards were reworked, becoming at times both grotesque and notably racist.

6. Though the British-born Burnett likely did not intend it, perhaps United States audiences read it as a thinly veiled metaphor for the United States' former colonial state with the English "motherland"?

7. Certainly the text's sensational topic of sudden and potentially lost inheritance was a compelling one, as McLoughlin Brothers in 1893 and Milton Bradley in 1908 produced multiple editions of a "Lost Heir" game, complete with a card depicting a "Wrong Boy" (generally loafing about and looking disreputable) in addition to a card of a true "lost heir" boy (generally looking like a model child-citizen).

8. The Western, and often Eurocentric, perspective of many of the games can be confirmed through games such as those put forth by Elmer E. Johnson, president of the co-educational The Regents Institute in Brooklyn. Clustered together in instructions and advertising are "A Trip Through the United States," "A Trip Through Europe," and "The World Visited." For many game manufacturers and probably players in the United States, there was the United States, Europe, and then the rest of the World, writ large and undistinguished.

9. Burnett, too, was given her due at times, though Alcott may have the distinction of being the only woman portrayed in the original G. M. Whipple

and A. A. Smith game. Ives's chapter in this collection also discusses the representation of women in "Author" games.

10. George S. Parker and Co.'s 1886 "The Dickens Game" is also modeled after "Authors," though the sets of cards are based entirely on Dickens's novels and characters.

11. Other Robin Hood–themed games of the era include George S. Parker and Co.'s 1886 *Ivanhoe* (based on Sir Walter Scott's novel) and McLoughlin Brothers' circa-1890 *The Bugle Horn, or Robin Hood and His Merry Men.*

12. For an analysis of socialization practices embedded in fairy-tale based games, see my "Socialization."

Works Cited

Abbot, Anne. *Doctor Busby and His Neighbors: A Story*. Salem, MA: W. & S. B. Ives, 1844.

———. "Edward's Cap and Edward's Grandfather: Or, Playground Peace and Peace of Nations." Abbot, *How* 91–120.

———. "How to Spoil a Good Citizen." Abbot, *How* 5–90.

———. *How to Spoil a Good Citizen and Other Stories*. Boston, MA: Crosby and Nichols, and S. G. Simpkins, 1848.

Alcott, Louisa May. *Little Women*. 1868. Peterborough, Ontario, Canada: Broadview, 2001.

American Card Company. *Union Playing Cards*. New York, circa 1863.

Beissel Heath, Michelle. *Nineteenth-Century Fictions of Childhood and the Politics of Play*. London: Routledge, 2018.

———. "Oh Golly, What a Happy Family!: Trajectories of Citizenship and Agency in Three Twentieth-Century Book Series for Children." *Jeunesse: Young Peoples, Texts, Cultures* 5.1 (Summer 2013): 38–64.

———. "Socialization: Civilizing Child's Play." *The Long Nineteenth Century (1800–1920)*. Ed. Naomi Wood. Vol. 5. *A Cultural History of the Fairy Tale*. Ed. Anne Duggan. London: Bloomsbury, 2021. 149–66.

Bernstein, Robin. "Toys Are Good for Us: Why We Should Embrace the Historical Integration of Children's Literature, Material Culture, and Play." *Children's Literature Association Quarterly* 38.4 (Winter 2013): 458–63.

Boone, Richard G. "History Games: General Statement to Teachers." *The Game of United States History: Illustrated by Bryant Venable*. Ed. Wilbur F. Gordy. Cincinnati, OH: The Cincinnati Game Co., 1903.

Burnett, Frances Hodgson. *Little Lord Fauntleroy*. 1886. London: Penguin Puffin, 1994.

Carroll, A. B. *A New Game of Authors*. Rev. ed. Chicago, IL: A. Flanagan, 1889.

C. L. B. *Tyche: The Fireside Oracle*. Chicago, IL: J. S. Goodman, 1876.

Cohen, Lara Langer, and Meredith L. McGill. "The Perils of Authorship and Nineteenth-Century American Fiction." *The Oxford History of the Novel in English*. Vol. 5: "The American Novel to 1870." Ed. J. Gerald Kennedy and Leland S. Person. Oxford: Oxford University Press, 2014. 195–212.

Colwell, F. A. *The Race for the Pole*. Woonsocket, RI: F. A. Colwell, 1896.

Dodge, Mary Mapes. *The Protean Cards*. New York: Scribner & Co., 1879.

E. G. Selchow & Co. *Carnival of Characters from Dickens*. New York: E. G. Selchow & Co, 1876.

Gaskell, Charles A. *Gaskell's Popular Historical Game or History Made Interesting to Young and Old*. Chicago: United States Publishing House, 1884.

George S. Parker & Co. *The Dickens Game*. Salem, MA: George S. Parker & Co., 1886.

———. *The Good Old Game of Oliver Twist*. Salem, MA: George S. Parker & Co, circa 1880.

———. *Ivanhoe: A Social Game*. Salem, MA: George S. Parker & Co., 1886.

Hill, Albert A. *Right and Wrong, or the Princess Belinda*. 1876.

Hofer, Margaret K. *The Games We Played: The Golden Age of Board and Table Games*. New York: Princeton Architectural Press, 2003.

Johnson, Elmer E. *A Trip Through the United States*. Brooklyn, New York: Educational Game Company of America, 1895.

The Lion and the Eagle, or the Days of '76. E. H. Snow, 1883.

McLoughlin Brothers. *The Bugle Horn, or Robin Hood and His Merry Men: A Mirthful Game*. New York: McLoughlin Brothers, [1890].

———. *Game of the Lost Heir*. New York: McLoughlin Brothers, 1893.

———. *Game of the Mariner's Compass*. New York: McLoughlin Brothers, [1890].

———. *Game of Nations*. New York: McLoughlin Brothers, [1890].

———. *Game of Nations*. New York: McLoughlin Brothers, 1898.

———. *Improved Authors: The Queens of Literature*. New York: McLoughlin Brothers, circa 1890.

———. *Improved Star Authors*. New York: McLoughlin Brothers, 1887.

———. *Queens of Literature*. New York: McLoughlin Brothers, 1886.

Milton Bradley Company. *Game of the Lost Heir*. Springfield, MA: Milton Bradley Company, 1908.

———. *Game of Nations*. Springfield, MA: Milton Bradley Company, 1908.

———. *The North Pole Game*. Springfield, MA: Milton Bradley Company, 1907.

Nesbit, Edith. "Fortunatus Rex & Co." *Forbidden Journeys: Fairy Tales and Fantasies by Victorian Women Writers*. Ed. Nina Auerbach and U. C. Knoepflmacher. Chicago: University of Chicago Press, 1992. 192–205.

Pardon, George Frederick [Captain Rawdon Crawley]. *The Handy Book of Games for Gentlemen*. London: Charles. H. Clarke, 1860.

Parker Brothers. *The Game of Robin Hood*. Salem, MA: Parker Brothers, 1893.

———. "Rules for Playing." *The Game of Authors*. New ed. Salem, MA: Parker Brothers, 1897.
———. *Sherlock Holmes*. Salem, MA: Parker Brothers, 1904.
The Russell and Morgan Printing Company. *Fauntleroy Playing Cards*. Cincinnati, OH: Russell and Morgan Printing Company, [1890].
Smith, W. C. *Centennial, Seventy-Six*. Warsaw, MO: W. C. Smith, 1876.
Tilley, Roger. *A History of Playing Cards*. London: Studio Vista, 1973.
Wilhelm, N. O. *Literary Whist, or Games of Great Men*. Chicago: A. Flanagan, 1887.

Chapter 9

Gaming the Great Exhibition of 1851

Children's Board Games, Display, and Imperial Power

MEGAN A. NORCIA

The first world's fair, the Great Exhibition of 1851, drew six million visitors to London to see more than 100,000 exhibits that "illustrated every conceivable branch of human industry from engines to dolls," including giant blocks of raw coal, the first facsimile machine, and the enormous Koh-i-Noor diamond, described as "the concretization of the jewel in the crown" (Hayward 135; Gill 159). Housed in Joseph Paxton's elaborately designed iron and glass structure, the Exhibition was dubbed a "Crystal Palace" by *Punch* humorists, and like Paxton's structure at Kew Gardens, this glass house also held the spoils of imperial exploration. It displayed the orderly classification characteristic of British scientific practice, encyclopedia writing, and museum curating in its thirty-part classification system, from raw materials to machinery, manufactures, and fine arts. The move to catalogue, organize, and classify grew out of eighteenth-century traditions of natural science and anthropology as well as cartography and ethnography. For visitors, moving through the displays offered a highly concentrated world tour, complete with interactive sensory experiences to "taste tobacco, snuff and chocolate drops, smell perfumes, and touch textiles and materials" and be "seduced" into "believing that they had indeed experienced the whole world" (Clemm 214).[1] Historians and cultural critics have theorized The Great Exhibition as a threshold event for tourism, manufacturing, consumerism, industrial design, commodity fetishism, and gender and social class construction.[2]

Even after its doors were closed, its displays packed up, and the dust swept away, the Exhibition continued to fascinate the British cultural imagination, historicized as "the pre-eminent symbol of the Victorian age" (Auerbach, *Great* 1). The collections, managed by Henry Cole, became the basis for the Kensington Museum and School, later the Victoria and Albert Museum. Crystal Palace images appeared on postcards, tea trays, paintings, commemorative coins, illustrated books, advertisements for Huntley & Palmers biscuits, and in "peep show" reproductions such as the *Lane's telescopic view, of the ceremony of Her Majesty opening the Great Exhibition, of All Nations* and William Spooner's *Perspective view of the Great Exhibition* (both 1851). Children's publishing firms created popular board and table games. These games promoted the Exhibition's ideology and used its methodology to contain, frame, and order the world to showcase British power and authority. These games prefigure late-century imperial propaganda agencies in "the educational system, the armed forces, uniformed youth movements, the Churches and missionary societies, and forms of public entertainment like the music hall and exhibitions" (MacKenzie 2–3). Mid-century board games were already doing this work by celebrating the Exhibition, privileging Britishness, and grooming players for membership in an imagined imperial community. Though dedicated international archivists, collectors, and historians have worked to uncover and preserve these rich artifacts in special collections, the games have not been part of a sustained cultural analysis of imperial discourse. They should be placed alongside Benedict Anderson's holy trinity—the map, the museum, and the census—as texts promoting national identity and fostering imperial ideology in young players.

Henry Smith Evans's c. 1855 *The Crystal Palace Game* uses the Exhibition's display methodology by surrounding a standard world map with boxed "displays." Evans identifies profitable commodities and the dangers of acquiring them through illustrations featuring threatening animals and resistant indigenous peoples. He casts child players as future imperial stewards, linking their success in the game to Britain's imperial triumphs. In contrast to Evans's straightforward celebration of imperial power, his rival Spooner's earlier *Comic Game of the Great Exhibition of 1851* satirized the Exhibition and Empire itself. Spooner's spiral game (with caricatures attributed to George Cruikshank) parodies the displays, the visitors, and the surrounding discourse, lampooning narratives of national and imperial progress. In their games about the nation's most famous "glass house," Evans and Spooner show the visibility and the fragility of the imperial narrative.

Commanding Resources in Henry Smith Evans's *The Crystal Palace Game*, circa 1855

Part of the developing mass market for children's books and toys in mid-eighteenth-century England, board games had become increasingly specialized by 1851, spanning topics from dynastic succession to industrialization and moral conduct, including the whimsical J. Passmore's circa-1840 *New and Favorite game of Mother Goose and the golden egg* and John Wallis's more troubling 1807 *New and fashionable game of the Jew*, which taught children mathematics and reinforced ethnic stereotypes. Games were part of the "trend in instructional play" that Andrew O'Malley has identified as "proliferat[ing] in the marketplace of late eighteenth-century England" (110). And the largest early subset focused on geography and history to groom players as stewards of an imagined imperial community. The proliferation of these games supports the Manchester School's contention that empire is as much about culture and ideology as it is about the movements of armies and navies. Board games are part of the story of how imperial ideology was transmitted to young people.

Unlike other prominent children's game publishers, like Darton and Wallis, Henry Smith Evans was an outsider. On his *Crystal Palace Game: A Voyage Round the World An Entertaining Excursion in Search of Knowledge Whereby Geography is Made Easy*, he identifies himself as a Fellow of the Royal Geographic Society ("F. R. G. S."), and on the frontispiece of his 1858 *Geology Made Easy*, his credentials include an LLD (a doctorate-level law degree or an honorary degree) and "Fellow of the Geological Society" (see Figure 9.1). Though these professional affiliations project a bookish, gentlemanly persona, Evans combined a colorful, combative character with a practical, professional interest in emigration.[3] In his early career, Evans joined John Clemmitt, Henry Chambers, and Richard Bullock in the firm Clemmitt, Evans, & Co in the New Inn, Old Bailey, offering services as "waggon and coach-office keepers, and general agents" ("Henry," *Law* 127). After the 1810 dissolution of the partnership, he formed Smyth and Evans, Colonial Agents and Accountants, providing advice, bookings, and supplies to emigrants ("Henry," *Law* 127). The work had its risks, and he was called to court in 1846 as "an insolvent debtor, having been filed in the Court of Bankruptcy" ("Henry," *London* 5478). Considered in this context, Evans's game extends his professional interest in profitable emigration, as evident in the game's display cases, chart of "possessions," and inscriptions of raw materials.

The game is formal in appearance, a brightly colored world map printed on linen, bordered on three sides with fourteen illustrated inset display boxes. There was also an accompanying booklet, now missing from extant archival copies.[4] The top border features the title and two large ovals: the first features the Crystal Palace, flags flying; the second depicts Queen Victoria's visit to the Crystal Palace surrounded by her family and state officials. These ovals are positioned as the apex of progress on top of all the boxed displays. This reflects how the Exhibition itself represented the privileged position of England and its Empire in relation to other nations. Deborah Philips affirms that the Great Exhibition itself "place[d] the royal family firmly at the centre of British national identity.

Figure 9.1. Henry Smith Evans identifies himself as a Fellow of the Royal Geographic Society on his Crystal Palace Game. Courtesy of Maps and Research Programs, National Library of Australia.

The Great Exhibition was organized and designed by Prince Albert and was ceremonially opened by his admiring wife Queen Victoria" (96). The placement and size of the ovals reinforces their importance as an organizing force and a representative symbol of British family life and domestic culture.

On the central map, England and its territories are heavily outlined in red, extending the Exhibition's ideological work. Jeffrey Auerbach notes that through the Exhibition "visitors learned what 'belonged' to them" ("Great" 101). Evans's game helps players determine this with proprietary outlines and a very specific accounting of territory in a central chart labeled "British Possessions." It enumerates import and export statistics, lists the "population of colonies" as 4,674,335, and measures the breadth of the "Colonial Empire" at 2,153,246 square miles. In a pre-Foucauldian move, this chart displays the power and authority the Empire commanded over both territory and inhabitants. An emblem above features a small image of a ship positioned on top of a globe; a legend proclaims, "Britain upon whose Empire the sun never sets." Through these instruments of traditional cartography (charts, powerful visual images, meaningful labels), the game communicates imperial might. The chart echoes the Great Exhibition's "elaborate classification" system so "the world appeared as an orderly, compartmentalized space in which the visitor could stroll and inspect at leisure whatever struck their fancy" (Clemm 213). Evans's game replicates both the ideological insistence of the Exhibition and its spatial methods.

The geography of the Exhibition itself was carefully arranged with an east wing to house foreign countries and a west wing reserved entirely for Britain and its colonies, reflecting "how much the Empire was at the heart of the British self-perception" (Clemm 213). The move privileges the breadth of the Empire just as Evans does on his chart. Evans further underscores England's importance by placing it *twice* on the map. To the far west, the numbered spaces begin with an English lighthouse, ending at the eastern edge at number 82, where England is visible again on the horizon as the beginning and end of travel and exploration. This map follows Clemm's contention that the Great Exhibition offered "not so much a realistic representation of the countries that appeared in the Crystal Palace, but an impression of the world as it looked on the 'psychological map' of the early Victorian Empire" (223). On this "psychological map" England is the referential homeland: New Zealand is marked as "Antipodes of Greenwich"; west of Africa a sea route is labeled "homeward course"; and territories from "Barbadoes" to "Timbo" are marked with incorporation dates, suggesting that they are called into being on the map through colonization.

Following the numbering, players begin the game on the left in England, proceed along the west coast of Africa, then around the Cape and up to the Middle East and the Arabian Peninsula. They then travel to India, East Asia, Russia, and down America's west coast, then back out to the Pacific islands, Australia, over to Central America, South America, up America's east coast to Greenland, and then across the Atlantic back to England.[5] The distribution of the stops works out so that 20 percent focus on the Pacific islands, Australia, and New Zealand. Australia and New Zealand alone contain eight stops, compared to only three stops for the entire Indian subcontinent. Given the recent discovery of gold in Australia, Evans may be privileging an opportunity for quick profit. An illustration near Australia depicts "Gold Diggings," part of Evans's overall interest in profitable harvest and trade. Words emblazoned across and alongside territories identify commodities and resources. Over Hindoostan, Evans inscribes "cotton, silk, spice, indigo, tea, and sugar"; the region of central Africa under the Mountains of the Moon is distinguished for wood, gold dust, ivory, and palm oil; South Africa is "rich in gold, wool, wine, and ivory." Off the coast of Australia an image of men panning for gold draws a direct sight line from the image to the mapped territory of Australia.

The identification of territories with their commodities reflects the Great Exhibition's display strategies featuring "captured exotic objects and peoples, the spoils of war and aggressive commercialism" (Gill 157). In particular, the East India Tea Company showcased "India" through a display of primitive-looking tools and raw materials, as well as luxury items and elaborate jewelry, showing it as "a profitable resource, which was in need of the expert control that the East India Company offered" (Clemm 214). The Koh-i-Noor diamond display has been interpreted as "represent[ing] in itself the final submission of the subcontinent following that of the Punjab annexed in 1849" (Gill 157). This display of colonial riches is a persuasive inducement. Gaming the Empire means moving pieces on a board, thinking strategically, calculating, gathering resources and prizes, and then returning home, just as adventure heroes did in the plots of novels by R[obert] M[ichael] Ballantyne, G[eorge] A[lfred] Henty, and W[illiam H[enry] Kingston. London's position at both the beginning and the end of Evans's game underscores for child players that they too are products of Empire who have been sent to circulate in the colonial world and then to return to the home shores where all imperial products and labor tend. Winning this Great Game meant, as Auerbach argues, "find[ing] new sources of raw materials" and "new markets for their manufactured goods" ("Great" 101). The raw materials were an important resource but the colonies were important as well, as markets "for British industrial prowess" (Philips 97).

Auerbach notes that the Exhibition "project[ed] an image of wealth and control" in keeping with the same narrative presented at the British Museum and the India House ("Great" 102). The Great Exhibition mapped Britain's supremacy, technological prowess, and colonial might much like maps of the period. Geographer J. B. Harley states that "Cartographers manufacture power" (244). The Empire's power in Evans's game is based on commanding wealth, and it displays opportunities for mining, harvesting, exploiting, and trading. He shows not only how to traverse imperial space, but also how to manage it. This requires a global enterprise whose steady, coordinated activity of colonial outposts, plantations, ports, and factories is assured through the installation and supervision of civil servants, military officers, merchants, and even teachers and parents in the metropole. John MacKenzie relates that "teachers were enjoined to stimulate children's interests in the value of the Empire by revealing the manner in which their diet and clothing relied on supplies of foodstuffs and raw materials from it" (186). As early-nineteenth-century geography primer writer Priscilla Wakefield remarked, the reader "will soon perceive that he cannot procure his usual breakfast, or clothe himself in his accustomed dress, without the assistance of his fellow-creatures who inhabit countries beyond the ocean" (190). Though Wakefield takes for granted (or overlooks entirely) the coercion involved in what she gently characterizes as "assistance" from fellow-creatures who labored in fields, forests, paddies, and busy ports, colonized populations did not have much choice or share in the profits, unlike emigrants (190).

Evans's professional interest in opportunities for colonial development extended beyond the game and his work as an emigration agent; he also published geology and geography texts marketed to help emigrants. Known best for *Map of the World on Mercator's projection*, featuring lithography by John Anthony L'Enfant (who also did the lithography on the *Crystal Palace* game), Evans published variations of this work from 1847 to 1852.[6] The titles are overtly speculative about opportunities for colonial profit, including *British Colonies: their capabilities and resources*;

Corn-Field map of the world, showing where food for man grows advantageously, including Rice, Maize, Cocoa, Coffee, Tea, &c; and Map of all the known coal-fields of the world, for extending oceanic steam navigation, the primary and carboniferous formations are distinctly marked in which gold is found. The titles promise that careful study of the texts will help emigrants make strategic, profitable choices. Many of the same commodities listed in the titles (e.g., rice, cocoa, coffee, tea, and gold) also appear on the *Crystal Palace* map, connecting adult emigration to children's play.

Evans's commercial interest in emigration drives his practical approach in the game. Gillian Hill, who helped curate a 1970s British Library exhibit, glimpsed the now-lost accompanying game booklet. She noted that it provided not only place descriptions, but practical advice for the voyage: "'All Provisions, Wine, Spirits, and Sugar being shipped 'duty free.' [. . .] Contracts could be made to supply the Sailors with provisions, &c., according to an agreed dietary table from 10d. to 1s. per diem, and the Cabin Passengers, including Wine, &c., at 3s. 6d. to 5s.'" (qtd in Hill 14). Since the provision of spirits and duty-free goods are outside children's typical interests, Evans may have counted on families playing the game together, or perhaps he took a long view of the children as future emigrants. Whatever his intent, Evans's work found a broad market. Eric Richards's research on emigration estimates that from 1853–94 almost eight million people left Britain and Ireland for destinations outside Europe (145). Practical advice established Evans's authority and may have led players to his other emigration books.

Even as he promoted emigration, Evans also acknowledges the many dangers facing those working in colonial offices as clerks, in churches and schools as ministers and missionaries, in forts as soldiers, and at ports and plantations as overseers, managers, shipping agents, and sailors. Across the map, ships face maelstroms; sea monsters off the Cape of Good Hope; volcanoes, typhoons, and opposition from indigenous peoples; and fierce wilderness predators. Evans showcases the dangers in harvesting, acquiring, and shipping goods and resources, which must be overcome with courage and duty. While the bulk of Evans's game promotes a positive, profitable imperial narrative, supported by symbolic imagery, tables, and cartographic devices, it also features two deaths that disrupt this plot.

Most of the territory on Evans's map features commodities instead of indigenous peoples. When they do appear, indigenous peoples are featured as part of the exotic scenery, such as kangaroo hunters contemplating a church, or as victims awaiting English rescue from slavers or ferocious animals. Two notable exceptions to this rule appear between the Marquesas and Sandwich Islands on spaces 42 and 46. The spaces depict the deaths of Englishmen at the hands of South Pacific islanders (see Figure 9.2). Both images bristle with spears and bodies at sharp angles, illustrating William Moebius's claim that "[j]agged lines and those that run at sharp or odd angles to each other usually accompany troubled emotions or an endangered life" (151).

Space 42's "Captain Cook Killed" juxtaposes the peaceful tropical setting of "Owhyhee" in Kealakekua Bay with the violent clash arising over the theft of a cutter. In the foreground, with one of his men fallen at his feet, Cook stands with legs astride, one hand held palm up in a quieting or commanding gesture. His bright blue and yellow clothing distinguish him from the undifferentiated mass of spear-wielding islanders shaded in gray. Generally regarded as the greatest eighteenth-century explorer, Cook had enjoyed many triumphs, voyaging to Tahiti, along the coasts of New Zealand and Australia where he claimed territory for Britain, and to Antarctica. On this final voyage, he had charted the Sandwich Islands, present-day Hawaii. Rather than illustrating Cook's accomplish-

Figure 9.2. In Henry Smith Evans's Crystal Palace Game, spaces 42 and 46 depict the deaths of Englishmen at the hands of South Pacific islanders. Courtesy of Maps and Research Programs, National Library of Australia.

ments by a formal portrait or showing the explorer on his ship, Evans chooses to depict his death. In Space 42, Cook is vastly outnumbered, but remains calm and authoritative, unaware that an islander prepares to strike him down from behind. Space 42, by showing Cook about to be stabbed from behind, comments on the Hawaiians' nature, not Cook's.

In a work that otherwise celebrates emigration and colonization, it is a discordant moment. The islands (and the islanders) are mapped as the end of Cook's story; regardless of what stories of their own they may have to tell, they are visible only as Cook's killers and are marked with the "firm, immutable authority of the inscription" (Moebius 144). This move occludes their narratives and layers Cook's story over theirs. It also puts Evans's map within the corpus of texts memorializing Cook in a particular way. James Akerman discusses this tradition: "as part of the volumes commemorating Cook's discoveries and achievements the map became a way of leading the entire British nation, defined at the at time above all others by its naval prowess, on a memorializing and celebratory (if virtual) journey" (58). Memorializing Cook celebrates his work of discovery and imperial inscription.

The other space featuring an Englishman's death, Space 46, memorializes another seemingly benevolent imperial aim: spreading religious salvation. In space 46, islanders brandish clubs, running through the waves to attack an unarmed fallen man who holds up a hand in supplication or defense. Given the location, the man is likely Reverend John Williams (1796–1839) of the London Missionary Society who from 1817 proselytized in the South Pacific's Society Islands, Raiatea, Samoa, and elsewhere until he was killed on Erromango Island, present-day Vanuatu.[7] Four years following Williams's death, his friend George Baxter painted two companion pieces in England: *The Reception of Reverend John Williams at Tanna in the South Seas* illustrated first the islanders' positive reception of Williams when he landed in the islands, and second his violent death at their hands. Baxter's source material may have influenced Evans. In both images the fight is represented as unfair in numbers, position, and arms. The Erromangoans rush from right to left (reversing the traditional flow of reading text in the West, thus signaling a type of disruption or "backwardness"). They brandish clubs over an unarmed, fallen man, ignoring his raised hand. With these elements, Baxter portrays the attack on Williams as unjust, casting the islanders as villains. The "cultural assumptions" at work here draw from a well-stocked visual library of imperial relations that extend beyond these individual actors (Doonan 48). The ready visuals Evans appropriated from contemporary paintings of Williams's death suggest that an "imperial printing plate with a well-defined picture existed with identical copies in wide circulation throughout the empire [depicting] an inferior native and a superior European" (Mangan 22). In Evans's game, the Erromangoans and Hawaiians are stock characters from an imperial imaginary. Homi Bhabha asserts that the "exercise of colonialist authority" relies on the "production of differentiations" between the ruling power and those it purports to rule, marking the latter "with the visible and transparent mark of power" (111). Evans imprints that "mark of power" by representing the Hawaiians and Erromangoans as unjust, dangerous antagonists in imperial interaction. Edward Said, in his discussion of Rudyard Kipling's *Kim*, has called this "the vantage of controlled observation" (155). Said indicates that visibility is an exercise of power, leading to control and containment. Just as the exhibits were contained in their glassed galleries at the Exhibition, so too is Evans displaying images, charts, and inscriptions to make power visible, while occluding other inscriptions.

These illustrated deaths of Cook and Williams underscore the anticipated violence of the contact zone, where one set of peoples impose their authority over others through maps, trade, or religious practices. Images offer "the immediacy of their testimony" when the "historical moment is literally there before our eyes" (Berger 31). As spatial theorist Henri Lefebvre puts it, "nationhood implies *violence* [. . .] a political power controlling and exploiting the resources of the market or the growth of the productive forces in order to maintain and further its rule" (112). Lefebvre's identification of the violence undergirding nationhood (and by extension imperialism) is difficult to resolve in a society that prided itself in its rule of law and commitment to ending slavery. Yet it was also an Empire that met resistance with force, as seen six years after the Exhibition in its response to the nationalist uprising described in the press as the "Indian Mutiny." Though the Crystal Palace itself relied on the metaphoric transparency of its glass divisions and nicely ordered galleries, Evans's game acknowledges some messier realities of the contact zone.

While part of the imperial narrative demonstrating the dangers of exploration and conquest, Cook's and Williams's deaths may also fulfill a ludic function typical in period board games. Games designed in the tradition of the *Game of the Goose* featured built-in "death" squares that booted players out of the game if they were unfortunate enough to land on them.[8] In Evans's game, these deaths are offset by spaces offering wealth, imperial glory, and a measure of immortality. After all, Baxter's painting placed Williams firmly in the public eye as a martyr, whose death crowns his ministry. Since neither Cook nor Williams were emigrants, the use of the "death space" might also offer players the impression that emigration offered a more profitable and safer route than exploration or missionary work, both in the game and beyond the board. When the player wins, the Empire does as well. In his study of nations as "imagined communities," Benedict Anderson argues that though a citizen of a particular nation will never interact with his thousands of fellow citizens, "he has complete confidence in their steady, anonymous, simultaneous activity" (26). Children's games honed this sense of consistent, coordinated corporate action, reinforcing that players were all rehearsing the activities of Empire through exploration, trade, and colonial management.

Though Evans's map does depict two deaths, most of the violence of colonization is displaced onto the many scenes in which animals are threatening (or are threatened by) human incursion into their territory: a giant snake looms as large as a hut; a tiger attacks Indians mounted on elephants; a kangaroo flees while warriors with spears gaze across a wilderness broken only by the lone spire of newly constructed church; a white man and child stare at an ostrich that has breached the fence of their compound; and a man shoots an angry polar bear while elsewhere another bear attacks a man. Ferocious animal behavior suggests that British intervention is necessary to subdue these wild beasts and ensure peace and prosperity. It may also signal the coded resistance of indigenous peoples to colonization. In her work on hunting culture, Harriet Ritvo theorizes that depictions of "[d]ead wild animals, especially if there were a lot of them, symbolized the British suppression of the Afghans or the Ashante more compellingly than their pampered captive cousins. Rows of horns and hides, mounted heads and stuffed bodies, clearly alluded to the violent, heroic underside of imperialism" (248). When considered in this context, Evans's depiction of ferocious wild animals takes on an imperial charge.

Despite these obvious dangers, Evans's game offered would-be imperial actors a way to inscribe their own stories on the map, experiencing adventure, fame, and monetary gain while joining what was framed as a Christian, civilizing mission and ending the cruel enslavement of peoples by rival imperial powers. One of the larger displays along the bottom depicts one of these nations (perhaps the United States) engaging in taking of slaves (see Figure 9.3). A white man brandishes a sword over

Figure 9.3. Henry Smith Evans's 1851 *Crystal Palace Game* depicts the taking of slaves. Courtesy of Maps and Research Programs, National Library of Australia.

the heads of a group of bound people while his confederate attempts to wrest a baby from its mother. Since Britain had abolished the importation and trade of slaves in 1808 and then subsequently banned slave owning in its colonies, this image reinforces the Empire's moral authority and its duty to intervene in such scenes. This moral authority was also impressed upon children in their geography texts. Mid-nineteenth-century children's author Viscountess Mary F. E. Boscawen, for example, acknowledges that English colonies were "formed, partly for commercial purposes," but "even more in the hope of establishing settlements of Negroes, who should be instructed in religion and civilization. [. . .] The Negroes intended to be placed here are chiefly those slaves who have been set free by the vessels sent from England to put down the slave-trade in these parts" (241–42). In addition to being profitable, imperial work also served a larger purpose.

We cannot underestimate the compelling nature of this imperial narrative, especially because of the way it was, and continues to be, marketed to children and their parents. As Chris Gosden and Chantal Knowles posit, "Colonialism was made up of a mass of small processes with global effects" (xix). In other words, imagine a child's hand moving a piece across the sea to Africa. What were the global effects of such a move? What happened inside the head of that child while that hand was moving? How did it affect the child's conceptions of Africa, Empire, and Britishness in ways that played out later in written discourse, social interactions, critical voting contexts, consumer experiences, or through a career choice, emigration, or military service? The "smallness" of a hand on a game piece during a family game night, an afternoon's play with a governess, or a rainy day with friends could have global consequences. In Australia, for example, emigration was an urgent enterprise. Colonization programs encouraged 100,000 free settlers to relocate there in the 1830s, and the 1851 gold rush added another incentive. In addition, emigrants were also transported, including 160,000 men, women, and children by the 1860s (Parsons 13). Yet as Eric Richards's research shows, from 1837 onward, emigrants were increasingly "self-financing" (choosing to emigrate under their own power, not as slaves, transports, or indentured servants); and, statistically, most were "young and usually slightly better off and more skilled and literate than most of the home population," including miners, agriculturalists, and capitalist entrepreneurs (145, 142). This demographic likely would have purchased and played this game.

Copies of the game have survived its child players, and this persistence tells a story about the families who purchased and played it. In their work, Gosden and Knowles discuss how objects in museum cases "are always in a state of becoming. [. . .] The physical circumstances of the object change continuously, but so also do its sets of significances as it accumulates a history" (4). In 2006, the South Australian Maritime Museum offered child visitors of its *South Australia on the Map, 1606–2006* exhibition a photocopy of Evans's *Crystal Palace* game board. The photocopies mark the changing imperial and postimperial landscape across the intervening 152 years, underlining Gosden and Knowles's point about shifting "sets of significances" (4). In 1854, when Evans's game was marketed in *The Family Herald* as a game for families to enjoy together, the game was an object celebrating the Great Exhibition and a learning tool for families to compete for imperial resources ("Henry" 796). Yet just as the images of Cook's and Williams's deaths fixed their historical significance and established a singular narrative, representing South Pacific islanders as unscrupulous and dangerous, this game's significance is not only determined by the Great Exhibition, but as an emigration guide for citizens of the metropole. This was a less visible significance, but layered with the celebration of the Exhibition, the two narratives told an alluring story. As a contemporary artifact, however, the game presents an added layer of significance; for the future, it acts as a curio of the past, selected and reproduced in a former colony to help its citizens trace and construct their own historical and postcolonial identity in line with, or in opposition to, its closures. The "physical circumstances" of the object and its world have changed tremendously, yet its survival, preservation, and distribution offer a glimpse into the world it came from and the one we now inhabit.

Prizing Subversion: William Spooner's *Comic Game of the Great Exhibition of 1851*

Though the Exhibition sought to promote international harmony, it also provoked "some quite jingoistic responses" from visitors, and competition rather than collaboration (Clemm 208). Publications such as *Punch* subverted the Exhibition committee's goal of international harmony, seeing a chance to expose and mock "the foreign 'other' as a means of asserting British superiority and national identity" (Auerbach, "Great" 189). Foreign visitors to the Exhibition aroused "both fear and fascination" in the British public (Auerbach, "Great" 187). As Pearson contends, the humanity on display at the Exhibition was more interesting to *Punch* than the actual exhibits: "the Exhibition offers a chance to glimpse humanity in microcosm—all races and classes, and both sexes, accommodated under the same transparent roof. They are all observable, all contained, in what *Punch* thinks of as a great zoo" (202). The view of the Exhibition as a great zoo may have inspired William Spooner's A *Comic Game of the Great Exhibition of 1851* (see Figure 9.4). Satirizing the Exhibition, its goals, and its visitors, *Comic Game* is a colored lithograph with a spiral track; its seventy-six spaces parody the Exhibition's displays through caricatures attributed to George Cruikshank (Shefrin 14). The winner is the first to reach the central Crystal Palace space. As Jill Shefrin has noted, Spooner appears to have used a humorous print souvenir as inspiration: Thomas Onwhyn's 1851 *Mr. Goggleye's Visit to the Exhibition of National Industry to be held in London on the 1st of April 1851: with a catalogue containing notes & remarks on the most remarkable works in the exhibition* (14). *Mr. Goggleyes* featured twenty-three joined pages of exhibit parodies that unfold in an accordion-like strip.[9] These include a device for extracting sunshine from cucumbers, a means of building castles in the air, and an Irish scarecrow modeling clothing" (Onwhyn 6, 9). While Spooner's exhibit parodies differ, his work is in the tradition of Onwhyn's and *Punch*'s work.

Figure 9.4. Satirizing the Exhibition, its goals, and its visitors, William Spooner's *A Comic Game of the Great Exhibition of 1851* is a colored lithograph with a spiral track. Courtesy of University of Toronto Libraries.

Though some of Spooner's games were fairly straightforward and educational, designed in the restrained, formal style of Evans's *Crystal Palace* game (e.g., *Voyage of Discovery*, *Travellers of Europe*), others were comic, punny, and absurd. He spoofed moral games in *Cottage of Content* and sent up aristocrats in *Funnyshire Fox Chase*. Spooner's range of approaches indicates that he made deliberate choices about how to represent his topics. *Comic Game* was published near the end of a twenty-year career, when Spooner knew his craft. Though he could have rendered the Crystal Palace formally, he chose a spiral track in the tradition of the *Game of the Goose*, "a gambling game popular in western Europe from around the sixteenth century" (Dillon 337). Characterized by Adrian Seville as the "most important spiral race game ever devised," *Goose* came to England as John Wolfe's 1597 *Newe and most Pleasant Game of the Goose* (1001 7). The spiral form departs from a linear track of Exhibition displays, and Spooner uses it to subvert the importance of the center, traditionally reserved for triumphant displays of British power and supremacy like St. Paul's or the Crystal Palace. Spooner's center pushes the Crystal Palace to the background behind a British gentleman and ladies strolling past caricatured Native American, Chinese, and Turkish peoples and regarding these foreigners with a mixture of frank curiosity, fear, and hostility, as one would do in *Punch*'s "great zoo."

In style and arrangement, Spooner's game questions the notion of progress in arts and manufactures. Unlike the real Exhibition, which had designated wings and courts, grouping nations with their respective colonies, Spooner's arrangement is entirely arbitrary, beginning with China, jumping to France, England, Holland, Prussia, Spain, Egypt, Turkey, over to America, and then back to Germany. From there it is Russia, Scotland, Africa, Australia, Asia, Ireland, South America, Italy, Switzerland, Sweden, and Belgium. The track through these countries is not determined by geography, size, importance, or colonial relationships. The displays, caricatures by George Cruikshank, feature both punny jokes and serious satirical jabs.[10] With an exhibit of "anti-crush" clothing modeled by two dour tourists, Spooner mocks the crowded Exhibition space, as well as Prince Albert and the committee's hopes for the Exhibition. Following the European revolutions of 1848, the Chartist revolts, and the "Hungry Forties" lean decade in Britain, the Exhibition was billed as a chance to refine and educate the tastes of the English public and to stimulate British manufacturing through comparison with other nations. Prince Albert hoped that "developing a taste for art would elevate the character and habits of British men and women and provide greater incentive for British manufacturers to produce high-quality, aesthetically pleasing work" (Auerbach, *Great* 15). Spooner mocks that hope with his display of cleverly punned products. One panel features a seasick bottle of "pale" ale that has doubled the Cape; another shows an "alarum" "belle/bell"; and another the merry Damascus "blade" (Spaces 58, 14, and 32). Spooner's cheeky puns bring together the adult audience of *Punch* with their appetite for satire and caricature, with a burgeoning child audience eager for nonsense verse.[11]

Advancement in Spooner's game is determined by "paying" or "taking" forfeits. Of the seventy-six total spaces, sixty-one (or 80 percent of the game) focus on taking or paying. For Spooner, the Exhibition highlights profit, and in his exhibits, profits are made and lost quickly and randomly, rather than acquired slowly and steadily with careful strategizing.

The game's economics of wealth include more "Pay" spaces (51 percent) than "Take" (29 percent). Unlike Evans's vision of profitable emigration, in Spooner's game players pay more for the Exhibition than they take away from it, just as does the imperial experience. Space 29, for example, labeled "[z]oological Magnet to attract shillings and sixpences," features a hippopotamus pacing in front of a pointing crowd. Like the depicted viewers, players must "Pay 3," because exhibitions are showy spectacles designed to part people from their shillings. This fits neatly within the game's take-or-pay economy, with emphasis on the "pay." Characterizing the Exhibition as profit-based spectacle, Spooner uses the gamed space to undercut the Exhibition's goal of celebrating manufacturing and arts, and educating public tastes.

Players "take" or "pay" according to how the featured exhibits, and, more pointedly, technology, add value to the life of humanity or detract from it. For instance, players who land on a steam plough may "Take 2." The caption explains, "Steam plough to do the work while Farmers eat and drink" (Space 15; see Figure 9.5). Advances in ploughing could certainly reduce a farmer's labor and facilitate a more efficient harvest. Yet the foreground features the farmer leaning back smoking a pipe, looking not unlike the locomotive plough doing his labor in the background. The farmer's body is outlined by cross-hatching lines, which for Moebius "often signa[l] vitality or even a surfeit of energy, rendering the scene crowded, nervous, busy, as if each line were a living organism, part of a giant organism. Swabs of plain colour provide relief from such jungles of line" (151). These "jungles of line," the equivalent of visual noise, surround the farmer, creating a mood of "nervous, busy" energy at odds with his own body, washed in plain colors. By shifting the focus from the labor-saving plough to the farmer, Spooner prompts viewers to consider how the farmer uses his newfound leisure. The farmer drinks, smokes, and samples pineapple, rather than sitting down to a good, wholesome English dinner, reading books, making art, or practicing science. The plough offers him the "take" of labor savings, but this leads to the "pay" of sloth, idleness, self-importance, and possible overindulgence. His table is spread with decanted wine and a pineapple, recalling the Exhibition's goal to bring the public into contact with commodities and products from faraway places, but on this dandified farmer's table, they seem slightly ridiculous. Alongside some of the other exhibits, the game offers insight into the mingled feelings of excitement and suspicion inspired by the Industrial Revolution's promised progress. Even space 48's lighter "[d]omestic telegraph," which allows a wife to "call to Husband in the Library, Scold children in the Nursery & order Cook in the Kitchen," disrupts domestic harmony within a "networked" home (see Figure 9.5). As the wife telegraphs, the cook and husband eye it askance and the children topple chairs in fear. These inventions suggest that industrialization alters human relationships and can lead to unproductive leisure.

Spooner identifies more dire consequences of technological innovation in "The last Continental fashion in Iron work" exhibit: space 4 features a dancing iron cannon with bayonets for arms, swords for legs, and a cannon ball for the head, topped perhaps by a globe (see Figure 9.6). Rather than celebrating ingenuity and progress, Spooner's anthropomorphized display presents ironwork that offers more effective ways of *destroying* humanity, rather than *elevating* it. Players must "Pay 3" in acknowledgment of the human cost this invention exacts in battle. Calling it a "Continental fashion" mocks British consumption of foreign (especially French) fashion trends and alludes to the Continental "fashion" of the 1848 European revolutions (Space 4). If Britons follow this "fashion," it will introduce the destruction emblematic in the ironwork display.

Figure 9.5. In William Spooner's *A Comic Game of the Great Exhibition of 1851*, spaces show how players "take" or "pay" according to how the featured exhibits, and more pointedly technology, add value to the life of humanity or detract from it. Courtesy of University of Toronto Libraries.

Figure 9.6. In William Spooner's *A Comic Game of the Great Exhibition of 1851*, the "Last Continental Fashion in Iron Work" highlights how technological innovation can destroy humanity. Courtesy of University of Toronto Libraries.

To avoid France's revolutionary "fashion," the Exhibition promoted patriotic consumption. Auerbach acknowledges that "[t]here may also have been an element of indoctrination involved, a belief that educating workers would foster stronger social ties and keep them out of Chartist mischief" ("Great" 11). Yet somewhere along the way, "[p]opular commentators took this to signify a competition between different nations and a chance for Britain to outdo them all" (Clemm 213). Spooner's mockery of inventions and industrial progress lampoons the Exhibition's earnest hopes to use displays of skilled manufacturing and ingenuity to spark productive competition and nationalist identification. Spooner represents nations alongside their distinctive products (e.g., Dutch tulips, Spanish sherry, Australian wool), and their problematic cultural practices. In space 1, an image of a Chinese man holding a shoe with a tightening key is labeled, "CHINA, with a model shoe for making the foot small & beautifully less." This technology achieves its "beautifu[l]" goals by painfully disfiguring the body. Lest the English viewer feel too smug, Spooner cannily links this four spaces later to the English practice of tight-lacing, showing an Englishwoman using "The Waist Contractor and Tight Lacing Machine" to constrict her waist into an alarming wasp shape (see Figure 9.6). Though British women would later make their bid for suffrage based on the idea that they could save their colonial sisters from practices such as foot binding, *sati*, the harem, and child marriage, Spooner shows that this intervention is needed at home.

The same mix of satiric playfulness and vicious skewering appears in representations of colonial territory. Gill notes that the Exhibition represented Britain's perceived superiority over Africa and Asia "as an effect of industrial skill rather than the result of military conquest" (159). For Spooner, colonial displays are as ridiculous as the imperialists who seek them. Players who land on Indian curry and Mogul sauce, depicted as fireworks in a bottle, will Pay 3, rebuking both the tame British palate and the over-adventurous memsahib who dares to diversify her family's fare. Exhibition visitors reinforced their notion of what it meant to be British by observing other countries' displays and defining British identity "by its relation to, and position in, the rest of the world" (Philips 96). Space 60 represents Ireland as "a broth of a boy" with a club and a bottle, mouth open in song, followed by Space 61's "Tumbler of punch and the Matarials" (*sic*, see Figure 9.6). At 61, viewers may "Take 1," suggesting that they gain at the expense of the Irish who cannot govern themselves moderately. The game's exhibits and central space show "the process of Britons defining themselves against, and in comparison to, other nations and peoples" (Auerbach, "Great" 107). Africa is introduced in relation to Britain with the caption "Africa with the chain Great Britain has broken" (Space 50). The single display case for the entire African continent features a smartly dressed African man with exaggerated features holding two lengths of broken chain. The costume choice suggests that a freed Africa will adopt English dress and social practices. He is followed at space 51 by a load of tusks, "Cocoa Nut and Box of Ivories." There, viewers "Take 2," perhaps in congratulation for helping Africans break the yoke of slavery, or in recognition that a newly freed Africa offers a profitable commodity market to exploit. Like Evans's game, Spooner's *Comic Game* encourages commodity identification with territory. In the Australia display box at Space 54, a kangaroo with a cargo pack is captioned, "AUSTRALIA. Kangaroo & Wool," framing a colonial territory in terms of goods to be extracted. Spooner's display of colonial territories demonstrates that the Exhibition is less about the unique cultures of Africa, Ireland, and Australia than it is about extracting and circulating their commodities.

Spooner offers a "prize" space to would-be emigrants to Australia.[12] At Space 55, the display features a giant, wheeled "Domestic & Travelling Kettle" with a family sitting at table inside. Choosing to travel inside a vessel of British culture isolates them from their new colonial surroundings. One cannot appreciate the view of Sydney's harbor from within a teakettle. Unlike Evans who built his professional career on a pro-emigration platform, Spooner satirizes emigrants who barricade themselves with their own cultural traditions. The teakettle not only limits emigrants' experience of the world around them, but can destroy them—a kettle is made for boiling water, after all, and this one has steam issuing from its spout. Spooner highlights the self-destructive nature of emigrants' choices, when they insist on the trappings of Britishness despite making a new home abroad, or rely too much on potentially dangerous technology, connecting to the displays of ironwork weapons, constricting shoes, and tight-lacing machines.

Perhaps because of its emigrants' blinkering or its inhabitants' self-destructive behaviors, the game predicts the demise of Britain's imperial power. Spooner introduces England in a shared display with a past empire, not a current rival. The display, "John Bull and Brother Bull of Nineveh," at space 8 features a nattily dressed British John Bull complete with top hat beside a turbaned Assyrian bull (see Figure 9.6). By introducing the British Bull with a Bull of the past, Spooner highlights transitions of power. He alludes to this with the Roman Empire also in the display of Italy as "A model brigand," followed by "Relics from Herculaneum," ordinary pots and pans with comic faces (spaces 66 and 67). These humdrum relics are the ancient empire's only remnants, an Ozymandian caution. Though Auerbach characterizes the Exhibition as a "cultural battlefield" on which "competing visions of Britain fought for ascendency in a struggle to define Britain's past, present, and future," Spooner presents viewers with a sobering vision of Britain's future (*Great* 5). Far from celebrating the Exhibition as the apex of progress, Spooner's game glimpses its diminution at the very moment when the Exhibition was lauding its prosperity.

Seen at best as playful and punny, at worst as subversive or even anti-imperialist, Spooner's game is a satirical parody, an "imitation characterized by ironic inversion [. . .] repetition with critical distance, which marks difference rather than similarity" (Hutcheon 6). Spooner and Cruikshank visually reproduce the Exhibition with ironic differences in order to defamiliarize and critique its excesses. Readers are called to see it differently and look more carefully. This may take a cue from Onwhyn's *Mr. Goggleyes'* exhibit of spectacles and binoculars captioned, "Glasses, for enabling everybody to take the same view of everything, so that there will never be no disagreement on nothing!" (7). Was the goal of the Exhibition to showcase difference or to promote a singular view? Chris Hopkins also notes that the name of the "hero, Mr Goggleye, may suggest that his wonder at the exhibition is part of an indiscriminate and deluding love of spectacle, rather than a realistically progressive attitude" (55). In other words, looking at a glass house is not the same as seeing it.

Taken together, Spooner's and Evans's games commemorate the Crystal Palace by "creat[ing] little universes of meaning," in Clifford Geertz's phrase, with their own rules governing advancement (25). The games reveal how children's play dispenses the kind of cultural ideology promoted by the Exhibition in its setup, displays, and subsequent discourse. David Cannadine points out that the British Empire was "culturally created and imaginatively constructed artifact" a vast, varied space that Britons had to "imagine and envisage" (3). Wrapping one's head around the immense imperium is a formidable task. The Exhibition offered one way to make the far-reaching Empire visible to child players. Games were another. Yet in both games, visibility is a trick—for Evans, the apparent visibility in the curated images of Cook's and Williams's deaths occlude indigenous narratives. For Spooner, visibility is a lure, a spectacle, designed for profit; when visitors look too closely, they see the absurdity of the pig locomotive, or they glimpse the larger problems of labor and leisure represented by the farmer, or the self-destructive nature of technology in the iron work display.

Evans's and Spooner's games both use visuals to bolster and challenge narratives of imperial power, but they have also become part of the imperial archive. For Evans, displays, charts, and lists of commodities make the authority and power of the Empire visible to child players and promote emigration. For Spooner and Cruikshank, the structures of exhibitions are questionable and the visuals that seem exciting and innovative at a glance quickly become absurd, messy, or even dangerous when examined closely. Spooner's game challenges the narrative of imperial might and progress even as it acknowledges its bewitching power. He questions the committee's goal to promote harmony and manufacturing, and interrogates whether technology and progress really benefit human life, using a liberal "prize" distribution to satirize visitors' unthinking awe of the Exhibition and its displays. He amuses, but also indicts, the player touring his Exhibition. Evans's game, on the other hand, uses the framework of the Exhibition to make imperial power visible to inspire awe and acquisitiveness, rather than cynicism and skepticism. Employing the cartographic tradition, inset images and charts, and textual interventions on the face of the map, he displays the world within a comprehensive, highly visible imperial hierarchy. Rather than indicting players or demanding that they question the authority of the

Exhibition or the Empire, Evans's game urges them to join the imperial enterprise and share in its profits. His game offered homeward trails across the oceans, as well as lists of commodities to help players and would-be emigrants traverse the Empire. For both of these games, so divergent in approach, method, and perspective, the Great Exhibition provided a meaningful visual threshold to showcase and critique imperial power.

Notes

1. Diane Dillon discusses George Shove's souvenir lady's glove, which bore a printed map of the Exhibition and surrounding London sites: "Shove illustrated the relative positions of other prominent destinations, picturing St. Paul's Cathedral across two fingers, the Colosseum on the thumb, and Kensington Gardens near the wrist" (315).

2. Called a "myth-making venture" and a screen onto which Britons have projected "their hopes and fears, values and beliefs," the Great Exhibition is read differently across critical schools (Gill 153; Auerbach, "Great" 108). For Auerbach, the Exhibition's significance has been "refracted through a Victorian lens: Whiggish historians seeing it as a shining example of mid-Victorian peace, progress, and prosperity; Marxists as an egregious symbol of industrialization and the formation of rigid social classes; postmodernists as an imperial and commodity spectacle" ("Great" 89–91).

3. On 12 March 1844, the *Morning Post* details the controversy Evans sparked. Called to court to answer for "offensive" language to Deputy-Chairman of the Stock Exchange Mr. Hutchinson, Evans's "volley of abuse" convinced everyone that "his language was well calculated to provoke a quarrel" ("To James" 7e). To avoid indictment, Evans agreed to "withdraw, in the fullest manner, all the offensive expressions" ("Police" 7b). Evans admits that his charges were "without foundation" and "regret[s] that in a moment of irritation I ever made them" (7b).

4. The *Athenaeum*'s 1855 review questions the usefulness of the book, positing that it "asks a great many questions without giving answers; and in place of necessary information, we have not unfrequently bad puns and wretched street slang" (704). The review offers an example of the book's "balderdash": "reflect on the vast extent of the British Empire, 'on which the sun never sets'—to which curious notion add, 'nor the tax-gatherer goes to bed!!' [. . .] You are also at liberty to turn two summersaults, by way of exemplifying the revolutions of the globe," expostulating that "Mr. Evans cannot think this pleasantry!" and advising the purchaser "to put the 'Key' into the fire. Without it the board is perfectly intelligible" (*Athenaeum* 704). The book disrupts notions of decorous play and learning.

5. Along the way, Evans marks routes between places for the practical traveler: San Francisco to Sandwich Isles 2,300 Miles, translating to "12 Days Sail" and "Gulph Stream 150 Miles a Day" (Spaces 42, 75, 76). These estimates set emigrants' expectations of time through space.

6. *Map of the World on Mercator's Projection shewing the British Possessions, with the date of their accession, population, &c., all the existing Steam Navigation, the Overland Route to India, with the proposed extension to Australia, also the route to Australia via Panama* (1847) was later titled *Emigration Map of the World* (1849). Another title is *Geographical and physical map of the world on Mercator's projection, shewing the coal fields, all the existing steam navigation, the overland route to India with the proposed extension to Australia* (1851).

7. Christian missionary Allen Gardiner also perished in Tierra del Fuego in 1851, but from sickness and starvation.

8. In traditional play, Goose has sixty-three spaces, with a death space and a prison or "well" space "requir[ing] the player to remain unless and until rescued by another" (Seville 1003).

9. This is similar to Onwhyn's earlier work *A Railway Adventure that Mr. Larkin Encountered with the Lady of Captn. Coleraine. Showing the Power of Platonic Love* [1841].

10. By the 1850s, Cruikshank was a prolific artist; his 800 works include illustrations for Charles Dickens, the Temperance Society, and his own *Comic Almanack* (1835–1853). Spooner's game was familiar territory; Cruikshank also illustrated Henry Mayhew's comic novel *1851: or, The adventures of Mr and Mrs [Cursty] Sandboys and family who came up to London to "enjoy themselves," and to see the Great Exhibition* (1851).

11. The tradition of irreverent children's nonsense verse was in its infant stages at mid-century with Edward Lear's 1846 *A Book of Nonsense* and with Lewis Carroll's 1865 *Alice's Adventures in Wonderland* on the horizon.

12. Doubling down on his cynical impression of Exhibitions, Spooner liberally awards "PRIZE[s]" throughout the game to every country: the wool-toting kangaroo gets one, as does a seedy-looking American with a ticket to a Jenny Lind concert, Spain with a Cuban cigar, Egypt riding a bucking crocodile, and so forth (Spaces 33, 23, and 27). Indiscriminate prize distribution suggests that if all earn prizes, then none of them are actually extraordinary. The "prize" designation itself is worthless; it is not a "pay" spot, so players do not acquire wealth, nor do they advance in the game. The "prize" is simply an empty honorific.

Works Cited

Akerman, James R. "Finding our Way." *Maps: Finding our Place in the World.* Akerman and Karrow 19–63.

Akerman, James R., and Robert W. Karrow, Jr., eds. *Maps: Finding our Place in the World.* The Field Museum, in association with The Newberry Library. Chicago and London: University of Chicago Press, 2007.

Anderson, Benedict. *Imagined Communities; Reflections on the Origin and Spread of Nationalism.* London: Verso, 2000.

Auerbach, Jeffrey. "The Great Exhibition and Historical Memory." *Journal of Victorian Culture* 6. 1 (2001): 89–112.

———. *The Great Exhibition of 1851; a nation on display.* New Haven: Yale University Press, 1999.

Berger, John. *Ways of Seeing.* London: British Broadcasting Corporation and Penguin Books, 1974.

Bhabha, Homi. *The Location of Culture.* London and New York: Routledge, 1994.

Boscawen, Mary F. E., Viscountess Falmouth. *Conversations on Geography. Or, The Child's First Introduction to Where he is, What he is, and What else there Is besides.* London: Longman, Brown, Green, and Longmans, 1854.

British Newspaper Archive (*BNA*). British Library in collaboration with findmy past.com. https://www.britishnewspaperarchive.co.uk/. Accessed 20 October 2020.

Cannadine, David. *Ornamentalism: How the British saw their Empire.* Oxford: Oxford University Press, 2001.

Clemm, Sabine. "'Amidst the heterogeneous masses': Charles Dickens's *Household Words* and the Great Exhibition of 1851." *Nineteenth-Century Contexts* 27. 3 (September 2005): 207–30.

Dillon, Diane. "Consuming Maps." *Maps: Finding our Place in the World.* Akerman and Karrow. 289–343.

Doonan, Jane. *Looking at Pictures in Picture Books.* Exeter, UK: Thimble Press, 1993.

Evans, [Henry] S[mith]. *The Crystal Palace Game. A Voyage Round the World An Entertaining Excursion in Search of Knowledge Whereby Geography is Made Easy.* London: Alfred Davis & Co., [1855]. National Library of Australia Map NK 2981 http://nla.gov.au/nla.obj-230670288.

Geertz, Clifford. "Blurred Genres: The refiguration of social thought." *Local knowledge; further essays in interpretive anthropology.* New York: Basic Books, Inc., 1983. 19–35.

Gill, Hélène. "Discordant and ambiguous messages in official representations of Empire: Versailles 1845, Crystal Palace 1851." *International Journal of Francophone Studies* 7. 3 (2004): 151–67.

Gosden, Chris, and Chantal Knowles. *Collecting Colonialism: Material Culture and Colonial Change.* Oxford and New York: Berg 2001.

Harley, J. B. "Deconstructing the Map." *Writing Worlds: Discourse, text and metaphor in the representation of landscape.* Ed. Trevor J. Barnes and James S. Duncan. London & New York: Routledge, 1992. 231–47.

Hayward, Arthur L. *The Days of Dickens: A Glance at Some Aspects of Early Victorian Life in London*. 1926. Archon Books, 1968.

"Henry Smith Evans' *Crystal Palace Game*." *The Family Herald*. 12 (1854): 796.

"Henry Smith Evans." *The Law Advertiser for the year 1831*. 9 (1831): 127.

"Henry Smith Evans." *The London Gazette* 20676 (27 November 1846): 5478. www.thegazette.co.uk/London/issue/60676/5478.

Hill, Gillian. *Cartographical Curiosities*. British Library Board. Scarborough, UK: G. A. Pindar & Son, 1978.

Hopkins, Chris. "Victorian modernity? Writing the Great Exhibition." *Varieties of Victorianism: The Uses of a Past*. Ed. Gary Day. Houndmills, Basingstoke, Hampshire: Palgrave, 1998. 40–46.

Hutcheon, Linda. *A Theory of Parody: The Teachings of Twentieth-Century Art Forms*. NY and London: Methuen, 1985.

Lefebvre, Henri. *The Production of Space*. Trans. Donald Nicholson-Smith. Oxford: Blackwell, 2000.

MacKenzie, John M. *Propaganda and Empire: The Manipulation of British Public Opinion, 1880–1960*. Manchester: Manchester University Press, 1984.

Mangan, J. A. "Images for confident control: stereotypes in imperial discourse." *The Imperial Curriculum: Racial Images and Education in the British Colonial Experience*. Ed. J. A. Mangan. London and New York: Routledge, 1993. 6–22.

Moebius, William. "Introduction to Picture Book Codes." *Word & Image* 2. 2 (1986): 141–58.

Myers, Walter Dean. *At her Majesty's Request: An African Princess in Victorian England*. New York: Scholastic, 1999.

Onwhyn, Thomas. *Mr. Goggleye's Visit to the Exhibition of National Industry to be held in London on the 1st of April 1851: with a catalogue containing notes & remarks on the most remarkable works in the exhibition*. London: Timy Takem'in, 1851.

O'Malley, Andrew. *The Making of the Modern Child: Children's Literature in the late Eighteenth-Century*. New York: Routledge, 2003.

Parsons, Timothy H. *The British Imperial Century, 1815–1914: A world history perspective*. Lanham, MD: Rowan and Littlefield, 1999.

Pearson, Richard. "Thackeray and Punch at the Great Exhibition: authority and ambivalence in verbal and visual caricatures." *The Great Exhibition: New Interdisciplinary Essays*. Ed. Louise Purbrick. Manchester: Manchester University Press, 2001. 179–205.

Philips, Deborah. "Stately pleasure domes—nationhood, monarchy and industry: the celebration of exhibition in Britain." *Leisure Studies* 23. 2 (April 2004): 95–108.

"*Police Intelligence. Mansion House*." *Morning Post* (London). 13 March 1844. 7b. *BNA*.

Review of *The Crystal Palace Game: A Voyage round the World* by Smith Evans [sic]. "Reviews." *Athenaeum*. 16 June 1855. 704.

Richards, Eric. "Human Traffic." *The Victorian World*. Ed. Martin Hewitt. London and New York: Routledge, 2012. 141–59.

Ritvo, Harriet. *The Animal Estate: The English and Other Creatures in the Victorian Age*. Cambridge: Harvard University Press, 1987.

Said, Edward. *Culture and Imperialism*. New York: Vintage Books, 1993.

Seville, Adrian. "The Sociable *Game of the Goose*." *Proceedings of the Board Game Studies Colloquium* XI. 1000–1014. http://www.giochidelloca.it/storia/lisbona.pdf.

Shefrin, Jill. Introduction. *Ingenious Contrivances: Table Games and Puzzles for Children based on an exhibition at The Osborne Collection of Early Children's Books*. Toronto: Toronto Public Library, 1996. 7–9.

Spooner, William. *Comic Game of the Great Exhibition of 1851*. London: W. Spooner, 1851.

Sunderland, David. *Managing the British Empire: The Crown Agents, 1833–1914*. The Royal Historical Society. Suffolk: Boydell Press, 2004.

"To James Hutchinson, Esq." *Morning Post* (London). 12 March 1844. 7e. *BNA*.

Wakefield, Priscilla. *Sketches of Human Manners, Delineated in Stories, intended to illustrate the Characters, Religion, and Singular Customs, of the inhabitants of different parts of the world*. 6th ed. London: Harvey and Darton, 1821.

Whitehouse, F. R. B. *Table Games of Georgian and Victorian Days*. Hertfordshire and Birmingham: Priory Press, 1971.

Chapter 10

Teetotum Lives

Mediating Globalization in the Nineteenth-Century Board Game

SIOBHAN CARROLL

In 1866, George Augustus Sala described himself as driven abroad by "the great whirling teetotum of life," which "spun round [and] fell [. . .] athwart a spot on the map marked 'United States of America'" (42).[1] Soon thereafter "the teetotum"—a dreidel-like spinning device used in nineteenth-century board games—takes Sala to Cuba, then to Africa (43). Caught up in a seemingly endless sequence of business travel, he eventually comes to feel as though he himself has become "a teetotum; and to wheel about [. . .] was my doom" (Sala 115). Seemingly arbitrarily, Sala interrupts his account of his life as a Special Correspondent to the *Daily Telegraph* to acknowledge that "there must have been something wrong in the manner they taught boys geography in our time" (42). He claims that his "sectional" knowledge of the world, garnered through "isolated scraps of puzzles" ill-prepared him to grasp the scale of the geographies and historical events he is called on to witness (Sala 42). In these passages, Sala draws on images familiar from nineteenth-century geographical education—the whirling teetotum of the geographical game genre and the jigsaw puzzles that sometimes doubled as gameboards—to convey his rapid, chance-driven, and seemingly irrational progress across the world. His metaphor of gameplay conveys both the excitement of his economically driven travel and his perceived lack of control over its direction, culminating in his portrait of himself, not as an objective observer, but as an object in motion: the iconic teetotum, whirled about by forces it cannot control.

The following essay takes up the objects that inspired Sala's imagery, examining how the material artifact of the nineteenth-century board game encoded Britons' attitudes toward the accelerations, circulations, and space-time compressions of incipient globalization. Familiar to twenty-first-century players via family games like *Monopoly* and *The Game of Life*, the race game, in which players are asked to identify themselves as objects competing in chance-driven motion across space, was ideally suited to expressing the bewilderment and powerlessness felt by nineteenth-century Britons in an increasingly internationalized world. The teetotum, too, as a whirling representation of unstable fortune, served as an icon of instability whose invocation spoke to the vulnerabilities of what Matthew Kaiser has called the Victorian "world in play," an unsettled and unsettling world of competition and change (2). Produced to sate a burgeoning desire for geographical education, these play objects ostensibly prepared players to embrace this brave new world of incipient globalization. As we shall see, however, the early-nineteenth-century board games produced by John and Edward Wallis invited players to regard the spatial transformations created by space-time compression with suspicion. By mid-century, this early suspicion had been replaced by a cheerful embrace of travel and empire, an embrace that was perhaps most provocatively enacted in the games of William Spooner. In tracing the broad arc of this ideological transformation from the eighteenth century through the Victorian period, I aim to illustrate the unstable potential of the board game form to both support and criticize spatial, economic, and cultural transformation.

Traveling Games

The material artifact of the board game has long been associated with travel. In Europe, the earliest and most influential board game on record is the *Game of Goose* or *Jeu de l'Oie*, a gambling game in which players race markers around a spiral game-board track, with the first person to land exactly in the winning space claiming the pool. Pictures of geese mark favorable squares on which a player may be advanced by the amount of the throw, while penalty squares send a player backward, or force him to pay into the pool. As Adrian Seville notes, in "this traditional form, the game [of Goose] was evidently a game of human life," as indicated by the notorious penalty square of "*death*, on space 58" upon which "the unfortunate player [. . .] must begin the game again" (par. 8). Just as the *Game of Life* (the *Game of Goose*'s twentieth-century descendant) envisions life as an American road trip, the *Game of Goose* envisioned its players encountering objects familiar from European journeys. Game squares such as "*bridge*—go on to 12" or "*inn*—lose two turns" could very well reproduce the sights that players had seen on their way to the inn at which their own *Game of Goose* was being played (Seville par. 8).

The *Game of Goose* quickly became an icon associated with border-crossings and spaces of travel. It reputedly made its first appearance in the sixteenth century as a diplomatic gift given by Francesco de' Medici to King Philip II of Spain—an object that, even at this early date, signified a connection between different parts of the world (Seville par. 8). By the seventeenth century, the game had become a common sight in European inns, where it was used as a gambling game to entertain travelers. Instantly recognizable, the *Game of Goose* again served as a mediator of social relations between people from disparate places, who would not necessarily need to share a language in order to interact via the game's familiar rules. When in 1770, Oliver Goldsmith wished to summon the lost life of the village inn in "The Deserted Village," the inn's obligatory copy of the "royal game of goose" connotes both the sociality the game once enabled and a nod to the cruel fortune that has plunged the inn's "tottering mansion" into ruin, and sent the villagers spiraling out into a world reshaped by enclosure, emigration, and international trade (l. 232, 238).

During the latter half of the eighteenth century, board games became more explicitly associated with the kinds of knowledge needed to engage in global circulation. The emergence of the geographical game can be traced to 1645 when the French geographer Pierre Duval used the *Game of Goose* system as the basis for *Le Jeu du Monde* (*Game of the World*). In *Le Jeu du Monde*, players raced along a spiral track in which squares were occupied by tiny maps of different countries. Players racing along the track would presumably learn to recognize the maps of these different nations and their corresponding ideological associations. ("France," unsurprisingly, is the country featured in the winning square.) By the late eighteenth century, British publishers eager to capitalize on a growing market for children's educational items had taken up the idea and were producing their own geographical games for British and

American audiences. Not only did geographical games sell well, but they also allowed British publishers to maximize their profits by eking more use out of old cartographical engravings. British game publishers reprinted old maps in slightly altered form as game boards across which players would race. As Jill Shefrin has noted, they also reproduced the form of "travelling maps" by printing their games on paper that was subsequently attached to canvas or linen, then folded into a slipcase for packing and travel (92). Advertisements on slipcases and gameboards would reinforce this association of board game with traveler's map by directing interested players to the publisher's cartographical wares (see Figure 10.1). Before a player even examined a geographical game's informational contents, its haptic and visual aspects already promised to orient the player to the world.

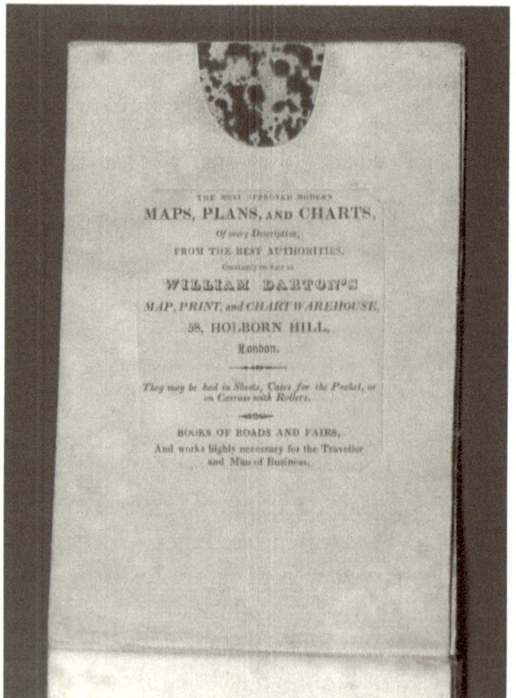

Figure 10.1. The advertisement on this slipcover for *Walker's New Geographical Game Exhibiting a Tour Through Europe* (London: W. & T. Darton, 1810) reinforced the association of board game with traveler's map and directed interested players to the publisher's cartographical wares. Courtesy of Special Collections, University of Delaware Library, Newark, Delaware.

The popularity of British geographical games was fueled by a growing perception of the utility of geographical study to Britain's domestic, commercial, and imperial interests. As early as 1726, Isaac Watts noted "the utility of geography for 'commerce' with distant places" (qtd. in Smith 139). By 1800, Watts's observation had become as commonplace as the dependence of British power on "burgeoning maritime trade (including slavery), empire, the navy and the transportation of goods [. . .] created a considerable demand for geographical education" (Elliot and Daniels 20). By the late eighteenth century, geography was perceived as foundational to practical subjects like navigation; it was foundational too for the cartography required in agricultural estate management, making it an important area of study even for those whose business never took them overseas. The practicality of geography undergirded its rise as "an important component of the polite knowledge craved by the middling sort," a rise both reflected in and spurred on by early-nineteenth-century marketing of "games, textbooks, globes and other apparatus" to the middle classes (Elliot and Daniels 21). By the time of the 1851 educational census, geography's position had been solidified in curriculums across the nation. Not only was geography the content-oriented course most often taught to children in both public and private schools, but it had also become the third most-taught subject in evening schools for adults, where it was prioritized behind "Writing" and "Reading" and above other subjects such as "Mathematics," "History," and "Modern Languages."[2] Potentially encompassing science, politics, history, mathematics, religion, and foreign languages, Victorian geography as taught by the games that were associated with it served both as a foundation for practical skills and as a general-knowledge course, in which students could be introduced to a wide variety of information organized within a spatial frame.

The rise of the British board game thus took place alongside what Roland Robertson has argued was a period of "incipient" globalization taking place roughly from 1750–1875 (59). While some of the knowledge inculcated by geographical games directly reflected Britain's developing sense of national and imperial identity, other games inculcated a sense of the geopolitical relations between European powers or sought to envision globe-spanning trade networks involving nations with which Britain was not immediately concerned. As such, they participated in what Manfred Steger refers to as globalization's tendency to "intensify worldwide social interdependencies and exchanges while at the same time fostering in people a growing awareness of deepening connections between the local and the distant" (13). As we shall see, even games that pretended to engage only with local or national landscapes implicated themselves in these larger processes, encoding in the materiality of board games changing British attitudes toward the accelerations, circulations, and space-time compressions of incipient globalization.

Resisting Circulation

At the dawn of the nineteenth century, the typical British board game was, like the *Game of Goose*, a race game in which players move markers across a board, competing to be the first to successfully land on the final square (see Figure 10.2). Geographical game boards tended to be

Figure 10.2. Like other race games, *Walker's 1810 New Geographical Game Exhibiting a Tour through Europe* required players to move markers across a board, competing to be the first to successfully land on the final square. Courtesy of Special Collections, University of Delaware Library, Newark, Delaware.

structured either in a spiral form, featuring a circular racetrack that included, or was positioned beside, images of famous locations, or in a cartographical form, in which players would be directed to certain locations on a map of a city, nation, or continent. In such games, players typically had little actual influence over their motion, which was determined by a roll of dice or a spin of the more politic teetotum, the device that would rise to become a nineteenth-century icon of the vagaries of fate. Players landing on particular squares would be directed to its accompanying educational information, about which, in some games or methods of play, they would then have to answer questions. A player whose teetotum-spin propelled her to square 55 of John Wallis's 1795 *Complete Voyage Round the World: A New Geographical Pastime*, for example, would learn that "Canton" is "a city in China, and is the only Chinese seaport in which the Europeans are permitted to trade" and that its city wall was "five miles in circumference." Unfortunately for the player, these educational details come at a cost, as "the traveller must stay one turn" in Canton to learn this information and thus fall behind in the race that could win her the game (Wallis). While a few games like Robert Sayer's 1787 *New Royal Geographical Pastime for England and Wales* rewarded players for accumulating geographical knowledge, the vast majority of geographical games associated learning with penalty, a practice that one could excuse as poor game design if it did not often appear to have been deliberate.

Indeed, the early-nineteenth-century games published by the Wallis family—the most important and prolific of England's early game publishers—appear somewhat critical of the spatial transformations for which they ostensibly prepared their players. Edward Wallis's 1820 *The British Tourist*, for example, features a game system diametrically opposed to the values of the Romantic-era tourist culture invoked by its title. In this game, players are repeatedly penalized for their desire to "*view* [. . .] *fine ruins*," such that the opportunity to view "*Tintern Abbey*" can cost a player the game (E. Wallis, *British* 3, 9). Meanwhile, if a player is "*born in London*," he will be rewarded for his indifference to rural beauties (E. Wallis, *British* 3, 9). Finding himself in Wordsworthian landscapes such as that featured on square 12, "A FARM-HOUSE at BROOMFIELD," this member of modern commercial society "*will be at a loss for amusement, and must therefore spin again*" (E. Wallis, *British* 4). *The British Tourist* thus displays a satirical edge that associates the shallow world of the global metropolis with the kind of rapid motion encouraged by the board game form.

While other Wallis games are less obviously satirical, they are similarly characterized by a suspicion of the forms of travel they ostensibly celebrate. Thus, while the title of Edward Wallis's 1835 *Locomotive Game of Railroad Adventure* might suggest a nineteenth-century version of *Ticket to Ride* that touts advances in speed, technology, and far-flung global connections, this game instead highlights moments of stoppage and friction. The excitement of the railway journey is ascribed not to speed and motion, but to incidents such as missing one's train, losing one's fiancé, and the apparently frequent peril posed by loose pigs on the tracks. The game appears to celebrate the advent of railway travel; however, it emphasizes the moments when the railway *fails* to propel its players into the fast-paced movement that would win them the game. In portraying the railway as a place of disorder and even danger, the game reifies contemporary resistance to the railway as an uncertain new technology that disrupts social order and entails "an enervating lack of individual control" over one's mobility (Dorré 23).[3] Given the board game's association with gambling, we can also read this game as anticipating the critiques of economic speculation that would come to be associated with railway companies in the mid-1830s and 1840s. In either case, the board game serves as a device for critiquing the railway as an enabler of problematic forms of physical and economic circulation.

Games such as Edward Wallis's 1830–33 *Game of the Star-Spangled Banner, or, The Emigrants to the United States* similarly call players' attention to the negative dimensions of the spatial movements featured in the game. As its title suggests, this game addresses itself to potential emigrants to the United States, and to the family members of those contemplating such a voyage. Ostensibly neutral or positive in its attitude toward emigration, the game in its rule book reflects contemporary British anxiety over the large numbers of people leaving England—flying, in the words of one contemporary commenter, "from a future charged with evils [. . .] to a hostile or at least a rival country," rendering "the lot of the remaining population still more miserable" (Haussez 123). While the *Game of the Star-Spangled Banner* allows its players occasional moments of triumph—landing on a "Gold Mine, in Georgia," for example, allows the player to move forward, with the somewhat sardonic cry of "*that's the way to go a-head*"—the player is just as likely to be propelled forward by dangers such as forest fires (flying for "your life" from a terrifying blaze allows the player to move ahead to site 116) (E. Wallis, *Game* 9, 1). Penalty sites in which players are vomited on by turkey vultures paint a less-than-desirable vision of life in America, while penalty sites demanding that players inquire into the state of a "slave plantation" and bear witness to the "odious practice" of lynching, suggest that players would suffer morally, too, from absorption into the American body politic (E. Wallis, *Game* 1). The morally chaotic nature of the United States is reinforced by the visual appearance of the game itself, which does not feature clearly demarcated squares. Instead, the stages of a player's journey are indicated by numbers placed on top of images that dissolve into and overlap with each other, so that the peril of a forest fire threatens to consume a nearby town, and a cry of protest against lynching also intrudes into a space on natural history. The numbers are not always easy to read, and their direction can be hard to anticipate, rendering the emigrant's movement into the United States a confusing search and hop across a disorderly landscape. As with the accident-prone *Railroad Adventure*, emigration is positioned as an adventurous encounter with mobility that the player should not find particularly appealing. Far better, the game implies, to stay in the comfort of British domestic space than to risk gambling on a future in America.

While the early-nineteenth-century Wallis board games associated themselves with traveling maps, they also included subversive commentary on the types of travel for which they were extensively preparing their players. Middle-class families wary of contaminating their homes with the values of the marketplace could have their ludic cake and eat it too, in the form of games that familiarized children with contemporary forms of mobility while simultaneously highlighting the annoyances, injustices, disorders, and dangers associated with these circuits of global movement. Like the earliest version of *Monopoly*—originally a satire of capitalism rather than a celebration of it—these early-nineteenth-century games modeled the *unfairness* of commercial society, encouraging a kind of double consciousness in which things players knew they should value, such as the picturesque, education, and hard work, became handicaps that would prevent them from *winning* in a world of rapid movement, superficial social relations, and amoral dedication to lucre. The educational objective of such games was not just the accumulation of geographical facts, but the construction of a self that could resist false imperatives to win at all costs. However such designs may have worked out in real life, scenes of geographical gameplay in children's literature reinforce this reading, for they never feature sore losers. Instead, as the beaming characters in Mrs. Richardson's 1866 children's book *Little Harry's Troubles* pronounce, the experience of losing at a "geographical game" is a happy one, for it teaches the female loser to love the "beautiful" place in which the "teetotum" has cast her, and inspires the male loser to "grow up a strong useful man" (75).

Embracing the Teetotum Life

While Wallis games were popular in the early decades of the nineteenth century, the kinds of games published at mid-century were of a different ideological cast. This development is most visible in the games published by the innovative Victorian publisher William Spooner. "One of the most engaging and distinctive printsellers and publishers of the nineteenth century," Spooner introduced a series of visually striking games that reflect a more positive view of mobility (Worms). Crucially, in many Spooner games, players get to choose the direction of their travel, giving them a limited degree of agency over their movement. In Spooner's 1847 *The Pirate and the Traders of the West Indies*, for example, trader players spin a teetotum to determine the direction of the winds and then *choose* to move in one of two directions along intersecting oceanic pathways. Whereas Edward Wallis's games emphasized the costs of movement, games such as *The Pirate and the Traders of the West Indies* emphasize the cost of remaining in place: all players in this game must pay a penalty each time they find themselves unable to move (rule book vi). By introducing a limited degree of player agency and by altering the kinds of actions rewarded by the game system, Spooner games such as *Pirate and the Traders* signaled a transformation of the ideological character of the British board game from games that resented or invited suspicion of new forms of mobility into games unabashedly celebrating human circulation.

This celebration is overt in games such as Spooner's *The Travellers of Asia*, which praises the space-time compressions of a new era of rapid "global transit" (rule book, v). Whereas a "few years ago, the passage betwixt Europe and Hindoostan was rarely performed under five or six months," the *Travellers of Asia* rule book observes, "now a regular transit is established, and the mail-steamers are dispatched every six weeks" (v). Such indeed is the justification for the game's existence: given that new circuits of transportation make it increasingly likely that Britons will find themselves in foreign spaces, relying on their game-inculcated acquaintance with "the Geography, manners, and Customs of those whom we are called to rule" (Spooner, *Travellers* v). Embracing Victorian Britain's role as imperial power would require embracing a new era of global circulation, the game indicates, an era in which the spatial education provided by board games would prove essential to players' success.

Not only should travel to foreign places be accepted as a matter of course, Spooner's games argue, but foreigners' presences within the domestic sphere should also be accepted as a natural consequence of Britain's rise to global prominence. A participant in Spooner's *Comic Game of the Great Exhibition of 1851* would have brought caricatures of the multiracial crowds visible in London into the space of the home. While the illustrations (attributed to George Cruikshank) exaggerate the racial features of exhibition-goers, the game's text foregoes xenophobia in favor of a self-congratulatory portrait of Britain's place in the world, as when, in square 50, "Africa with the Chain Great Britain has broken," the (non-minstrelized) caricature of a well-dressed black man reflects back Victorian Britain's image of itself as the moral leader of the globe (Spooner, *Comic*).

While Square 50 of the *Comic Game* suggests a condemnation of the commodification of human bodies, the cartoonish exaggeration of those bodies on the game board creates a visual connection between the circulation of foreign bodies and the circulation of the foreign and domestic commodities celebrated as wonders. Caricatured human bodies are juxtaposed with caricatured objects, and in certain squares, the line between living being and object is decidedly blurred. Players move objects representing themselves across the board, landing on squares that feature anthropomorphized objects such as the queasy beer bottle depicted on square 58, which we are told is a "Pale Ale that has doubled the Cape." Meanwhile, squares such as 5—"The Waist Contractor and Tight Lacing Machine"—depict British bodies as actively produced by commodities. These familiar satires of fashion trends are accompanied by squares such as 48—"Domestic telegraph to call to Husband in the Library[,] Scold Children in the Nursery[,] & order Cook in the Kitchen" (Spooner, *Comic*). These squares convey the marvel invoked by the real objects on display while humorously suggesting how such objects might transform British domestic life. British identity, as the *Comic Game* suggests, does not stand apart from the global marketplace, but is actively shaped by it. Square 55—"Immigrants Domestic and Traveling Kettle"—for example, depicts a teakettle transformed into a giant immigrant transportation device, driving home the game's suggestive parallel between bodies and commodities. Such squares suggest that if one wants access to the wondrous foreign commodities on display in the Exhibition, one must also be willing to accept the entrance of foreigners into British domestic space. While the *Comic Game*'s gentle satire could serve xenophobic as well as multicultural purposes, the essential wonder conveyed by the game, as well as its own winking status as a commodity that serves as a souvenir of the Great Exhibition, suggests that players should view global circulations of people and objects in a positive light.

This laughing embrace of commodity-based circulation continues through Spooner's other Exhibition-related game, the 1851 *Harlequin's Rambles Through Europe*. Unlike the *Comic Game*, *Harlequin's Rambles* humorously engages with the geographical game genre designed to mediate young Britons' relations with the world. The spaces and monuments it represents are of the kind illustrated in a typical geographical game and gesture toward an educational experience that will familiarize players with an accurate representation of the world. Nevertheless, the gameboard subverts this promise, allowing players to hopscotch across such "European" nations as the North Pole and Egypt. This is not a reproduction of geographical reality so much as it is a reproduction of the lively juxtaposition of nations and cultures featured in the Crystal Palace: the directions the game encourages its player to follow—"left," "right" or "forward"—are not the compass directions one follows across Europe, but the directions one follows across a crowded Exhibition Hall (Spooner, *Harlequin's*). As with the *Comic Game of the Great Exhibition of 1851*, *Harlequin's Rambles* metaphorically reproduces the experience of the Great Exhibition for players by having them hopscotch through a sea of objects and peoples. The experience of hopscotching through a profusion of inventions, material goods, and people produces disorientation rather than comprehension; but this, the game suggests, is an experience we should take pleasure in. Unlike the satire-edged games of Edward Wallis, Spooner games poke fun at the speed and disorientations produced by space-time compression, encouraging players *not* to resist the rise of new global circulations, but to go with the flow.

Spooner's more positive sentiments toward global mobility may well reflect the publisher's own experience. As a young clerk, Spooner had traveled to Ireland on business for Hurst and Robinson.[4] When he struck out on his own as a publisher, Spooner set himself up as the first printer of the *Dublin Review* in London—the Catholic periodical founded and maintained by figures such as Michael Joseph Quin, Cardinal Wiseman, and Daniel O'Connell, that would, in its later years, prove a significant agitator for the rights of Irish Catholics within the British Empire.[5] While biography never suffices as explanation, the limited information we have for Spooner suggests that, unlike John and Edward Wallis, he was personally acquainted with international travel and worked with immigrants in London, including those who were speaking of (though not necessarily sympathetic toward) the grievances of the colonized. In publishing games that celebrate international circulation and that speak of Britons' duty to familiarize themselves with the "Geography, manners, and Customs of those whom we are called to rule," Spooner was very likely reflecting the perspective of London businessmen who saw not only travel but also cultural engagement as necessary to Britain's economic growth (*Traveller's* rule book v).

Games in Circulation

William Spooner's circulatory games can be productively contrasted with games such as *The New Game of the Royal Mail or London to Edinburgh*, whose creation was sponsored by the L & N. W. Railway around 1850. Such games served as forerunners of our own era of corporation-driven gamification, in which companies attempt to reshape players' attitudes toward their products via games tailored to promote certain products or services. Small, portable, and likely designed to be played on a train, the *New Game of the Royal Mail* displays no ambiguities in its celebration of rapid circulation. Its game system more closely resembles the kind of railway-centric race games seen in twenty-first-century culture: it asks players to race train engines across its board, awarding the win to the first player to reach Edinburgh. With rules printed on the game board, the *New Game of the Royal Mail* retains elements of earlier British board games, such as the penalties applied to visiting tourist sites—landing on square "76. Penrith," for example, forces a player to "Remain here for one turn, and visit Druidical Remains"—but the *New Game of the Royal Mail* also introduces the concept of traffic control, so that "An Engine stopping at a Station with Signal against it must remain there one turn." The resulting game, unlike Wallis's earlier *Locomotive Game of Railroad Adventure*, offers a non-satirical celebration of speed and acceleration. As the title of the game suggests, the *New Game of the Royal Mail* implies that the real purpose of the railway is the acceleration of communication networks, rather than tourism or the transportation of products. Speed is to be embraced as a good, not because it enhances products, but because it brings the disparate elements of the nation's imagined community closer together.

In the latter half of the nineteenth century, British game publishers saw their influence diminish, while American publishers such as the prolific McLoughlin Brothers, along with familiar names such as Parker Brothers and Milton Bradley, came to dominate the Anglophone archive. Given the long dominance of the American marketplace by British game publishers, it is unsurprising that games such as the Parker Brothers' 1888 *The Amusing Game of Innocence Abroad* inherit William Spooner's innovations in player agency, or that these games also express an earlier generation's skepticism toward travel. In *The Amusing Game of Innocence Abroad*, for example, players spend a great deal of the game trying unsuccessfully to get on the road. As the instructions note, "[e] ach player at the outset goes on a shopping expedition [. . .] and after having purchased several articles, reaches the depot and is fairly started on his journey" (*Amusing*). "Fairly started" is an exaggeration. Despite the title's deliberate echo of Mark Twain's 1869 *The Innocents Abroad*, the players never succeed in leaving the country, or indeed, getting much beyond their local territory. However, unlike in Wallis's *Game of Railroad Adventure*, the stoppages that plague these American tourists are caused not by accidents but by their own relentless consumerism: their need to pause for refreshments, for new luggage, for new and more fashionable hats. The game offers an ironic commentary on the purpose of travel, suggesting that tourists participate in the accelerated circulations of the global marketplace both as consumers and transported objects. The latter suggestion emerges not only from the players' identification with game pieces but from lines that, as in Wallis's *British Tourist*, emphasize the tourist's desire to get on with travel rather than enjoying the picturesque qualities of tourist destinations. Thus players are told that "[t]he large mountain, up which runs a stage line, affords the possibility of a pleasure trip to its top. [. . . B]ut the purpose of the players being to arrive at the City as quickly as possible all such delays even spent 'amid such delightful scenery' are to be avoided if possible" (Parker). Whatever the purpose of American tourism, the game suggests, it is neither to bind the imagined community together nor to see the world, but instead represents an opportunity for conspicuous and grandly inconvenient excesses of consumption.

A contrasting view of American transatlantic circulation is on display in the McLoughlin Brothers' 1890 *Game of Round the World*, published to capitalize on the press generated by Nellie Bly's successful whirlwind tour of the globe (see Figure 10.3). At the top of the brightly colored game board, the intrepid female journalist gazes across the board at the looming face of Jules Verne, the man whose fictional celebration of the possibilities of global transportation had inspired Bly's real-life global race. The silhouette of Verne's fictional traveler, Phileas Fogg,

Figure 10.3. The McLoughlin Brothers' 1890 *Game of Round the World* capitalizes on the press generated by Nellie Bly's successful whirlwind tour of the globe. Springfield, Massachusetts: Milton Bradley & Co., [ca. 1890]. Courtesy of Special Collections, University of Delaware Library, Newark, Delaware.

flees into the distance behind his creator, while the author's gaze rests approvingly on the woman writer-turned-traveler who has translated the speculations of Verne's imagination into reality. Between the two writers, the spiral-shaped race game invites players to imaginatively participate in the highlights and hardships of Bly's journey. Fiction and news, geography and narrative, meet and merge on a game board space that flattens out global geography and reuses the traditional shape of the spiral race game to celebrate new transportation technologies that even—as Bly's resolute figure declares—a woman could use.

Game of Round the World recalls the geographical representations of earlier games but, given its attachment to a real-world "game" of rapid travel, it also encapsulates nineteenth-century board games' transformation from critics of incipient globalization into tools for its conceptualization. Like many spiral geography games from earlier in the century, the images featured in its squares cast "national and international places into jarring proximity," a proximity that, as Edlie Wong observes, does not "represent the 'real' geography of Bly's travel" (302). As Wong argues, the game's haphazard geographical representations seem to put the lie to the proclamations that had accompanied Bly's journey, which the *New York World* credited with awakening a new "interest in geography and in books of travel" as the public attempted to follow or even anticipate her progress (2). The *New York World* encouraged the latter with "The Nellie Bly Guessing Match," a "contest offering a free first-class trip to Europe [. . . for the reader who submitted] the guess nearest to the final travel time" (Wong 298). As the contests attracted a frenzied interest from the American public, the prize was increased to include a £50 prize. Before they got the opportunity to play the *Game of Round the World*, fans of Bly already resembled *Game of Goose* players, gambling on the progress of a marker across a board. Criticisms lobbed at Bly's journey also recall the resistances encoded in early board games, as when the editor of the *Petit Journal* bemoaned Bly's realization of "the American system of education" in her "daring journey," which demanded the "passing of a thousand interesting places without visiting them" (qtd. in Wong 302). Both the *Petit Journal* and the *New York World* credit Bly with embodying the kind of circulation envisioned in board games, a circulation accelerated by the technologies and cultures of an incipient globalization as opposed to the interests of local place. That Bly's game-like journey was itself then reproduced in board game form signals the triumph of a late-nineteenth-century vision of rapid human mobility; the emergence of our own gamified world of rapid transit and communication.

In reflecting on his "teetotum existence," then, George Augustus Sala invokes the board games of his youth to both represent and explain his implication in global systems of circulation (119). His economic ambitions have led him to leave home and hopscotch across the globe, often, he claims, with very little understanding of the larger contexts of the places or events he encounters. In making this claim, Sala invokes the geographical board game's status as a problematic inculcator of knowledge: a game whose system encourages players to embrace rapid circulation over intellectual and physical dwelling, and one that prepares players to accept both their detachment from local place and—as Sala's narrative suggests—a loss of control over their movements, which will now be driven by the vagaries of market forces and determined by transportation and communication infrastructure. As I have suggested here, Sala's invocation of board games is both accurate and overly simplistic: while the systems of nineteenth-century games did indeed create a vision of a flattened, globalized space that rewarded rapid travel over place-based engagement, the games of both the Wallis and Spooner eras complicated this formal tendency of race games via satire and (in the case of Spooner) by introducing a limited degree of player agency. After mid-century, however, board games lost their subversive edge, a development that was likely linked to the growing role played by railway companies and newspapers in creating games as components of wider advertising campaigns. The games we see at the end of the century appear to encourage a more straightforward embrace not only of the technologies of transportation and communication but also of a global culture in which the player was encouraged to see herself as an object in global circulation. In examining the material artifacts of nineteenth-century board games, we gain more than just fresh insight into Victorian spatialities; these games also anticipate our own era of globalization and "gamification," in which video games and apps serve both to implicate us in systems of global consumption and to mediate our relationship to the twenty-first-century environment. The kind of data a player of *Pokémon Go* transfers to Niantic may be a new development, but the idea that a game prepares us to move through space towards predetermined destinations is not. We may no longer spin teetotums to determine our progress through virtual space, but arguably many of us continue to live what Sala would have referred to as a "teetotum existence," moving in global currents made visible by gamification.

Notes

1. Portions of this essay revise and extend my argument in "Play."

2. The most commonly taught subjects were reading, writing, arithmetic, and geography. See Great Britain's 1851 Education Census tables cxxx, cxxxi, and ccx.

3. For Victorian attitudes toward railway and horse-based transportation, see Dorré 21–62.

4. See Charles Maturin's correspondence with Spooner, in particular the letter dated 8 November 1823.

5. For a brief history of *The Dublin Review's* early years of publication, see Casartelli.

Works Cited

"A Boon for Geography." *New York World*. Dec. 21, 1889: 2. *Newspaper Archive*. Accessed 3 December 2016.

Carroll, Siobhan. "'Play You Must': *Villette* and the Nineteenth-Century Board Game." *Nineteenth-century Contexts* 39.1 (2016): 33–47.

Casartelli, L. C. "Article 1. Our Diamond Jubilee." *The Dublin Review, 1836–1910*. 118. 18 (1896): cclxxi. *Newspaper Archive*. Accessed 1 April 2017.

Dorré, Gina M. *Victorian Fiction and the Cult of the Horse*. Burlington: Ashgate, 2006.

Duvall, Pierre. *Le Jeu du Monde*. Paris: Chez l'auteur, P. Du Val d'Abbeville, 1645.

Elliot, Paul, and Stephen Daniels. "'No *Study so Agreeable* to the Youthful Mind': Geographical Education in the Georgian Grammar School." *History of Education* 39. 1 (January 2010): 15–33.

Goldsmith, Oliver. "The Deserted Village." Ed. Austin Dobson. London: Henry Frowde, 1906. 23–37.

Great Britain. *Census of Great Britain, 1851, Education. England and Wales. Report and Tables*. London: George E. Eyre and William Spottiswoode, 1854.

Haussez, Charles Le Mercher de Longpré, baron de. *Great Britain in 1833*. Philadelphia: E.C. Mielke, 1833.

Kaiser, Matthew. *The World in Play: Portraits of a Victorian Concept*. Stanford: Stanford University Press, 2012.

Maturin, Charles. Letter to William Spooner. 8 November 1823. MS British Library. Add MS 41996 A-Y. ff. 40. London.

McLoughlin Brothers. *Game of Round the World a Novel and Fascinating Game with Plenty of Excitement by Land and Sea: With Nellie Bly, the World's Globe Circler*. New York: McLoughlin Brothers, 1890.

L & N. W. Railway. *The New Game of the Royal Mail or London to Edinburgh*. London: John Jaques & Son, 1850.

Parker Brothers. *The Amusing Game of Innocence Abroad*. Salem: Parker Brothers, 1888.

Richardson, Mrs. *Little Harry's Troubles: A Story of Gipsy Life*. Edinburgh: Johnstone, Hunter and Co., 1866. Google Books. Accessed 25 October 2018.

Robertson, Roland. *Globalization*. New York: Sage, 1992.

Sala, George Augustus. *Under the Sun: Essays Written mainly in Hot Countries*. London: Robson and Sons, 1872.

Sayer, Robert. *A New Royal Geographical Pastime for England and Wales, Etc*. London: Robert Sayer, 1787.

Seville, Adrian. "The Geographical *Jeux de l'Oie* of Europe." *Belgeo* 3–4 (2008): 1–14. https://journals.openedition.org/belgeo/11907. Accessed 25 October 2018.

Shefrin, Jill. *The Dartons: Publishers of Educational Aids, Pastimes & Juvenile Ephemera, 1787–1876*. Los Angeles: Cotsen Occasional Press, 2009.

Smith, Johanna M. "Constructing the Nation: Eighteenth-Century Geographies for Children." *Mosaic* 34. 2 (2001): 133–48.

Spooner, William. *Comic Game of the Great Exhibition of 1851*. London: William Spooner, 1851.

———. *Harlequin's Rambles through Europe: A Game*. London: William Spooner, 1851.

———. *The Pirate and the Traders of the West Indies*. London: William Spooner, 1847.

———. *The Travellers of Asia*. London: William Spooner, 1843.

Steger, Manfred. *Globalization: A Very Short Introduction*. New York: Oxford University Press, 2003.

Wallis, Edward. *The British Tourist: A New Game*. London: E. Wallis, 1820.

———. *Game of the Star Spangled Banner, or, The Emigrants to the United States*. London: Edward Wallis, c. 1833.

———. *Locomotive Game of Railroad Adventure*. London: Edward Wallis, 1835.

Wallis, John. *Complete Voyage Round the World: A New Geographical Pastime*. London: John Wallis, 1796.

Wong, Edlie L. "Around the World and Across the Board: Nellie Bly and the Geography of Games." *American Literary Geographies: Spatial Practice and Cultural Production, 1500—1900*. Ed. Martin Brückner and Hsuan L. Hsu. Newark: University of Delaware Press, 2007. 296–324.

Worms, Laurence. "Spoonerism." 29 June 2012. *The Book Hunter on Safari: The Blog of Ash Rare Books*. https://ashrarebooks.wordpress.com/2012/06/29/spoonerism/. Accessed 10 October 2018.

Section IV

Books, Boards, and Other Objects

Chapter 11

What Did They Play, and What Does This Say?

A Quantitative and Cultural Analysis of British Collected Games in the Nineteenth Century through the *Games Research Database*

MAURICE SUCKLING

Introduction: What is GARD? And What Doesn't It Tell Us?

The Games Research Database (GARD) is currently the most comprehensive games database of its type in the United Kingdom. A not-for-profit academic resource curated by British game historians Richard Ballam, Edward Copisarow, Neil Darbyshire, Mike Goodall, James Masters, Jeremy Secker, and Michael Thomson, the GARD lists 3001 different game and/or game-related entries by name. The games range in time period from 1650 to 1990, with games between 1650 and 1750 existing primarily in facsimile. After 1750, each of the following periods accounts for one-quarter of the database's holdings: 1750–1870 (120 years), 1870–1910 (40 years), 1910–1950 (40 years), and 1950–1990 (40 years). The vast majority of the listings cover Britain, with some sparse exceptions of France, Germany, and the United States. To my knowledge, there is currently no better single resource through which to glean what people in Britain played during the nineteenth century. Using GARD, we may also speculate on nineteenth-century culture and its game players.

We should, however, outline GARD's current contents in order to clarify what we can learn from it. Foremost, GARD is a work in progress, still being implemented and expanded, and still adding data, such as manufacturer details. According to two curators of GARD, Edward Copisarow and Richard Ballam (a collector whose games are now housed in the Bodleian) in a correspondence with the author, the database *primarily* represents popular games from the late nineteenth century onward. Many of those games appear in multiple listings: "Chess," for example, has thirty-one sublistings, excluding compendia and other references to chess with different titles, such as a traveling chess set titled *Staunton Legacy/Chess Drayton*; "counters" has forty-seven sublistings. At the same time, the database does not fully reflect *all* sorts of games: it excludes what Copisarow and Ballam term "dexterity" or "activity" games (such as Charades); games not requiring equipment (such as I Spy); or games played with standard equipment (such as a pack of cards to play Poker). The database underrepresents wooden game boards and other non-printed games, for instance, games with marbles, spinning tops or other artifacts (such as counters), and pub games (such as darts; shove ha'penny; skittles; or cribbage). In addition, as Ballam clarified to the author, GARD assimilates the collections of individual collectors, each one inevitably skewed by personal interests or chance.

GARD then does not and cannot claim to show us precisely what people were playing nor does it give us an entirely accurate breakdown of the games that were commercially produced. Nevertheless, in Ballam's opinion, it does provide a fair sample of British-manufactured indoor games. But most significantly for my purpose, GARD, though, incredibly useful in offering researchers examples of historic games, fails to organize its holdings into useful categories. In this essay, then, I categorize the GARD database's nineteenth-century contents by game types and themes. My method is quantitative, though I do offer some light cultural analysis in relation to game types, themes, and mechanics. In my analysis, I have excluded entries that do not yet include images or which do not include dates of manufacture (around 1,087 entries of the 3,001). In my examples, unless otherwise noted, I draw explicitly from GARD holdings. Interspersed with the empirical data, I will also offer brief thoughts on continuities and discontinuities between the nineteenth century and our own times. Despite these caveats, GARD still has considerable riches to divulge and is an excellent means through which to attempt to tackle my question: What did they play and what does this say?

GARD Game Types

With specific reference to the nineteenth century, we might break down the database into many of the same categories (and example games) that Richard Ballam suggested in his 2016 Oxford lecture:

- Board Games: Strategy (Chess) or Race
- Card games and Dominoes
- Dexterity games (Shove ha'penny, Jenga)
- Word games (Scrabble)
- Question & Answer games
- Party games (Pictionary, Charades)
- Games of chance (Lotto)
- Jigsaws and other Puzzles
- Teaching toys (Alphabets)
- Pastimes (Scrapbooks)
- Equipment (counters, dice)
- Books, catalogues and Trade lists

But to include the full spread of GARD's games, I have expanded on Ballam's categories, as I explain below.

Board Games—Race Games

Race games are board games in which players use pawns or similar pieces and race their pieces to an end point. These games most frequently utilize dice or teetotums to generate a random movement score. The board usually has penalties or bonuses on different spaces, knocking pieces back or advancing them. Sometimes the games include a mechanic that bumps other pieces back too or has other implications on movement if two pieces occupy the same space. Usually these games are meant for two or more players and have around a thirty-minute play time. Examples for these types of games include *Snakes and Ladders*; *Cowes at Home*; and *The Five Navigators*.

Board Games—Abstract Strategy

In these games, players take turns to make moves determined by strategy and defined by regulated rule sets, rather than through random movement and/or random conflict mechanics. These games may have some thematic wrapper like the Crusades, or military hierarchy, or fox and geese, but there is almost no narrative quality beyond a title, and perhaps some tangentially (at best) relevant artwork. Usually for two players (though occasionally more), the games often have a play time of around forty-five minutes or more. Examples for these types of games include Chess; Draughts; and Halma.

Other Strategy and/or Board Games

These games might be board games, but they may perhaps combine cards in some way, or they are less abstract in conception, perhaps incorporating some asymmetrical design, or greater levels of simulation detail in a wargame. Examples for these types of games include Polemos and Invasion.

Card—Dominoes—Tiles

These games are largely predicated on collecting sets or matching elements to be the first to deplete or complete a hand. Usually luck (in the hand distribution) and memory (tracking who has which cards) are the key mechanics. Usually for two to six players, sometimes more, these games typically have around a thirty-minute play time. Examples for these types of games include Happy Families; Piquet; and Poor Old School Soldier and His Dog.

Dexterity

The games require physical abilities such as throwing, shooting, flicking, and blowing. Sometimes these are sports like croquet, tennis, table tennis, or whiff whaff. On other occasions, they are reimagined versions of sports in a miniaturized format, such as golf or table croquet.

Word

In these games, players complete words or construct words through rebus or other puzzles, and other players decipher them, try to identify missing words in sequences, or to match words together. Usually engaging three or more players, these games usually involve around thirty minutes of play time. Examples for these types of games include *Word Making*; *Beaux and Belles*; and *Geography of Europe*.

Question and Answer Games

Question and Answer games are usually on cards and survey a range of topics from general knowledge to more specific areas of interest such as geography, natural history, and history. Sometimes these games are connected to scoring systems involving the collection of points and avoiding the reduction of points by giving wrong answers. Usually engaging more than three players, these games take around thirty minutes play time. Examples for these types of games include *Scripture Questions and Answers*; *Structure of the Earth*; and *The Welcome Intruder*.

Party

Games predicated on drawing and "parlor games" like charades, riddles, and fortune telling.

Lotto

In these games, cards listing items are completed by the random appearance of those items in a sequence. The first player to complete the whole card is the winner. Usually these games include three or more players.

PUZZLES

Games include dissected puzzles, and, particularly later in the nineteenth century, jigsaw puzzles. These also include 3D puzzles in various materials.

TEACHING TOYS

These may be instructional toys or cards that are aids to discussion rather than elements of a more complex game design. Examples for these types of games include *Amphibiological Conversation Cards*; *Bible Characters*; *Birds Booklet*; or *Birds On Blocks*.

PASTIMES

Scrapbooks often include game-derived elements such as cards or images from games or toys. Certainly, scrapbooks were *of themselves* a nineteenth-century cultural phenomenon, but—as the GARD collections indicate—they often included games. As a result, I include them in my categories.

EQUIPMENT

These include dice, counters, shakers, teetotums, pieces for various games.

LISTS

Trade lists outlining game titles, sometimes with some details.

OTHER TOYS

Toys that don't fit neatly into the category for teaching toys. Examples for these types of games include *Changeable Portraits*; *Periscopes*; *Miniatures*; *Thaumatropes*; and *Conjuring Tricks*.

Unclear—Probably

These games appear to be in line with the some of the category definitions above, but need further study in order to verify them.

Unclear—Compendia

These games are compendia of other games, such as chess, draughts, ludo, various card games, and, as a result, do not fit clearly into any single category.

Unclear—Other

Games that either clearly do not fit into any of the categories above or, more frequently, require closer analysis in order to discern their most appropriate category. An entry with 'Race' in the title may *not* be a race game: *The Donkey Race*, for example, is a puzzle, while the *Numerical Puzzle* is an abstract strategy game, not a puzzle at all.

As may already be apparent from the descriptions and examples above, the taxonomy I outline (based on Ballam) is certainly open to debate. Should riddles be considered party games or word games? Should *Magic Cards* be included in "Other Toys" (as they are in my schema) or as "Cards"? Should *Miniatures* be included as "Other Toys" (as they are in my schema) or as "Equipment"? When is a semi-abstract game "abstract" enough to be *Abstract*, or "other" enough to be *Other*? Jaques's *Polemos* (c.1885) is perhaps the most complex strategy game in our date range, but it is also a wargame with some of the complexity of *Kriegspiel* and as such would be recognizable to modern wargamers. In fact, *Polemos* shares the same name (from the Greek, meaning a divine embodiment of war) with a modern series of rules developed by Baccus in Sheffield, England, for 6mm wargames for a variety of different eras. Yet *Polemos* is still an abstraction of war, as all wargames must be. As a result, I consider it to be of a sufficiently different nature (closer—albeit not that much closer—to simulation) to move it into the "Other" category, away from the likes of Chess, Draughts, Solitaire, and Halma.

Dating is also problematic. In almost all cases, GARD gives dates as "circa." Only in some instances do we have specific dates printed on the board or in the rules or on some other part of the published game. The current survey includes all c.1900 manufactures, yet excludes c.1800, on the supposition that the c.1900 listings will be more confident datings, while the c.1800 will less likely be so and could therefore extend further back into the 1700s, thus distorting our understanding of nineteenth-century manufactures. Perhaps this analysis should have included them. But where would we stop? c.1799? c. 1798? Up to c.1901? Up to c.1902, or c.1903? In the interests of coherence, I have included only the dates c.1801–c.1900.

Of course, other researchers might create different categories based on their research interests, and the database, by providing no categories at all, allows that freedom. At the same time, it's likely that other researchers will (as I have) base their categories on those already commonly used by games specialists such as Ballam. By categorizing the GARD collection, I hope to open up the conversation to other researchers more broadly, including those who work primarily in fields outside of games such as history, English, and cultural studies.

GARD Game Breakdown by Categories and Date

- 3,001 entries (many with multiple sub-entries—132 of which affect the date range in question)
- 1,481 without date of manufacture information. Of these, three look to be nineteenth century from appearances, and a further three appear to be board/race games from the nineteenth century, again from appearances. As per the rationale above, however, they were still excluded from this study.
- 1,520 entries with dates.
- 741 entries within date range (c.1801–c.1900). Three additional entries appear to be within the date range and thirty-seven listings appear to be cross listings of the same item, most often with a slight name variation.
- 132 multiple sub-entry listings.

This study then combines the 741 entries within the date range combined with the 132 multiple sub-entry listings, or 873 nineteenth-century listings, leading to the following breakdown of game types.[1]

Table 11.1. Game Types Shown in the 873 Nineteenth-Century Listings on GARD

Game Types	Number	Overall Percentage of Listings
Board Games - Race	118	8.9%
Board Games - Abstract strategy	332	25%
Other strategy/and board	20	1.5%
Card/dominoes/tiles	89	6.7%
Dexterity	140	10.6%
Word	17	1.28%
Q&A	26	2%
Party	23	1.7%
Lotto	24	1.8%
Puzzles	64	4.8%
Teaching toys	101	7.6%
Pastimes	5	.38%
Equipment	82	6.2%
Lists	8	.6%
Other Toys	32	2.4%

All tables and figures in this chapter were created by Maurice Suckling to visually represent GARD nineteenth-century listings data.

We could further organize "unclear" game types into the categories that likely describe them:

Table 11.2. A Categorization of Listings with Unclear Game Types on GARD

Game Types	Number	Overall Percentage of Listings
Probably Race games	78	5.9%
Probably Abstract Strategy	8	0.6%
Probably Other Board:	5	0.38%
Probably Card	21	1.6%
Probably Teaching	9	0.68%
Probably Q&A	4	0.3%
Compendia	4	0.3%
Other	116	8.7%

We could then represent those statistics more visually:

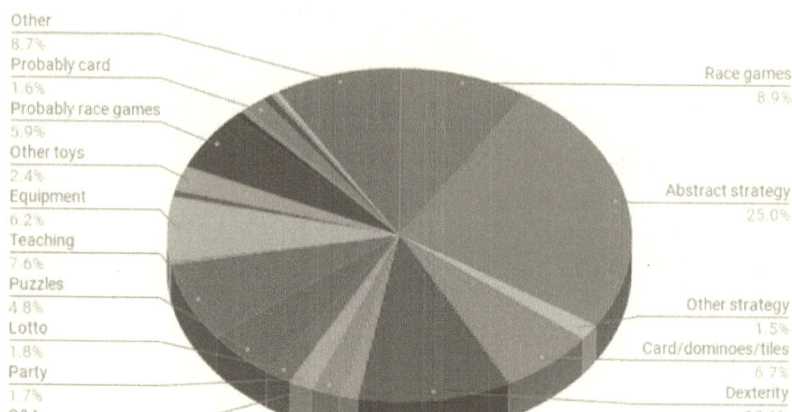

Figure 11.1. GARD listings' game types data (Tables 11.1 and 11.2) represented as percentages.

Games designated as "Probably" can collate into the corresponding categories:

Table 11.3. Categories for the Listings That Are Described as "Probably"

Game Types	Number	Overall Percentage of Listings
Board Games—Race / Probably Race Games	196	9.5%
Board Games—Abstract strategy / Probably Abstract Strategy	340	27.2%
Other strategy/and or board/ Probably	25	2%
Card/dominoes/tiles	110	6.7%
Dexterity	140	10.6%
Word	17	1.28%
Q&A / Probably Q&A: 30	30	2.4%
Party	23	1.8%
Lotto	24	1.9%
Puzzles	64	4.8%
Teaching toys / Probably	110	8.8%
Pastimes	5	.38%
Equipment	82	6.2%
Lists	8	.6%
Other Toys	32	2.6%

This leaves relatively few games that cannot be collated into definitive categories:

Table 11.4. Breakdown of Unclear Listings in GARD

Game Types	Number	Overall Percentage of Listings
Compendia	4	.3%
Other	116	9.3%

We could also represent the resulting statistics more visually:

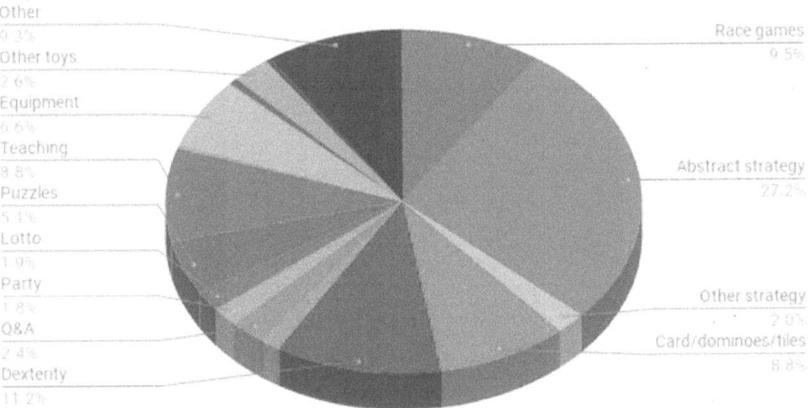

Figure 11.2. GARD listings' game categories data (Tables 11.3 and 11.4) represented as percentages.

Rearranging those categories, including those designated as "Probably" into an order of frequency clarifies these findings further:

Table 11.5. Board Games Breakdowns from Previous Tables Organized in Order of Frequency

Game Types	Number	Overall Percentage of Listings
Board Games—Abstract Strategy etc.	340	27.2%
Board Games—Race Games, etc.	196	15.7%

continued on next page

Table 11.5. Continued.

Game Types	Number	Overall Percentage of Listings
Dexterity	140	11.2%
Unclear/Other	116	9.3%
Teaching Toys etc.	110	8.8%
Card/Dominoes etc.	110	8.8%
Equipment	82	6.6%
Puzzles	64	5.1%
Other Toys	32	2.6%
Q&A etc.	30	2.4%
Board Games—Other etc.	25	2%
Lotto	24	1.9%
Party	23	1.8%
Word	17	1.4%
Lists	8	0.6%
Pastimes	5	0.4%
Unclear etc.	4	0.3%

Once we incorporate the "probables," abstract strategy games have a clear preponderance at more than one-quarter of the listings, with dexterity games and race games each around 10 percent.

Popularity and Sales

We can say more about the popularity of games than this, however. The database also tells us about multiple instances of the same titles, giving a clearer sense of the popularity of specific games. Abstract strategy games may be the most popular category by instances, but 35 percent (118 of 340) of titles so categorized above are accounted for in just *six* different games and their close variations, albeit by a variety of publishers:

- Chess (26–36, depending on whether we include variations or not)[2]
- *Halma* (20)
- *German Tactics* (9); *Asalto* (2); *Fox and Geese* (13); *Wolf and Lamb* (1).[3]
- Draughts (12–13, depending on variations)
- Board solitaire (6)
- *Go Bang* (9)[4]

This gives us a picture of a marketplace largely dominated very a small number of unique titles. Chess and Draughts need no explanation. *Halma* was, as these figures purport to show, a popular nineteenth-century game now little heard of in mainstream gaming cultures. With a checkered 16x16 board, like a double-sized chess or draughts board, it also has a game mechanic reminiscent of draughts, allowing pieces, which otherwise move one space per turn (and just one piece can be moved by a player per turn) except when jumping opposing pieces. But, unlike draughts, jumps do not remove opposing pieces from play. The game is also playable by two or four players.

Board solitaire may also need little explanation. The board is often a thirty-three "spaced" board as a player attempts to remove each of the thirty-two marbles or pegs by jumping over them (similar to draughts). *German Tactics*, *Asalto*, *Fox and Geese*, and *Wolf and Lamb* also utilize the "jump over to remove" mechanic, but are asymmetrical two-player games. One player attempts to hem in the "fox," or more potent but less numerous piece(s), while the "fox" player attempts to remove the "geese" pieces piecemeal to win by degrees—diminishing the "geese" player's capacity to surround the "fox." *Go Bang* is a 14x14, up to a 20x20-square, board. It is also a two-player game in which players take turns to move one piece, as they attempt to surround the other player's pieces, whereupon they are removed from play. The player who removes the most pieces wins.

Clearly, there are a number of overlapping mechanics, boards, and design elements across these games, which already represent a high proportion of the kind of abstract strategy game being played at the time.

However, GARD doesn't typically include sales figures, other than in one instance I've located in my data set. The game box of the phrenology-themed card game *Perfect Man*, published c.1890, boasts advertised sales figures of "115,000 copies sold to date." This figure—part of the game's own marketing copy—certainly sounds impressive. If true and if proven high in relation to other games, it would be worthy of closer examination. Perhaps this game had special cultural relevance. But verifying sales figures is difficult, and certainly not possible from inside GARD.[5]

Themes

GARD doesn't allow searching by theme, and the listing summaries, where extant, frequently do not detail theme in any way. However, as part of this analysis, I have catalogued theme for all 873 items in my data set. If we ignore the most abstract of games, such as Halma, and only ascribed theme to titles where it can be clearly distinguished, then we can generate a chart with the X axis showing the game theme and the Y axis showing the number of instances.

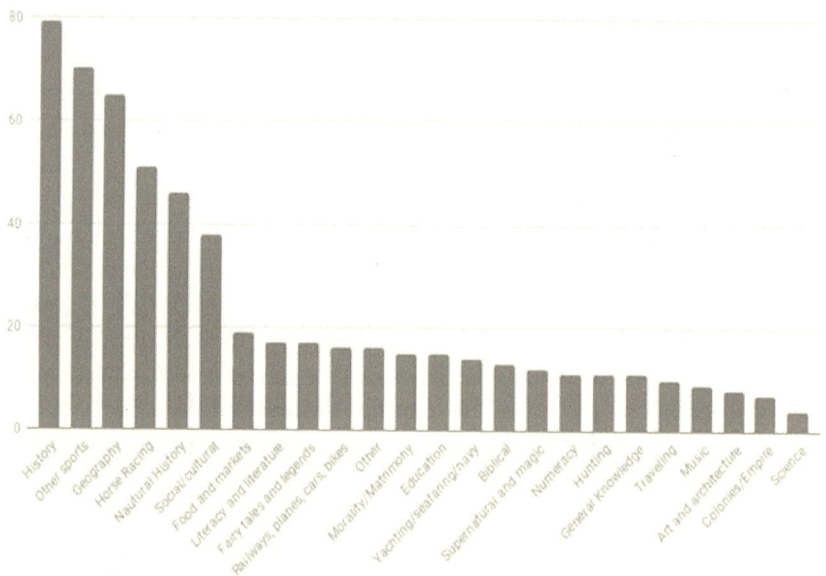

Figure 11.3. Data from Table 11.5 represented in percentages.

In creating this chart, I also allowed games to have multiple categories whenever appropriate. So, some titles, such as *Life of Nelson* (a puzzle) have two themes: Navy and History. The game *Trade and Empire* is counted as both Colonies/Empire and Food and Markets. The game *Travelling in India* is counted under three themes: Traveling, Geography, and Colonies/Empire. The thematic categories can be further clarified as follows:

- "History" (79 items) focuses predominantly on monarchs of England, and Britain, but includes an overlap with all war-themed games (14). It also includes unique entries, such as *Suffragetto*, a suffragette-themed strategy game.
- "Other sports" (70 items) includes all sports other than horse racing.
    - o Croquet: 20
    - o Table tennis: 7; and Ping pong: 4
    - o Golf: 8
    - o Rugby: 5
    - o Billiards: 4
    - o Rowing/boat race: 4
    - o Skittles: 4
    - o Bowls: 3
    - o Cricket: 3
    - o Football: 3
    - o Archery: 1
    - o Badminton: 1
    - o Boxing: 1
    - o Quoits: 1
    - o Tennis: 1
- "Geography" (65 items) focuses predominantly on England and Wales, but also Scotland, France, Europe, and the world.

- "Horse racing" (51 items) includes steeplechase.
- "Natural history" (46 items) includes animals, birds, zoology. *Fox and Geese* games have been included here: the game may be abstract but the thematic reference is clear. Snakes and Ladders, however, is excluded, as its theme is not considered to be natural history in any real sense.[6]
- "Social/cultural" (38 items) includes a wide spread of themes such as rural sports, trade cries of London, Twelfth-night, and toothache.
- "Yachting/seafaring/navy" (22 items) includes some historical content, such as Nelson, or Columbus, but also some contemporary topics, such as *Cowes at Home*, and *The Regatta*, as well as some that demonstrate the theme in a more broad sense, such as *Beside the Broad Ocean*, and *Our Ship*.
- "Food and markets" (19 items) covers a wide variety of themes, including market day, trade, groceries, fruit, cookery, county fair, the progress of butter (how the process of making it moves from a cow to the finished product in a home), and the dairy.
- "Literacy and Literature" (17 items) includes games related to English language and literature:
  - Literacy/grammar/pronunciation: 11
  - Literature: 4
  - Poets: 1
  - Storytelling: 1
- "Fairy tales and legends" (17 items) includes Dick Turpin, Robin Hood, Dick Whittington, Little Pigs, and Red Riding Hood.
- "Other" (16 items) encompasses items not included in other categories:
  - Faces: 5
  - Dress/costumes: 2

- Auction: 1
- Courts: 1
- Furniture: 1
- Hieroglyphics: 1
- Natural Philosophy: 1
- Nursing: 1
- Phrenology: 1
- Seasons: 1
- Technology: 1

- "Railways, planes, cars, bikes" (16 items) focuses on transportation.
  - Railways: 9
  - Bicycles: 3
  - Planes: 3
  - Cars/taxis: 1
- "Morality/matrimony" (15 items) includes themes of courtship, and proverbs relating to moral rectitude.
- "Education" (15 items) includes games which explicitly teach a subject or skill.
  - Education: 11
  - French: 4
- "War" (14 items) is limited to only titles where the theme was expressly war. Clearly, one might argue this category should include chess and close variants, but these are too abstract to legitimately qualify. Most games included here are no less, or are perhaps even more, abstract in terms of the gameplay, but their titles more directly build specific associations with the theme, and so more clearly deliver on it in terms of surface perceptions.
- "Biblical" (13 items) include direct references to the Bible and Christianity.

- "Supernatural and magic" (12 items) includes a range of otherworldly themed games:
  - o Magic: 5
  - o Astrology: 3
  - o Fortune Telling: 3
  - o Ghosts: 1
- "Numeracy" (11 items) teaches numeracy skills
- "Hunting" (11 items) includes deer, duck, and other general hunting themes.
- "General knowledge" (11 items) categorizes general knowledge–themed Q&A games.
- "Traveling" (10 items) includes mostly walking games, but also travel in general, but not travel if expressly in another format, i.e., railways or seafaring.
- "Music" (9 items) includes educational and Q&A games.
- "Art and Architecture" (8 items) also includes games involving construction or building.
  - o Art: 3
  - o Architecture: 3
  - o Construction/Building: 2
- "Colonies/Empire" (7 items) includes games expressly on the theme of British colonies/British Empire.
- "Science" (4 items) includes Astronomy

From this schema, we may draw some brief conclusions. As you see from the data above, for the nineteenth-century games, abstract strategy games at 27 percent are by far the most frequently included game type in the database, and race games and dexterity games fall second with around 10 percent of the included games. My data, further, identify the most prevalent themes for these games as sports, history, geography, and natural history.

Considered from our broad understanding of nineteenth-century culture, these themes match what we might expect. We find the vaunted British love of sports and of horse racing in particular much in evidence.

Natural History too is popular, as are contemporary transportation and seafaring-themed games.

But other British concerns show up less than we might have anticipated. Take for example war (14 items) and references to the Colonies/Empire (7 items). Using the broadest classification of "war," we find conflicts relating to Britain, the East India Company, British subjects, or British possessions averaging more than one a year for the entire century. Yet games only refer to the Boer War and the Crimean War twice each, the Indian Mutiny and Trafalgar once each, with another game referring to potential future war with an unstated continental power attempting invasion of southern England. For a state with a vast empire forged and maintained by martial exploits, this is sparse reference indeed. It might be that political or psychological sensitivity to bereavements from recent wars may factor significantly here; likewise, games might be considered a medium more appropriate for entertainment than for serious concerns. Similarly, Colonies/Empire are not referenced nearly as much as we may have expected. Some art elements of travel games and general knowledge games may subtly include these themes, and that may complicate or deepen the breadth of themes.

Also not especially prevalent are Biblical themes (15 items), together with moralizing (15 items) and science (11 items). Certainly we might find more religious or scientific themed games in the amorphous category of general knowledge. But even taking that into account, we find is a marked disparity between the British interest in sports of all kinds, history, geography, and natural history than with science. If there were a database like GARD to support it, would a parallel study in Germany over the same time span demonstrate a higher relative interest in science and engineering? Or might it demonstrate similar cultural preferences? We can say that the British in this timespan, through their games, were most concerned with sports of all kinds (especially horse racing), history, geography, natural history, and social/cultural topics.

Continuities

What else might we take from the database? I suggest GARD also has something to tell us about continuities and discontinuities between the nineteenth century and our own times. I would suggest five key continuities:

- The retention of matching categories of game types.
- The preoccupation with justifying the existence of games / of spending the time to play them / of tolerating their subject matter.
- An equivalent popularity of dexterity/twitch games.
- The parallel existence of sheer whimsy.
- The use of what today we might call "licenses," or prominent cultural touchstones such as fairy tales, or myths.

The types of games evident in nineteenth-century Britain are still with us. GARD shows us games providing a range of experiences—from word games to shooting games, from general knowledge to parlor games—almost all of which modern gamers still find engaging. Strategy games, race games, Q&A, parlor/puzzle games, cards, dexterity games, teaching games: we still have all of these, even if in different degrees of popularity, and with some new game types added and new technologies altering dynamics of some of these game types. In many ways the nineteenth-century games prevalent in Britain helped establish remarkably durable gameplay formats and commercial categories with expected gameplay mechanics.

The GARD's nineteenth-century games also demonstrate a strong strain of moral justification.[7] In addition to the data already presented, we can see this in titles like *Cheating*, which comes with the following descriptor: "This looks a very dreadful title, but the game is very harmless, and a Clergyman's family would find it full of fun without a savour of evil." Although Morality/Matrimony is a category showing only fifteen titles, there are also titles expressly themed around the Bible (13). Here we see a moral justification in the broad sense, as in a pastime worthy of the conscientious spending time on it. So we should also add Education (15 items); Literacy and Literature (17 items); Numeracy (11 items), much of the History (79 items), Geography (65 items), and Natural History (46 items) categories are also highly pedagogic in formulation: these games subtextually demonstrate their social worthiness by the edifying quality of their content. This is no less so than the type of questions posed within the General Knowledge (11 items) which we might describe as aspirant *higher brow* than present in the more trivial modern formulation. Music (9 items), Art and Architecture (8 items), Colonies and Empire (7 items), and Science (4 items) also demonstrate the same evident subtext. Even if we put to one side the categories of War (13 items) and Food and Markets (19 items), where there is a mixture of this educational subtext and more flippant or tangential connections to the theme, we can see that the clear majority of our thematic categories are concerned with demonstrating a moral legitimacy. We might end up saying that perhaps only the Horse Racing (51 items), Hunting (11 items), Other Sports (70 items), Supernatural and Magic (12 items), and some of Other (16 items), and some of Social/Cultural (38 items) are very clearly shorn of this subtext. We may end up saying around 65 percent of the content nineteenth-century gamers were experiencing had this evident morally legitimizing quality.

It would be difficult to put any figures on how much modern gamers experience content concerned with the same kind of moral legitimacy. It is unlikely to be anywhere near close as a percentage as in the nineteenth century. Yet I suggest we find continuities in the concern of the value of game playing, and the debate surrounding the justification of the time sink. Certainly the economic value of games in our times far outstrips that which any nineteenth-century game maker could have imagined, and we see studies of games (and how to make them) becoming increasingly more culturally acceptable in academic curricula. Nevertheless, the debate is clearly far from settled. For all the considerable content shift, we have not yet moved as far away from nineteenth-century anxiety over the worthiness of games as we may wish that we had.

In today's AAA space, we have a preponderance of first-person-shooter (FPS) titles, Massively Multiplayer Online Games (MOG), Action, Stealth, and Adventure titles, among many others that give a very different complexion to the industry. Although shooters may be manifestly different in the video game form, the database shows us eight games that were explicitly shooting games, and 140 Dexterity/Activity games (including those eight shooting games) that have a parallel with modern "twitch" games predicated on a player's dexterity. As noted, too, the database is considered to underrepresent Dexterity/Activity games. There are longstanding precedents, then, and modern gamers are not unique in their proclivities for this kind of twitch-based activity.

We find a parallel relish in sheer whimsy too. GARD holds eleven parlor games, though the curators acknowledge that this area is underrepresented; "miniaturized" sports, such as bowls and skittles (an additional two others are already listed as "Parlour" games); five "puff" games (indoor sports, or adaptations of sports where players blow); and seven other games of a comic or whimsical nature, such as *Brag and Grab*; *Cheating*; *Changeable Portraits*; and *Comic Answers to Queer Questions* ("enough to make a cat laugh"). We might even draw parallels between the miniaturized sports and the trend for executive desk toys. Consider the "puff" mechanic features in the PlayStation 5 where players blow on the controller to effect in-game actions). Likewise we might draw parallels between the comical/whimsical titles in GARD and modern card games such as *Fluxx* (where the rules frequently change); or *Dobble* (where there are a large variety of different rules with the same deck of cards for quick fire games); or *Six Degrees of Kevin Bacon* (where players try to trace connections between actors back to Kevin Bacon, with as few steps as possible); or *Cards Against Humanity* (where players fill in the blanks to statements on cards for comic effect). Nineteenth-century gamers would not have found games offering potentially offensive content like *Cards Against Humanity*, but they too had games that delighted in fun for fun's sake.

On the surface, our license- and franchise-laden world of behemoth media brands seems to have little in common with the nineteenth-century world of seemingly cottage-industry games. The publishers whose games survive in GARD are not typically long-lived nor do they produce games on any great scale. Yet just as today's game world is dominated by franchises such as *Call of Duty*, *Assassin's Creed*, and *FIFA*, we can detect something similar through GARD, though in perhaps in ways not obvious. We might liken the popularity of *Call of Duty* and the whole First-Person Shooter (FPS) genre as somewhat akin to the popularity of chess, draughts, or *Halma*, with similar game types also benefiting from the market's predilection for and settling on a certain kind of game. Our FPS titles are clearly markedly different from nineteenth-century abstract-strategy games, but we do see a continuity in terms of the market coalescing around popular titles, which seems to drive the publication of "Me Too"–type titles.

Today in games, as in other media areas, we find a predominance of *bankable* brands. The commercial logic is highly persuasive in reducing financial risk. But just as the likes of *Assassin's Creed* now trades on a recognition of its previous iterations and a preexisting consumer base, so too do we see this in the nineteenth century. Though the Fairy Tales and Legends category (17 items) is a small category with not even three percent of items total, its games trade on recognition of culturally resonant stories, such as Dick Turpin or Robin Hood. Such games come with a built-in marketing strategy: people have already heard of the theme. The same kind of built-in marketing strategy exists with the History (79 items), Geography (65 items), and Natural History (46 items) categories as well as with War and Yachting/Seafaring/Navy categories. Even when new, these games were being sold to people who most certainly had already heard of the theme and had some preexisting associations with it. We might, then, be looking at well over 50 percent of the market being populated with titles that traded on what we might call brand recognition. Wherever we place that figure for our own game industry, whether we look at divisions of it, such as the AAA video game world, or the indie world, or board games, we must surely acknowledge that this as a familiar dynamic.

But the continuity of about recognizable *brands* may extend to sports as a theme. The nineteenth-century interest in sports—Horse Racing and related horse sports (51 items) and Other Sports (70 items), accounts for more than 20 percent of the categorized themes—is still evident in the modern popularity of titles such as *FIFA*, *2K Basketball*, and *Madden*, whatever their percentage of the market. It is perhaps also worth stating that chess has remained a cultural mainstay. Our marketplace may include far more games, but chess remains popular in both analog and digital forms.

I note four key discontinuities from the database between then and now.

- Different popularity of specific game types
- The emphasis of sheer luck within game types
- Different thematic concerns
- A lack of narrative-games

The mix of the available game types in the nineteenth century appears notably different from what we have today. Race games have considerably diminished in popularity. (I might editorially add, thank goodness.) They are almost entirely predicated on sheer luck. For example, mathematician Katie Steckles mentioned how she and her family had been playing Snakes and Ladders remotely for several years, simply by use of an algorithm that rolled the dice and handled their moves: they never actually sat down to play the game at all—they just checked in from time to time to see who had won the most games so far. We still have Snakes and Ladders/Chutes and Ladders, Ludo (and variations), *The Game of Life*, and some others in this category, but their popularity has assuredly waned. Abstract-strategy games are now nowhere near as common, even taking into account the cultural persistence of chess and draughts. Halma, as mentioned, is now little heard of. For sure, we aren't entirely bereft of more modern abstract strategy games, but they are now a decidedly minor and sporadic entry within the games marketplace where once they dominated. We might argue that match-three-puzzle digital games like the hugely popular *Candy Crush*, and *Bejeweled*, are our modern equivalents, but I think this is distorting when we look more closely at the type of cognitive processing involved with these games. I think a truer comparison with the playstyle of nineteenth-century abstract strategy games would be games such as *Hive*, *Santorini*, or *Patchwork*—although these are all notably more complex and varied than their antecedents.

This overall different complexion of the marketplace also touches on the second significant discontinuity. Today, utilizing the mechanics of sheer luck is less popular, existing only at the more casual end of the industry in its entirely undiluted form. Even in board games we see far more complex (and I might add interesting) mechanics, with luck mitigated by the use of, say, Card-Driven Game systems, with each card having a variety of uses and optimum opportunities whereupon it may be played.

History, Geography, Natural History, and even Horse Racing are now far less popular as themes, and when those from the first three categories are now present they are usually wrapped within games far less overtly pedagogic in nature. The majority of the History, Geography, Colonies and Empire categories, and some of the Social/Cultural category are, to a large extent, not just pedagogic in nature, but also have a clear subtext, if it can even be said to run that deep, concerned with national identity. Perhaps the dearth of games themed on colonies and the Empire may surprise us, but through these other categories we can still see the preponderance of this national-identity theme. Here is a third key discontinuity. There is no such equivalence today. Britain and Britishness as clear themes, overt or subtextually, are little in evidence. Many U.S. games are not even given a different U.K. release—for sound commercial financial reasons—so the text comes in American English, not British English. Even major British franchises such as the hugely successful *GTA* series are more concerned with American culture—and the commercial logic of being so concerned.

We also see a fourth major discontinuity in the dearth of narrative-led or narrative-immersed games. To some extent this relates to the markedly different complexion of the industry then and now. But this touches not just on theme, but on a whole design approach in relation to theme. A race game about railways might thematically be about railways, because there are images of railways and train tracks on the board, and perhaps train pawns for the players. But this is mostly what we might call "surface" theme. The themes rarely go deeper into the game design, such that the narrative quality of that theme is then delivered through the formulation of the mechanics. Modern board games, such as *Churchill* or *Twilight Struggle*, don't just apply the theme as content over an essentially narrative agnostic design (like a race game, with different text in the boxes with different board art); they mesh design and theme together to deliver the key narrative expectations and possibilities that the choice of subject matter engenders. Not all modern designers may be happy to consider narrative as key to this design approach, but I would expect many would be happy to agree there is a *deeper* use of theme in the majority of modern games than is apparent in nineteenth-century games. This lack of narrative games in the nineteenth century is one of the key differences in game types in our own times, where role-playing games, in many design variations, in both analog and digital form, are a significant part of the landscape of modern games.

Conclusion

British game producers seemed to believe that British gamers cared about five key things with regards to cultural values (or could be made to care about them):

- national identity, about a sense of themselves and their place in Europe and the world, especially as it related to geography and history
- sports, especially those with horses
- natural history (and this too, to some extent compounds the idea of national identity)

- strategy, bereft of luck—these make players feel smart when they win, or compete to a certain level
- whimsy, whether with or without luck

For all our (perhaps lazy or skewed) perception of the Victorians as avid churchgoers in a heavily religious society, religion shows itself to be a relatively minor concern, as evidenced through these titles. But the culturally influential Evangelical movement was also opposed to games generally, putting it in the same category of other morally trivial activities such as dancing and theater-going, and this might have suggested that religion wasn't an appropriate topic for games. At the same time, the database shows us education themes too, with learning French almost one-third as popular as a theme as the Bible!

We do see one game, *Invasion*, on the topic of the invasion of southern England from the continent clearly speak to a concern over the—as it turned out—imminent future. But this is just one game, so it doesn't provide enough evidence to draw invasion out as a key anxiety, even if it was evident—and prescient. Certainly, we don't see a preponderance of this theme in games as we do in contemporary "Invasion" literature. This seems to convey that games in nineteenth-century Britain are entertainment, strive to be education, but remain a long way from literature or art. In our own times, games as literature or art is still a debate, even if emergent university programs suggest the debate being won in some circles.

What the extracted data further say about nineteenth-century British gamers is that they had little real concern about science (other than natural history) or engineering. They liked twitch games to roughly the same significant extent modern gamers do. They didn't have "deep" gaming experiences lasting hours, nor experiences with involved narratives. They enjoyed whimsy, yet this balanced with their concerns over education and "cultural worthiness." Their games were generally not experimental and were usually repetitions of known types with usually only minor and surface alterations. They also cared about Britishness and a sense of distinctive identity through history, geography, and cultural traditions.

What does this say about the game makers? They were commercially, and in terms of design focus, deeply conservative. We do not see any examples of wildly different game designs, even in the small numbers we could expect with outright commercial disasters the database might have captured. The same basic design approaches are repeatedly in evidence—most particularly in abstract strategy games and race games. Perhaps we can also say that the constant re-use of the race game format with barely any innovation in evidence over a century is suggestive of restricted conceptions of what games could be—a lack of belief in their value and potential importance. Perhaps this also speaks to a society with a constrained sense of individualism. (If so, does this tell us about Britain as well as the timespan? Here a parallel study with a different nationally focused database could be revealing.) That said, the games produced still provided a range of experiences or game types we recognize today. In that regard these games tell us of game developers who were both lacking in innovation—stuck in cycles of insipid repetition—and yet also visionary—tapping into a broad swath of the core enduring gameplay formats. The world of nineteenth-century board games is then both vastly different from our own times—not just in obvious respects such as technology, but also with regard to shifting game types, an emphasis on luck, theme, and a lack of narrative-games—but then it is also remarkably like our own times—the same sorts of game experiences are available—there is whimsy, dexterity games, a preponderance of effective "franchise licenses"/cultural touchstones being used through games, and a surrounding debate concerning the justifiability of games as a pastime.

So what next? The 1,087 titles without dates might be dated. The 245 "Unclear" titles might be explored in an attempt to clarify them. The sets of lists within the database, which indicate well over another one hundred games, could be categorized within our date range. The taxonomy I employ here and the categorizations and allocations I extract and compose might also be examined and stress tested. All of which would give us a substantial bump in accuracy so we could get more precise data, giving us a clearer picture to refine or revise the summaries and conclusions drawn here. More of the games might also be played, so we could say something more substantial about them. In many ways, this look at GARD and the nineteenth century is just beginning to unearth the database's still barely tapped riches.

Notes

1. This excludes titles from inside the listed "List" items, which are worthy of closer study. They include numerous different game types spread liberally across the preexisting categories used above.

2. Some of the titles listed here as chess variations, such as *Homo*, *King of the Castle*, *Modern Naval Warfare*, or *Siege of Paris* may, on closer inspection be more closely considered draughts, *Halma* or hybrid variations. Two entries included in this list also appear to be double-listed, as *Staunton Legacy* and as *Travelling Chess*.

3. *Fox and Geese* has ten entries within the date range, with one outside it. *Double Fox and Geese* has two entries, for double-sized boards. There is also an erroneous entry of *Fox and Geese* (Double) that actually links to *Balance Cupolette*.

4. There are cross-listings here, with five titles listed under *Go Bang* and a further four listed under *Go-Bang* with only one of these titles appearing to be a unique instance.

5. There may be other examples of sales related information on printed matter within the 1,481 entries without date information, excluded from my data set.

6. Arguably *Snakes and Ladders* carries the theme of karma or some other philosophical or religious connotation. But it is has not been ascribed a theme in these lists here.

7. This parallels the findings of literary studies on amusement (frivolity versus instruction/moral purpose) in general.

Works Cited

Ballam, Richard. "200 years of fun and games." Lecture. University of Oxford. http://podcasts.ox.ac.uk/200-years-fun-and-games; Accessed 29 January 2016.

Knizia, Reiner, and Katie Steckles. "Board Games: Movers and Shakers." Old Fire Station, Oxford. https://www.oxfordsparks.ox.ac.uk/content/board-games-movers-and-shakers; Accessed 28 June 2016.

The Games Board. Eds. Richard Ballam, James Masters, Jeremy Secker, Michael Thomson, Neil Darbyshire, Mike Goodall, and Edward Copisarow. http://www.gamesboard.org.uk/.

Chapter 12

Professor Hoffmann's Victorian Puzzles and Stage Magic

ANDREW RHODA

Professor Louis Hoffmann popularized stage magic and puzzles, improving the understanding and acceptability of both these hobbies in Victorian society and beyond. Yet despite Hoffmann being a notable figure in the United Kingdom until well into the twentieth century, his works are little known outside of the community of those who collect or study puzzles and stage magic. Hoffmann began writing on magic in a series of articles for *The Young Gentleman's Magazine*, which became *Every Boy's Magazine* during the serialization (Findlay and Sawyer 5–6). On the recommendation of that magazine's editor, he expanded his articles into *Modern Magic* (1876), then followed that success with several translations of French works on magic, including Robert Houdin's *Secrets of Conjuring and Magic* (1878) and *Secrets of Stage Conjuring* (1881) and L. P.'s *Drawing Room Conjuring* (1887). Hoffmann returned to his own writing on stage magic with *Tricks with Cards* (1889), *More Magic* (1890), *Later Magic* (1903, expanded in 1911), the short volume *Magical Titbits* (1911), and *Latest Magic* (1918). Though he wrote several novels for children and his original essays on stage magic were geared toward a young audience, Hoffmann developed the subjects of stage magic into an area of study suitable for adults as well, even adults of some social standing. Alongside these important works on magic, Hoffmann revealed his interest in puzzles and other games, translating in 1892 the German *The Illustrated Book of Patience Games*, then writing his own groundbreaking 1893 volume *Puzzles, Old and New*. This essay will serve as a brief introduction to the author and his works, demonstrating their importance in the joint history of magic and games.

Negotiating Reputation in the Victorian Age

Professor Hoffmann was the pseudonym of Oxford-educated London barrister Angelo John Lewis. Born in London on 23 July 1839, Lewis attended Oxford University before being "called to the Chancery Bar in 1861" (Findlay and Sawyer 1). To become a barrister in Victorian society, one took a series of oaths to perform the occupation responsibly. These oaths, as Albert Pionke notes, also elevated the oath taker into a higher social class: "By taking an oath witnessed by God, individuals who in private were already learned, or wealthy, or well-connected became members of the elite public, authorized by those already in positions of power to exercise their influence over other's behavior and to maintain the newly resanctified Victorian social system" (617). Physicians' oaths, for example, which included a "provision that graduates will work for the good of their patients and not themselves" actually increased their social standing, transforming doctors into gentlemen as well as conferring their medical credentials (Pionke 618). This increase in social standing was true for the legal profession as well, which included different oaths for different types of lawyers (618). Those who became barristers continued to advance in society: election to the House of Commons placed a junior barrister on the path to appointment as Queen's Counsel, and eventually, if successful, to a position as judge and in the House of Lords (Pionke 620).

Hoffmann clearly considered the possibility that publishing on stage magic and later puzzles might negatively affect his professional and social prestige. In an October 1896 interview in *The Windsor Magazine* with George Knight, Hoffmann explains his decision to use a pen name:

> I remarked that I should want [*Modern Magic*] produced anonymously—I didn't expect that it would do a practicing barrister any good to pose as the author of a work on conjuring. But Mr. Edmund Routledge urged that such a course would be prejudicial to the book, and I consented to a nom de plume. "While you are about it," Mr. Routledge observed, "be a Professor." I hit upon "Hoffmann" as a name of uncertain

> nationality and left the public to imagine, if they chose, that some distinguished German or American wizard was giving away the secrets of his craft. (362–63)

Later commentators such as L. E. Hordern have noted Hoffmann's concern as well, stating explicitly that "[i]t could have been thought at the time that writing books on *puzzles* was incompatible with his profession" (vi). In addition, Slocum and Botermans argue that Lewis used his pen name as his professional life might have been harmed by his hobbies involving trickery and deception (49). It is not so surprising, then, that Lewis the barrister became Professor Hoffmann to publish his works on puzzles and stage conjuring, distancing himself from the deception and trickery associated with them. With the pseudonym, Hoffmann felt free of societal and professional pressures and published on these subjects, beginning with *Modern Magic*.

Modern, More, and Latest Magic

Modern Magic was one of the few publications on the practice of stage conjuring when it was first published in 1876. Hoffmann wished to train others in how to perform the feats they had seen performed on stage. However, he found the state of the literature on stage magic "scanty":

> Until within the last few years it would have been difficult to name a single book worth reading upon this subject, the whole literature of the art consisting of single chapters in books written for the amusement of youth (which were chiefly remarkable for the unanimity with which each copied, without acknowledgement, from its predecessors), and handbooks sold at the entertainments of various public performers, who took care not to reveal therein any trick which they deemed worthy of performance themselves. (Hoffmann, *Modern* 1)

Hoffmann attributed the lack of sufficient works on stage conjuring techniques to the previous nature of the field in which "the more important secrets of the art have been known but to few [people], and those few have jealously guarded them, knowing that the more closely they concealed the clue to their mysteries, the more would those mysteries be valued" (*Modern* 1). Contemporaneously, however, the majority of stage tricks were accessible to the Victorian audience to purchase and Hoffmann declares that even amateurs "at a sufficient expenditure of shillings or guineas" might purchase such knowledge (*Modern* 1–2). In addition, these purchases would only provide access to the mechanics of the particular trick. In this sense, Hoffmann's work attempted to improve the state of conjuring literature by working against books that covered the practice of tricks "so briefly and scantily as to be practically useless" (*Modern* 2). Hoffmann's intention was to create a manual that would be of utility to those wishing to pursue stage magic.

Hoffmann's focus on usability speaks to his concern for educating the reader in performance. Hoffmann notes that previous manuals only describe the mechanics of the magic trick, and that to teach a reader how to perform the trick is a different matter (*Modern* 2). Instead, Hoffmann hoped "to teach sleight-of-hand generally, as well as particular tricks; and to conduct the neophyte from the very A B C of the magic art gradually up to those marvels which are exhibited on the public stage" (*Modern* 2). It did not take Hoffmann long to implement this pedagogical focus, even outlining the rules that would be the basis of his instruction (*Modern* 3–10).

At the end of *Modern Magic*, Hoffmann broadens his discussion to include actual stage performance. His concluding chapter deals with aspects of presentation of the magic tricks learned earlier, noting that the magician preparing for a performance should first understand fully the instructions for the tricks selected for the performance (*Modern* 502). For Hoffmann, one combines understanding the instructions with diligently training oneself to perform the trick mechanically, so that each part of the performance is rehearsed to the point where the performer executes the tricks effortlessly (*Modern* 502). Once one masters the "mechanical portion of the illusion, he must now devote himself to its dramatic element, which, as regards the effect upon the spectator, is by far the more important portion" (*Modern* 502). To that end, Hoffmann encourages the reader to develop this portion of the performance, and even provides an example of how one would script such an act (*Modern* 503–505). Hoffmann closes the section by writing, "The above example will show how, by the exercise of a little tact and ingenuity, a simple piece of parlour magic may be elevated to the dignity of a stage trick" (*Modern* 505). The magician does this, Hoffmann writes, by (mis)directing the audience with the physical acuity in executing the tricks in addition to arranging the constituent magic tricks in the performance in such a way that the next trick builds upon the last (*Modern* 505). Hoffmann encourages this attention to the construction of a performance, describing it as "a comparatively simple feat being employed to prepare the minds of the spectators for the greater marvel to follow" (*Modern* 505).

Hoffmann teaches his reader how to develop the verbal setting for a single trick, known as patter, as well as how to situate that single trick in a larger performance for a greater effect. For Hoffmann, "[t]he programme should consist not of a number of absolutely unconnected tricks, but of a series of ten or a dozen *groups* of tricks" (*Modern* 506). Hoffmann recommends how to set up the performing area, so that the audience does not inadvertently see how a trick is being performed (*Modern* 508). As an example of such an occasion, Hoffmann describes the situation in which a magician has been requested to perform in the drawing room of a private residence, instead of a proper theatrical space (*Modern* 509). Hoffmann describes the setup of the room for the performance, including a full diagram of the stage and the placement of the seats (*Modern* 509). He indicates they "should be arranged at the opposite end of the room, leaving as wide a space between as can well be obtained, as many 'changes,' etc. are effected during the journey from the audience to the table, and the longer this journey is, the more time is available for the necessary manipulations" (*Modern* 509). In envisioning an event where the amateur magician would be called upon by acquaintances to give a conjuring demonstration, it would appear that Hoffmann is envisioning a situation where performing stage magic for groups of acquaintances would be both an acceptable and common way to practice one's conjuring skills.

Hoffmann's second book on conjuring, *More Magic*, seeks to bring the reader up to date with more recently discovered techniques:

> Conjuring, like other arts, has been "moving on" during the past eleven years. Old methods have been improved, and new have been devised. "Eternal progress is eternal change," and the "how it's done" of 1889 differs in a good many particulars from the "how it's done" of 1878. (1)

Hoffmann's reasoning for writing a separate work was that addition of the new information to *Modern Magic* would make a subsequent edition an unwieldy reference guide (*More* 1). Hoffmann structures his sequel as a work intended to supplement *Modern Magic*. Each chapter covers the same topics presented in *Modern Magic*, describing innovations or improvements to the existing techniques or new tricks developed since the publication of the first book. With this extensive reference to the previous book, *More Magic* assumes that the reader has purchased or has access to *Modern Magic*. In so doing, Hoffmann appears to have had a particular audience in mind for his publications, specifically an audience that has the economic resources to purchase both volumes.

Published in the year before Hoffmann's death, *Latest Magic*, in contrast, provides stage conjuring techniques of Hoffmann's own devising: "The tricks described in the following pages are of my own invention, and for the most part are entirely new departures: not only the effects produced, but the appliances by means of which they are produced, being original" (vii). J. B. Findlay and Thomas Sawyer note that *Latest Magic* is of a lesser quality than either *Modern Magic* or *More Magic*; however, they do stress that the text "is monumental in that it contains so much of Professor Hoffmann's original material—a fitting last legacy for a giant figure in the field of magic" (2). Hoffmann notes that "few of the items described have been submitted to the supreme test of performance in public, but all have been thoroughly thought out; most of the root-ideas having in fact been simmering in my mind for more than two years past" (*Latest* vii). He adds, "[s]hould any of my modest inventions be found, as is not improbable, susceptible to further polish, the keen wits and ready fingers of my brother wizards may safely be trusted to supply it" (*Latest* vii). Through his work, Hoffmann hoped to expand the number of his fellow magicians who would develop his contributions in the future. It would seem that Hoffmann was able to do just that by contributing to stage magic's social acceptability. Even as early as 1896, when Knight interviewed Hoffmann, Hoffmann's publications seem to have increased the acceptability of the art form such that Hoffmann felt free to explain why he initially published under a pseudonym. In elevating the status of stage magic for the amateur practitioner, Hoffmann was leading the way for those *brother wizards*.

As with his other works on magic, *Latest Magic* divides into sections based on the nature of the trick or the apparatus involved in the trick (ix–x). For example, in "Concerning Patter," like in the last chapters of *Modern Magic*, Hoffmann gives advice to potential performers. He includes this section "to enable the reader to form a better estimate of the effect of the trick presented, duly clothed and coloured, to the mind of the spectator" (*Latest* 192). As with his earlier books, Hoffmann was concerned not only with instructing his readers in how to perform the tricks, but also in how to present those tricks and craft an effective magic performance.

At the same time as he was offering his own "modest inventions," Hoffmann only revealed a limited number of tricks by fellow practitioners, choosing those most well-known in the trade: "A first-class stage trick has frequently taken months, or even years, to bring to perfection, and while it remains a novelty, has a high commercial value. I have purposely limited my disclosures to such illusions as have been sufficiently long before the public to be fairly regarded as common property" (*Modern*, 2nd ed. iii). Hoffmann did not wish to "deprive [other magicians] of the value of the stage tricks that they have developed and use in their performances" (*Modern*, 2nd ed. iii). John Nevil Maskelyne praised Hoffmann's "loyal[ty] to the profession; he never exposed any novelty that was at the time creating a sensation." (qtd. in Finlay and Sawyer 8). However, Harry Leat, in *Forty Years In & Around Magic*, was less complimentary: "Hoffmann was doing in those days what every journalist is doing in these, and that is looking for copy. As a matter of fact, Hoffmann started writing against the interests of Magic, exposing tricks in papers not solely written for the benefit of Magicians" (qtd. in Finlay and Sawyer 8). As Hoffmann was writing for a general audience, and not solely for the professional magician of the day, some like Leat saw Hoffmann's work as a dilution of the secrecy of that art of stage magic. They did not see the wider popularization of stage magic as a way to increase the appreciation for the art form, as Hoffmann did.

Though some, like Leat, felt that Hoffmann's work could do harm to the art of magic, Findlay and Sawyer found "the net effect of *Modern Magic* and Hoffmann's other magic works was one of marked and lasting benefit to magic" (8). Findlay and Sawyer also indicate that Hoffmann felt that "there were no hard feelings between the other magicians and himself" (8). Some magic store owners did not feel the quite the same way; however Hoffmann "pointed out that everyone benefited in the end; the professionals invented new and better tricks, and the dealers, although their prices had to be lower, now had an increased number of customers" (Findlay and Sawyer 8–9).

The first edition of two thousand copies of *Modern Magic* sold out "in about six weeks," and in 1914, *Modern Magic* had published its thirteenth edition, indicating the popularity of the book (Findlay and

Sawyer 7). In fact, Findlay and Sawyer identify at least seventeen editions of Hoffmann's *Modern Magic*, and his other works on stage magic went through multiple editions and multiple versions as well (49–55).

Ultimately, Professor Hoffmann taught his readers both individual tricks and the art of stage magic as a whole. In the closing chapter of *Latest Magic*, Hoffmann comments, "When I first began to discourse of magic, I had the whole field, in a literary sense, to myself. That state of things has long since ceased to be. Fertile brains and ready writers have taken up my task, and magic has now a worthy literature, growing day by day" (222). Hoffmann had blazed the trail, and others followed. In bringing information about these little-known subjects to light, Hoffmann gave those who had an interest in stage magic and puzzles the knowledge to which they previously had not had access.

From Magic to Puzzles

Modern Magic did for stage magic what *Puzzles Old and New* did for mechanical and pencil and paper puzzles about seventeen years later. Hoffmann's work on puzzles is noteworthy on a number of fronts. His work was comprehensive and detailed; he "was the first to describe in the minutest detail [all the] *mechanical* puzzles available commercially at the time" (Hordern vi). His work was carefully and copiously illustrated, providing "a wealth of accurate drawings" (Hordern vi). In addition, he wrote from the position of an authority, as "he either possessed or had access to the puzzles he was describing" (Hordern vi). These characteristics made his book the standard in its field for generations. As L. E. Hordern writes in his forward to the 1988 reproduction, "for some 80 years or more (until the advent of modern color printing techniques), [Hoffmann's] book stood alone, head and shoulders above the rest. For this reason, collectors of mechanical puzzles often refer to *Puzzles Old and New* as the 'Bible' of that industry, and the puzzles described as 'Hoffmann' puzzles" (vi). Remarkably, now after more than a century, this work is still considered a foundational document in the literature of mechanical puzzle collecting.

When Hoffmann published his *Puzzles Old and New*, he did not have the benefit of even the most basic categories, let alone the expanded taxonomies and nomenclatures that he inspired (Slocum and Botermans v). Consequently, Hoffmann's first task in writing on puzzles was to define his territory: "In view of the varieties of taste, some preferring a mathematical, some a mechanical problem—one person a trial of skill, another an exercise of patience—it seemed desirable to have as many categories as possible" (*Puzzles* vii). As Hoffmann explains, he grouped a wide variety of puzzles into discernable categories, either by the action needed to solve the puzzle, such as "Puzzles Dependent on Dexterity and Perseverance" (chapter 1), or a key physical feature of the puzzle, such as "Puzzles with Counters" (chapter 6) or "Wire Puzzles" (chapter 8) (*Puzzles* ix–xvii). Three chapters in *Puzzles Old and New* focus on pencil-and-paper puzzles: "Arithmetical Puzzles," "Word and Letter Puzzles," and "'Quibble' and 'Catch Puzzles," chapters 4, 5, and 9 respectively.

Ultimately, Hoffmann's groupings align into two general categories: mechanical puzzles, generally defined as "a self-contained object, composed of one or more parts, which involves a problem for one person to solve by manipulation using logic, reasoning, insight, luck and/or dexterity"; and pencil-and-paper puzzles, mathematical problems or word-based riddles that can be worked out with pen and paper, but which lack the physical manipulation required for the mechanical puzzle (Slocum and Botermans v). Perhaps due to his interest in stage magic, discussion of mechanical puzzles accounts for the majority of the chapters in *Puzzles Old and New*, with only three chapters devoted to pencil-and-paper puzzles.

Unlike other puzzle books of the time, Hoffmann omitted the "very wide class of verbal puzzles, comprising conundrum, enigmas, charades, etc." in order to focus largely on mechanical and pencil-and-paper puzzles (*Puzzles* viii). These types of puzzles were familiar enough that Hoffmann provided no preamble or description to those chapters, only a short section in the "Key to Chapter IV" in which he explained the properties of numbers (*Puzzles* 174). Hoffmann also provided hints and solutions to the puzzles that he featured in the book at the end of each chapter, with the exception of the first chapter where the hints are included in the descriptions (*Puzzles* 1).

However, creating broad categories only went so far. Hoffmann faced another crisis of nomenclature: the games followed no uniform titling system, even with puzzles of almost the same design. "For example, there are some half-dozen 'cross' puzzles, more or less unlike, yet all having a fair claim to the title, and being scarcely distinguishable by any other" (Hoffmann, *Puzzles* vi–vii). The opposite problem is also true; take the famous *Fifteen Puzzle*, for example. The original designer, Noyes Chapman, a postmaster in Canastota, New York, had his patent for the puzzle denied assumedly because it was too similar to a patent granted a year earlier to Ernest U. Kinsey for "Puzzle-Blocks" (Slocum and Sonneveld 101–102). As soon as Matthias Rice produced the first commercial version of the puzzle—*The Gem Puzzle*—in December 1879, others began manufacturing versions under titles such as *The Mystic Square*, *The Boss Puzzle*, *The Game of Fifteen*, *The Game of 15 and 34*, and *The Sliding Block Puzzle* among others (Slocum and Sonneveld 11–17). The puzzles sold well in Boston, and by February of 1880, *The Fifteen Puzzle*, in all of its many titled forms, was wildly popular (Slocum and Sonneveld 19).

This variety of names for essentially the same puzzle extended across the field: "A mechanical puzzle is frequently described in the price-lists of different dealers by different names, the 'Arabian Mystery' of one being, say, the 'Egyptian Paradox' or the 'Ashantee Difficulty' of another" (Hoffmann, *Puzzles* viii). As with the "cross" puzzles, that issue also extended in the opposite direction: "[Other puzzles] are of necessity nameless, it being impossible to devise any short title which shall give any idea of the nature of the problem" (Hoffmann, *Puzzles* viii). Faced with this difficulty, Hoffmann standardized the naming, often providing the titles by which those puzzles are known today.

In his book, Hoffmann devotes substantive space to the Richter Company's line of ceramic stone geometric dissection puzzles—or, Anker or Anchor Stone Puzzles after the Richter Company's ship anchor insignia (Slocum and Gebhardt 23). Hoffmann begins his section on the Richter puzzles by discussing the Anchor Stone Building-blocks, which Hoffmann refers to as the "the *ne plus ultra* of Toydom, and delight of every kindergarten and schoolroom which is fortunate enough to possess a set of them" (*Puzzles* 74). While Hoffmann introduces this set of building blocks, they were actually first produced by Richter in 1880, when Gustav and Otto Lilienthal sold their invention and transferred the patent for the stone building blocks to Richter (Slocum and Gebhardt 14). Hoffmann refers to the use of these blocks in education settings, which is because Gustav Lilienthal was the protégé of educator and social scientist Jan Georgens, which Richter used in his advertising for these stone building blocks (Slocum and Gebhardt 14).

Hoffmann devotes the beginning of the chapter to Richter and the building blocks as a way to introduce the company's puzzles, as they were made of the same material as the blocks, which because of their popularity were a widely known toy from Richter. He then moves on to Richter's puzzles as a way to structure the next part of the chapter.

He begins by describing *The Anchor Puzzle*, which was a stone set of Tangram pieces that were produced in 1890 that used the same material as the building block sets (Slocum and Gebhardt 21). As early as 1878, Richter had been working with Jan Georgens on producing educational publications leading to "a series of pamphlets and educational material called New Kindergarten (*Neuer Kindergarten*)" (Slocum and Gebhardt 19). As Georgens was a student of the educator Friedrich Fröbel, most of the content of these materials were drawn from Fröbel's methods (Slocum and Gebhardt 19). Tangram problems appeared in these publications, with a set of cards being produced in 1878 under a different title (Slocum and Gebhardt 20–21). These cards became the basis for the problems included with *The Anchor Puzzle*, with a few additional designs added in from other books (Slocum and Gebhardt 24). Hoffmann includes some examples of these problems after his explanation of *The Anchor Puzzle* (*Puzzles* 78–79).

Hoffmann also briefly introduces subsequent stone puzzles produced by Richter, listing *The Tormentor*, *The Pythagoras Puzzle*, *The Cross Puzzle*, *The Circular Puzzle*, and *The Star Puzzle* in the next sections (*Puzzles*). Hoffmann includes images of problems after the description of each puzzle, as with *The Anchor Puzzle* (*Puzzles*). After *The Star Puzzle*, Hoffmann ends his description of the Richter puzzles with a note, informing the reader that these individual puzzle sets can be paired with the others to produce unique configurations provided in the problem books (*Puzzles* 90). Slocum and Gebhardt estimate that "Richter produced about 3.5 to 4 million problem books, and Anchor Puzzles, from 1891 until 1924" (138). This estimate does not include the sales figures for the other puzzles in the series, which Slocum and Gebhardt also describe (138). While Hoffmann does go on in the chapter to describe other similar puzzles, with these figures in mind, it is not surprising that Hoffmann chose to begin his chapter on combination puzzles with the popular Richter series.

Hoffmann dedicated his second chapter in *Puzzles Old and New* to mechanical puzzles. The take-apart mechanical puzzle depends for its solution "on some trick or secret": "The *crux* propounded is to extract a marble or other small object from some outer receptacle which has no visible opening large enough to allow of its passage, or which cannot be opened without the knowledge or discovery of some secret" (*Puzzles* 50, 20). The disentanglement puzzle "consists of the removal of a ball or ring from a silken cord, passed backwards and forwards through openings in a piece of wood or bone in a more or less complicated manner"

(*Puzzles* 25). At the end of the chapter, Hoffmann introduces another category of mechanical puzzle, the dexterity puzzle, with "The New Egg of Columbus." To solve this puzzle, one must use gravity to guide the weighted ball inside the egg to its proper place to stand the egg on end (*Puzzles* 47, 72–73). By including these puzzles in his chapter, Hoffmann makes them some of the most recognizable puzzles in the nineteenth century. In fact, the puzzles listed in *Puzzles Old and New* even came to be known by Hoffmann's name.

Hoffmann dedicates his eighth chapter to wire puzzles, providing twelve puzzles similar in concept to the disentanglement puzzles featured in chapter 2. "The Heart," "The Two Balls," "The Ariel Puzzle," and "The Balls and Rings" all require the parts of the puzzle to be removed from one another (Hoffmann, *Puzzles* 302–308, 309–14). Some of the puzzles, such as "The United Hearts," The Unionist Puzzle," and "The Eastern Question," require two parts of a puzzle to be removed from each other (Hoffmann, *Puzzles* 302–307). The final puzzle of the chapter, "The Handcuff Puzzle," requires the solver to disconnect four interlocked rings (Hoffmann, *Puzzles* 307–308).

In cataloging these puzzles, Hoffmann created the first work that categorized mechanical puzzles. Such information about the mechanics and classification of puzzles had been previously unavailable. Hoffmann's *Puzzles Old and New* strongly influenced the field of puzzles, gathering the popular mechanical puzzles of the era and bringing them to the forefront. At the time mechanical puzzles were often placed together with pencil and paper puzzles in a general category of "puzzles." Hoffmann educated his readership in all of the different types of puzzles and educated them in how these puzzles worked.

When Hoffmann began writing on stage magic and puzzles, both topics were obscure and viewed with some suspicion. In his works, Hoffmann sought to familiarize his audience with these subjects and thereby popularize them as well. He also succeeded in linking the two fields, as the popularity of his conjuring books increased the visibility of this landmark publication on puzzles. His works are still valuable resources and references to scholars of stage magic and mechanical puzzles. For the latter, Hoffmann was the first to define separate and specific categories for puzzles based on their attributes. As evidence of these books' enduring popularity, parts of both *Modern Magic* and *Puzzles Old and New* have been republished as separate works (Findlay and Sawyer 62–63). Hoffmann and his works still provide a rich field of study or those interested in either puzzles or stage magic.

Works Cited

Findlay, J. B., and Thomas A. Sawyer. *Professor Hoffmann: A Study*. Tustin, CA: Sawyer, 1977.

Hoffmann, Professor. *Latest Magic: Being Original Conjuring Tricks*. New York: Spon & Chamberlain, 1918.

———. *Magical Titbits*. Illustrated by H. L. Shindler. London: Routledge, 1911.

———. *Modern Magic: A Practical Treatise on the Art of Conjuring*. American ed. London: Routledge, 1876.

———. *Modern Magic: A Practical Treatise on the Art of Conjuring*. 2nd ed. London; New York: Routledge, 1877. *Victorian Popular Culture*. Accessed 23 October 2015.

———. *More Magic*. London: Routledge, 1889.

———. *Puzzles Old and New*. London: Warne, 1893.

Hordern, L. E. Foreword to This Edition. *Puzzles Old and New*. By Professor Hoffmann. London: Breese, 1988. v–vi.

Knight, George. "Professor Hoffmann and Conjuring." *The Windsor Magazine: An Illustrated Monthly for Men and Women*. October 1896: 362–64.

Pionke, Albert D. "'I Do Swear': Oath-Taking among the Elite Public in Victorian England." *Victorian Studies* 49.4 (2007): 611–33. *Project Muse*. Accessed 14 September 2015.-

Slocum, Jerry, and Dic Sonneveld. *The 15 puzzle: How It Drove the World Crazy; the Puzzle That Started the Craze of 1880; How America's Greatest Puzzle Designer, Sam Loyd, Fooled Everyone for 115 years*. Beverly Hills: Slocum Puzzle Foundation, 2006.

Slocum, Jerry, and Dieter Gebhardt. *The Anchor Puzzle Book: The Amazing Stories of More Than 50 New Puzzles Made of Stone*. Beverly Hills: Slocum Puzzle Foundation, 2012.

Slocum, Jerry and Jack Botermans. *Puzzles Old and New: How to Make and Solve Them*. Seattle: University of Washington Press, 1986.

Chapter 13

"An Endless Round of Delights"

Materializing the Toy Theatre

JENNIE MacDONALD

> The Juvenile Drama grew out of the Adult Drama, the toy theatre was just exactly the big theatre in miniature; actors, costumes, scenery, were all faithfully copied from actual productions on the London stage, and reproduced for their miniature performance. The origin of every toy theatre play is to be found upon the living stage . . .
>
> —George Speiaght, *Juvenile Drama: The History of the English Toy Theatre*[1]

Stocked with dolls and dollhouses, tin soldiers, spinning tops, pull-toys, carved wooden animals, books, and magazines, the Victorian nursery presented a veritable wonderland. Perhaps a less familiar plaything of that time, the toy-theatre commanded children's devotion and pocket money during its golden age from the 1810s to the 1850s.[2] Capitalizing on a feverish demand for toy theatres and plays, enterprising publishers created small-scale theatre stages designed after their full-size counterparts. They dispatched artists to live performances to sketch the scenery and costumed characters and to note major incidents and spectacles. Dependent upon dramatic story for its appeal, the toy theatre succeeded best as a vehicle for visually spectacular plays featuring courageous heroes and heroines; outrageous villains; supernatural figures and remarkable locations; battles, chases, and other exciting events; and magic and special effects. A succession of toy theatre publishers across the century printed important texts dramatized on the live stage, including plays by William Shakespeare (*A Midsummer Night's Dream*, *Hamlet*, *Julius Caesar*, and *The Tempest*); Gothic novels (*The Castle of Otranto*, *Blue Beard*, *The Castle Spectre*, and *The Iron Chest*); legends and fairy tales (*Aladdin*, *Jack the Giant Killer*, *The Sleeping Beauty*, and *Tom Thumb*); and pantomimes featuring the trickster-magician Harlequin and often derived from the same works that inspired main-piece plays (*The Castle of Otranto; or, Harlequin & the Giant Helmet*, *Harlequin Blue Beard*, and *Harlequin Robin Hood*).

The scenes and dialogue were abridged and published as playbooks. These were sold alongside printed sheets of characters, scenery, stage wings, and tricks for pantomimes, resulting in a set for each play. Initially the sheets were printed in black and white (plain); later, pre-colored sheets could be had, although pre-colored sheets were categorically condemned for eliminating the creative fun of coloring and decorating. Writing in 1871, John Oxenford commented on the absurdity of the pre-colored miniature theatres:

> [When] at some of the West-end toy-shops I see a little theatre, evidently offered for sale complete, with all the performers and decorations, brilliantly illuminated, and ready for immediate action, I sometimes wonder how it can find a purchaser. In my day [such] a piece would have been regarded with the indifference with which an angler would contemplate a basket of killed fish offered as a substitute for his expected day's sport. (67)

As an object of critical inquiry, the toy theatre has in the past largely been disregarded, a manifestation, in part, of toy-theatre practitioner and historian George Speiaght's prediction that future critics would presume "such a small and insignificant subject as Toy Theatres should not be submerged beneath a ponderous weight of criticism and research" (*Juvenile* 200). Fortunately, this view is changing, thanks to increasing interest in adaptation and children's studies, popular and material culture, and noncanonical theatrical texts and forms such as pantomime.[3] As a paper souvenir, child's toy, dramatic repository, and material embodiment of historical practices and performances, the toy theatre presents a nexus of research potential.

John Storey posits a definition of "popular culture" that is helpful for thinking about the toy theatre as "a site of performance" and also as an object that embodies and represents popular culture (Introduction 1). Toy theatres were devised, printed, and sold by contributors to what Storey would call one of the "new culture industries"; consumption or use of the toy theatre contributed to the "'making' of popular culture" (Introduction 1). Storey's aim is to bring attention "to the study of popular culture more generally, a renewed interest in the historical conditions of existence of popular texts and practices," which an examination of toy-theatre practices offers (Introduction 1). Similarly, Daniel Cook and Nicolas Seager propose a material-studies approach to later iterations of canonical works. Rather than encountering such iterations as secondary, defined by their relationship to original texts and potentially viewed as "derivative" or "debased," Cook and Seager propose thinking about such iterations as "afterlives" (2). "Afterlife," they find, "is a capacious term that includes critical reception, remediation, and creative appropriation [which] levels distinctions of value and priority [. . .] and flexibly accommodates a range of creative and other efforts by which works persist and are transformed" (Cook and Seager 2). Such an approach sets aside hierarchical views that privilege the source text; it also democratizes considerations of marginalized forms such as children's toys and pantomime.

The toy theatre stands as a ready site for consideration from many angles: its beginnings as a live theatre souvenir, as an early form of fan culture, and as an emblematic example of nineteenth-century popular culture. In its textual content, it contains new versions, miniaturized, often from eighteenth-century and later fictions. In its consumers' acts of acquisition, consumption, and advocacy, it represents popular culture in the guise of afterlife. In the spirit of Cook and Seager's aspiration to "move away from what we might call narrative and narrative qualified media and develop a grammar of immersive experience," I propose the term *materializing* for discussing the toy theatre as an object whose users engage with it on a material level; reviewing ways in which it has been considered materially significant; and examining the value it offers as a material repository for historical theatrical performances (5). I illustrate this strategy through a discussion of the 1841 toy-theatre version of the early Victorian pantomime *The Castle of Otranto; or, Harlequin & the Giant Helmet.*

Material Experience

> In their play, children actively appropriate cultural commodities, making their own discriminations and judgments, while combining and reworking them in myriad ways.
>
> —Goldstein, Buckingham, and Brougère, *Toys, Games, and Media*[4]

Jeffrey Goldstein, David Buckingham, and Gilles Brougère identify toy theatres as precursors of twentieth- and early-twenty-first-century interactive and intertextual children's toys. Although various types of toy theatres had been in use on the Continent during the eighteenth century and earlier, in England they date from the early nineteenth century. The printer William West is credited with creating the first sheets of characters and scenery in 1811, which were based on Thomas Dibdin's 1806 pantomime, *Harlequin and Mother Goose; or, The Golden Egg*, as well as miniature stages to gratify enthusiastic children.[5]

West's success quickly drew other printers to the business. Many created their own versions of the same popular plays—multiple versions of the same titles appear in the lists for different printers—and some copied or printed those of others. The industry became wildly competitive and even engendered its own form of dynastic succession as later printers took over or purchased plates from earlier ones and families got into the business. Speiaght lists more than 100 "Publishers of the Juvenile Drama" and their published plays (*Juvenile*, Appendix A). Of these, the most prolific were West, J. H. Jameson, Hodgson and Co., J. K. Green, and the Skelt family. Green, Skelt, and others revolutionized the industry by issuing smaller half-penny sheets to appeal to a wider audience.

As a "site of performance," in the event of a child's acquiring and decorating the sheets, as well as the production (or nonproduction, as discussed below) of a play, the toy theatre functions as a "cultural commodity," to use Goldstein, Buckingham, and Brougère's term (3). As Liz Farr points out, "Its genesis complicates passive models of consumption, because its early consumers, despite their youth, were not merely submissive recipients of market products, but active agents who helped shape the materials through which they could explore their playful fantasies" (44). This shaping of materials, the sheets, rehearsals, and productions varied from child to child, but commonalities can be found in responses to the materials and the prospect of production.

The many published recollections of the toy theatre are especially engaging in their details of the writers' acquisition and decoration of the character and scenery sheets. Although the cost seems negligible today, even a penny could be dear to a nineteenth-century child. According to Ruth Goodman, for example, a boy who was a school monitor would be paid approximately one half-penny per day (287). At a penny each (prior to the half-penny craze), just an eight-sheet set of character sheets could cost a school monitor the equivalent of sixteen days' pay. Arthur comments on the sixty-four half-penny sheet set of "Green's *Jack Sheppard* [which] beat every other play published for the number of sheets of characters and scenes; that is required in its fulness [*sic*]—some fabulous number it was, which the savings of no ordinary pocket-money could ever hope to procure; it required a rich uncle (after dinner) or a godfather in a good temper to finance the youthful manager for the drama in question" at a cost of thirty-two pence, plus the playbook, which cost four pence (44). In John Leech's satire with the unwieldy title *Young troublesome, or Master Jacky's holidays from the blessed moment of his leaving school to the identical moment of his going back again, showing how there never was such a boy as that boy*, Master Jacky receives just such a gift from a benevolent figure, Captain Clarence (see Figure 13.1).

Figure 13.1. On the left of John Leech's illustration for *Young troublesome*, Captain Clarence presents a miniature theatre to Master Jacky, and, on the right, the boys work on their performance. Courtesy of the Baldwin Library of Historical Children's Literature in the Special Collections, George A. Smathers Libraries at the University of Florida, Gainesville, Florida.

The prospect of acquiring a complete play made the toy theatre a pricey venture for a child without such a benefactor, however. In addition to the sheets, G. K. Chesterton noted other necessities, evidently affordable for him: "I only had to pay a shilling a sheet for good cardboard and a shilling a box for bad water colours" (148–49). Also required were the building or purchase of a miniature theatre, unless a child already possessed one or was fortunate enough to be given one; cardboard and paste to stabilize the characters and tin slides for moving them across the stage; metal lamps and colza (rapeseed) oil for lighting; a stage curtain (preferably green calico); and special effects such as the "red fire" essential for the perennially popular toy-theatre play depicted in *Young troublesome*, *The Miller and His Men*. The toy theatre arrives "in a forward state of preparation" and is further prepared by Master Jacky and his young siblings (see Figure 13.1).

The event of coloring the sheets prompted special commentary in the recollections, particularly to distinguish purchasers of plain sheets requiring decoration from the unworthy purchasers of pre-colored sheets. Robert Louis Stevenson in 1883 elaborates on the magic of the coloring (painting) activity:

> I cannot deny that joy attended the illumination; nor can I quite forgive that child who, wilfully [*sic*] forgoing pleasure, stoops to "twopence coloured." With crimson lake (hark to the sound of it—crimson lake!—the horns of elf-land are not richer on the ear)—with crimson lake and Prussian blue a certain purple is to be compounded which, for cloaks especially, Titian could not equal. The latter colour with gamboge, a hated name although an exquisite pigment, supplied a green of such a savoury greenness that today my heart regrets it. Nor can I recall without a tender weakness the very aspect of the water where I dipped my brush. (219)

And yet, for Stevenson, accompanying the act of creation was the death of creation: "Yes, there was pleasure in the painting. But when all was painted, it is needless to deny it, all was spoiled. You might, indeed, set up a scene or two to look at; but to cut the figures out was simply sacrilege"; furthermore, "nor could any child twice court the tedium, the worry, and the long-drawn disenchantment of an actual performance" (219–20). Around a decade later, Charles Dickens Jr., too, found the greatest pleasure in "the preparations—the painting the scenery, the painting and cutting out the characters, the pasting, the gumming, the thousand and one messes and snippings, and general causes of litter and untidiness, which were so dear to the boys of my time" (526).

After all of the efforts to decorate the sheets, an actual production could be hazardous in many ways, especially to the well-being of the toy theatre itself. Dickens Jr. mentions the footlights and oil, which would be lit for the performance. Often, though, this would end with the characters "cremating themselves on the footlights" or the scenery catching fire and, like so many of the real-life theatres, the miniature one would come to a charred finish (Arthur 44). In a later illustration for *Young troublesome*, Master Jacky's "Grand evening rehearsal of the Miller and his Men" culminates in a "terrific explosion in the Housekeepers room" (see Figure 13.2). In his Foreword to Wilson's 1932 history, Charles B. Cochran recalls the end of his interest in toy-theatre productions at age nine:

Figure 13.2. On the right of John Leech's illustration for *Young troublesome*, the boys set their toy theatrical on fire. Courtesy of the Baldwin Library of Historical Children's Literature in the Special Collections, George A. Smathers Libraries at the University of Florida, Gainesville, Florida.

> In working up to the climax, with revolving mill, red fire, and so on, I felt the lack of four or more hands. Pushing on a character in a tin slide, lighting the red fire, manipulating a trap and working the wheel, while at the same time speaking the lines of the characters, made me lose my presence of mind.
>
> The character in the tin slide caught fire, the flames spread to the wing; I burnt my hand, and then the great conflagration! My theatre was reduced to ashes. (7)

"In the main," Cochran concludes, "I agree with Mr Wilson that the pleasure of the toy theatre was in anticipation rather than in realization" (8–9). What with following the stage directions in the playbook, moving multiple characters on and off stage, speaking the dialogue, and managing the special effects, it is little wonder that Chesterton found "the work" "too heavy": "If I am ever in any other and better world I hope that I shall have enough time to play with nothing but toy theatres; and I hope that I shall have enough divine and superhuman energy to act at least one play in them without a hitch" (149). Possibly the best-known example of successful toy-theatre production is fictional: in William Makepeace Thackeray's *Vanity Fair: A Novel without a Hero*, Master George and "young Todd" "visited all the principal theatres of the metropolis—knew the names of all the actors from Drury Lane to Sadler's Wells; and performed, indeed, many of the plays to the Todd family and their youthful friends, with West's famous characters, on their pasteboard theatre" (161).

Primary sources that record playing with toy theatres often overlook the playbook or script. Of course, if a toy-theatre manager chose to produce his play, he could simply improvise the events and dialogue or recreate them from memory if he had seen the play in the theatre. He could acquire a published copy of the live theatre script; in the early days this was probably the only option available. He could purchase a toy theatre, or "Juvenile Drama," playbook for four pence; these were the abridged versions that included the dialogue and action as derived from the live theatre production and also directions specific to the sheets concerning which scenery and which character image to use.[6]

In other cases, the quality of the script becomes a point of debate. For Stevenson, "The fable, as set forth in the play-book, proved to be not worthy of the scenes and characters. [. . .] Indeed, as literature, these dramas did not much appeal to me. I forget the very outline of the plots"

(218). Suzanne Rahn has commented on "the poor literary quality of toy theater scripts. The original plays on which toy theater plays were based were for the most part moral-formulaic melodramas or simple-minded pantomimes. Even when the original was itself of high quality"—Shakespeare, Walter Scott, or Dickens, for example—"not much was likely to survive the minifying process" (33). Theo Arthur in 1891, however, offers an appealing view: "The books of the words (price 4*d.*) supplied by the [. . .] firms were in their way masterpieces of adaptive art. How remarkably well pruned for the youthful reader the speeches all were!" (45).[7] Like the brisk and sometimes rough sketches of the characters and scenes, the playbooks mirror and even comment on their real-life counterparts as they eliminate excess and offer to the young impresario (a miniature himself) everything necessary for a minified production on a minified stage in a minified auditorium, a room in a family home.

Material Importance

> [I]n my time a toy theatre was about the most popular present you could give a boy, and when some philanthropist presented me with an unusually fine specimen, a perfect Drury Lane among its brethren, I anticipated an endless round of delights.
>
> —Charles Dickens Jr., "Glimpses of Charles Dickens"[8]

A historiography for the English toy theatre dates from the later Victorian era. Playwrights and critics such as John Oxenford in 1871 and Theo Arthur in 1891, and authors such as R. L. Stevenson in 1883 and G. K. Chesterton in 1909 published essays celebrating the toy theatre. Following the era of periodical documentation, came the histories. A. E. Wilson, dramatic critic of *The Star*, in 1932 led the way with *Penny Plain Two Pence Coloured: A History of the Juvenile Drama*, followed by Speiaght in 1946 with *Juvenile Drama: The History of the English Toy Theatre* (revised in 1969 as *The History of the English Toy Theatre*). The latter is now viewed as the standard text on the subject, although a combined reading of Wilson and Speiaght offers a more complete understanding of the material life of the toy theatre. More recently, in his 1992 *Toy Theatres of the World*, actor Peter Baldwin has contextualized the English toy theatre within a wider history and includes Germany,

France, Austria, Denmark, Spain, and North America, as well as Italy, Sweden, Norway, Holland, and Czechoslovakia.

The toy theatre was not the only form of domestic entertainment available to children; however, it prompted fond, even elegiac, reminiscences from notable men long after their days of playing with toy theatres were over and when toy theatres had largely been co-opted or subsumed by other toys and activities. As a material object of the humblest origins—paper, ink, paint, and paste—for its advocates the toy theatre embodied and made material their ideas of the world.

For Stevenson, the unpainted sheets represented the very font of imagination: "Every sheet we fingered was another lightning glance into obscure, delicious story; it was like wallowing in the raw stuff of story-books" (216–17). Stevenson recognized the toy theatre's failings even as he acknowledged its influence upon his work and his life:

> Indeed, out of this cut-and-dry, dull, swaggering, obtrusive and infantile art, I seem to have learned the very spirit of my life's enjoyment; met there the shadows of the characters I was to read about and love in a late future; [. . .] acquired a gallery of scenes and characters with which, in the silent theatre of the brain, I might enact all novels and romances; and took from these rude cuts an enduring and transforming pleasure. (225–26)

One of the first to document this influence on Stevenson's adventure novels, Chesterton saw in his own experiences of the toy theatre "[a]ll the essential morals which modern men need to learn. [. . .] Artistically considered, it reminds us of the main principle of art, the principle which is in most danger of being forgotten in our time. I mean the fact that art consists of limitation; the fact that art is limitation" (150). Of the efforts to create and produce his own toy-theatre play, Chesterton declared, "[a]ll this gives me a feeling touching the real meaning of immortality" (149). For Speiaght, completing his history during World War II while stationed at the island of Colombo in Ceylon (now Sri Lanka), the essentiality to humanity of "little absurdities" such as the toy theatre could not be overstated:

> [A] civilised society is one whose members can devote themselves to Toy Theatres! It is, anyhow, not a question of Toy Theatres instead of Hospitals; the question is, can we have

> Toy Theatres as well as the Atom Bomb. I can only answer that we *must!* If the humane and urbane pattern of life is to survive upon this planet, man must be able to relax among toys and nonsense; a passionate interest in little absurdities is a necessary safety valve in the March of Progress. (201)

Others asserted the material importance of the toy theatre in terms of its tragic decline. For Arthur, the generations growing up in the 1830s–50s, "will conclude that the present generation knows not that resource from which their parents derived great amusement and, probably, unconscious instruction, and may, perhaps, with us, deplore the fact that the theatrical stationer has to be classed, with the Dodo and Megatherium, as utterly and totally extinct" (46). Not only did the loss of the toy theatre and its industry—figured as the "theatrical stationer"—rank with the extinction of iconic species, but also, as Alan Powers notes from his unique position as chairman of Pollock's Toy Museum Trust, "with the loss of childhood," "a more general sense of lost folk art vigor in the face of Victorian gentility," and the understanding that "English toy theatres were superseded in the trade by German chromolithographed ones, which were more magnificent, but offered less interaction for the child" (12). For all of these writers, however disparate their reasons for celebrating the toy theatre, their valuations of it as a mechanism for a material encounter consistently appears in their comments.

Faced with the toy theatre's vanishing from shops and homes, historians took an additional approach: asserting its value as a historical record of real-life theatre productions. According to A. E. Wilson, the miniature theatre provides important and irreplaceable information:

> We know how much were the pains taken to ensure accuracy in reproducing plays in miniature [. . .] these little sheets afford a record of what theatrical productions were like a hundred years or more ago, and of the old fashions and conventions, such as we do not otherwise possess. It is a complete picture of the British theatre as it was and of a kind that has ceased to exist [. . .] even [a contemporary description] hardly gives us so graphic an idea as one of the West or Webb or Redington prosceniums which were sold for one penny or twopence. (77–78)

Wilson outlines the many components of live theatre captured by toy theatre artists. Of special note are the "sheets of characters," which represent not only "a portrait gallery of old favourites [actors] in miniature," but also "afford us an excellent idea of stage dressing in those far-off days. [. . .] In Hodgson's 'Macbeth,' for instance, Macbeth and Macduff wore the gigantic feathered bonnets, such as were worn by Scottish regiments of that time; they were then thought quite appropriate to the period of the play" (79).

Most important for Wilson were the sheets of scenes and scenery "as a record of scene-painting and designing," particularly those scenes "picturing actual localities," especially of London (80). Theatrical publisher Hodgson, for example, published around 1830 *Life in London* which featured "Burlington Arcade, Tattersall's, Almack's, Cribb's Parlour, Temple Bar (when the archway stood in Fleet Street), Fleet Street [. . .] and Leicester Square" (80). Contemporary locations featured in the harlequinades of the ever-popular pantomimes on the live stages and were reproduced in toy theatre form, mirroring scene-painting practices begun during the previous century.[9] The real-life completion of Trafalgar Square represented in the harlequinade sequence of James Robinson Planché's 1840 stage pantomime *The Castle of Otranto; or, Harlequin & the Giant Helmet*, for example, was translated to J. K. Green's 1841 toy-theatre version. In his Foreword to Speiaght's *Juvenile Drama*, actor Ralph Richardson summed up the toy theatre's historical value: "It is so much a pocket-diary of that which had its being in the real-life theatre of last century, a chronicle in little, as it were, of the brave old days of transpontine delights" (viii).

Materializing Live Theatre / Pantomime

> But, indeed, I have a dream at times that is not all a dream. [. . .] There in a dim shop, low in the roof and smelling strong of glue and footlights, I find myself in quaking treaty with great Skelt himself, the aboriginal, all dusty from the tomb. I buy, with what a choking heart—I buy them all, *all but the pantomimes*; I pay my mental money, and go forth; and lo! the packets are dust.
>
> —Robert Louis Stevenson, *Memories and Portraits*[10]

Like the toy theatre, overlooked because of its purpose as souvenir and child's toy, live theatre pantomime has garnered less critical attention than canonical plays due to its long association with the non-patent, or "transpontine" (on the south side of the Thames) theatres as an "illegitimate" dramatic form and later as the formulaic children's entertainment that even Stevenson disparaged in his dream of procuring toy-theatre plays, "all but the pantomimes" (227). Like the toy theatre, too, pantomime enjoyed enormous popular success from its early-eighteenth-century appearance on live theatre stages and throughout the nineteenth century.

According to Judith Flanders, "[b]y the middle of the nineteenth century, pantomime took up an ever larger proportion of many theatres' calendars: the investment in the spectacle was huge, and the audience to witness it equally huge. In Leeds in 1885 the Grand Theatre made an annual profit of £2,067, of which £1,766, or 85 per cent, came from its ten-and-a-half week run of *Sinbad the Sailor*" (305). The "regular ingredients of the pantomime: spectacle, slapstick, gender role reversal and topical allusion" that Jeffrey Richards investigates made it a perfect source for toy-theatre adaptation, as did the nineteenth-century practice of presenting new pantomimes during the Christmas season, which was steadily becoming a child-centered, gift-giving holiday (xiii). Central to Storey's concept of "the new popular culture" was "the development of a whole range of culture industries" owned and controlled by the new urban middle class and which included "publishing, music hall [. . .] and the invention of the 'traditional' Christmas" (Introduction 4). The "customs that survived or were revived or invented" as part of the traditional Christmas "all had one thing in common: they were commodities that could be sold for a profit" (Storey, "Class" 199). In the new popular culture, pantomime and toy theatre starred as culture industries.

Pantomime plays—also called harlequin plays—feature on many toy-theatre publishers' lists. According to Antonia Fraser, in the toy theatre world, "[the] Harlequin series was always popular with children" because of its spectacle, exciting events, ridiculous characters in absurd situations, gorgeous costumes, and magical transformations (134). These types of plays can be difficult today to imagine. Although O'Brien is concerned with eighteenth-century pantomime, he acknowledges that, although "these performances were [. . .] sketchy at best,"

> that same shortfall of primary evidence [. . .] also serves a useful purpose in reminding us how much of the past of any cultural practice—performance, reading, talking, thinking, feeling—is irretrievable. In particular, the challenge of re-creating and thinking about eighteenth-century British pantomime underscores how inadequate the printed word is as a means to capture the full texture of embodied performance. (xx)

Scholars of nineteenth-century pantomime fare better due to "the often incredibly detailed reviews and the evocative engravings in the new illustrated magazines" (Richards xi). Together with real-life scripts, music, reviews and engravings, as well as playbills and programs, the near-three-dimensionality and direct adaptation of the toy-theatre sheets and plays offer a rich approximation of contemporary live theatre plays, particularly the strange and wonderful pantomimes.

Wilson, again extolling the value of toy theatre as historical evidence and embodiment of live theatre, details elements of pantomime captured for the miniature stage: "the processions of pantomime giants, 'big-heads,' ogres, and other fearful wild-fowl of the time [. . . the] old-time Harlequinade [. . .] pursued through many scenes [. . . featuring] the 'tricks'—the magic changes of scene and objects performed at the touch of Harlequin's bat [. . .] which commanded the wonderment and admiration of the pantomime-goer of old" (82). Together with contemporary reviews of the live pantomime *The Castle of Otranto; or, Harlequin & the Giant Helmet*, the toy-theatre version can be read as a reconstruction, a commentary, and a material representation of a historical production.

According to Richards, in 1839 the Covent Garden audience had "demanded a traditional pantomime" (84). For the 1840 Christmas pantomime, resident playwright Planché obliged with his *The Castle of Otranto; or, Harlequin & the Giant Helmet* (adapted from Horace Walpole's seminal Gothic novel, *The Castle of Otranto*, first published on Christmas Eve, 1764), which opened on 26 December 1840. Framed by a clever allegorical story featuring the triumph of the genii of Burlesque over the Spirit of Romance and her heroic "Romances," it hewed to traditional pantomime form: first a very truncated version of the most spectacular events of the novel, including the giant helmet in the courtyard, the ghost descending from the portrait, the gigantic disembodied legs and arms, and the massive sword. Prince Manfred, the usurper, tries to get rid of his wife, Hippolyta, and prevent his ward Isabella from eloping with the rightful heir, Theodore. Following Manfred's defeat, the characters are transformed into the classic *commedia dell'arte* characters. The harlequinade chase scenes through London's environs ensue, ending with a panorama concerning political issues such as the return of Napoleon's remains to France and the opium war with China. The *Theatrical Journal*'s review of the revival the following year reads almost as a toy-theatre review might:

> And now to wield our magic pencil, and endeavour to paint the wonders that we have beheld at Covent Garden. If beauty

> of scenery, grouping of characters, and mechanical changes of the most surprising nature be a test of merit, then surely is this Pantomime worthy of every praise—but the "vis comica" is wanting; the pantomimic actors are made subservient to the pencil of the scene painter, and the machinery of the carpenter. ("Covent Garden" 2)

Captured by Green in a half-penny toy-theatre version published to coincide with the revival on Christmas Day 1841, the sheets invite a young impresario to "paint the wonders" and perhaps restore the lamented "vis comica" (comic force) in a jocular presentation. Considered next to the original live theatre script, the playbook generally retains the dialogue of the main story and the harlequinade; the major omission is the panorama sequence featuring much of the contemporary news commentary. The set consists of a fourteen-page playbook (reissued at least once, in 1854, as *Harlequin and the Giant Helmet*), eight sheets of characters, ten sheets of scenery, four sheets of wings, and two sheets of "Green's New Tricks in Harlequin and the Giant Helmet."

Figure 13.3. Title sheets, such as this one from J. K. Green's 1841 version of *The Castle of Otranto; or, Harlequin & the Giant Helmet*, highlight the practices of nineteenth-century pantomimes. Courtesy of Hugo's Toy Theatre and HCC Brown's Reproductions, Wilburton, Ely, Cambridgeshire, UK.

The sheets reveal a number of things to a modern viewer who might be unfamiliar with pantomime practices. The title sheet includes the numbers and types of sheets, the printer's information, date of publication, and in this case the agent, J. Redington (see Figure 13.3).[11] It presents the main characters and indicates their transformations: Manfred and Hippolyta are two of the pantomime's "big heads," and Hippolyta, played by a male actor, turns into a Clown designed after the indelible (Joseph) Grimaldi. The subsequent sheets give alternate poses for the main characters and present numerous sublunary characters such as Romance, Burlesque, and their respective armies; Blue Devils and Spirits (fairies); other big heads such as Manfred's servants Tremblino and Farfromboldo; "supers" (multicharacter sets) of Union Jacks and Jills and a Mob; and many stereotypical Londoners.

Adapted from the original backdrops by the famous Grieves scene-painting family, the evocative sheets of scenery include the land of Romance, the many-towered and battlemented Castle of Otranto, the courtyard with the enormous helmet topped with feathers and inhabited by a face (one of the character sheets offers a matching beaver to attach to the helmet as a kind of special effect), Trafalgar Square with Nelson's Column, "Furnished Lodgings," and a London street of shop fronts (see Figure 13.4). The wings include sets for the castle scenes and the lodgings. The "New Tricks" sheets provide an idea of how some of the real-life pantomime tricks looked in performance (see Figure 13.5). Wilson indicates that on the live stage the tricks were often accomplished by drops; on the toy-theatre stage it was probably a matter of replacing one object with another to suggest a transformation. An example from the playbook indicates how complex a scene involving tricks could be. The "Furnished Lodgings" scene features Clown and Pantaloon, who is always the one on the receiving end of the joke. Errors in the original have been corrected.

Scene 8, No. 8. Furnished Lodgings
Enter Clown, and Pantaloon, plate 8. and Landlord plate 7. L. H.[12]
CLOWN—How much is your Lodging's per Week?
LANDLORD—One Sovereign, Gentlemen.
PANTALOON—Oh! that will do. Let us have some tea, directly.
Exit Landlord, Clown, and Pantaloon, R. H.[13] *re-enter same side Clown and Pantaloon, sitting at the Tea Table, followed by Landlady, plate 7.*

Figure 13.4. The scenery sheets included in the toy theatres, such as this sheet from J. K. Green's 1841 version of *The Castle of Otranto; or, Harlequin & the Giant Helmet,* were adapted from the original backdrops by the famous Grieves scene-painting family. Courtesy of Hugo's Toy Theatre and HCC Brown's Reproductions, Wilburton, Ely, Cambridgeshire, UK.

Figure 13.5. This plate from J. K. Green's 1841 *Harlequin and the Giant Helmet* suggests how some of the pantomime "tricks" looked in performance. Courtesy of Hugo's Toy Theatre and HCC Brown's Reproductions, Wilburton, Ely, Cambridgeshire, UK.

Clown—Some prime Hyson [green China tea], this, Marm.
Landlady—Yes Sir, capitol.
Clown—Send in my box of Fruit, if you please:
Exit Landlady, R. H. *re-enter with trick, (Box of choice Fruit.) plate 2, No. 9 at the same time the table to be drawn off,* R. H. *re-enter Clown, and Pantaloon, plate 8: and Harlequin plate 6.—the trick to change to the Fruit, and to be drawn off* R. H. *and the trick of the (Pudding,) plate 2. No. 5. to be pushed on.*
Clown—Oh! Here's a Plummy Pudding!
The trick to change to the Clown's Head, and to be drawn off R. H. exit all the Characters, R. H. re-enter same side, Clown, with cap on, Landlady, and Pantaloon, plate 8.
Clown—My eye's, what a Figure Head!
Landlady—You wretch! give me my cap, or I will tear your eyes out!
Pantaloon—That's right, give it him, missis.
Exit the whole, L. H. Harlequin dancing after them, plate 2. (*Castle*, 12–13)

Between sliding the required characters and tricks onto the stage, speaking the dialogue, and exiting (removing) the whole group, it is no wonder would-be toy-theatre impresarios could be daunted into never producing a play. Oft-quoted drama critic William Archer seized upon the potential benefit to this, declaring in 1887, "[i]t is precisely because performances never came off that the toy theatre is so infinitely preferable to its so-called real rival. [. . .] It is the very gymnasium of the imagination" (105).

Conclusion

> Children's culture is now highly intertextual: Every "text" (including commodities such as toys) effectively draws upon and feeds into every other text. [. . .] Each play event is part of a broader flow of events that crosses from one medium or "platform" to another.
>
> —Goldstein, Buckingham, and Brougére, *Toys, Games, and Media*[14]

Of note concerning the toy-theatre version of *The Castle of Otranto; or, Harlequin & the Giant Helmet* is its status as the offspring of the pantomime staged at the Theatre Royal Covent Garden. In 1840, the London theatres still operated under the restrictions imposed by the 1737 Licensing Act, which granted only Covent Garden, Drury Lane, and the Haymarket theatres licenses to produce *legitimate* or *spoken word* performances. Pantomime could feature songs but not dialogue. This made the harlequinade transformations and chase scenes perfect pantomime fodder, making up for lack of dialogue with visual spectacle and comedy. How, though, could a pantomime or *illegitimate* production—with dialogue—appear on the licensed stage at Covent Garden?

This was also the case as early as 1806, when Thomas Dibdin's *Harlequin and Mother Goose; or, the Golden Egg* was produced at Covent Garden, a fact that, as Molly Clark Hillard points out, "troubles the very definitions of 'popular' and elite" and a fact that can be attributed to a more general movement of pantomime from the unlicensed theatres to the licensed theatres thanks to "permeable boundaries" created by considerations of profit (181). The Theatre Regulation Act of 1843 abolished the patent theatre privileges, but they had already become so compromised that it is likely the public hardly noticed.

Nor, it seems, did parents protest the insinuation into their homes and children's spheres of the many toy-theatre plays derived from previously illegitimate dramatic forms such as pantomime. Hillard, reflecting on O'Brien's interpretation of pantomime in the legitimate theatres, dramatically finds "pantomime [. . .] figured as the thing of the streets brought into the respectable home" (182). In the home, it is made manifest in the form of the seemingly innocent toy theatre.

In many ways, the toy theatre introduced children to the adult world. In its acquisition they learned the value of money and engaged with the commercial sphere as well as making choices about plays, plots, and potential. In decorating the sheets, they learned patience, fortitude, and something of aesthetics and artistic materials. The production, or even nonproduction, of the plays taught children about leadership, practice, and imaginative engagement. "That the original plays were written primarily for adults," Rahn comments, "also gives the toy theater a special value. Toy theater plays push gently and enticingly against the boundaries of what was (and is) considered appropriate for children" (35). In the toy-theatre world, children could make so many of their own decisions. Perhaps this was part of the appeal of the pantomimes, which in their elevation of marginalized or strange characters such as Harlequin and Clown, "not only provided characters with whom such audience members could identify, but gave those characters agency and power" (11).

Key to the toy theatre's history are four eras: the golden age of production and consumption (c. 1808–1830), revival (1870s), nostalgia (1870s and later), and historicization (1932 and later). During the later nineteenth century, other forms of entertainment rapidly displaced it, notably optical toys such as the Zoetrope, the Praxinoscope, and especially, the Magic Lantern; mechanical toys; illustrated magazines; and photography (see Fraser, 122–41). The "fundamental cause for the decline of the Toy Theatre," according to Speiaght, "must [. . .] be found on the stage itself" in the emergence of increasingly cerebral and decreasingly spectacular plays by the likes of Oscar Wilde, George Bernard Shaw, and Henrik Ibsen (163).

And yet, despite its paper foundation, the toy theatre, which bridges so many areas of social, material, and theatrical culture, can bear scrutiny.[15] As Chesterton exulted, "Exactly in so far as it is limited, so far it could play easily with falling cities or with falling stars. Meanwhile the big theatres are obliged to be economical because they are big. [. . .] You can only represent very big ideas in very small spaces" (151).

Notes

1. See *Juvenile* 14.

2. Boys appear to have been the target demographic for toy theatres, if the recollections in primary sources are representative. Certainly, in the adult world, the role of theatre manager was typically filled by men. Because toy theatres were a form of familial and domestic entertainment, however, it's likely that girls also played with them, perhaps also acquiring, decorating, and producing the plays and not simply acting as assistants to boys. Liz Farr, for example, notes that like her male contemporaries, actress Ellen Terry was a "juvenile theatrical" producer (43). This remains a compelling area for further research.

3. Recently, a number of researchers have found historical evidence of costume and scenic design practices. Valerie Cumming created "some tolerably accurate costumes and accessories for twenty-first century performance" using four *Old Oak Chest* toy theatre sheets from 1817 (53). Likewise, Rachel Bryant Davies described in detail the toy theatre recreation of *The Giant Horse, or The Siege of Troy*, produced at Astley's Amphitheatre in 1833: "These sheets for rep-

licating *Giant Horse* are especially exciting," she notes, "since they enable [. . .] an almost unprecedented insight into how the original performance represented the mythical past" (156).

4. See p. 3.

5. Ironically, Dibdin was the godson of David Garrick, who famously tried to undermine the popularity of pantomime with "his own contribution to the form—*Harlequin's Invasion*, first produced in 1759 and staged as a Christmas entertainment for many years afterward," effectively making Dibdin and Garrick the live theatre's godfathers of the toy theatre (O'Brien xxiv).

6. Oxenford explains, "[t]o compensate for the absence of gesticulation, the same personage is represented several times in different attitudes, and a playbook, composed expressly for miniature theatricals, with short dialogues and long stage directions, indicates the precise figure to be used in each particular situation" (67).

7. Modern scholars are finding much to mine in the toy-theatre scripts. Holly Furneaux, for example, finds "the careful manner in which Dickens's plot is reduced does allow for social critique" in its distillation of contemporary institutional endangerment of the child protagonist (217).

8. See Dickens 526.

9. Speiaght notes "a certain movement towards architectural realism in scene-painting" during the eighteenth century. At Covent Garden, for example, "William Capon painted for John Kemble a series of vast architectural canvases, carefully studied from actual remains" (*Juvenile* 19).

10. See Stevenson 227. Emphasis added.

11. Redington was succeeded by his son-in-law, Benjamin Pollock. See Speiaght, *Juvenile* 223.

12. Left hand (stage right).

13. Right hand (stage left).

14. See Goldstein, Buckingham, and Brougére 2–3.

15. Modern toy theatre practitioners, educators, and artists are expanding its creative aesthetic and power to engage new generations, using subjects ranging from *Dante's Inferno*, a 2008 "satirical toy theatre movie" to organizations employing toy-theatre design to help explore underserved communities concerns about "wrongful conviction, bullying, unreasonable searches and seizures, and racial profiling, as well as less direct issues such as ocean pollution" (de Rooy 102; Bell 445).

Works Cited

Archer, William. "The Drama in Pasteboard." *The Art Journal* (April–May 1887): 105–108, 140–44. *HathiTrust*. Accessed 23 April 2021.

Arthur, Theo. "The Toy Theatre." *The Era Almanack and Annual* (1891): 43–46. *HathiTrust*. Accessed 23 April 2021.

Baldwin, Peter. *Toy Theatres of the World*. London: A. Zwemmer, 1992.

Bell, John. "Can Theatre Change Lives and Impact Underserved Communities?" *Theatre Survey* 57.3 (September 2016): 441–51.

The Castle of Otranto; or, Harlequin & the Giant Helmet. Green's Juvenile Drama. London: J. K. Green, 1841.

Chesterton, G[ilbert] K[eith]. *Tremendous Trifles*. London: Methuen, 1909. *HathiTrust*. Accessed 23 April 2021.

Cochran, Charles B. Foreword. Wilson 7–9.

Cook, Daniel, and Nicolas Seager, eds. Introduction. *The Afterlives of Eighteenth-Century Fiction*. Cambridge: Cambridge University Press, 2015. 1–19.

"Covent Garden." *Theatrical Journal*. 2. 55 (1841): 2–3. *British Periodicals Collection II*. Accessed 19 December 2019.

Cumming, Valerie. "Costume or Clothes? Dressing the 1815 Season at the Sans Pareil Theatre." *Nineteenth Century Theatre and Film* 29. 2 (Winter 2002): 51–57. *Literature Online*. Accessed 24 November 2019.

Davies, Rachel Bryant. *Troy, Carthage and the Victorians: The Drama of Classical Ruins in the Nineteenth-Century Imagination*. Cambridge: Cambridge University Press, 2018.

Dickens Jr., Charles. "Glimpses of Charles Dickens." *The North American Review* 160. 462 (May 1895): 525–37. *JSTOR*. Accessed 23 April 2021.

Ennis, Daniel J. "Afterpieces." *The Encyclopedia of British Literature 1660–1789*. Ed. Gary Day and Jack Lynch. *Blackwell Reference Online*. 2015. Accessed 23 April 2021.

Farr, Liz. "Paper Dreams and Romantic Projections: The Nineteenth-Century Toy Theater, Boyhood and Aesthetic Play." *The Nineteenth-Century Child and Consumer Culture*. Ed. Dennis Denisoff. *Ashgate Studies in Childhood, 1700 to the Present*. Aldershot, Hampshire, and Burlington, VT: Ashgate, 2008. 43–61.

Flanders, Judith. *Consuming Passions: Leisure and Pleasure in Victorian Britain*. London: HarperCollins, 2006.

Fraser, Antonia. *The History of Toys*. 1966. London: Hamlyn, 1972.

Furneaux, Holly. "'Worrying to Death'—Reinterpreting Dickens's Critique of the New Poor Law in *Oliver Twist* and Contemporary Adaptations." *The Dickensian* 101. 467 (Winter 2005): 213–24. *Literature Online*. Accessed 24 November 2019.

Goldstein, Jeffrey, David Buckingham, and Gilles Brougère. Introduction. *Toys, Games, and Media*. Ed. Jeffrey Goldstein, David Buckingham, and Gilles Brougère. London: Erlbaum, 2006. 1–7.

Goodman, Ruth. *How to Be a Victorian: A Dawn-to-Dusk Guide to Victorian Life*. 2013. London: Penguin, 2014.

Green, J. K. *Green's Characters and Scenes in* The Castle of Otranto; or, Harlequin & the Giant Helmet. London: J. Redington, 1841.

Hillard, Molly Clark. *Spellbound: The Fairy Tale and the Victorians*. Columbus: Ohio State University Press, 2014.

Leech, John. *Young Troublesome, or, Master Jacky's holidays from the blessed moment of his leaving school to the identical moment of his going back again, showing how there never was such a boy as that boy*. London: Bradbury and Evans, [n.d.] Baldwin Library of Historical Children's Literature in the Special Collections, George A. Smathers Libraries. University of Florida. https://ufdc.ufl.edu/UF00028393/000001 Accessed 23 April 2021.

O'Brien, John. *Harlequin Britain: Pantomime and Entertainment, 1690–1760*. Baltimore: Johns Hopkins University Press, 2004.

Oxenford, John. "The Toy Theatre." *The Era Almanack and Annual* (1871): 67–68. *HathiTrust*. Accessed 23 April 2021.

Powers, Alan. "The Toy Theatre: The Revival and Survival of an English Tradition." Goldstein, Buckingham, and Brougére 11–18.

Rahn, Suzanne. *Rediscoveries in Children's Literature*. 1995. London: Routledge, 2011.

Richards, Jeffrey. *The Golden Age of Pantomime: Slapstick, Spectacle and Subversion in Victorian England*. London: I. B. Tauris, 2011.

Richardson, Ralph. Foreword. Speiaght, *Juvenile* vii–viii.

de Rooy, Ronald. "Divine Comics." *European Comic Art* 10.1 (Spring 2017): 94–109. Accessed 23 April 2021.

Speiaght, George. *The History of the English Toy Theatre*. 1946. Boston: Plays, 1969.

———. *Juvenile Drama: The History of the English Toy Theatre*. London: MacDonald, 1946.

Stevenson, Robert Louis. *Memories and Portraits*. 1884. New York: Scribner's, 1898. Googlebooks. Accessed 23 April 2021.

Storey, John, ed. "Class and the Invention of Tradition: The Cases of Christmas, Football, and Folksong." Storey, *Making* 197–212.

———. Introduction: Making Popular Culture. Storey, *Making* 1–13.

———. *The Making of English Material Culture*. London: Routledge, 2016.

Thackeray, William Makepeace. *Vanity Fair: A Novel without a Hero*. Vol. 3. Kensington Ed. New York: Scribner's, 1903. *HathiTrust*. Accessed 23 April 2021.

Wilson, A. E. *Penny Plain Two Pence Coloured: A History of the Juvenile Drama*. New York: Macmillan, 1932.

Chapter 14

The Game of Authors, 1861–1900

A Case History

MAURA IVES

The *Game of Authors* was one of the most popular and commercially successful card games in nineteenth-century America. By 1886, Milton Bradley, noting the game's "educational features," along with various "improved methods applied to it" over the years, declared the *Game of Authors* (henceforth referred to as *Authors*) to have had "a permanence and an aggregate sale probably never equalled by any other modern social game" (225). Among the factors that supported the appeal and longevity of *Authors* were an easily mastered form of play (matching cards to form a set), an ostensibly "educational" benefit derived from memorizing the names of authors and the titles of their works, and the clever marketing tactics of the game's various manufacturers. After its initial publication in 1862, multiple companies produced versions of *Authors* throughout, and beyond, the nineteenth century. A 1996 exhibit of games from the Stuart and Marilyn R. Kaplan Playing Card Collection included seventy-six pre-1900 author games, and by Stuart Kaplan's estimate, more than 200 versions of the game have been created (*Play* 3). While *Authors* continued to be popular in the early twentieth century, Stuart Kaplan's company, U.S. Games Systems, Inc., is currently the only company that still produces author games, "spurred by a sense of its own modest contribution to American literacy and by the desire to keep in print a legacy from the past" (insert 1).

As significant as *Authors* is in the history of American games and the development of American literary culture, there has been little scholarship on the games, with some recent exceptions, such as Michelle Beissel Heath's *Nineteenth-Century Fictions of Childhood and the Politics of Play*.[1] Beissel Heath devotes a chapter to the role of card and other parlor games in the promotion of respectability, citizenship, and patriotism. As Beissel Heath's work demonstrates, the popularity and content of *Authors* was tied to debates about youth culture and leisure; other discussions of *Authors* have represented them as mechanisms for canon formation.

The examination of extant games remains crucial for understanding their place within larger cultural and literary discourses, including the alignment of nineteenth-century American author games with celebrity culture, especially since the actual content of the games has yet to be fully taken into account. Shifts in marketing of author games, reflecting a split between child and adult audiences, were expressed through changes in their content as well as their material and visual design, resulting in a split between games marketed to children or adapted for classroom use, and games that targeted adults, especially women; at the same time, the content of *Authors* expanded to include more women writers and to incorporate nonliterary content and creators. The popularity of *Authors*, the relative simplicity of game play, and the ease with which the theme of "authors" could be customized also led to the emergence of do it yourself (DIY) versions of the game, connecting it to other popular nineteenth-century amusements such as scrapbooking, and further questioning its role in shaping or stabilizing the American literary canon.

Origin and Early History

On 5 December 1861, publishers G. M. Whipple and A. A. Smith of Salem, Massachusetts, registered the copyright for "The Game of Authors" along with "The Game of Anybody & Everybody &" (Account). According to Bruce Whitehill, A. A. Smith was also the game's author (76). Smith is identified elsewhere as Augustus Smith, a teacher "who invented the game with the help of his female seminary students in 1861" (Smith and Saunders 48). Smith's role dwindles in later accounts of the game's authorship. Steward Culin credits the game's creation to an unidentified "young man [. . .] helped by some of his female acquaintances," explaining that when the "young man" approached A. A. Smith in hope of having a few copies printed, Smith offered to print some copies for free in return for the opportunity to manufacture it (35). By the end of the century, not only had Augustus Smith the teacher disappeared from the narrative entirely, but the game's authors were all female: a "coterie of bright young ladies" in Charles Trow's account or "a number of young ladies" in the instruction sheet for Parker Brothers' version of the game (Trow 24; qtd. in Beissel Heath, 21). According to Beissel Heath, Parker Brothers' emphasis on the game's "feminine origin" reflects the efforts of game publishers throughout the century to legitimize card games by associating them with domesticity and the "home circle," along with other positive values (21). *Authors* has sometimes been attributed to Anne Abbot, the creator of *Doctor Busby* (as discussed below), but there is no evidence to support the claim that she was responsible for *Authors*, and if she had been, one suspects that she and her publisher would have announced her involvement as a selling point.[2]

Neither the game's mode of play nor its focus on authorship were entirely new. As a matching game, *Authors* has been linked to predecessors in the United Kingdom, Europe, and the United States. One nineteenth-century source compares *Authors* to an earlier British game titled "Spade, the Gardener"; Bruce Whitehill connects it to a German game, *Quartet*; and an American version, *Presidential Quartets*, had been published in Boston two years before *Authors* (Champlin and Bostwick 40; 8). *Authors* also resembles the British game *Happy Families* (published no later than 1861)[3] but *Happy Families* itself may have derived from the *Game of Trades*, published in Salem by W. & S. B. Ives in 1845, or an earlier Ives game, *Doctor Busby*, published in 1843 (Whittet 14; Beissel Heath 29).[4] Of the American games that preceded *Authors*, Abbot's *Doctor Busby* is the one to which *Authors* is most frequently linked. But while *Doctor Busby* and similar games may have contributed to the basic design of *Authors*, the concept of an author-themed game already existed in the form of *Uncle Tom's Cabin*, copyrighted by the Ives Brothers in 1852, and the *Game of Uncle Tom*, copyrighted by V. S. W. Parkhurst in Rhode Island that same year. Parkhurst's game was also divided into numbered "Families." *Authors* and its precursors are all based on sets of four cards, each representing a 'family' group. In *Spade the Gardener*, the numbered cards below ten are removed from a set of regular playing cards, with families constructed from the four remaining suits: "the King of Spades is called Spade, the Gardener; the Queen, Spade, the Gardener's Wife; the Knave, his son; the Ace, his servant, and the Ten, his dog" (Champlin and Bostwick 40). In *Trades*, the families consist of a "tradesman" card and the cards representing his tools, while *Doctor Busby's* families are based on various members of the Busby household (Whittet 68–69). Game play for all of these games involved collecting a complete set of related cards, with the "families" of earlier games replaced in *Authors* by a "book" of cards representing an author and their works.[5] Whipple & Smith's *Game of Authors* included "twenty sets of four Cards each," with "each set consisting of the name of an Author and names of three of his productions." One of the players deals the cards, then the player to the right of the dealer "commences the game by drawing from his right hand neighbor, such Cards are he may desire to complete his sets [. . .] until he demands a card not in the hand of his neighbor, who then continues the game in like manner" ("The Game").

As Laura Cohen and Meredith McGill indicate, the history of *Authors* "exemplifies the continuing insecurity of intellectual property" in the latter half of the century, since contemporary copyright law did not cover playing cards (210). Paula Petrick notes in her history of Selchow & Righter that "piracy in the world of game and toy makers was easy and widespread" at midcentury, and "any enterprising lithographer with a press and paper could copy a popular game and peddle it in shows with little fear of prosecution" (418). It was not long before *Authors* attracted the attention of competing publishers. In 1863, New York publisher John H. Tingley advertised a *New Game of Authors*, matching Whipple & Smith's price of fifty cents ("New"). It is often impossible to know whether "new" instances of *Authors* were actually new, and in what sense. Card games, like books, could move from one publisher to another through several means. Some examples probably represent a new printing with essentially the same content as an existing game; others may be new printings from old plates transferred from one publisher to another; in other cases, a company may repackage its existing stock of printed cards in a new box with a new title. Milton Bradley capitalized upon other publishers' habit of reissuing the same content year after year by assuring potential purchasers that "Our Author Game is revised late every summer," with "numerous additions" of "popular authors and new works of old authors"—in contrast to "those stereotyped editions of ten years' standing" sold by others ("Social"). But other departures from the original content of the game seem to have emerged very early. In the same year that Tingley offered its "new" game, T. Ellwood Zell of Philadelphia advertised what may be the first genre-specific version, "The beautiful *Game of the Four Poets*" ("A New").

Despite the increasingly crowded field of *Authors*-type games, sales were strong. Porter and Coates's *Instructive Game of Authors*, issued in 1872, sold 36,000 copies in one year ("Correspondence" 301). Still, as the century progressed, publishers sought to maintain or boost the game's sales through additional modifications to the games' content, methods of play, and design. Joining the genre- and region-specific games of the 1860s were quotation games, games focused on specific writers (William Shakespeare, Charles Dickens) and titles (*Alice in Wonderland*, *Ivanhoe*), and McLoughlin's *Queens of Literature*, which included only women writers. Although genres of writing other than British and American literature were present in the early years (such as Porter and Coates's 1872 *Instructive Game of Mythology*), the end of the century saw games focused on celebrity figures other than literary authors (missionaries), artists other than writers (composers or "musical authors"), and sacred texts. Game publishers also introduced variations in game play, of which McLoughlin's 1875 *Game of Cribbage Authors* was perhaps the most extreme. In 1876, McLoughlin's *Star Authors* allowed players to "form books, sequences, star books and star sequences, each having a different value" (*Catalogue*). While most *Authors* remained relatively inexpensive at fifty cents per game, some companies sought to differentiate their offerings through variations in packaging, design, quality—and price. Cards printed only on the side that included the names of authors or texts gave way to cards with attractive designs on their formerly blank backs. Milton Bradley advertised its "extra" version of *Authors Improved*, with "[e]xtra quality of cards, lithographed back and front, and put up in an elegant embossed muslin box, in imitation of a book or album" as early as 1867; at one dollar, the "extra" version cost twice as much as the basic game ("Social"; "Popular"). Milton Bradley's catalogue would eventually include four versions of its game: *Authors Improved* ("72 waterproof enameled cards, with portraits"), *Authors, Household Edition* ("an elegant set of lithographed cards with beautiful designs"), *Authors, Plain Edition* ("A good set of 33 cards on buff ticket stock"), and *Selected Authors* ("A game of Authors in neat box, with illuminated lithographic label") (*Catalogue*). Similarly, the description of Parker's 1891 *Game of Authors* reveals how important the design, quality, and packaging of the cards had become; the cards were "round cornered, enameled on face and back," with the backs decorated with "an owl sitting beneath the full moon," and the cards came either in "a small cloth case or in a large lithographed covered box" ("Parker's").

The Game of Authors and Authorship

There were some author-oriented games available in the United Kingdom (at least one of which, *Characters from Charles Dickens*, may predate *Authors*),[6] but although a "Game of Authors" was advertised for sale in Sydney as early as 1861 (with 1862 advertisements declaring it to be "very popular in England"), I have been unable to find any other evidence of the popularity, or even the availability, of *Authors* in Britain, nor is there any way to know what resemblance the games advertised in Sydney bore to their American counterparts ("Christmas"; "Game"). Most scholarship on *Authors* therefore focuses on its relation to the commercial and cultural value attached to the concept of "authorship" in mid- to late-nineteenth-century America. Cohen and McGill find that the game's focus on identifying authors and matching them with their works "serves to consolidate literary property under the purview of authorship," with the later addition of "engravings or photographs of authors, further solidifying players' mastery of authorial identity" (210). However, the game's role in establishing or reinforcing a literary canon bears further study. Cohen and McGill argue that the game "condensed the field of authorship by equating 'Authors' writ large with the particular writers it assembled," and that "[t]he selective elevation of these authors to 'Authors' helped reinforce what we have come to know as a national literary canon, while demonstrating how canons can be formed through mass cultural phenomena as well as through more familiar, top-down, critical or institutional fiat" (210). Author lists can be counted on to include figures "we have come to know" as canonical such as Nathaniel Hawthorne, but they also included (and retained) authors who have since fallen out of the canon, such as Charles Dudley Warner and Richard Grant White (both included in McLoughlin's 1889 *Improved Authors with Portraits & Autographs*).

We do not know what drove author selection in *Authors*. While one might assume that copyright would be a factor in the selection of an author, Cohen and McGill's reminder that copyright laws did not extend to playing cards challenges that assumption. Other economic factors are worth considering, such as whether and how the list of authors intersected with game publishers' marketing strategies, which included presenting the games as educational toys, as wholesome alternatives to undesirable activities such as gambling and drinking alcohol, as tasteful décor, and as part of the material culture of literary celebrity. The marketing of the games as an alternative to gambling and other vices favored writers who supported the temperance movement, such as Isabella M. Alden (better known by her pseudonym "Pansy"), Elizabeth Phelps, T. S. Arthur, Louisa Alcott, H. W. Beecher, Harriet Beecher Stowe, and others. At the same time, while we might assume that game publishers are likely to have had some rationale for the selection of authors represented in *Authors*, there is little evidence to show that those who played the games cared which authors were represented in them, and Milton Bradley's practice of updating the list every year backfired with at least one reviewer: the *Christian Union* complained that "[o]f the game of Authors, announced by the same house as "improved" and "revised," we can only say that the selection of authors in the last edition of it is rather whimsical, and the selection of their works still more so" ("Literature" 62). The only players who could be counted on to care about author selection were educators who used the game to teach literature, and some versions of *Authors* responded to the possibility of the cards being used as teaching tools. Professor A. B. Carroll's *A New Game of Authors or Graded Literary Cards* included a listing of the "Periods of American literature," and a review of Carroll's game recommended it to teachers as "a great help in leading pupils into acquaintance with authors and their works" ("State" 377). But teachers also seem to have dealt with the question of author selection by making their own games, or instructing their students to do so, as I discuss later.

A more nuanced evaluation of the relationship of author games to the developing American canon requires focused research in primary sources, including extensive examination of extant copies, analysis of contemporary responses to the games as they evolved, as well as study of publisher's correspondence and any other materials that would shed light on publishers' rationales for author selection. Unfortunately, early versions of the game are scarce, making it difficult to gauge how the various games' rosters of authors shifted over time (remembering, of course, that extant copies with 1861 copyright dates may have been printed years later, and thus may not reflect the content of original editions of the game). We may never know who was included in Whipple & Smith's 1863 *Extant Authors*, of which no copy seems to have survived. We can, however, get some sense of the early author lists from two Whipple and Smith printings of *Authors* held by the American Antiquarian Society

(AAS), both of which bear the 1861 copyright but no printing date. The Worcester Historical Museum holds another very early game, the *Boston Game of Authors*, published by Degen, Estes & Co. in 1864. The author lists of these early games provide a benchmark for tracking and evaluating changes in later versions of the game.

The AAS games bear out Beissel Heath's observation that the games were originally "divided between a U. S. and British literary legacy," with British authors dominating early versions (36): fifteen of the authors in the AAS copies are British, including the only women included (Charlotte Brontë and Elizabeth Barrett Browning). The remaining British authors include the past and present Poets Laureate (William Wordsworth and Alfred, Lord Tennyson), highly canonical poets such as John Milton and Shakespeare, two eighteenth-century authors (Oliver Goldsmith and William Cowper) and a mix of later novelists and nonfiction writers (William Bulwer, Dickens, Charles Kingsley, T. B. Macaulay, John Ruskin, Sir Walter Scott, Thackeray, and Scottish geologist Hugh Miller).[7] The Americans in the deck were New Englanders Hawthorne, William H. Prescott (both born in Salem), Washington Irving, and Henry Wadsworth Longfellow. While it overlapped significantly with the Whipple and Smith game, the *Boston Game* includes more women (four of the twenty authors) and more Americans. The *Boston Game* replaced Goldsmith, Kingsley, Ruskin, and Hugh Miller with Felicia Hemans, for a total of thirteen British writers, three of whom were female. On the American side, the *Boston Game* removed Prescott, but added Edgar Allan Poe, Thomas Bulfinch, George Curtis, and "Miss Cummings" (Maria S. Cummings) for a total of seven Americans, including the first female American writer to be featured in the game. But later games did not necessarily follow the *Boston Game*'s lead in selecting American authors: Porter & Coates's 1872 *Instructive Game of Poets* included only two Americans, William Cullen Bryant and John Greenleaf Whittier, and the later games for which I have author lists include few (if any) women. Authorship as represented in these and later *Authors* was also not always, or even primarily, literary, as Hugh Miller's inclusion in Whipple and Smith showed. A copy of McLoughlin Brothers's 1877 *The Game of Familiar Quotations from Popular Authors* also held by AAS includes cards featuring the works of "Statesmen" (including Daniel Webster, Niccolo Machiavelli, Cardinal Armand Richelieu, and William Gladstone) and "Generals" (Napoleon Buonaparte, George Washington, Albrecht von Wallenstein, and Ulysses Grant) along with "Novelists" and "Poets."

While it is true that the authors featured in later nineteenth-century *Authors* were often American and male (and always white), that they represented a mix of canonical and contemporary (living) writers, and that fiction and nonfiction writers were more prevalent than poets, this was not always the case in early games, and we currently lack information about how the author lists changed over time, especially with respect to women authors. Louisa May Alcott, often said to be the first woman to have been included in *Authors*, was preceded by Brontë, Browning, Hemans, and Cummings, and possibly also by Harriett Beecher Stowe, who appeared in Porter & Coates's 1872 game.[8] Women writers were included in at least some of Milton Bradley's various editions of *Authors Improved*; the AAS holds an 1870s copy of the game that includes the British novelists "Miss Muloch" (Diana Mulock) and "Mrs. Charles" (Elizabeth Rundle Charles). This admittedly limited data indicates that women were scarce but not absent, and that American women writers appeared less frequently than their British counterparts. Women authors became more visible in 1886, when McLoughlin introduced its first all-female game, *Queens of Literature*. Of the sixteen authors included in *Queens*, five were British (Brontë, Browning, and Hemans, along with George Eliot and Jean Ingelow). But the majority of the women in *Queens* were American, with an emphasis on novelists and essayists. Alongside Alcott and Stowe were temperance novelist Isabella M. Alden, regionalist writers Sarah Orne Jewett and Mary N. Murfree, reformers Margaret Fuller Ossoli and Elizabeth Stuart Phelps, and poets Lucy Larcom, Alice and Phoebe Cary, Celia Thaxter, and Adaline [*sic*] D. T. Whitney. The canon of "queens" was also not only strongly tilted toward American writers, but toward living ones: all of the British authors in the list except for Ingelow were dead, while all of the Americans (except for Margaret Fuller and the Cary sisters) were alive. McLoughlin included women in other games as well; eleven of the eighteen authors in Baylor University's copy of McLoughlin's [1888] *Improved Game of Star Authors. Game B* were female, including many of the authors included in *Queens* (Alcott, Alden, Brontë, Browning, Eliot, Hemans, Ingelow, Phelps, and Thaxter) along with Frances Hodgson Burnett and Harriett Beecher Stowe. Parker Brothers followed McLoughlin with its game of *Literary Women* in 1893; I have not been able to find a copy of this game, or any other instance of an all-female author game prior to 1900. And apart from Milton Bradley, McLoughlin, and Parker Brothers's late interventions, women were still scarce in many late *Authors*: of the 100

American authors in the Lilly Library's copy of Carroll's *New Game of Authors*, only twelve were female, and other late-nineteenth-century *Authors* (including McLoughlin's) still excluded women entirely.

The Game of Authors and Celebrity Culture

In 1873, the first "portrait" author games were offered by West and Lee and E. I. Horsman. In these games, authors' portraits appear on the cards. Portraits may have appeared on game boxes before they appeared on cards, though after portrait cards were introduced, shrewd manufacturers might have included portraits on the box without changing the design of the cards themselves.[9] Even without the inclusion of portraits, the shift in the representation of authorship from an organizing principle for book titles or quotations to a form of celebrity was visible in games such as the 1872 *Instructive Game of Authors*, which included "short biographical notices" to "familiarize one with each writer" ("Novelties, Games, Etc."). Eventually, both portraits and authors' autographs were included, as in McLoughlin's 1889 *Improved Authors with Portraits & Autographs*. West and Lee's claim that a "single portrait" in the game could be "worth the price of all" played upon the market value of celebrity images in the era of photography and celebrity cartes de visite, which had made images of the famous commercially available ("Portrait"). Photography became a selling point for Parker Brothers, whose "illustrated and improved" version of the game included "exact reproductions of authors' photographs on every card" ("Parker's").

Author games were perfectly situated to satisfy the desire for intimacy and affiliation that animated the material culture of celebrity. Playing a game that featured portraits of literary celebrities brought famous writers into the homes, and leisure activities, of their fans. Selchow and Righter leveraged this aspect of celebrity culture by presenting *Vignette Authors* as a means of virtual access to fame, with players "sitting as it were, face to face with the author" (69). This is the only advertisement I have found in which a list of authors appears, but the purpose of the list is not to reveal the names of the authors so much as to let the purchaser know which authors' portraits are included. The advertisement closes with the assurance that "most" of the living authors "furnished us with their photographs for the special use of this game"—thereby vouching for the authenticity of the images, while further situating the game as a direct link between players and the authors themselves ([Selchow and Righter] 69). The game as proxy for the author emerges even more strongly in games focused upon individual writers, such as the *Carnival of Characters from Dickens*, which combined affiliation with a literary celebrity with an appeal to quality in the form of "a high-toned literary game" ("Carnival").

Not everyone approved of supplying authors' portraits, or the equation of literary celebrity with other forms of fame (or infamy). This was an especially sore point with respect to games that invoked religious associations. The *Catholic World* protested the inclusion of portraits for writers represented in the *Game of Quotations from Catholic American Authors*, declaring it inappropriate for Catholic writers to have their faces "printed on playing-cards, where we usually find actresses and id omne genus [all that sort], to be mauled over by unrespecting hands and to be joked about in the frame of mind which one carries to the gaming-table" ("Talk" 556).[10] The development of a card game based upon the Bible also raised concerns about the game eroding the stature of the texts represented within it. A letter to the editor of the *Christian Advocate*, alarmed by a recent notice for *The Game of Old Testament Characters*, argued that such a game would "lower the Holy Scriptures" (Parker). The author of the letter, J. Parker, based his argument on *Authors*' success in erasing the distance between players and famous authors: "I was at a friend's house where they were playing that game, and they said, "Give me Billy Shakespeare"; other names were used the same way. It lowered the name of Shakespeare very much." Parker's discomfort illustrates the tension between "cultural authority and marketability" that accompanied the rise of literary celebrity in the nineteenth century and to the risks that participation in celebrity culture carried for *Authors*, since "lowering" the stature of authors might interfere with efforts to use games' cultural and aesthetic value as a selling point (Moran 20).

Marketing Cards in the Temperance Era

But *Authors* games were vulnerable in other ways, the more so because they were central to the efforts of game publishers to establish a positive reputation for card games. Beissel Heath credits *Authors* with "helping to secure games from the taint otherwise associated with games and playing cards," pointing to efforts by game manufacturers (and aficionados) to "promote games as respectable for children and families [. . .] by emphasizing didacticism and morality [. . .] along with femininity and the home" (23, 16). Since card games were especially tainted by their association with gambling (and by extension, alcohol), there was considerable debate throughout the century about the dangerous potential of card games to destigmatize card playing and render young players vulnerable to vice. Author games per se were often seen as harmless, so much so that sanctimonious adults who mistook *Authors* for less appropriate games figured in humorous anecdotes as early as 1874, when the editor of the *Ladies Repository* told the story of a Scottish missionary who

> horrified our American and Methodist notions [. . .] by saying, one evening, after tea, "The ladies propose cards; but I think we will have prayers first." Visions of euchre and poker and whist were dissipated when, after a season of devotion, the cards were produced and found to be the harmless child's "game of authors." (Wentworth 3)

At the same time, the popularity and apparent wholesomeness of *Authors* meant that they frequently served as the example for the slippery slope argument that any card game paved the way to less savory activities. Hiram Haydn Collins's 1880 *Amusements: In the Light of Reason and Scripture* voices the usual arguments against cards as "the tools of the gambler," questioning the distinction between games such as *Authors* and regular playing cards. For Collins, even "temperate" use of card games represented "a questionable use of precious time and immortal powers" that was almost certain to "carry recreation over to dissipation, which is sinful" (127–28). Even worse, Collins asserted, card playing in the home "has often paved the way straight into immoral uses of these games in immoral places" (129). Other writers were less adamant about the dangers of card games, but echoed Collins's sense that there were more profitable ways to use one's time. Girls and young women especially were advised not to allow leisure activities such as card games to distract them from more suitable occupations, such as learning how to manage a household (H.).

The mixed reception to *Authors* prompted game manufacturers to market the games as benign educational toys that could prevent children and young adults from seeking card games outside the home and/or from playing games that were more conducive to gambling and drinking. Claxton, Remsen. & Haffelfinger met potential objections head on, ominously warning "parents" that "[a]ll need occasional recreation, and if it cannot be found at home, they will seek it abroad, perhaps in the haunts of vice" (153). Publishers also hedged their bets by cultivating additional marketing strategies, such as representing the games as distinctive because of their intellectual, cultural, and aesthetic value. Advertisements for Whipple and Smith's games featured the heading "For Every Intelligent Household" (5e). And advertising for Schafer's *Game of Authors* offered a somewhat more subtle appeal to the educational aspirations of purchasers, locating the game in the domestic realm as a "Home Amusement" and foregrounding its claim to be "both Amusing and Instructive" (3d). In contrast, Milton Bradley pulled no punches, claiming that their games were "RATIONAL, MORAL, INSTRUCTIVE and AMUSING and entirely different from the MASS OF TRASH formerly offered to the public," cleverly sidestepping the question of whether their games were "moral" or "trash" by promoting them as decorative household objects ("Social" 90). Milton Bradley packaged its "extra" version of *Authors Improved* to resemble a book or album, highlighting its domesticity and aligning it with the social rituals of friendship and exchange associated with gift books and literary and autograph albums ("Social" 90). West and Lee's efforts to deflect negative associations went even farther by disassociating the cards from their use in game play. Arguing that the artistic merit of the authors' portraits made the game itself "an article of artistic merit and value," West and Lee claimed that it was "worthy of a place on the centre-table of the most cultivated and refined, even if never used as a pastime" ("Portrait").

West and Lee's game, clearly marketed to adults, reveals another important aspect of the marketing of *Authors* both as a children's game and as a game for adults. Copies of *Authors* game (no publisher identified) were offered as a premium for subscribers to the *Youth's Companion* as early as 1871 "(Premiums" 346). But games marketed to young women and homemakers on the basis of their decorative value were not necessarily intended to be played by anyone, especially not young children. In addition, the efficacy of *Authors* in preventing "vice" rested on the game's ability to keep young men at home by encouraging them to spend time with their families—and with young women. Fictional representations of the game identify it as a means for unmarried men and women to socialize; as Trow put it, *Authors* was among the social games that were universally understood as "a potent factor in drawing the sexes nearer to each other" (22). One of the only versions of the game specifically marketed to children seems to be the 1897 *Young Folks Authors*. Two game boxes from Kaplan's collection literally illustrate the split audience for *Authors*. The box for Parker's 1897 *The Game of Authors, Salem Edition* features four young women and one young man seated at a table, playing the game; as Kaplan notes, this is "one of the very few covers showing people playing the game" (*Play*). But the box for Parker's 1896 *Game of Authors* features a group of elementary school–aged boys and girls marching behind a boy holding a banner with the game's title.

Do-It-Yourself Games

A little-known result of *Authors*'s popularity was the emergence of DIY games, in which players either played the game without cards or created their own. The adaptation of *Authors* for classroom use was discussed as early as 1876, when A. F. Blaisdell described how students might make up a set of cards for "an extended course in Milton, Cowper, the Novelists, or Shakespeare," then "meet at the house of a mutual friend, and spend a couple of hours some evening playing the game" (267). Similar articles offering examples of author games for instructional purposes appeared well into the twentieth century.

But DIY games were offered as opportunities for entertainment also. In 1881, Mary Sherwood's *Home Amusements* suggested that the game "is a very common one [. . .] but it can be rendered uncommon by the preparation of the cards among the members of the family" (34). Sherwood offers suggestions to vary the game by "using the names of kings and queens, and the learned men of their reigns, instead of authors," or "the popes [. . .] with their attendant great men" (35). In suggesting ways to vary the point values of cards, she provides us with a sense of which authors she and her readers might expect to include: "the Dickens cards may count but one, while Tupper will be named sixteen; Carlyle can be two, while Artemus Ward shall be sixty" (Sherwood 35–36). Although Sherwood's list reflects standard authors likely to be represented in purchased games, other references to DIY games acknowledge that part of the fun of creating one's one games included "introducing recent books and new authors" ("Authors," 39). While Sherwood views DIY games as a family activity, Mary C. Myer recommended a self-made *Authors* game as a way for women "who sojourn during the summer months of rest and health" to find "interesting employment for the hands" (209).

Myer's game reflects the shift from authors' works to authors' images, as she directs her readers to cut out portraits of authors from publisher's catalogues and magazines and attach them to cards. The portrait cards—without the names of the authors or titles of their works—are passed among the players, who write down their guesses as to the authors' identities. Myer's description of the game's "value" in "render[ing] familiar the faces of dear and cherished friends, who speak none the less tenderly, instructively and profitably in print and between covers, than do other loved ones in person, and by word of mouth" further demonstrates the alignment of late-nineteenth-century author games with celebrity culture (209).

Conclusion

Arguably, late-nineteenth-century American author games are best understood in terms of the rise and material culture of literary celebrity. The game's author lists overlapped with other contemporary registers of canonicity, or at least celebrity (such as Jeanette Gilder and Joseph Benson's *Authors at Home*), but also demonstrated canonic fluidity by their shifting content and by their ability to inspire DIY game creation, allowing players to assemble their own canons through self-made sets of cards. DIY game creation mirrored a split in the game's audience toward the end of the century. For young adults, DIY games offered private amusement or an instructive pastime not unrelated to scrapbooking—itself described by Ellen Gruber Garvey as a way of managing information overload (4). For educators and students, DIY became a more explicitly educational undertaking in which students could create author lists from literature familiar to them. Understanding author games, then, requires both examination of the games themselves, and more careful consideration of their audiences and the uses they made of the games they played.

Notes

1. Beissel Heath discusses *The Author Game* in her 2017 book and in her chapter for this collection.

2. In 2017, the *Huffington Post* distributed a column from *Country Living*, in which an "antiques specialist" explained that the game was "[c]reated in 1861 by journalist Anne Abbott" ("Country").

3. Morris and others indicate that the game was available at the time of the Great Exhibition in 1851, but the earliest advertisement I can find for it is in December 1861, where it is presented as "Jaques' New Game, Happy Families" (4).

4. The "Improved and Illustrated Game of Dr. Busby" was advertised in March 1843, and the following year Abbot followed the game's publication with a book, *Doctor Busby and His Neighbors*.

5. For an insightful discussion of the significance of Doctor Busby's representations of the family, see Whittet 65–68.

6. *Characters from Charles Dickens* also arranged cards in "books," which consisted of four characters from one of Dickens's novels, but game play differed—players dealt a card instead of asking for a card, and the dealt card had to be matched by the players to the left until the "trick" of four cards was completed (Melby). Another author-related game, Mrs. Blackwell's 1862 *The Game of Quotations from the Poets* is held in the British Library.

7. This author list seems to have been current as early as 1865, when a reference to "Game of Authors" in August Bell's story "My Cousin Annice" involves a character who, in playing the game, mistakenly calls for a "Huge Miller" card.

8. I have not found evidence for this claim, which appears in a 1980 review of feminist criticism by Nina Auerbach, whose comment may pertain to contemporary rather than historical Authors ("her [Alcott's] chief distinction today is her appearance as the only woman in the children's game of Authors," 263).

9. One of the American Antiquarian Society's Whipple & Smith games includes a box with two portraits.

10. See "Talk," 548–62.

Works Cited

Abbot, Anne. *Doctor Busby and His Neighbors: A Story Illustrated by the Games of Doctor Busby and Master Rodbury*. Salem: W. & S. B. Ives, 1844.

Account Book for copyright registrations in the U. S. District Court for the District of Massachusetts, 1860–1864. Archive.org. https://archive.org/details/MAAccountBook18601864. Accessed 4 May 2021.

Auerbach, Nina. "Feminist Criticism Reviewed." *Gender and Literary Voice*. Ed. Janet M. Todd. New York: Holmes and Meier, 1980. 258–68.

Author's Improvd [*sic*]. Milton Bradley, [1870s]. American Antiquarian Society. Games Box 82 Item 5.

Beissel Heath, Michelle. *Nineteenth-Century Fictions of Childhood and the Politics of Play*. London: Routledge, 2017.

Bell, August. "My Cousin Annice." *Flag of Our Union*. 15 July 1865: 1.

Blackwell, Mrs. *The Game of Quotations from the Poets*. London: Dean and Son, [1862].

Blaisdell, A. F. "'Authors' adapted to Class Use." *The New England Journal of Education* 3. 23 (3 June 1876): 267.

Bradley, Milton. "Uses and Abuses of Games." *Good Housekeeping* 2. 8 (February 20, 1886): 225–26.

Carroll, A. B. A *New Game of Authors, or Graded Literary Cards American*. Rev. ed. Seventh Thousand. Burlington, IA: Bishop Bros., [1889].

"Carnival of Characters from Dickens." Advertisement. *The Independent* 29 November 1877: 13.

Champlin, John D[enison], and Arthur E[lmore] Bostwick. "Authors." *Young Folks Cyclopedia of Games and Sports*. 2nd ed. Rev. New York: Henry Holt, 1899. 39–40.

Characters from Charles Dickens. [London, Jaques & Son, ca. 1858.]

"Christmas Presents and New Year's Gifts." Advertisement. *Sydney Morning Herald*. 23 December 1861: 6.

"Claxton, Remsen & Haffelfinger Have Just Published: [. . .] New and Original Games." *American Literary Gazette and Publisher's Circular*. 11. 6 (15 July 1868): 153.

Cohen, Lara Langer, and Meredith L. McGill. "The Perils of Authorship: Literary Property and Ninteenth-Century American Fiction." *The Oxford History of the Novel in English: Volume 5: The American Novel to 1870*. Ed. J. Gerald Kennedy and Leland S. Person. Oxford: Oxford University Press, 2014. Oxford Scholarship Online. Accessed March 2015.

"Correspondence. Philadelphia." *Publisher's Weekly* 88 (20 September 1873): 301–302.

"Country Living Appraises Circa-1890 Game of Authors Cards: What's It Worth?" *HuffPost* November 19, 2012. Updated December 6, 2017. https://www.huffingtonpost.com/2012/11/18/country-living-whats-it-worth_n_2156336.html. Accessed 4 May 2021.

Culin, Stewart. "The Exhibit of American Games at the Fair." *Putnam's Monthly Historical Magazine, devoted to Genealogy, History and Archaeology*. 2 (September 1893): 35–37.

"For Every Intelligent Household." Advertisement for Whipple and Smith's games. *Times* 4 November 1863. 5e.

"Game of Authors." Advertisement. *Sydney Morning Herald*. 29 January 1862: 6.

The Game of Authors. [Salem, Mass.]: G. M. Whipple & A. A. Smith, [1861]. American Antiquarian Society. Games Box 89. Item 3.

The Game of Familiar Quotations from Popular Authors. New York: McLoughlin Brothers, 1877.

The Game of Trades. W. S. B. Ives, [1845–60]. Victoria & Albert Museum of Childhood. http://collections.vam.ac.uk/item/O26713/the-game-of-trades-card-game-w-s-b/. Accessed 4 May 2021.

Garvey, Ellen Gruber. *Writing with Scissors: American Scrapbooks from the Civil War to the Harlem Renaissance.* New York: Oxford University Press, 2013.

Gilder, J[eanette L[Leonard]. and J[oseph] B[enson]. *Authors at Home: Personal and Biographical Sketches of Well-Known American Writers.* New York: Cassell, 1888.

H., S. C. "Mistress and Maid." *Women's Journal.* 1872. Rpt. *Friends' Intelligencer.* [Philadelphia] 30. 18 (28 June 1873): 284–86.

"Holiday Whispers Concerning Toys and Games." *The Riverside Magazine for Young People* 2. 13 (January 1868): 4.

"The Improved and Illustrated Game of Dr. Busby." *Salem Gazette.* 7 March 1843: 3.

The Instructive Game of Poets. 1872. *Past Times: Children's Games and Their Literary Inspirations.* The Lilly Library, Indiana University, Bloomington, Indiana. https://collections.libraries.indiana.edu/lilly/exhibitions_legacy/games/authors.html. Accessed 4 May 2021.

"Jaques' New Game, Happy Families." *Morning Chronicle.* 13 December 1861: 4.

"Literature and Art." *Christian Union.* 10 January 1872: 61–63.

Melby, Julie L. "Tired of Bridge? Play Dickens." 9 August 2011. Graphic Arts blog. Graphic Arts Collection, Princeton University Library. https://www.princeton.edu/~graphicarts/2011/08/tired_of_bridge_play_dickens.html Accessed 4 May 2021.

Myer, Mary C. "Entertainments." Table Talk. 12.6 (June 1897): 209.

Moran, Joe. *Star Authors: Literary Celebrity in America.* London: Pluto Press, 2000.

Morris, Frankie. *Artist of Wonderland: The Life, Political Cartoons, and Illustrations of Tenniel.* Charlottesville: University of Virginia Press, 2005.

"New and Original Games for the Holidays." Advertisement for John H. Tingley. *American Literary Gazette and Publishers' Circular* 2.2 (16 November 1863): 55.

"New and Popular Games for the Holiday Season." Advertisement for the Boston Game of Authors. *The Youth's Companion.* 37. 52 (29 December 1864): 207.

"A New Game for the Holidays." Advertisement for T. Elwood Zell's *Game of the Four Poets. American Literary Gazette and Publishers' Circular.* 2.2 (16 November 1863): 55.

"Novelties, Games, Etc." *The Publishers' and stationers' weekly trade circular.* 11 (12 September 1872): 257.

"Parker's Games." *The American Stationer.* 22 October 1891: 898.

Petrick, Paula, "The House that Parcheesi Built: Selchow & Righter Company." *Business History Review* 60.3 (Autumn 1986): 410–37.

Play Your Cards! Catalogue of exhibition at the Bruce Museum, Greenwich, CT. December 2, 1995–February 4, 1996, with additional six-page descriptive insert. Stamford, CT: U. S. Games Systems, 1995.

"Portrait Authors." Advertisement. *Lippincott's Magazine*. 15. 85 (January 1875): [137].

"Premiums." *The Youth's Companion*. 26 October 1871: 345–50.

Schafer's *Game of Authors*. Advertisement. *The Christian Union*. 27 May 1874: 3d.

S[herwood], M[ary] E. W. S. *Home Amusements*. New York: D. Appleton, 1881.

[Selchow, E. G., and J. H. Righter]. *Wholesale Catalogue of Games and Home Amusements*. Jersey City, NJ: The Jersey City Printing Company, 1 October 1888.

Smith, Linda Joan, and Richard Saunders. "Authorized Entertainment." *Country Home* (August 1995): 48–52.

"Social Games and Home Amusements, Published and Manufactured by Milton Bradley & Co" Advertisement. *Publisher's Uniform Trade List Directory*. Philadelphia: Howard Challen, 1868. 90.

"State News." *Iowa Normal Monthly* 9.9 (April 1885): 376–84.

"Talk About New Books." *Catholic World* 67. 400 (July 1898): 548–62.

Trow, Charles E. *Prose and Verse*. Salem, MA: Barry Printing Company, 1900.

Wentworth, Reverend E. "Celestial Memories." *The Ladies' Repository: A Monthly Periodical devoted to Literature, Art, and Religion*. 34. 1 (January 1874): 1–5.

Whitehill, Bruce. "Games of America in the Nineteenth Century." *Board Game Studies* 9 (2015): 65–87.

Whittet, Ethan. *The Mass Production of Old England*. Dissertation. Department of English, Northeastern University. 3 January 2017. 65–68.

Contributors

Michelle Beissel Heath, professor and director of graduate studies in the English department at the University of Nebraska, Kearney, specializes in children's literature and in nineteenth-century British literature. With essays published on children's citizenship, play, gender, and literary texts in *Children's Literature*, the *Journal of the History of Childhood and Youth*, and *Critical Survey*, among others, Beissel Heath is the author of *Nineteenth-Century Fictions of Childhood and the Politics of Play*.

Erin N. Bistline, PhD, specializes in nineteenth-century transatlantic literature and book history, with focus in ecocriticism and animal studies. A contributor to *Victorian Writers and the Environment* and *Romantic Women Writers Reviewed*, Bistline co-edited a special issue of CEA *Critic* focused on games and gaming. She is a full-time lecturer in the Department of English at the University of Tennessee-Knoxville.

Catherine S. Blackwell, PhD, researches long-nineteenth-century transatlantic literature, material culture, and legal artifacts. A nationally certified paralegal for more than twenty years, Blackwell has published a scholarly edition of the Anna Seward / Joseph Weston debate from *The Gentleman's Magazine* as well as articles on British and American women writers, including Louisa May Alcott. She is associate editor of the digital *Victorian Women Writers Reviewed* project and the forthcoming *Routledge Research Companion to Romantic Women Writers*.

Andrew Byers, PhD, researches the history of U.S. and European militaries in the nineteenth and twentieth centuries. He is co-editor of *The Role-Playing Society: Essays on the Cultural Influence of RPGs* and

Biopolitics and Utopia: An Interdisciplinary Reader. With essays published in *Foreign Affairs* and the *Journal of Military History* among others, Byers most recently authored *The Sexual Economy of War: Discipline and Desire in the U.S. Army*.

Siobhan Carroll, associate professor of English at the University of Delaware, works on intersections between nineteenth-century literature and the imperial and environmental imaginaries. Her *An Empire of Air and Water: Uncolonizable Space in the British Imagination, 1750–1850* was the 2015 runner-up for the first book prize of the British Association for Romantic Studies. She has published on nineteenth-century board games in *Nineteenth-Century Contexts* and in a forthcoming collection on Romantic cartography.

Heather Fitzsimmons Frey, assistant professor of arts and cultural management at MacEwan University in Edmonton, Canada, researches the arts and performance for, by, and with young people. A director and dramaturge, she serves on the International Theatre for Young Audiences Research Network Board of Directors. She is the editor of *Ignite: Illuminating Theatre for Young People* and has a co-authored chapter forthcoming in the *Cambridge Handbook of Material Culture*.

Sean Grass, professor of English at Rochester Institute of Technology, specializing in Victorian literature, particularly the Victorian novel, print culture, the book market, and life writing. Author of *The Self in the Cell: Narrating the Victorian Prisoner*, *Charles Dickens's Our* Mutual Friend: *A Publishing History*, and *The Commodification of Identity in Victorian Narrative: Autobiography, Sensation, and the Literary Marketplace*, Grass serves as president of the Dickens Society and as the executive secretary for the North American Victorian Studies Association.

Ann R. Hawkins, assistant provost for graduate education and research at the State University of New York System Administration, has published widely in textual criticism and book history. She has published scholarly editions of *Romantic Women Writers Reviewed, 1788–1792* (9 vols) and of three nineteenth-century Silver Fork novels; edited *Teaching Bibliography, Book History, and Textual Criticism*; and co-edited *Women Writers and the Artifacts of Celebrity* and two special issues of CEA *Critic* (one on games and gaming). She serves as series co-editor for SUNY

Press's History of Books, Publishing, and the Book Trades. As Rachael Miles, Hawkins writes award-winning historical romances (which all include period games).

Maura Ives, professor and head of the English Department at Texas A&M University, specializes in nineteenth-century print and digital textual studies. Her work focuses on British Victorian women writers (especially Christina Rossetti and Jean Ingelow), with attention to bibliographical and literary subgenres such as musical settings, religious writing, and celebrity print and material culture. She is the author of *Christina Rossetti: A Descriptive Bibliography*, the North American collaborator on the *Christina Rossetti in Music* digital project, and co-editor of *Women Writers and the Artifacts of Celebrity*.

Miles A. Kimball, professor of technical communication at Rensselaer Polytechnic Institute, has worked as a technical writer and knowledge management consultant in the defense and telecommunication industries. He has published broadly on e-portfolio pedagogy, information design, graphic design, digital humanities, and the history of data visualization. An Associate Fellow of the Society for Technical Communication, Kimball has received the Ken Rainey Award for a lifetime of quality research and significant contributions to the field and the Jay R. Gould Award for Excellence in Teaching.

Jennie MacDonald, PhD, author, playwright, and researcher, has edited *Schabraco and other Gothic Tales from the* Lady's Monthly Museum, *1798–1828*. Her other publications investigate eighteenth- and nineteenth-century Gothic literature; theater and children's culture; adaptation and paratext; and visual and material culture. An award-winning playwright, she regularly contributes to online audio and visual productions. Her work with nontraditional student writers prompted her current research into affect theory, writing, and publishing.

Megan A. Norcia, professor of English at SUNY Brockport, researches nineteenth-century imperialism, particularly imperial geography, castaway tales, and nineteenth-century children's games. She has published *X Marks the Spot: British Women Map the Empire, 1790–1895* and *Gaming Empire in Children's British Board Games, 1836–1860*. Her essays have appeared in *Victorian Literature and Culture*, *Children's Literature Annual*, *Victorian*

Review, and *The Lion and the Unicorn*, among others. She is happiest when up to her elbows in archives.

Andrew Rhoda is the curator of puzzles of the Jerry Slocum Mechanical Puzzle Collection at the Lilly Library, Indiana University's rare materials library, where he manages the collection of more than 35,000 mechanical puzzles. Rhoda has published on the history of puzzles, concentrating on the nineteenth and early twentieth centuries, and he has presented internationally on mechanical puzzles to the Association for Games and Puzzles International and the International Puzzle Collectors Association's International Puzzle Party.

Kristin Flieger Samuelian, an associate professor of English at George Mason University, focuses on intersections between popular/print culture and literary texts from the late eighteenth through the mid-nineteenth century. Her essays have appeared in *Studies in Romanticism*, *ELH*, and *Nineteenth-Century Contexts*, among others. Author of *Royal Romances: Sex, Scandal, and Monarchy in Print, 1780–1821*, Samuelian looks at discourses of national identity in British Romantic-period writing about dance, dancing, and dancers in her 2021 *The Moving Body and the English Romantic Imaginary*.

Mark Schoenfield, professor of English at Vanderbilt University, is the co-winner of the 2009 Colby Prize for *British Periodicals and Romantic Identity: "The Literary Lower Empire."* A Guggenheim Fellow, Schoenfield writes on material culture, within the context of institutions and the knowledge they produce. In addition to research on periodicals, he writes on law and literature during the Romantic era, including his first book, *The Professional Wordsworth: Law, Labor, and the Poet's Contract*. Schoenfield has published on both the boxer Daniel Mendoza and the game-like representation of violence in *Blackwood's Magazine*.

Maurice Suckling, assistant professor in the Games Simulation Arts and Sciences program at Rensselaer Polytechnic Institute, has worked in the games industry for more than twenty years. With more than fifty published video game titles to his name, including *Civilization VI*, *Killing Floor 2*, and *Planet of the Apes: Last Frontier*, Suckling has design credits on three published board games and has co-authored *Video Game Writing:*

From Macro to Micro. His research interests include storytelling in games, games as narrative systems, history in games, and the history of games.

Matthew Von Vogt, PhD, works at the intersection of theory and practice within the visual culture of the long twentieth century. His research addresses intermediality, with a focus on how visual and material objects comment on what cinema is and how we experience it. An independent scholar, Von Vogt has published articles in *The Cine-Files* and *Culture, Theory and Critique*.

Allison Whitney, associate professor of film and media studies at Texas Tech University, specializes in film technology, genre cinema, and the relationship between technological history and film form. She has published on race and class in American maternal melodrama, colonial narratives in science fiction, contemporary horror films, religion and cinema, sonic literacy, and dance in Weimar film culture. She is currently developing a digital humanities project on oral histories of film exhibition culture in Texas and the Southwest.

General Index

To highlight the international and ethnological components of many nineteenth-century games, we have included content referred to in passing here. We also have included here words that today would be considered fraught: racial slurs or at the least racially inflected terms, such as creole. These words are part of the historical past that this book examines, but they also represent aspects of that past which need interrogation. To not index these words would be to continue to overlook and elide their presence and silence that interrogation.

§ game subjects or components. *See also* games index
† pre-World War I authors, game designers, game theorists, etc.
‡ long-19thC artist, engraver, illustrator
° long-19thC publishers
◊ long-19thC periodicals

Abbot, Anne †: *Dr. Busby and his Neighbors*, 25, 193–209, 210n1, 333–34, 346n4, 346n5; "Edward's Cap and Edward's Grandfather," 196, 199; "How to Spoil a Good Citizen," 196
Abella, Jennifer, 29
Adams, John Quincy §, 204
Advertisements, 11–14, 17–20, 24, 31n15, 31n18, 99, 130–31, 133–36, 145, 147, 216, 246, 336, 340, 343, 346n3
Afghans §, 226
Africa §, 202, 203, 219, 227, 231, 241, 243; Cape of Good Hope, 220; caricatures of, 235, 253; Mountains of the Moon, 220; products of, 200, 220, 235; south Africa, 220; west coast, 220
African Americans §, 83n4; "Negro," 227; Game of Uncle Tom, 333
Akerman, James, 224, 239
Albert, Prince Consort (England) §, 207, 219, 231
Alcott, Louisa May †§, 24, 129–30; 142–44; in *Game of Authors*, 204, 207, 210n9, 337, 339, 346n8; *Little Women*, 129–30; 145, 148, 204
Alden, Isabella M. "Pansy" †, 337, 339
Alexander and Macnab (croquet petticoat sellers), 134–35

Alger, Horatio †, 198
Alken, Henry Thomas ‡, 87
Allen & Ginter °, 78–79
Allen, Michael, 112
Amateur Sportsman †, 12
amateurs and amateurism, 17, 22; and boxing, 41–43, 47, 52–54, 62; and baseball, 73; and the hunt, 91; and magic, 296–98; and theatricals, 155, 159, 169n6
America, 25, 62; households in, 3, 140; spending in, 3, 13; revolutionary war in, 143, 199, 202. *See also* United States
Anderson, Benedict, 216, 226
Anderson, Nancy Fix, 8, 93, 95
Angiolini, Gasparo †: *Don Juan*, 53
Animal §, 8, 11, 12, 14, 23, 44, 57, 69, 73, 74, 81, 87, 88, 97, 98, 103–104, 216, 222–23, 226, 280, 307; and animal husbandry, 11–12; and Animal Welfare movement, 23, 87; ape, 103; ass (donkey), 102; bear, 11, 16, 56, 95, 226; birds, 280; Blink Bonny (racehorse), 94; bull, 7, 11, 56, 89, 95, 103, 236; chicken, 74; cocks, 7, 11, 95, 103; cow, 31n17, 102, 280; crocodile, 239n12; deer, 11, 94, 282; dog / hound, 12, 22, 87, 89–104, 118, 119, 121, 333; duck, 282; eagle, 202, 203, 208, 301; elephant, 226; fish, 308; fitchew, 91; flamingo, 141–42; fox, 80, 88; frog, 113; hare, 88, 92; hedgehogs, 141–42; hippopotamus, 232; horses, 7, 8, 11, 12, 22, 44, 64n5, 73, 87–107, 200, 260n3, 279, 280, 282–83, 285, 287, 288–89; kangaroo, 226, 234, 239n12; lion, 201; marten cat, 92; mouse, 203; mule, 102; Nailor (racehorse), 104; ostrich, 226; owl, 335; ox, 12, 44; pig, 31n17, 237, 250; pigeon, 103; polar bear, 196; rabbit, 11; sheep, 12, 31n17, 102; snake, 226; Spectre (racehorse), 104; stag, 88; tiger, 103, 226; turkey vulture, 251; wolf, 121
Aniseed †, 101–102
Annual Review ◊, 62
Anson, Adrian Constantine "Cap" ¥§, 71–72, 77, 83n4, 83n9
Antarctica, 223
anthropology, 52, 253; and photography, 74–75, 83n7
Arabia §, 220; *Arabian Mystery*, 302
Archer, William †, 324
Aria, Mrs. [Eliza Davis Aria] †, 162
Arthur, T[imothy] S[hay] †, 337
Arthur, Theo †, 311, 313, 315, 317
Arts, 11, 21, 41, 48–49, 58, 60, 73, 132, 215, 231, 232, 297
Ashante §, 226; *Ashantee Difficulty*, 302
Ashby-Sterry, Joseph †, 149
Asia §, 202, 220, 231, 235; East Asia, 220; *Travellers of Asia*, 252
Assyria §: "brother bull" of, 236; and Nineveh, 236
Astley's (Amphitheatre), 11, 327n4
Athenaeum ◊, 140, 147, 238
Auerbach, Jeffrey, 216, 219, 221, 229, 231, 234, 235, 236, 238n2
Austen Leigh, James Edward †, 92
Austen, Cassandra, 2
Austen, Jane †, 1, 2, 29, 31, 52, 53; *Persuasion*, 31; *Pride and Prejudice*, 2, 52–53; *Sense and Sensibility*, 1
Australia §, 223, 228, 231, 235, 239n6; and kangaroo, 234; products of, 220, 234; and Sydney harbor, 235, 336
Austria §, 182, 316

Austria-Hungary §, 176, 180
Azerbaijian: *Hounds and Jackals*, 3
Aztec, 3

Baldwin, Peter, 315
Ball, Robert ¥, 56
Ballam, Richard, 265–67, 271, 272
Barbados (West Indies) §, 220
Baring, Evelyn †, 180, 184
Barrington, Bishop Shute †, 50–51
Baseball §, 69–86; and American League, 69; and Boston Beaneaters, 70–71, 78; and Buchner Gold Coin 79–80; and Chicago White Stockings, 70, 72, 83n9; and exclusion of women and minorities, 75, 83n4; and Gypsy Queen, 71–72, 76; and National League, 69, 72, 81, 295; and physiognomy of players, 73–76, 82.
Beau Geste (1939 film), 4
Beckford, Peter †, 91
Beecher, H[enry] W[ard] †, 337
Beeton, Isabella †, 136
Beissel Heath, Michelle, 21, 25–26, 28, 141, 143–44, 145–46, 332, 333, 338, 341–42, 345n1
Belcher, James ("Jem") ¥, 60, 62
Belfast News-Letter ◊, 138, 144
Bell, August †, 346n7
Bell, John °, 327n15
Bell, R[obert] C[harles] †, 30n13
Benedict, Frank Lee †, 135
Benson, Joseph °, 345
Benson, Mary Margaret, 29
Bentley, Richard °, 113
Bentley's Miscellany ◊, 113
Berger, John, 225
Bertillon, Alphonse ‡, 74, 75
Bhabha, Homi, 225
Bible §, 270, 281, 283, 284, 290, 341; *Bible Characters*, 270; *Old Testament Characters*, 341; and Pharisee, 138
Bistline, Erin N., 7, 21, 22–23, 148n2
A Bitter Bondage (novel), 99–100
blackface §, 163, 169n9
Blackwell, Catherine S., 21, 23–24
Blackwell, Mrs. †, 346n6
Blackwood's Magazine ◊, 60
Blaine, Delabere †, 12, 14
Blaisdell, A[lbert] F. †, 344
Blake, Kathleen, 8
Bly, Nellie †, 257–58
Boddice, Rob, 97
Boddy, Kasia, 54, 55
body, 28, 46, 71, 104, 190; aesthetics of, 9, 42, 54, 234; discourses of, 21, 42–43; display of, 42, 44, 49, 50–54, 58, 73–76, 146, 232; movement of, 43, 47, 48, 50, 57
Boone, Richard G., 202
Bootblacking, 199–200; and Warren's, 111–12, 124, 125, 200
Boscawen, Mary F. E. †, 227
Bostwick, Arthur, 333
Bourdieu, Pierre, 114
boxing §, 3, 8, 11, 16, 54–64, 65n9, 113–14, 121–22, 279; and Enlightenment values, 55, 57; and immorality, 56, 62; and performance, 21–22; and professionalism, 41–47; and "science," 23, 42–43, 55–56, 57–61
Bracey, Robert, 5
Brewster, Paul, 3, 29
Bristol Magpie ◊, 16
Bristol, Olivia, 6
British Newspaper Archive (database), 10, 147
Bronte, Charlotte †, 207, 338, 339
Brougére, Gilles, 310, 324, 327n14
Broughton, Jack ¥, 55–56, 65n8

Brown, Bill, 70
Brown, Mr. [John] (Queen Victoria's warden), 94
Browning, Elizabeth Barrett †§, 207, 338, 339
Bryant, William Cullen †§, 338
Buckingham, David, 310, 324, 327n14
Bulfinch, Thomas †§, 338
Bullfinch, Bob †, 100–101
Bullock, Richard, 217
Bulwer, William †§, 338
Buonaparte, Napoleon §, 177, 178, 320, 338
Burke, Edmund †, 48
Burnett, Frances Hodgson †§, 199, 210n6, 210n9, 339; and *Little Lord Fauntleroy*, 199, 200, 207
Burns, Robert †§: "To a mouse," 203
Burrowes, William (bootmaker), 130, 131
Bury and Norwich Post ◊, 14
Butler, James (bootmaker), 132
Butler, Sarah, 30
Byers, Andrew, 21, 25
Byron, George Gordon, Lord †, 22, 55, 64; *Childe Harold's Pilgrimage*, 14, 42, 64n4
The Bystander ◊, 98

C., A. W. †, 98
Cannadine, David, 237
Capon, William ‡, 327n9
caricatures §: of the Crystal Palace, 216, 229; of men, 198, 210n5; of minority groups, 231, 253; of women, 134. *See also* Africa; blackface; Italy; stereotype; racial minorities
Carlisle Journal ◊, 92
Carlyle, Thomas †§, 344
Carr, Raymond, 93
Carroll, A. B. †, 204, 337, 340
Carroll, Lewis [Charles Dodgson] †, 8, 24, 129, 144, 195, 208, 239; and *Alice's Adventures in Wonderland*, 129, 140–42, 143, 145, 148, 208, 239n12, 335; *Alice's Adventures Underground*, 141
Carroll, Siobhan, 21, 26
Carter, John, 17
cartography, 215, 219–23, 235–36, 239n6, 247, 249. *See also* maps
Cary, Alice †§, 339
Cary, Phoebe †§, 339
Casartelli, L[ouis] C[harles] †, 260n5
Catholic (religion), 254, 341; and Irish, 255
celebrity, 58, 78, 164, 335, 337, and celebrity culture, 54, 332, 340–45
Central America §, 220
Chadwick, Henry †, 70, 80–82, 83n10
Chafin, William †, 91
Chambers, Henry, 217
Champlin, John Denison, 333
Chandler, James, 48
Chapman, Noyes †, 301
Charles, Elizabeth Rundle [Mrs. Charles], 339
Charnwood †, 94
Chartist movement, 231, 234
cheating, 30n11; and croquet, 137, 138–43, 147; *Cheating*, 284
Cheltenham Examiner ◊, 92
chess (equipment): chessboard 20, 177; chess men, 20; traveling set, 266, 292n2
Chesterton, G. K. †§, 312, 314–16, 326
children §, 25, 124, 210n7, 233, 253; and educational play 4, 20–21, 28, 90, 245–47, 325–26, 332; and family play 4, 156–57, 199; and

games, 5, 19–20, 23, 27, 168n2, 169n5, 206, 207, 233, 251–53, 307, 309–12, 315–17, 319, 324–26, 344; and imperialism 26, 216–17, 220–21, 226–28, 237–38; and literature, 19–20, 124, 193–95, 207, 210n4, 217, 239n11, 293; and morality 16, 195–96, 205–206, 342–44; and patriotism 25–26, 143–44, 195, 201–202
Children's Friend ◊, 195
China §, 231, 324; and Canton, 249; and foot-binding, 234, 236; and Opium War, 320; and Go, 25, 175, 179
Christianity, 281; "muscular," 16
Christmas, 92, 98, 99; and dance, 63; and Dickens, 111–12, 126n1; and games, 153, 160, 166, 319, 320, 321, 336, 327n5; and gift-giving, 19, 20, 141, 319; and Lewis Carroll, 141
Chromolithography, 76–82, 317. *See also* lithography
Churchman's Family Magazine ◊, 129, 144, 147
Clark, Alex B. (bootmaker), 131
class (social orders), 19, 25, 88, 251, 319; and anti-theatrical prejudice, 158, 162–63, 168, 169n6; and consumerism, 9, 14–15; and education, 25, 200, 247; and gaming, 16, 23, 47, 55, 56, 58, 88, 95, 101, 123; and gender, 43, 97, 154, 157, 162, 168n5; and Great Exhibition, 215, 229, 238n2; and income, 13–14, 136; and professionalization, 42, 177, 294
Claxton, Remsen & Haffelfinger °, 342–43
Clay, Henry §, 204
Clemm, Sabine, 215, 219–20, 229, 234
Clemmitt, Evans, & Co., 217
Clemmitt, John, 217
Cleopatra §, 162
Coates, Edward A. (professor), 72
Coates, Henry T. : *See* Porter and Coates
Cobbett's Political Register ◊, 102
Cochran, Charles B., 313–14
Cohen, Laura Langer, 204, 334, 336
Coleridge, Christabel †°¥, 169n6
Collins, Hiram Haydn †, 342
Colomb, Philip H. (Captain, Royal Navy) †¥, 187
Colón-Semenza, Gregory, 114
colonialism §, 202, 210n6, 255; and agents, 217–18; in games 4, 26, 202, 279, 282–84, 288; and Great Exhibition, 219–35; in literature, 210n6. *See also* emigration
Columbus §, 280
Colwell, F. A. †, 203
commedia dell'arte, 320
Connoisseur ◊, 55, 58, 65n7
connoisseur, 22, 41, 52, 59, 63. *See also* professionals
consumer, 9–10, 76, 82, 228, 286; and consumer economy, 22, 70, 72, 158, 215, 216, 256
consumption, 42, 46, 73, 76, 161, 233, 234, 256, 259, 309–11, 326; and consuming, 11, 73, 83n5, 102, 115, 161
consumption (tuberculosis), 155
Cook, Captain James §, 223–26, 228, 237
Cook, Daniel, 309
Cooper, Abraham, R.A. ‡, 98
copyright, 334, 336; infringement, 140, 142, 148
Cormack, Malcolm, 8, 98
Cornhill Magazine ◊, 137, 144, 147

costs (financial): of books, 12–15, 17–20, 315; of clothing 131–36; in games, 22, 252, 276–78; of magic tricks, 299; of stables 101
Court Magazine and Belle Assemblée ◊, 62, 64n4
COVID-19, 30
Cowper, William †§, 338, 344; translation of *Odyssey*, 54
Coyners, Henry John ¥, 96
Crawley, Captain Rawdon [pseud. of George Frederick Pardon] †: *Handy Book of Games for Gentlemen*, 207
creole, 57. *See also* stereotypes
cribbage (equipment), 20
criminal §, 56, 74, 114, 122, 206
The Critic ◊, 96, 102
Cronin, Richard, 63
croquet §: addiction to, 145–46; as battle, 138, 143; costs of, 129, 136, 140; death by, 129, 145, 146, 147, 148; and flirtation, 129, 136, 138–39, 142, 144, 146; and marriage market, 132, 134, 138, 147; and mixed-gender competition, 130, 136–38, 143, 144, 146, 148n2; popularity of, 130, 137, 138; rules of, 137, 139–43; satire of, 132, 133–35, 138, 144, 145; and seduction, 132, 134, 136, 138–39, 143; and "science," 143; and playing sets, 130–34, 144
croquet boots: and goloshes, 133–34; prices of, 130–31, 132–33, 136, 144, 147; sexual allure of, 131, 132, 134, 136, 138; styles of, 130–34, 136, 139; and waterproof, 133–34
croquet petticoats, 24, 147; in crinoline, 134–37; prices of, 134–36, 145; sexual allure of, 131, 134, 136; styles of, 134, 136
Cruikshank, George ‡, 64, 205, 216, 229, 231, 236, 237, 239n10, 253
Crystal Palace §, 26, 215, 216, 217–38
Cuba §, 243; and cigars, 239n12
Culin, Stewart, 332
Cummings, Maria S. †§, 338, 339
Curtis, George †§, 338
Czechoslovakia §, 316

Dallas, E[neas] S[weetland] †§, 115
dance §, 21, 22, 23, 41–65, 113, 121, 290, 324; and ballet, 50–51, 53, 149n6; Morris, 16; as science, 42–43, 48–49, 51–52, 61; theorization of, 51–52; and waltz, 62. *See also* sexuality
Daniel, William Barker †, 12, 14
Darbyshire, Neil, 265
Dart, Gregory, 63
Darton and Wallis °, 217
Darwin, Charles †, 74
de Bauclas, L †, 62
de Younge, Annemina †, 156–57, 162, 165, 169n7
de' Medici, Francesco, 245
death §, 147, 298, 312; in games, 90, 181, 223–36, 237, 239n8, 245; in the hunt, 95, 98, 101; in literature, 45, 47, 88, 90, 115, 129, 145, 146, 148
Degen, Estes & Co. °, 338
Denmark, 316; King of, 98
Derby Mercury ◊, 17, 19
Derbyshire Advertiser ◊, 134
Derrida, Jacques, 113
Dibdin, Thomas †, 310, 325, 327n5
dice (equipment), 178, 181, 249, 267, 268, 270, 287
Dickens, Catherine (Katey) Elizabeth Macready, 111
Dickens, Catherine (Thomson Hogarth), 111

Dickens, Charles (Charley) Culliford Boz, 111, 125, 312–13, 315
Dickens, Charles John Huffam †§, 23, 29, 99, 111–26, 195, 205–206, 211, 239n10, 312, 313, 315, 327n7, 327n8, 335, 336, 338, 340–41, 344, 346n6; and Christmas, 111–12, 125, 126n1; and play, 112–26; and trauma, 112–20, 123–26; childhood, 112; *All the Year Round*, 99; *Bleak House*, 115; *David Copperfield*, 23, 112, 119, 123; *Great Expectations*, 23, 111–27; *Hard Times*, 23, 29, 113, 115; *Life of Grimaldi*, 113; *Little Dorrit*, 113, 115; *Mystery of Edwin Drood*, 23, 125–26; *Oliver Twist*, 113, 205; *Our Mutual Friend*, 113, 124–25; *Pickwick Papers*, 113, 115; "The Signalman," 114
Dickens, Henry Fielding, 111–12, 126n1
Dickens, John, 112–13
Dickens, Jr., Charles †: "Glimpses of Charles Dickens," 312–13, 315, 327n8
Dickens, Mary (Mamie), 111
Dickens, Sr., Charles, 315, 327n7
Didelot, Charles ‡°¥, 50–51
Didelot, Rose ¥, 51
Dillon, Diane, 230, 238
Disderi, Eugene ‡, 76
Dodge, Mary Mapes †, 195, 207
Dolby, George, 111, 113
Doonan, Jane, 224
Dorset, Mrs. [Catherine Ann Turner] †, 20
Doubleday, Abner ¥, 82n1
Downing, Karen, 54, 58
Drama, Juvenile, 153–68, 307–26, 326n2
Dublin Review ◊, 254, 260n5
Dublin Weekly Nation ◊, 132
Dublin, 134; and International Exhibition of Arts and Manufactures, 132
Duval, Pierre †, 245

E. G. Selchow and Company °, 205. *See also* Selchow and Righter
E. I. Horsman °, 340
Eakins, Thomas ‡, 73, 75
East India Company §, 220, 283
Echalaz, Cornet Richard Charles ¥, 95
Eckroth, Stephanie, 20
Edinburgh Evening Courant ◊, 135
education, 24, 43, 195, 200, 216, 296; and *Census of Great Britain 1851: Education*, 260n2; and *Game of Authors*, 331, 337, 342–45; and games, 16, 19, 28, 230, 281, 282, 284–85, 290, 302–304, 336; and geography, 243–60; and Great Exhibition, 231–32, 234; and home theatricals, 157, 159, 237n15; and military 180, 188; of women 161, 166
Edward Copisarow, 265, 266
Edwards, Lionel ‡, 97, 98
Egan, Pierce †, 55, 58; "A Boxing we will go," 41, 64n2; *Boxiana*, 60, 63; *Life in London*, 62–64
Egypt §, 3, 231, 239n12, 254; and Cleopatra, 162; *The Egyptian Paradox* 302
Eliot, George †§, 207, 339
Elliott Avedon Virtual Museum of Games, 5, 29
Elmhurst, Edward Pennell †, 92
emigrants and emigration §: advice for 221–22, 238, 239n5, 239n6; anxieties about, 245, 250, 251; benefits of, 224, 226; costs of 228, 232; cultural isolation of 235–37

empire, 24, 26, 161, 237–38, 238n4, 239n12, 244, 247, 279, 288; Assyrian, 236; British, 6, 26, 215–38, 255, 282, 284, 283, 284; Roman, 236
England §, 12, 63, 121, 142, 154, 167, 195, 198, 199, 207, 224, 227, 250, 310; and games, 15, 16, 54, 61; 91, 92, 121, 208, 219, 220, 230, 231, 236, 249, 271, 290, 279, 283, 336; and Great Exhibition, 217, 218. *See also* Great Britain
engravings, 2, 9, 12, 16, 50, 51, 94, 97, 98, 194, 246, 320, 336
Entertainment Software Association, 3
ephemera, 9, 21, 25, 76, 88, 90
Erromango (Vanuatu) and Erromangoans §, 224–25
Essex, Earl of [Arthur Algernon Capell, sixth earl of] †, 140; and plagiarism, 140
ethnography, 215; and photography, 74–75
Evangelical movement, 290
Evans, Henry Smith †, 26, 216–29, 230, 232, 235, 236, 237, 238, 239n5
Evening Freeman ◊, 132
Every Saturday ◊, 134

F. Ad. Richter & Co.°, *See* Richter Company
fairy tales, 205, 207, 211n12, 280, 284, 286, 308; Aladdin, 308; Blue Beard, 308; Cinderella, 208; Jack the Giant Killer, 308; Little Pigs, 280; Red Riding Hood, 280; Sleeping Beauty, 308; Tom Thumb, 308
Faithfull, Emily °, 140
fan culture, 27, 83n4, 309; 258, 340
Farr, Liz, 310, 326n2
femininity, 53, 58, 134, 140, 146, 157, 170, 207, 208, 333, 343, 346n8; of clothing, 132–34; and domesticity, 157, 207, 342 and duty, 141–42, 144, 146 and fair play, 142–44; and female authorship, 207–208; and games, 208, 333
Field, James ¥, 56
Fildes, (Samuel) Luke ‡, 125
Fine Art Union °, 99
Fitzsimmons Frey, Heather, 21, 24, 27
Flanders, Judith, 319
Forster, John †: Life of Charles Dickens, 112, 115, 125, 126n1
Foucault, Michel, 43
France §, 51, 122, 153, 154, 176, 180, 199, 231, 234, 245, 265, 279, 316, 320; and Francophobia, 50–51. *See also* Games: Charades
Franklin, Benjamin †§, 206
Fraser, Antonia, 319, 326
Freud, Sigmund †, 113, 114–15
Friedrich Wilhelm III of Prussia, 177
Fröbel, Friedrich (educator), 303
Fuller Ossoli, Margaret †§, 339
Furneaux, Holly, 327n7

Gale (database), 10, 30n14
Gallini, Giovanni Andrea Battista †‡°¥, 49
Galton, Francis †¥, 74, 75
game counters (equipment), 89, 90, 207, 266, 301–302; in war games, 183, 185, 188, 190. *See also* totum; teetotum
game culture, 25, 26
game studies, 8, 27; Ludic Cultures, 8; Cultures of Play, 8
games: *See* Games and § entries here
Games and Research Database, 27, 265–92

Gardiner, Allen §, 239n7
Garrick, David ¥, 327n5
Garvey, Ellen Gruber, 345
Gaskell, Charles A. †, 202, 203
Geertz, Clifford, 237
gender, 16, 21; and differences between the sexes, 20, 100, 167, 229, 344; and cheating, 137, 140–43, 147; and mixed-gender sports, 97, 130, 136, 137, 144, 146, 148; and roles and expectations, 23, 24, 43, 100, 143, 147, 148, 159, 167, 215, 319. *See also* femininity; masculinity
General Magazine and Impartial Review ◊, 59
Gentleman's Magazine ◊, 55, 62
geography §, 19, 217, 219, 221, 227, 231, 239n6, 243–52, 254–55, 258–60, 260n2, 269, 279–83, 284, 287, 288, 289, 290
George [William Frederick] III of England §, 19
George Bernard Shaw †, 326
George S. Parker and Co. °, 205, 211n10, 211n11
Georgens, Jan (educator) †, 302–303
Germany §, 182, 186, 231, 265, 283, 315; and Wars of Unification, 179, 181, 185
Gilder, Jeanette †, 345
Gill, Hélène, 215, 220, 235, 238n2
Gillray, James ‡, 51, 54
Girl of the Period Miscellany ◊, 139, 149n5
Gladstone, William §, 338
Glendinning, Robert Edward ¥, 74
globalization §, 26, 243–44, 247, 248, 257–59
globe §, 19, 187, 219, 233, 238, 247, 253, 257, 259
Gluck, Christoph Willabald ‡, 49
Godey's Lady's Book and Magazine ◊, 142, 147
Godfrey, John ¥, 55
Godwin, William †: *Caleb Williams*, 43–47, 55, 59, 64, 64n6
Goldsmith, Oliver †§, 245, 338
Goldstein, Jeffrey, 310, 324, 327n14
Goodman, Ruth, 311
Goodrich, Caspar F. ¥, 187
Goodwin & Co. °, 82; and Goodwin Champions, 77; and Goodwin Round Album, 78; and Gypsy Queen 69, 71–72, 76; and Old Judge, 69–73, 75–76
Gordon, Sarah, 73, 74
Gosden, Chris, 227–28
Grand Theatre (Leeds), 319
Grant, Ulysses §, 338
The Graphic ◊, 101
Grass, Sean, 21, 23
Great Britain §, 7, 8, 10, 24, 88, 102, 130, 153, 222, 231, 256; compared to U.S., 200, 202–204, 206, 198–99; and empire, 216, 219, 227, 253; and games, 102, 223, 176, 180, 187, 247, 255, 279, 283, 284, 288, 290, 291, 336; and government, 102, 260n2; and Great Exhibition of 1851, 26, 194, 215–42, 253, 254, 346n3; and Hongkong, 132; and Little Britain, 122
Greece §, 54; and *Polemos*, 268, 271
Green, J. K. °, 310, 311, 318, 321–24, 325
Greenland §, 220
Greenwood, George †, 103
Greenwood, Hamar, Sir, MP, 103
Grieves scene-painting family ‡, 322
Grimaldi, Joseph ‡, 113, 322
Guerra, Doug, 7
Guinea §: Timbo, 220

Gunga Din (1939 film), 4
Gurevich, Eli, 3
Gygax, Gary, 4

Hacker, Morris, Jr. ¥, 74–75
Hamilton, Emma †, 20
harem, 234
Harley, J[ohn] B[rian] (geographer), 221
Harper's New Monthly Magazine ◊, 144, 147
Harris, J. °, 19, 20
Harrison, E[dward], Dr. †, 94
Harrow, Sharon, 8, 42
Harte, Francis Bret †§, 203
Harvey, Adrian, 8, 16, 42, 64n5
Hastings, Henry, fourth Marquis of, 138
Hawaii and Hawaiians §, 223–24, 225
Hawke, Martin ¥, 95
Hawkins, Ann R., 7. *See also* Rachael Miles
Hawthorne, Nathaniel †§, 7, 336, 338
Hayward, Arthur L., 215
Hemans, Felicia †§, 207, 338, 339
Hennelly, Mark, 113, 121
Herbert, Hilary A. ¥, 187
Herodotus †, 3
Hieover, Harry [Charles Bindley] †, 92
Hill, Albert A. †, 195, 208, 209
Hill, Gillian, 222
Hillard, Molly Clark, 325
Hodgson & Co. °, 310, 318
Hofer, Margaret, 6, 195, 210n3
Hoffmann, Professor Louis [pseud. of Angelo John Lewis] †, 27, 293–305
Hogarth, Georgina, 111
Hogarth, William ‡: *Four Stages of Cruelty*, 56
Holland §, 231, 316; and tulips, 234
Holt, Ardern †, 162, 169n7, 169n10
Homans, Jennifer, 49, 53
Homer †, 42, 60; *Odyssey*, 54
Hopkins, Chris, 236–37
Horse and Hound ◊, 93
Houdin, Robert †, 293
Houston, Gail Turley, 113
Hoyle, Edmond †, 2, 7, 17, 18, 29n4, 29n5, 55, 142
Huggins, Mike, 7, 101
Huizinga, Johan, 113–14
Humphries, Richard ¥, 57–59
Hutcheon, Linda, 236
Huxley, Thomas Henry †, 74, 75

Ibsen, Henrik †, 326
Iliad, 1; and Achilles, 46; and Hector, 46
Illustrated and Sporting News ◊, 97, 98, 99
Illustrated London News ◊, 149n5
Illustrated Sporting and Dramatic News ◊, 101
Illustrated Sporting and Dramatic Times ◊, 94–95, 97, 98
Illustrated Times ◊, 137
illustrations, 14, 16, 22, 64, 90, 97, 98, 99, 131, 197, 200, 210n5, 216, 239n10, 253
imagination, 53, 216, 256, 316, 324
immorality, 54, 100; of cards, 196, 342; of dance, 50–51, 54; of women, 146, 148n2. *See also* morality
imperialism: *See* empire
India §, 175, 220, 225, 226, 235; and Chaturanga, 175; and curry, 235; and Gunga Din, 4; and Hindoostan, 220, 252; and India House, 221; and Indian Mutiny, 225, 283; and Koh-i-Noor

diamond, 215, 220; and Mogul sauce, 235
indigenous peoples, 216, 222, 224, 226, 227
Ingelow, Jean †§, 207, 339
Ireland §, 18, 222, 229, 231, 234, 235, 254; and Catholics, 255; Lord Mayor of, 17
Irish Times ◊, 132
Irving, Washington †§, 338
Italy §, 45, 155, 176, 231, 236, 316; and Circus Maximus, 31; and Colosseum, 238n1; and Herculaneum, 236; and caricature of, 234
Itzkowitz, David C., 93
Ives Brothers °, 333
Ives, Maura, 21, 28
Ives, W & S. B. °, 195

J. and W. Jeffrey and Co. (boot seller), 132–33
Jackson, "John" Gentleman" ¥, 22
Jackson, Kenneth, 6
James, E. †, 103
Jameson, J. H. °, 310
Jamieson, Dave ¥, 83n5
Jane, Fred †, 191
Japan §: Army of, 180; and Meiji period, 180. *See* Games: Go, *Pokémon*, *Pokémon Go*
Jaques, Joe, 130, 131, 140, 141, 142, 271
Jaques, John, 130, 131, 140, 141, 142, 194, 271
Jewett, Sarah Orne †§, 339
Jews §, 57; and *New and Fashionable Game of the Jew*, 215; and Pharisee, 138. *See also* Mendoza
John Bull §, 234
John H. Tingley °, 334
Johnson, Ben, 92
Johnson, Elmer E. °, 210n8
Johnson, Tom ¥, 58–61
Jomini, Antoine-Henri †, 176
Jones, Charles †, 18
Joseph Hall Studio ‡, 70

Kaplan, Marilyn, 331, 344
Kaplan, Stuart, 331, 344
Kayyem, Marisa, 5
Kelly, Michael Joseph "King" ¥, 70, 76–77
Kemble, John †, 327n9
Kent Farmer, A †, 103
Kentish Gazette ◊, 132
Kernan, Alvin, 41, 64n3
Liman, Arthur, 5, 6
Kingsley, Charles †§, 338
Kinsey, Ernest U. †, 302
Kipling, Rudyard †: *Kim*, 225
Knight of the Fist †, 58
Knight, George †, 294
Knight, Thomas ¥, 56
Knowles, Chantal, 227, 228
Krauss, Rosalind, 75, 83n8
Kusnetz, Ella, 116, 123

L & N. W. Railway, 255
La Belle Assemblée ◊, 10, 48, 62
Ladies Cabinet of Fashion ◊, 146
Lady's Almanac for the &ear 1866 (Boston) ◊, 142
Lamprey, John ‡, 74
Landon, Letitia Elizabeth †§, 149n5
Landseer, Edwin ‡, 12
Larcom, Lucy †§, 339
Latta, Thomas Love ¥, 73
laws and legislation: copyright, 334, 336; Cruel Treatment of Cattle Act of 1822 (Martin's Act), 102–103; Dog Protection Act of 1919, 103; game laws, 11–12, 14, 17, 20, 103; Licensing Act of

laws and legislation *(continued)* 1737, 325; Theater Regulation Act of 1843, 325
Layard, George Somes †, 149
Leader and Saturday Analyst ◊, 95–96
Lear, Edward: and *Book of Nonsense*, 39n11
Leat, Harry †, 299
Leech, John †: and *Young troublesome*, 311–13
Lefanu, Miss (Alicia) †, 20
Lefebvre, Henri, 225
Legends, 205, 280, 286, 308; Robin Hood, 206, 211n11, 280, 287, 308; Dick Turpin, 280, 287; Dick Whittington, 280; *Sinbad the Sailor* (play), 319
Leicester Mercury ◊, 92, 131
leisure, 21, 25, 42–43, 157, 219, 232–33, 237, 340, 342
Lemoines, Henry †, 57
Lewis, Angelo John ¥: *See* Professor Hoffmann
Lewis, R. M., 137
Liddell, Alice, 141
Liddell's Living Age ◊, 147
Lilienthal, Gustav †, 302
Lilienthal, Otto †, 302
Liman Collection, 5, 6
Liman, Ellen, 5, 6
Lind, Jennie ¥§, 239n12
Linton, Eliza Lynn †, 149n5.
literacy, 24, 280, 284, 331
Literary Gazette and Journal of Belles Lettres ◊, 89
Literary Speculum ◊, 62
lithography, 9, 20, 221, 230, 334, 335. *See also* chromolithography
Livermore, W. R. °, 184, 185–86, 187
Liverpool Daily Post ◊, 132
Living Age ◊, 129, 147
London §, in games, 64n5, 202, 220, 238, 249, 253, 254, 255, 280, 318, 320, 322
London Evening Standard ◊, 134
London Journal ◊, 99–100
London Medical and Surgical Journal ◊, 94
London Review ◊, 131, 140, 142
London Society ◊, 138, 140
Longfellow, Henry Wadsworth †§, 338
Longman, Hurst, Rees, and Orme °, 11, 20
Lougy, Robert, 119
Louis XIV of France §, 163
Louis-Phillippe I of France, 53
Lovechild, Mrs. [Ellenor Fenn] §, 20
ludic play, 9, 23, 113, 114, 115, 119, 225, 251

Macaulay, T[homas] B. †§, 338
MacDonald, George †, 24, 154
MacDonald, Grace †, 24, 153–69
MacDonald, Jennie, 21, 27–28
Macdonald, Louisa Powell †, 154
Machemer, Theresa, 30
Machiavelli, Niccolo †§, 338
MacKenzie, John, 216, 221
magic, 27–28, 29, 48, 271, 282, 285, 293–305, 307, 308, 320, 326. *See also* Games
Malevich, Kasimir, 75
Mangan, J[ames] A[nthony], 225
map(s) §, 19, 216, 238n1, 243, 251; *Funnyshire Fox*, 89; and Henry Smith Evans, 218–26, 228, 237; and games, 245–46, 249. *See also* cartography
marketing, 74; of games, 28, 42, 90, 130–34, 247, 278, 287, 309, 331, 332, 336, 337, 341–43

marriage §, 18, 24, 53, 161, 167; of children, 234; market, 136, 147, 154, 169n3
Martin, C. E. (bootmaker), 134
Martin, Richard, 102–103
Marylebone Mercury ◊, 131
masculinity, 43, 44, 47, 54–61, 97, 100, 122, 207
Maskelyne, John Nevil, 299
Mason, Tony, 93, 95
Master of Harriers, 97
Master of the Hounds, 91, 93, 95, 96, 97
Master of the Hunt, 98
material culture, 21, 76, 210n4, 308; and literary celebrity, 337, 340, 345
materiality, 75, 76, 248
Maturin, Charles †, 260n4
Matus, Jill, 114–15, 126n3
May, Allyson N., 88
Maya, 3
McCarty Little, William †¥, 186–87
McGill, Meredith L., 204, 334, 336
McLoughlin Brothers °, 207–208, 210n7, 211n11, 256, 257, 335, 336, 338–39, 340
Medland, Thomas, R.A. ‡, 12
Melville, Herman †, 7
Mencius †, 3
Mendoza, Daniel †¥, 55, 57, 59, 63, 65n8; *Art of Boxing,* 57–58
Meredith McGill, 334, 336
Meynell, Hugo ¥, 93
Middle East §, 220
Mike Goodall, 265
Miles, Captain ¥, 56
Miles, Rachael [pseud. of Ann R. Hawkins]: *Charming Ophelia*, 29n2; *Chasing the Heiress*, 29n2; *Jilting the Duke*, 29n2; *Tempting the Earl*, 29n2
Miller, Hugh †§, 338, 346n7
Mills Commission (baseball), 82
Mills, John †, 92, 94
Milton Bradley °, 9, 210n7, 256, 257, 331, 334–35, 337, 339, 343
Milton, John †§, 42, 338, 344
minorities, racial, 74–75, 83n4. *See also* entries for individual groups
Miss Echo †, 149
missionary §, 239n7, 342; in games, 216, 222, 226, 243, 335; and London Missionary Society, 224
Mitford, Mary Russell †, 168n2
Moebius, William, 223–24, 232
Mondrian, Piet ‡, 75
morality, 55, 196, 283, 285, 290, 292n7; of at-home theatricals, 159, 163, 167–69, 204; and moral instruction, 16, 121, 195, 197, 204, 217, 230, 281, 284, 315, 316, 342, 343; of the U.K., 227, 253; of the U.S., 25, 204, 209, 251; of women, 142–46. *See also* immorality
Morgan, Lady [Sydney Owenson] †, 64n4
Morning Post ◊, 238
Morse, Deborah Denenholz, 137
Mulock, Diana †§, 339
Munkwitz, Erica, 97, 100, 148n2
Munnings, Alfred, Sir ‡, 87
Murfree, Mary N. †§, 339
Muybridge, Eadweard ‡, 22, 73–76, 82; and Zoopraxiscope, 83n6; *Animal Locomotion*, 69–70, 71, 73–75, 82, 83n7
Myer, Mary C. †, 344–45

nations and nationalism, 13, 25, 42, 44, 48, 50, 81, 143, 144, 181, 189, 190–91, 193–211, 218, 224–26, 231, 235, 239n12, 245, 248–49,

nations and nationalism *(continued)* 254, 256, 258; competition between, 26, 226, 234, 236; and national identity, 43, 199–203, 216, 218, 225, 229, 234, 247, 288–89
Native Americans, 202, 231
Naumann, Julius, 181, 184
Nelson, Horatio, Lord §, 280
Nesbit, Edith, 207
New Monthly Magazine and Literary Journal ◊, 62
New Sporting Magazine ◊, 42, 58, 64n4, 94, 97, 98, 100
New York World ◊, 258
New Zealand §, 219–20, 223
Newbery, John °, 19
Nicholson, T. E. ‡, 98
Nimrod [pseud. of Charles Apperley] †, 91
Nineteenth-century Collections Online (database), 10, 30
Norcia, Megan A., 7, 21, 26, 28, 88, 161
Northampton Mercury ◊, 103
Norway §, 316
Noverre, Jean-George †‡°¥, 49–50, 51, 52–53; *Médée et Jason*, 53

O'Brien, John, 319, 325, 327n5
O'Quinn, Daniel, 42
O'Connell, Daniel †°, 254
O'Malley, Andrew, 217
Odyssey (Homer), 54
Once a Week ◊, 98
Onwhyn, Thomas †, 229, 236, 239n9
Oriard, Michael, 8
Ovid †, 3
Oxenford, John †, 308, 315, 327n6
Oxford Magazine ◊, 56

Paget, Lady Florence, 138, 144, 145
Pall Mall Gazette ◊, 146
Panama §, 239n6
Panorama, 19, 320, 321
Pantomime §, 49, 308–10, 315, 318–26; and charades, 153, 159, 160, 169; and Harlequin plays, 218, 319–21, 325; and tricks, 308, 322, 324
Parke's Shew Room (game seller), 19, 20
Parker Brothers °, 206, 208, 211, 256, 333, 335, 339, 340–41, 344
Parker, J. †, 341
Parkhurst, V[ilen] S. W. †°, 333
Parliament, 95, 97
Parsons, Timothy, 228
Pasquin, Antony †, 18
pastoral, 76–81, 83n10
patience: as a game, 115; as a virtue, 28, 144, 193, 198, 293, 301, 325
patriotism, 21, 143, 196, 234, 332; in games, 1, 25, 195, 200, 201–204, 209
pawns (equipment), 178, 267, 289
peace §: in games, 64, 196, 199, 223; and prosperity, 226, 238; and military training, 184, 189–90; and Peace Society, 199
Pearson, Richard, 229
Peep-out †, 97
Perrins, Isaac ¥, 58–61
Persia §: *Prince of*, 4
Peterson's Magazine ◊, 135
Petit Journal ◊, 258
Petrick, Paula, 334
Pettit, Jean ¥, 55, 58
Phelps, Elizabeth Stuart †§, 337, 339
Philip II of Spain, 245
Philips, Anne K., 144
Philips, Deborah, 218, 221, 235
photography, 22, 69, 70, 69–85, 97, 98, 155, 326, 336, 340;

anthropometric, 74, 75; criminal bodies in, 74; racial minorities in, 74; stop-motion, 22, 69–76, 82, 83n7; and use of grid, 69, 74–75, 83n8
Pindar †, 15
Pinney, William ¥, 97–98
plagiarism, 140
Planché, James Robinson †, 318, 320; *Castle of Otranto; or, Harlequin & the Giant Helmet*, 308–9, 318, 320–22
Plantation §, 221–22, 251
Plato †, 3
play, 2, 10, 11, 23; of games, 1, 2, 346; ludic, 113–15, 119; orderly, 112–16, 119–21, 124–26. *See also* games culture
Poe, Edgar Allen †§, 338
Pollard, James ‡, 87
Pollock, Benjamin °, 327n11
Pope, Alexander †: "Essay on Criticism," 41, 64n1
Pope, S[tephen] W., 25
popular culture, 27–28, 42, 54, 76–77, 81, 308–309, 319
Porter & Coates °, 335, 338, 339
Porter, Robert °: *See* Porter and Coates
portraits: of authors, 340–45, 346n9; and *Changeable Portraits*, 270, 286; and games, 76, 335–36
power §, 126, 221, 225, 283, 294; geo-political, 25, 231, 247; imperial, 26, 177, 179, 187, 190, 215–16, 219, 221, 225–26, 228, 236–38, 253; military, 177–91; physical, 42, 53; and purchasing 9, 15, 20
Powers, Alan, 317
Prender, Mrs. ¥, 103–104
Prescott, William H. †§, 338
print culture, 9, 88. *See also* material culture; popular culture
professionalism, 3, 8, 18, 27, 81, 99; and baseball, 72–73, 75, 76; and identity, 27, 217–18, 221, 236, 294–95, 299; and military, 25, 176–78, 182, 189, 191; and satire, 134; and sports, 22, 41–43, 47–49, 52–52, 57, 58, 60, 64n5; and theater, 21, 167–69
Professor Hoffmann [pseud. of Angelo John Lewis], 293–304
Prussia §, 25, 176–83; General Staff of, 177, 179, 182, 186. *See* Games: *Kriegsspiel*
publishers: consortium of, 14, 18, 19, 254; stock of, 15. *See also* advertisements
Pullan, [Matilda Marian] Mrs. †, 157, 160, 169n7
Punch, or the London Charivari ◊, 133, 134, 144, 147, 149n5, 215, 229, 231
Punch's Almanack for 1863 ◊, 138
puzzles, 6, 27, 267, 270, 271, 273, 274, 276, 279, 284, 293–95, 300–304

Quin, Michael Joseph †, 254

R. and J. Dick (bootmaker), 131
race (ethnicity), 88, 229. *See also* entries on individual ethnic groups
race (games): *See* Games
Rahn, Suzanne, 315, 325–26
Railroad or railway, 189, 203, 239n9, 250, 251, 255, 256, 259, 260n3, 261
Raymond, C. W. ¥, 180, 186
Redington, J. °, 317, 322, 327n11
Regier, Alexander, 43
Reid, Captain Mayne †, 140, 141

Reinagle, Philip ‡, 12
Reynold's Miscellany of Romance, General Literature, Science and Art ◊, 98
Rhoda, Andrew, 21, 27
Rice, Matthias †, 302
Richards, Eric, 222, 228
Richards, Jeffrey, 319–20
Richardson, Charles †, 183
Richardson, Mrs. †: *Little Harry's Troubles*, 251
Richardson, Ralph, 318
Richelieu, Armand, Cardinal §, 338
Ritvo, Harriet, 226
Rogers, Fairman, 73
romance, 137, 138, 160, 316, 320; as character, 322; and Regency, 1, 29n2
Roscoe, Mr. †, 20
Routledge, Edmund °, 140, 143, 294
Royal Society for Prevention of Cruelty to Animals, 102–104
rules and rule books, 17–18, 19, 159, 169n7, 180–86, 188, 190, 208, 223, 237, 245, 250, 252, 255, 272; and baseball, 80; and board games, 89–91; and boxing, 51, 54–55, 57, 62, 63; competition among, 140, 148; debates on 137–40, 141–42; 253, 268, 271, 286, 296; and croquet, 130; in Great Expectations, 113–16, 119, 125; plagiarism of, 140–41, 142
Ruskin, John †§, 338
Russell Morgan Printing Company °, 200, 205
Russell, Gillian, 45
Russia §, 176, 180, 220, 231
Ruth, George Herman, "Babe" ¥, 83n5
Rutland, John Henry Manners, fifth Duke of †, 15
S., E. †, 101
Sabine, John †, 20
Said, Edward, 225
Salt, H. S. †, 100
Samuelian, Kristin, 21–22, 52
Sanborn, Vic, 29
Sandham, Miss (Elizabeth) †, 20
Sandwich Islands, 223, 239n5
Sarratt, J. H. †, 18
Sassoon, Siegfried †: *Memoirs of a Fox-Hunting Man*, 87
sati, 234
Saturday Review ◊, 95, 96, 103, 134, 138, 143, 145, 147, 149n5
savages §, 52, 114, 121, 203
Sayer, Robert °, 249
Sayre, Farrand ¥, 176, 185, 186, 188
Scandinavia §, 203
Schafer, Frank °, 343
Schoenfield, Mark, 21–22
science, 143, 215, 232, 247, and games, 282, 283, 285, 290; and military, 176, 183, 189; of motion, 21, 22, 23, 41–68, 76
Scotland §, 12, 91, 203, 231, 279, 318, 342
Scots Magazine ◊, 59
Scotsman ◊, 134
Scott, John ‡, 12
Scott, Sir Walter †§, 60, 211n11, 315, 338
scrapbooks, 267, 270, 332, 345
Scrutator [pseud. of Mr. Horlock] †, 96–97
Seager, Nicolas, 309
Sedgwick, Eve, 47
Sekula, Alan, 74, 75
Selchow & Righter °, 205, 334, 340–41
servant(s): civil, 221; domestic, 3, 13, 56, 136, 322, 333; indentured, 228

Seville, Adrian, 230, 239n8, 244–45
Sewell, Anna †, 87–88; *Black Beauty*, 88, 98
sexuality, 43; heteronormative, 45, 47, 160; homosocial, 47; and display, 51–53; in dancing, 50–54; in croquet, 133, 146; of clothing, 50; of dancers, 50–54
Shakespeare, William †§, 3, 14, 315, 335, 338, 341, 344; *Hamlet*, 47, 308; *Henry V*, 3; *Julius Caesar*, 308; *King Lear*, 3; *A Midsummer Night's Dream*, 308; *Tempest*, 308
She (1935 film), 4
Shefrin, Jill, 6, 229, 246
Sherborne Mercury ◊, 92
Sheridan, Richard Brinsley †, 62
Sherman, William T. (general) †, 183–84
Sherwood, Mary †, 344
Siegel, Elizabeth, 76
Skelt Family °, 310, 318
Slack, John, "Jack" ¥, 55–56, 58, 60
Slater, Michael, 112, 113, 126n1
slavery §, 62, 222, 225–27, 235, 247, 251; and slave(s), 59, 226–28; and trade, 226
Smart, Hawley †, 100
Smith, A[ugustus] A. †°, 28, 332–33. *See also* Whipple and Smith
Smith, Assheton ¥, 95–96
Smith, W. C. †, 204
Smyth and Evans (colonial agents), 217. *See also* Evans
Snowdon, David, 63
soldier(s): in games, 222, 268; toy or tin, 29n2, 307; and war, 176, 181, 183, 190, 196, 199, 207, 268; *Poor old School Soldier and his Dog*, 268
South America §, 220, 231
South Pacific: in games, 220, 223, 228; and Kealakekua Bay 224; and Raiatea, 224; and Samoa 224; and Society Islands, 224
South Sea Islands §, 203
Southey, Robert †, 49, 52
Souvenir: and games, 27, 229, 238, 254, 308–309, 318; and photography, 83
Spain §, 231, 239n12, 245, 316; and sherry, 234
Spalding, Albert †, 82
spectacle, 21, 41, 47, 48, 232, 237–38, 307, 319, 325, 307, 312–14, 319
Speiaght, George, 307–308, 310, 315–16, 318, 326, 326n1, 327n9, 327n11
Spencer, Herbert †, 74
Spooner, William †, xii, 22, 26, 88–91, 216, 217, 229–37, 244, 252–60
sport: and gambling, 29n5, 123, 207; as games, 2–4, 7–8, 10–12, 14–16, 18, 20, 25, 269, 279, 280, 281, 282, 283, 285, 286, 287, 289, 308; and professionalization, 54–64, 69–70, 72–83; and gender, 130, 137, 143–44, 148n8, 200; and rural or rustic, 12–16, 31n17, 64n5, 76–79, 81, 91, 92, 101, 137, 140, 280; and science, 21–22, 31n17
sporting culture, 21, 25, 42, 88–123
sporting goods, 24, 130, 132, 136
Sporting Magazine ◊, 58
Sporting Times ◊, 93
St. Clair, William, 13–14, 27
St. James's Magazine ◊, 100
St. Nicholas Magazine ◊, 195
Standiford, Lee, 111
Star [London] ◊, 31
Steckles, Katie, 287
stereotypes (ethnic), 87, 202, 253. *See also* caricatures and entries for individual ethnic groups

stereotypes (printing), 334
Sternberger, Paul, 5
Sterngrass, Jon, 137, 141
Stevenson, Robert Louis †§, 308, 312, 314–19, 327n10; *Memories and Portraits*, 318
Storey, John, 309, 319
Stowe, Harriet Beecher †§, 207, 333, 337, 339
Strachan, John, 60
strategy, 29n4; and boxing, 55, 61, 63; and games, 29n4, 267, 268, 271, 273, 274–77, 279, 282, 284, 286–88, 290–91; and military, 21, 25, 175–91
Strutt, Joseph †, 15, 16
Stuart and Marilyn Kaplan Playing Card Collection, 126, 331, 344
Stubbs, George ‡, 87
Suckling, Maurice, 21, 26–27, 149n3
suffrage, 97, 161, 224, 279. *See also* Games
Surtees, Robert Smith †, 87, 91
Susina, Jan, 141
Sutton, Richard, Sir ¥, 94
Sweden §, 231, 316; King of, 98
Swift, Eben †, 182
Switzerland §, 231

T. Ellwood Zell °, 334
T., J. P. †, 98–99
Tacitus †, 3
Taglioni, Filipo ‡¥: *La Sylphide*, 53
Taglioni, Marie ¥, 53–54, 57
Tahiti §, 223
Taplin, William †, 12, 14
Tarleton, Banastre †, 59
Taunton Courier and Western Advertiser ◊, 92
teetotum, 26, 89, 243, 244, 249, 252, 259–60, 268, 270. *See also* totum; counters
temperance movement, 196, 197, 337, 339, 341; and Temperance Society, 239
Tennyson, Alfred, Lord †§, 338
Terry, Ellen °¥, 326n2
Thackeray, William Makepeace †§, 314; *Vanity Fair*, 164, 207, 314
Thaxter, Celia †, 339
theater: at-home, 21, 153–68, 169n5 169n6; Covent Garden, 320, 321, 325, 327n9; Drury Lane, 314–15, 325; Haymarket, 131, 135; Sadler's Wells, 314; scenery, 27, 308, 310, 311, 313, 314, 318, 321, 322, 327n9. *See also* laws and legislation; toy theatre
Theatrical Journal ◊, 320
Thomas, Joseph, 91
Thomson, Michael, 265
Thornhill, Richard Badham †, 12, 14
Tilley, Roger, 195
Times (London) ◊, 115
Tompkins, John ‡, 12
Totten, Charles A. L. †°, 184
totum, 89–90. *See also* teetotum; counters
Town and Country ◊, 56
toy theatre, 28; character and scenery sheets, 308, 311–12, 316–18, 321–25, 327n6; and Gothic novels, 308; and plays, 308; *Dante's Inferno*, 327n15; *Castle Spectre*, 308; *Giant Horse, or The Siege of Troy*, 326–7, 327n3; *Harlequin and the Giant Helmet*, 321; *Iron Chest*, 308; *Jack Sheppard*, 311; *Macbeth*, 318; *Miller and His Men*, 312–13; *Old Oak Chest*, 326n3; *Sinbad the Sailor*, 319; playbooks, 308, 311, 314–15, 321. *See also* children; legends; fairy tales; Robert Lewis Stevenson

toys, 7, 19, 26, 27, 195, 217, 267, 271, 276, 286, 309, 310, 316, 317, 324, 326, 336, 342; mechanical, 304; pull, 307; teaching 267, 270, 273, 274, 276
trade (international), 220, 225, 226, 229, 244, 245, 247, 249, 255; and games, 252, 279, 280. *See also* slavery
Trafalgar Square, 318, 322
travel §: in games, 21, 219–20, traveling games, 266, 279, 292n2; virtual, 21, 224, 235–36, 239n5, 243–46, 250–59, 282–83, 292
Trollope, Anthony †, 24; *Small House at Allington*, 129, 137–40, 144, 146, 148; *Warden*, 1, 36, 152
Trow, Charles †, 333, 343
Tupper, Mr. †§, 344
Turkey §, 231
Turner, Francis Calcraft ‡, 87
Twain, Mark (Samuel Clemens) †, 195; *Innocents Abroad*, 256

U.S. Games Systems, Inc. °, 331
U.S. Military Academy (West Point), 186
United Kingdom, 9, 10, 26, 140, 265, 293, 333, 336
United States, 7, 9, 10, 25, 26, 69, 79, 154, 176, 177, 183; east coast, 220; South, 62; Uncle Sam, 203; west coast, 220
Universal Magazine of Knowledge and Pleasure ◊, 47, 49

Valentine, Mrs. †, 16, 157, 169n7
Vauxhill Gardens, 56
Venus de' Medici, 51
Veteran Sportsman †, 12
Victoria, Queen of England §, 94, 218, 219
video and computer games, 6, 4, 6, 13, 25, 30n12, 259, 285, 287
violence §, 114, 115–16, 196; in boxing, 43, 45–47, 121–22; in croquet, 141, 143; in *Crystal Palace Game*, 225, 226; in dance, 43, 45–47; and play, 124, 125
visual culture, 9, 20, 21, 27, 42, 82, 219, 332
Vizetelly, Frank †, 149n5
von Clausewitz, Carl †, 178, 190
von Meckel, Jakob ¥, 179, 180, 181
von Moltke, Helmuth (the Elder) ¥, 179, 180
von Müffling, Karl ¥, 179
von Reiswitz, Georg Heinrich Rudolf †¥, 179
von Reiswitz, George Leopold, Baron †¥, 177, 178, 179
von Schlieffen, Alfred ¥, 182
von Trotha, Thilo †¥, 180, 184
von Tschischwitz, Wilhelm †¥, 180, 184
von Verdy du Vernois, Julius †¥, 179, 181
Von Vogt, Matthew, 21, 22
von Wallenstein, Albrecht (general) §, 338

W. & S. B. Ives °, 333
Wakefield, Priscilla †, 221
Wales §, 249, 279
Walker's Hiberian Magazine ◊, 58
Wallice, Edward †, 249
Wallis, John †, 249
Walpole, Horace †: *Castle of Otranto*, 320
war §: American Revolution (1765–83), 143, 199, 202; Aroostook War (1838–39), 196; Austrio-Prussian (1866), 182; Battle of Trafalgar (1805), 283; Boer (1899–1902),

war § *(continued)*
283; Crimean (1853–56), 283; Franco-Prussian (1870–71), 179, 180; Napoleonic (1803–15), 176, 177; Russo-Japanese (1904–1905), 190; U. S. Civil War (1861–65), 72, 82n1, 176, 183, 184, 185, 186, 189, 190, 200, 201; World War I (1914–18), 182; World War II (1939–45), 191, 316
War College: French, 180; Italian, 180; Prussian, 179; United States Army 187–88; United States Naval 186–87
war games, 175–92
Ward, Artemus [pseud. of Charles Farrar Browne] †, 344
Ward, Joe ¥, 58, 59
Ward, Will ¥, 58, 59
Warner, Charles Dudley †, 336
Washington, George §, 338
Waterford News ◊, 130
Watkins, William †, 98–99
Watts, Isaac †, 247
Webb, H[enry]. J[ames] °, 317
Webster, Daniel §, 338
Wells, H. G. †¥, 191
West and Lee °, 340, 343
West Indies §, 252; Barbados, 220. *See also* Games
West Point (U.S. military academy), 180, 183, 186
West, William °, 310, 314
Western Daily Press ◊, 104
Whale, John, 58
Wheatley, Kim, 145–46
Whipple and Smith °, 28, 210n9, 332, 334, 337–38, 343, 346n9
Whipple, G. M. °: *See* Whipple and Smith
White, E. †, 18
White, Richard Grant †§, 336
Whitehead, Paul †: *Gymnasiad*, 65n7
Whitehill, Bruce, 332, 333
Whitman, Walt †, 7
Whitney, Adaline D. T. †§, 338
Whittet, Ethan, 333, 334, 346n5
Whittier, John Greenleaf †§, 328
Wilde, Oscar †, 326
Wilhelm, N. O. †°, 206
Wilhelm, Reverend †°, 183
Williams, J. L. †, 16
Williams, Reverend John, 223–26, 228, 237
Wilson, A[lbert] E[dward], 313–15, 317–18, 320, 322
Wilson, Andrew, 179, 181, 187
Wilson, John †, 60–61
Wiltshire Independent ◊, 92
Wiseman, Cardinal [Nicholas Patrick Stephen] †, 254
women §, 22, 196, 231; and bodies, 50, 234; and cheating, 140–43; and clothing, 130–36; and conduct or duty, 141–45, 146, 161–63, 166, 342; as emigrants, 228, 253–54; and exclusion, 75, 97; as game subjects, 204, 211, 335, 338–40; and hunting, 97–100, 103; and *Little Women*, 130, 142–48; and photography, 69, 74; as players, 3, 16, 19, 24, 137–38, 156–58, 161–63, 166, 332, 342–45; and 'tight-lacing' machines, 234, 236, 253; as writers, 20, 207–208; 335, 331–49
Woods, Livia Arndal, 146
Worcester Herald ◊, 20
Wordsworth, William †§, 249, 338

Yonge, Charlotte †°¥, 24, 148, 159; *Clever Woman of the Family*, 129, 144–46; "Strayed Falcon," 164; *Strolling Players*, 169

Games Index

Titles followed by * are derived from the *Game of Authors*

2K Basketball, 287

Adventures of Tom Sawyer, 6
Aldershot, 180
*Alice in Wonderland**, 335
Amphibiological Conversation Cards, 270
Amusing Game of Innocence Abroad, 256
Anchor Puzzle, 303
archery, 7, 8, 11, 279
Arabian Mystery, 302
Ariel Puzzle, 304
Asalto, 277
Ashantee Difficulty, 302
Assassin's Creed, 286
Author Game, 334, 345n1. See also *Game of Authors*
*Authors, Household Edition**, 335
*Authors Improved**, 335, 339, 343
*Authors, Plain Edition**, 335

backgammon, 17, 18, 20
back-sword, 11, 54
badminton, 279
bagatelle, 20, 113
Balance Cupolette, 292n3
ballet, 49–51, 53, 169n6
Balls and Rings, 304
baseball cards, 22, 25, 69–82, 83n3, 83n4, 83n5
bear baiting, 11, 16, 56, 95
beat your neighbor out of doors, 126n4
Beating the Bear, 16
Beaux and Belles, 269
Beggar My Neighbour, 114, 116–17, 121, 126n4
Bejeweled, 288
Beside the Broad Ocean, 280
Bible Characters, 270
bicycle, 7, 281
bilbocatch, 2
billiards, 2, 10, 18, 279
Birds Booklet, 270
Birds On Blocks, 270
blindman's bluff, 113, 160
blocks (building), 7, 302
bo-peep, 115
bocce, 29n2
Boss Game, 302. See also *Fifteen Puzzle*
*Boston Game of Authors**, 338
bowls, 279, 285

Box of Grammatical amusement, 20
boxing, 3, 8, 11, 16, 21–22, 23, 41–47, 54–64, 65n9, 113, 114, 121–22, 279
brag, 2
Brag and Grab, 286
British Tourist, 249, 256
The Bugle-Horn, or Robin Hood and His Merry Men, 211n11
bull baiting, 11, 56, 95, 103
bull fighting, 7
bullet pudding, 2

Call of Duty, 286
Candy Crush, 288
card games (generally), 2, 16, 28, 55, 115–23, 195–96, 199, 267–71, 273–74, 276, 284, 288
Cards Against Humanity, 286
*Carnival of Characters from Dickens**, 205, 341
carte de visite, 76, 340
carved animals, 307
cassino, 2, 29n4, 29n5
Centennial Games, 200
Centennial, Seventy-Six, 201–202, 204–205, 206–207
Changeable Portraits, 270, 286
*Characters from Charles Dickens**, 336, 346n6
Charades, 2, 10, 21, 24, 27, 153–68, 169n9, 266–67, 269, 301; charades in action 168n2, 169n7. *See also* riddles
Chaturanga, 175
Cheating, 284, 286
checkers, 4
chess, 7, 10, 11, 18, 43, 175, 177–79, 183, 266–68, 271, 277, 281, 286–88. See also *War-Chess*
*Children's Great People**, 206
Churchill, 289
Chutes and Ladders, 21, 288
Circular Puzzle, 303
climbing, 31n17
Clue (Cluedo), 4
cockfighting, 7, 11, 95, 103
Comic Answers to Queer Questions, 286
Comic Game of the Great Exhibition of 1851, 26, 216, 229–38, 238n3, 239n5, 253–54
Commerce, 2
Complete Voyage Round the World: A New Geographical Pastime, 249
Conjuring Tricks, 270
conundrums, 2, 301
Cottage of Content, 230
Cowes at Home, 268, 280
cribbage, 2, 10, 205, 266, 335
cricket, 7, 10, 31n17, 42, 80–81, 279
croquet, 22, 23–24, 99, 129–48, 149n3, 149n4, 269, 279; table croquet, 269
Crystal Palace Game, 26, 216–30, 237–38, 239n10, 239n12
cup and ball, 10

dancing, 21–22, 23, 41–54, 61–64, 64n5, 65n9, 290; dancing the frog hornpipe, 113; Morris dancing, 16
darts, 10, 266
dice, 4, 11, 55
*Dickens Game**, 211n10
DIY games, 332, 344–45
Dobble, 286
Doctor Busby, 25, 194, 203, 208–209, 210n1, 210n5, 333–34; *Improved and Illustrated* (1843), 346n4
Doctor Fusby, 194
dolls, 7, 215, 307; dollhouse, 307; paper dolls, 53
dominoes, 4, 267
Donkey Kong, 3

Donkey Race, 271
Dr. Jekyll and Mr. Hyde, 6
draughts, 18, 268, 271, 277, 286, 288, 292n2; draught men, 20
duels and dueling, 43, 45, 47, 56, 113
Duel (naval wargame), 187
Dungeons & Dragons, 4

Eastern Question, 304
écarté, 113
Egyptian Paradox, 302
enigmas, 10, 29n2, 301
euchre, 205, 342
*Extant Authors**, 337

Fauntleroy (playing cards), 200, 201, 205. *See also* General: Burnett
fencing, 42, 57; fencing-masters, 60
fetch, 29n2
FIFA, 286, 287
Fifteen Puzzle, 301–302
fishing, 8, 11; fishing-rod, 164
Five Navigators, 268
Fluxx, 286
football, 3, 11, 31n17, 279. See also *Madden*
forfeits, 113, 160
fort-da, 113
fortune telling, 269, 282
Fox and Geese, 268, 277, 280, 292n3; *Double Fox and Geese*, 292n3
fox hunting, 7, 8, 11, 16, 22–23, 87–104; equestrian fence-leaping, 87, 89
Friendly whispers for youth of both sexes, 20
Funnyshire Fox Chase, 22–23, 88–90, 230
gambling, 16–18, 55–56, 81, 113, 195–96, 199–200, 204–205, 207, 230, 244–45, 250, 258, 336–37, 342
Game of 15 and 34, 302. See also *Fifteen Puzzle*
*Game of Anybody & Everybody &**, 332
Game of Authors, 28, 204–206, 211n9, 211n10, 331–45, 345n1, 346n7, 346n8
*Game of Authors, Salem Edition**, 344
*Game of Cribbage Authors**, 335
Game of the District Messenger Boy, 4
*Game of Familiar Quotations from Popular Authors**, 338
Game of Fifteen, 302. See also *Fifteen Puzzle*
*Game of the Four Poets**, 334
Game of Goose (Jeu de l'Oie), 89, 239n8, 244–45, 248, 258; *Newe and most Pleasant Game of the Goose*, 230
*Game of Ivanhoe**, 211n11, 335
Game of Life, 244, 245, 288
Game of the Mariner's Compass, 202
Game of Nations, 202
*Game of Old Testament Characters**, 341
*Game of Quotations from Catholic American Authors**, 341
*Game of Quotations from the Poets**, 346n6
Game of Robin Hood, 206, 280, 287
Game of Round the World, 257–58
Game of the Star-Spangled Banner, or, The Emigrants to the United States, 250–51
Game of Trades, 333
*Game of Uncle Tom and Little Eva**, 333
*Game of Uncle Tom's Cabin**, 333
Game of United States History, 202–203
games of chance, 17, 27, 200, 267. *See also* gambling

Gaskell's Popular Historical Game, 202–203
Gem Puzzle, 302. See also *Fifteen Puzzle*
Geographical Recreations, or A voyage round the Habitable World, 19
Geography of Europe, 269
German Tactics, 277
Go, 25, 175, 179
Go Bang, 277, 292n4
Go Fish, 2
Gold Rush!, 6
golf, 279; miniature golf, 269
Good Old Game of Oliver Twist, 205–206
Great Men's Casino, 206
GTA [*Grand Theft Auto*], 289
guessing games, 3, 153–54, 157, 164, 165, 258

Halma, 268, 271, 277, 278, 286, 288, 292n2
Handcuff Puzzle, 304
Happy Families, 194, 210n1, 268, 333, 346n3
Harlequin's Rambles Through Europe, 254
hawking, 10, 11
Heart, 304
highland games, 7
Hive, 288
Homo, 292n2
hoops, 10; trundling the hoop, 11
horse racing, 7, 8, 11; as game theme, 279–80, 282, 283, 285, 287, 288
hot cockles, 2
Hounds and Jackals, 3
hunting, 11, 18, 226, 282, 285; rook-hunting, 113. *See also* fox hunting

ice-sliding, 113
*Improved Authors with Portraits & Autographs**, 336, 340, 346n9
*Improved Game of Star Authors**, 207–208, 339
*Instructive Game of Authors**, 335, 340
*Instructive Game of Mythology**, 335
*Instructive Game of Poets**, 338
Invasion, 268, 290

Jenga, 267
Jeu du Monde (Game of the World), 245
Jubilee!!, 19
jumping rope, 10

King of the Castle, 292n2
Kriegsspiel, 25, 176–85, 190; *American Kriegsspiel*, 183–86; Free *Kriegsspiel*, 181–82, 185–86; Rigid or "Strict" *Kriegsspiel*, 182

lacrosse, 7
Lara Croft: Tomb Raider, 4
leaping, 11
leap-frog, 113
Life of Nelson, 279
Lion and the Eagle, or the Days of '76, 201
Literary Whist, or Games of Great Men, 206
*Literary Women**, 339
Locomotive Game of Railroad Adventure, 250, 251, 255–56
Lost Heir, 210n7
lottery tickets, 2
Lotto, 267, 269–70
Ludo, 271, 288

Madden, 287
Magic Ring, 29n2

Magic Lantern, 326
Mansion of Happiness, 4
map maneuver games, 178–80, 188
marbles, 113, 266, 277
Master Rodbury, 194
Memory Game, 23, 24, 111–12, 125
Militaire, 183
Miniatures, 270, 271
Modern Naval Warfare, 292n2
Monopoly, 2, 4, 244, 251
Ms. *Pac-Man*, 3
Mystic Square, 302. See also *Fifteen Puzzle*

National Game of '76, 200
New and fashionable game of the Jew, 217
New and Favourite game of Mother Goose and the golden egg, 217
New Egg of Columbus, 304
*New Game of Authors**, 334
*New Game of Authors or Graded Literature Cards**, 337, 340
New Game of the Royal Mail or London to Edinburgh, 255–56
New Royal Geographical Pastime for England and Wales, 249
North Pole Game, 202
Numerical Puzzle, 271

One Hundred Events of US Colonial History, 200
Oregon Trail, 3, 6
Our Ship, 280

Panorama of London, or a Day's Journey round the Metropolis, 19
paper ships, 2
parlor or drawing room games (generally), 7, 19, 154, 158–60, 164, 167, 194, 269, 284–85, 293, 297, 332
Patchwork, 288
Patience, 115
Perfect Man, 278
Periscopes, 270
pig races, 31n17
ping pong, 279
piquet, 17, 268
Pirate and the Traders of the West Indies, 252
Pokémon, 4; *Pokémon Go*, 4, 259
poker, 266, 342
Polemos, 268, 271
Pong, 3
Poor Old School Soldier and His Dog, 268
Pope Joan, 20
Praxinoscope, 326
Presidential Quartets, 333
Prince of Persia, 4
Protean Cards, 207
pull-toys, 307
puss in the corner, 160
puzzles, 3D, 279
Puzzles, Anker or Anchor Stone, 302
puzzles, cross (generally), 301–302
puzzles, jigsaw, 29–30n8, 243, 267, 270
puzzle, mechanical, 6, 27, 300, 301–304
puzzles, pencil and paper, 27, 300–301, 304
Pythagoras Puzzle, 303

quadrille, 2, 17, 29n4, 29n5
quarterstaff, 54
Quartet, 333
*Queens of Literature**, 208, 335, 339
Quintain, 11
Quinze, 29n5
quoits, 29n2, 42, 279
Quorn Hunt, 93–94

race and steeple chase, 11, 20, 280
Race for the Pole, 202, 203
races and racing, 11, 202, 244–46, 249, 257, 259, 267, 271–76, 279, 282, 284, 287, 289, 291
rackets, 113
Regatta, 280
riddles, 2, 113, 160, 269, 271, 301; in charades 24, 154, 156–57, 161, 168n1
Right and Wrong, or the Princess Belinda, 208–209
Royal Race Course [and] Comic Steeplechase, 88
rowley-powley, 17

Saddle my Nag, 16
Saint Joan, 113
Santorini, 288
Scripture Questions and Answers, 269
Secret worth knowing, 20
see-saw, 10
*Selected Authors**, 335
Settlers of Catan, 4
Sherlock Holmes, 6, 206
shooting, 7, 8, 12, 14, 269, 284, 285
shove ha'penny, 266, 267
shuffle board, 17
Siege of Paris, 292n2
Signers of America's Independence, 200–201
singing, 11
Six Degrees of Kevin Bacon, 286
skittles, 113, 266, 279, 285
slanging, 113
Sliding Block Puzzle, 302. See also *Fifteen Puzzle*
Snakes and Ladders, 268, 280, 287–88, 292n6
Snapdragon, 2, 113
solitaire, 271; board solitaire, 277
Spade the Gardener, 333
spear throwing, 11
speculation, 2
spillikins, 2
spinning tops, 266, 307
*Star Authors**, 335
Star Puzzle, 303
strip jack naked, 126n4
Strategos, 184
Structure of the Earth, 269
Suffragetto, 279
Super Mario Brothers, 3
swimming, 8

tennis, 3, 8, 269, 279; table tennis, 269, 279
Thaumatropes, 270
three-card loo, 10
throwing stones, 11
Ticket to Ride, 250
tin soldiers, 307. *See also* toy soldiers
Tormentor, 303
tournaments, 4, 11
toy soldiers, 29n2. *See also* tin soldiers
Trade and Empire, 279
trade cries of London, 280
Traveller's Tour through the United States, 210
Travellers of Europe, 230
Travellers of Asia, 252–53, 255
Travelling in India, 279
treasure hunts, 292n2
Trip Through Europe, 210n8
Trip Through the United States, 210n8
Twelfth-Night, 280
Twilight Struggle, 289
Two Balls, 304

Unionist Puzzle, 304
United Hearts, 304

Victoria: an Empire Under the Sun, 6

Victoria II (sequel), 6
*Vignette Authors**, 340–41
vingt-un, 2, 29n5
Voyage of Discovery, 230

War-Chess, or the Game of Battle, 175, 183, 190
Welcome Intruder, 269
whiff whaff, 269
whist, 1, 2, 16, 17, 29, 113, 114, 122–23, 205, 342; *Literary Whist*, 206
Wolf and Lamb, 277
word games, 29n2, 267, 271, 284
Word Making, 269
World Visited, 210n8
wrestling, 3, 11, 42, 54

Yahtzee, 4
*Young Folks Authors**, 344
Yukon Trail, 6

Zoetrope, 326
Zork, 3

www.ingramcontent.com/pod-product-compliance
Lightning Source LLC
LaVergne TN
LVHW050146080826
844660LV00002B/99
* 9 7 8 1 4 3 8 4 8 5 5 5 3 *